Ferdia Mac Anna was born in 1955 in Dublin. He has worked as a television researcher, journalist, magazine editor and film reviewer, and for some years he toured Ireland as the rock and roll singer Rocky de Valera, first with the Gravediggers and latterly with the Rhythm Kings. He is the author of two novels, *The Last of the High Kings*, which has just been made into a Hollywood film, and *The Ship Inspector*, both of which are published by Penguin.

Ferdia Mac Anna lives in Dublin.

THE PENGUIN BOOK OF
IRISH COMIC WRITING

SELECTED AND INTRODUCED BY
FERDIA MAC ANNA

PENGUIN BOOKS

PENGUIN BOOKS

Published by the Penguin Group
Penguin Books Ltd, 27 Wrights Lane, London W8 5TZ, England
Penguin Books USA Inc., 375 Hudson Street, New York, New York 10014, USA
Penguin Books Australia Ltd, Ringwood, Victoria, Australia
Penguin Books Canada Ltd, 10 Alcorn Avenue, Toronto, Ontario, Canada M4V 3B2
Penguin Books (NZ) Ltd, 182–190 Wairau Road, Auckland 10, New Zealand

Penguin Books Ltd, Registered Offices: Harmondsworth, Middlesex, England

First published as *An Anthology of Irish Comic Writing* by Michael Joseph 1995
Published under the present title in Penguin Books 1996
3 5 7 9 10 8 6 4 2

Selection and Introduction copyright © Ferdia Mac Anna, 1995
All rights reserved

The moral right of the editor has been asserted

The acknowledgements on pp. ix and x constitute an extension of this copyright page

Printed in England by Clays Ltd, St Ives plc

Contents

Acknowledgements

Thanks to: Dr John Barrett (UCD); Dermot Bolger; Prof. Terence Brown (TCD); Ciaran Carty; Ann Clune (TCD); Kevin Connolly; Astrid Gerber; Nicholas Grene (TCD); Kate Holmquist; Prof. Brendan Kennelly (TCD); Sienna Mac Anna; Vanessa Mac Anna; Aisling Maguire; Geraldine Mangan; Tony Peake; the staff of the Rare Books Library of Trinity College; The Winding Stair.

Acknowledgements of Copyright Holders

The editor and publishers wish to thank the following for permission to use copyright material:

Attic Press for Eilís Ní Dhuibhne, 'A Visit to Newgrange' from *Blood and Water*;

The Samuel Beckett Estate and The Calder Educational Trust, London with Grove/Atlantic, Inc for an extract from Samuel Beckett, *Murphy*, Calder Publications Ltd, pp. 143–54. Copyright © Samuel Beckett 1938, 1963, 1977, and copyright © The Samuel Beckett Estate 1993;

Constable Publishers for Seán O'Faolain, 'The Confessional' from *The Collected Stories of Seán O'Faolain*;

Andre Deutsch Ltd for an extract from Molly Keane, *Good Behaviour*, pp. 10–13;

J. P. Donleavy for an extract from *The Ginger Man*, Penguin Books, pp. 97–101;

Fourth Estate Ltd for Michael Curtin, 'The Society of Bellringers' from *The Plastic Tomato-Cutter*, pp. 4–14. Copyright © 1991 Michael Curtin; and Nina Fitzpatrick, 'In the Company of Frauds' from *Fables of the Irish Intelligentsia*, pp. 47–54. Copyright © 1991 by Nina Fitzpatrick;

Greene & Heaton Ltd on behalf of the author, for Mary Morrissy, 'Bookworm' from *A Lazy Eye*, Jonathan Cape, pp. 3–11. Copyright © 1993 by Mary Morrissy;

Hamish Hamilton Ltd and Peters Fraser & Dunlop Group Ltd on behalf of the author for Frank O'Connor, 'First Confession' from *The Stories of Frank O'Connor*, 1953. Copyright © Frank O'Connor 1953;

HarperCollins Publishers Ltd for an extract from Myles Na Gopaleen (Flann O'Brien), *The Best of Myles*, 1987, pp. 24–34;

Katy Hayes for 'Forecourt', included in *Prizewinning Radio Stories*, The Mercier Press;

A. M. Heath on behalf of the Estate of Flann O'Brien for an extract from *The Third Policeman*, pp. 44–55;

Pat Ingoldsby for pieces collectively titled 'A Crisis for the Céilí Bands' originally included in the *Evening Press*;

Michael Joseph Ltd for an extract from Ferdia Mac Anna, *The Last of the High Kings*, 1991, pp. 62–7. Copyright © Ferdia Mac Anna 1991;

Noel McFarlane for 'Lucky Singing' from *True to Type: Stories by Journalists*, The Irish Times, pp. 33–41;

The Mercier Press for J. B. Keane, 'The Change' from *Irish Short Stories*, 1976;

The O'Brien Press Ltd for Padraig O'Siochfhradha, 'Death to the Master' from *Jimeen*, trs. P. Egan, P. Fallow and I. Ní Loaghaire; Brendan Behan, 'The Confirmation Suit' from *After the Wake*; and an extract from Brendan O'Carroll, *The Mammy*, 1994, pp. 9–17;

Pan Macmillan for an extract from Patrick McCabe, *The Butcher Boy*, pp. 9–16;

Pavilion Books Ltd for Patrick Campbell, 'The Hot Box' from *The Campbell Companion*;

Penguin Books Ltd for an extract from Hugh Leonard, *Home Before Night*, 1981, first published by Andre Deutsch. Copyright © Hugh Leonard 1979;

Poolbeg Press Ltd for James Stephens, 'A Rhinoceros, Some Ladies and a Horse' from *Desire and Other Stories*, 1980;

Random House UK Ltd for Bridget O'Connor, 'Here Comes John' from *Here Comes John*, Jonathan Cape; Bernard Mac Laverty, 'A Time to Dance' from *A Time to Dance*, Jonathan Cape; and Maeve Binchy, 'Holland Park' from *London Transport*, 1978;

Raven Arts Press for Eoin McNamee, 'The Lion Alone' from *The Last of Deeds*, 1989, and Sara Berkeley, 'The Catch' from *The Swimmer in the Deep Blue Dream*;

Reed Consumer Books Ltd for Joseph O'Connor, 'The Wizard of Oz' from *True Believers*, Sinclair-Stevenson, 1991; Aidan Mathews, 'Nephritis' from *Adventures in a Bathyscope*, Martin Secker & Warburg; Ann Enright, 'Revenge' from *The Portable Virgin*, Martin Secker & Warburg; and an extract from Micháel Mac Liammóir, *Put Money in Thy Purse*, Eyre Methuen, 1975, pp. 6–18;

Moya Roddy for 'The Day I Gave Neil Jordan a Lift';

Rogers, Coleridge and White Ltd on behalf of the author for Clare Boylan, 'Not a Recommended Hobby for a Housewife' from *A Nail on the Head*, Hamish Hamilton, 1983;

Sheil Land Associates Ltd on behalf of the author for Moy McCrory, 'The Wrong Vocation' from *The Sailing Ships of His Boyhood Dreams*, Jonathan Cape;

Spike Milligan Productions Ltd for an extract from Spike Milligan, *Puckoon*, Penguin Books, 1963, pp. 13–21;

The Sunday Independent for Roddy Doyle, 'A Christmas Story from Barrytown', *Sunday Independent*, 17.12.89;

Wolfhound Press Ltd for Seán Mac Mathúna, 'The Queen of Killiney' from *The Atheist*; and extracts from Mervyn Wall, *An Unfortunate Fursey*, pp. 11–9 and Billy Roche, *Tumbling Down*, pp. 28–34.

Every effort has been made to trace all the copyright holders but if any have been inadvertently overlooked the publishers will be pleased to make the necessary arrangement at the first opportunity.

Introduction

In the late 1980s, a British journalist came to Dublin to write a feature on the city's nightclubs which were undergoing a boom. He wanted to find out if it was true that the Irish were unique in Europe in their ability to ignore a recession. The journalist's Irish guide brought him to a glittery backstreet cavern where the bouncers enforced a notoriously strict and frequently baffling door policy. The journalist and his guide explained their mission and the bouncer shook hands, agreed that they had indeed come to the right spot and even joked with them for a while before beamingly refusing them entry. 'Sorry, yis are wearing jeans,' he explained. The journalist was wearing dark trousers, as was his Irish guide. 'But we're not wearing jeans,' they protested. 'Ah yes,' the bouncer smirked. 'But yis might as well be.'

Comedy, like the irrefutable Celtic logic of the nightclub bouncer, is a difficult thing to define. What makes one person laugh may leave another feeling indifferent. The only sure thing about comedy is that it is personal. Nobody can tell you what to laugh at or explain why something is funny. Attempts to persuade a person of the hilarity of a prose passage can often end in humiliation and resentment or at least, disgruntlement. About the best you can do with comedy is to recognize it when you see it.

I imagine that few writers in this anthology would describe themselves as comic writers. The label 'Comic Writer' is as limiting and slightly ludicrous as wearing a clown's red nose, and not something you'd like stamped on your passport. Comedy, humour and wit are so deeply ingrained in the Irish character that we in Ireland take them for granted. It runs through Irish writing even in work of an essentially tragic nature such as Pat McCabe's *The Butcher Boy*. Yet comedy or humour, along with literature and music, and, more recently, soccer, is one of our ways of communicating with the world, and an essential ingredient in our daily lives. You can find it in the wit and thrust of everyday conversation, the delight in wordplay and mischief, the rapture in telling and embellishing a good story and the sheer malicious glee of the Irish national pastime of 'slagging', a basic philosophy of humorously criticizing or insulting someone for the sheer sport of it. In Ireland, it often seems that anyone is capable of coming up with a remark that can haunt the victim for life. A few years ago, a disgruntled TD described the then Minister for Finance's contribution to the economic debate as 'having managed to *subtract* from the sum total of human knowledge'.

Dethroning the pompous is as ingrained in Irish writing as the delight in satire, parody and the grotesque. This spirit was traced in an unbroken line back to ninth century bardic literature by Vivian Mercier in *The Irish Comic Tradition*, the key work on the subject. Mercier points out that whereas writers from other cultures have to work hard to re-establish contact with their primitive or folk roots, the Anglo-Irish writer always has 'the past at his elbow'. In Ireland, the past is preserved in the Gaelic language and literature, 'in bilingual folklore, in Gaelic modes of thought and feeling and spirit which have become part of the rural Anglo-Irish dialects'. Writers as dissimilar as Swift, Joyce, Milligan and Beckett share a common heritage of the vitality, gaiety and spirit which stems from the early Gaelic comic writing tradition. Certainly, the writings of Swift and Joyce exhibit the early Gaelic writer's delight in the fantastical and the macabre. As Mercier points out, contact with folk speech and dialect also gave Anglo-Irish writers access to a living folklore and thus, myth. In Joyce's *Ulysses*, Bloom's Homeric wanderings around Dublin are a gradual yet effectively comic deflation of the noble, heroic spirit of serious literature as well as a gentle parody of Homer's epic. Mercier concludes that the Irish comic traditon, far from being peripheral activity, can in fact lay claim to being the central tradition in Irish literature. 'As Freud well knew, the Id manifests itself in the comic as well as tragic modes. Myth, ritual, the unconscious, all our sacred cows can be detected and studied in the comic if we trouble to look for them.'

At the World Cup championships in Italy in 1990, jittery Italian police herded hundreds of Irish soccer fans into a large pen before an important and potentially explosive match. Soon, the Irish fans were putting their faces to the bars and baa-ing. After a while, the police laughingly let the fans out. People who performed sheep impressions before an important life-or-death soccer match, they reasoned, were unlikely to be much of a menace to society.

As many commentators have pointed out, the ballyhoo surrounding the Irish international soccer team may have been good for tourism and national self-respect, but it has also served to distance us from reality. No amount of soccer games can cure the ills of unemployment, drugs epidemics, crime and disillusionment. But fantasy and belief in magic have always been a substantial element in the Irish character. Our early literature is steeped in magical deeds, from Finn McCool's exaggerated heroics to Saint Patrick driving the snakes out of Ireland. One of the first things an Irish child learns is how to turn a story into a saga. Our soccer stars are 'The Fianna' reborn, the modern version of the warrior heroes of our ancient folklore. Escapism is in our genetic make-up, and happily too.

It may be true that Ireland has never had to suffer the horrors of a world war, unlike Germany, Russia, France and many other European countries. Yet the catalogue of disasters to have beset so small a country is still fairly comprehensive – 800 years of British occupation, various disastrous uprisings and insurrections and political and social disunity, the twin holocausts of the famine and mass emigration and, in recent times, twenty-five years of violence in the North, not to mention the stifling power of the Catholic church. Against this backdrop, it is tempting to view the Irish love of comedy as a defence against hard times and oppression. The early Irish wakes, for example, were often frenetic, anarchic affairs. Traditionally held in the presence of the corpse, the wakes featured singing, dancing, the telling of obscene tales, even the odd orgy, as well as an amusement described as 'performing tricks on the corpse'. In *Finnegans Wake*, Joyce's word for wake was 'funferall'.

The Irish penchant for fantasy, magic and spiritualism has helped to set us apart, at least in the eyes of outsiders. To the Victorian poet and critic Matthew Arnold, the Celts, particularly the Irish, were 'sentimental', 'exotic', 'overly imaginative' and 'always ready to act against the despotism of fact'. Arnold felt that the blighted middle-class English were a dull lot. At home, the notion of the Irish as a spiritual, natural, pagan people, remnants of ancient pre-Christian civilization, was embraced by W.B. Yeats and other Anglo-Irish writers. The intoxication with mythical Ireland came to fruition in the 'Celtic Twilight' school where writers such as George Russell, George Moore and Lady Gregory sought to draw upon the past to create an indigenous literary culture. The 'Celtic Twilight' movement failed to impress James Joyce however, who renamed it 'Celtic Toilette'.

While the Celtic identity has been used to set the Irish apart from the British, the Celtic sensibility has also imbued British culture. It is no coincidence that many of the masters of 'English' stage comedy – Congreve, Wilde, Farquhar, Goldsmith, Sheridan, Shaw – were either Irish or grew up in Ireland.

Curiously, while we celebrate great writers such as Joyce, Beckett, Behan, O'Casey, Synge and Shaw for their humanism, their modernism and their innovative use of language, we are often slow to pay tribute to their comic gifts and to acknowledge the comic tradition that influenced and indeed inspired much of their great work. The only major critical work on Irish comic writing, Vivian Mercier's *The Irish Comic Tradition*, was published as long ago as 1962. Perhaps we prefer to regard comedy as a type of natural human fallout, a spontaneous emission that enables us to get through life, rather than an art form that requires toil and intellectual rigour.

If a writer's particular brand of comedy fails to impress a reviewer, then that writer's work stands a fair chance of being dismissed as shallow, unconvincing and laden with stereotypes or, at best, tolerated as harmless gas. In today's supercritical climate, the writer of comic literature can often feel vulnerable. As Spike Milligan put it, 'Naked, I had a body that invited burial.'

A noted writer, one who will not touch comedy, once remarked that he didn't much care for comic writing because it usually resulted in a happy ending and, as it saw it, 'Happiness is its own reward.' The writer's presumption that comic writing is 'happy' work is shocking, conjuring up an image of literary leprechauns, faces incandescent with glee as they compulsively churn out comic narratives like characters out of *Darby O'Gill and the Little People*. The implication that works as diverse and innovative as Swift's satirical masterpiece *Gulliver's Travels*, Laurence Sterne's playfully seditious *Tristram Shandy* and Flann O'Brien's hilariously surreal *The Third Policeman* are less deserving of praise or study than serious or tragic literature just because they are funny, is disturbing. *The Third Policeman*, with its crank philosophizing and lunatic bicycling policemen, is on one level an eccentric odyssey into Celtic gombeenism. But it can also be read as a complex, almost Kafkaesque meditation on creation, its unwittingly deceased narrator a symbol of man's futile desire to control his own destiny. Comic writing, at its best, provides as much subtle insight into ordinary life as any of the more po-faced sources.

Yet while experimentation has always been a part of Irish comic writing, clarity of story-telling and strong characterization remain important and fundamental requirements. In general, people are recognizably represented as people and dialogue and plot are easy to follow. In Spike Milligan's *Puckoon*, the author finds himself under attack by his protagonist regarding the deficient quality of the protagonist's 'legs', amongst other things. The interruption is a highly effective comic interlude as well as a lampoon of the traditional relationship between author and protagonist. But the indignation of the protagonist (also named Milligan) can also be viewed as mortal outrage, an individual railing against all-powerful fate. Comedy has also been utilized effectively as a weapon to rail against injustice. Jonathan Swift's *A Modest Proposal*, with its blackly comic suggestion that surplus babies could be eaten as the ideal solution to Irish poverty, succeeds in highlighting a social problem while indicting government complacency. Mervyn Wall's *The Unfortunate Fursey* sends up Irish monasticism, the cult of sainthood and the Irish attitude to sex in a bawdy and appealing fashion, while Eimar O'Duffy's unjustly neglected satirical novel, *King Goshawk and the Birds* satirizes Irish legend, myth and politics by bringing the fabled hero Cuchulain back to modern Dublin in the body of a scrawny shop assistant.

In modernist fiction such as 'Revenge', Ann Enright's quirky Nabokovian exploration of marital difficulty, and Aidan Mathews' 'Nephritis', a darkly playful tale of an individual's struggle with the imperialism of diagnosis, the comic spirit serves to sharpen the insight into human frailty, not obscure it. Could it be because comedy appears such an obvious, everyday commodity that we dismiss it so readily? Roddy Doyle, a superb, innovative prose stylist and the author of three fine comic novels, was acclaimed abroad while Irish critics remained sceptical. It wasn't really until Doyle's fourth novel, *Paddy Clarke Ha Ha Ha* (which was awarded the Booker Prize in 1993), that his talent gained critical acclaim in his home country. Having been acclaimed abroad, he has become yet another unimpeachable icon of Irishness.

Why then is comic writing so undervalued? You could blame the ancient Greeks, who invented theatrical comedy in 486 BC as mere light relief to their productions of tragedy (the word comedy is derived from the Greek word, *komos*, 'to revel'). Aristotle wrote that the difference between comedy and tragedy was that 'Comedy aims at representing men as worse than they are nowadays, tragedy as better.' Aristotle concluded that the origins and early history of comedy were obscure because it was given scant respect. If tragedy traditionally portrays man as noble and heroic, then comedy usually reveals him as an ass. Tragedy often enhances our self-image whereas comedy undermines it and subverts our exalted view of ourselves. As William Hazlitt wrote, 'For every joke, there is a sufferer.' I suspect that given the choice, most men would prefer to picture themselves as Stephen Dedalus rather than Leopold Bloom. That does not mean that the Leopold Blooms of this world are any less tragic, as Joyce showed.

Comedy is a way of laughing at the gods, of warding off the blows of cruel fate, of dealing with pain, of laughing in the face of death. As long as the 'craic is ninety', as the saying goes, then we're winning – even if we know deep down that it can only be for a short time.

One of the apparent contradictions in Irish comic writing is the way in which writers such as Eilís Ní Dhuibhne, Moy McCrory and Hugh Leonard among others, employ comedy as a way of heightening a sense of pathos or tragedy. Bridget O'Connor's unnamed narrator in 'Here Comes John' scatters acerbic insights into the hypocrisy of men. Underlying the bitterly comic put-downs however, is a sense of the grievous vulnerability of a person who has been hurt and abandoned many times and who will probably suffer the same fate again.

Another contradiction of Irish writing – and of Irish life – is that the language we use to express ourselves belongs to another country. All of the pieces here – with one exception, Padraig O'Siochfhradha's 'Jimeen' – were written in English. (Seán Mac Mathúna wrote in Irish for many years before turning to English in his collection, *The Atheist*.) Although our national tongue is undergoing something of a revival at present, it is unlikely ever again to play a dominant role in the lives of Irish people. Gaelic rhythms have influenced the English we speak in Ireland and flavoured our writing but, as Vivian Mercier points out, a great

deal of Irish comic writing is virtually indistinguishable from its
English counterpart. Mercier concludes that Irish humour, while
difficult to define, 'shows two distinct emphases – one on
fantasy and the other on the grotesque and the macabre. The
humour of other cultures besides the Irish displays one or other
of these emphases but I doubt whether both types of humour
have been simultaneously fostered to the same degree by any
other people.'

While it may be instructive to establish that the bardic tradition has influenced many Irish writers, either consciously or
unconsciously, the body of work produced defies easy categoriza-
tion. Writers such as Samuel Beckett and Aidan Mathews appear
to owe more to European or American influence than Irish
tradition. And what of those writers who grew up outside
Ireland? How does the work of Bridget O'Connor, Spike Milligan and J.P. Donleavy fall neatly into the Irish comic tradition?
Ireland is no longer as isolated as it once was. In an era of
television and emigration, we are being influenced by new ideas,
fresh perspectives and a modern global culture that is changing
all the time. The streets of New York and London are as much a
part of the Irish literary landscape as any Kerry town. Throughout, however, Irish writers' preoccupation with the grotesque
and the magical remains intact. Eoin McNamee's tale of a
bizarre preoccupation with unusual pets in a Northern city
street, which he uses as a metaphor for the Troubles in his story,
'The Lion Alone', is reminiscent of the playful surrealism of
Gabriel Garcia Marquez.

Nowadays there is great talk that Ireland is finally throwing
off the shackles of colonialism to become finally a modern
European nation. Dublin has almost as many coffee houses as
pubs. People point out that you would be hard-pressed to cross
the city without passing an espresso sign. Many of our social
commentators explain our deification of our popular icons – the
international soccer team, U2, Van Morrison, Neil Jordan,
Roddy Doyle – as the last symptoms of an inferiority complex

brought on by post-colonialism. The worship of success reveals us as a people still unsure of its identity, a nation which, to paraphrase a U2 song, still hasn't found what it's looking for.

But the commentators forget that we are at heart a nation of islanders, a magpie race diluted over a millennium by Vikings, Normans, English as well as the recent and continuing Anglo-American onslaught. We may not be as isolated or as self-obsessed as we once were, but we are skilled in subverting foreign influences to our own devices and in acting against 'the despotism of fact'. We will absorb 'Europeanness' just as we have absorbed the other influences. The other day I saw a sign in a restaurant window advertising 'Irish Lasagne'. We will drink cappuccinos and remain as peculiarly Irish as a Dolmen.

I had three reasons for compiling this anthology. The first was that nobody had ever compiled an anthology of modern Irish comic stories before and I thought it was about time someone did. Comic writing is a neglected and underrated area in Irish literature and I wanted to focus attention on it. The second reason was to demonstrate that the Irish comic tradition is in fine shape. Virtually every story contained here, from the charmingly wacky vision of James Stephens' 'A Rhinoceros, Some Ladies and a Horse' to Mike McCormack's darkly comic yet disturbing satire of the art world, 'Thomas Crumlesh 1960–1992: A Retrospective', explores and develops the Irish tradition of the fantastic and the grotesque. Finally, I wanted to show the diversity of talents in modern Irish writing and to provide a platform for some new voices. In these pages you will find the work of some of Ireland's most famous modern writers (James Joyce, Samuel Beckett, Flann O'Brien, Hugh Leonard, Molly Keane, J.P. Donleavy, Clare Boylan) alongside those of neglected authors (Eimar O' Duffy, Mervyn Wall) or emerging talents (Bridget O'Connor, Mary Morrissy, Eoin McNamee, Katy Hayes, Joseph O'Connor, Sara Berkeley, Billy Roche) as well as others who are uncategorizable (Spike Milligan, Pat Ingoldsby, Brendan O'Carroll). Some of the most memorable comic writing has been on the theme of childhood. I make no apologies for including classic stories by Seán O'Faolain, Bernard MacLaverty, Brendan Behan and Frank O'Connor. In these stories, the themes of innocence and pain appear as significant to comic writing as they are to so-called 'serious' literature. I have used the word story in its broadest sense and have included extracts from novels and autobiographical writings and essays. It seems to me that a failure to include an extract from a novel as darkly humorous and bizarre as Pat McCabe's *The Butcher Boy* would be a grave oversight. Similarly, I can find no justification for not including Patrick Campbell's celebrated comic essay 'The Hot Box' or an extract from Micháel Mac Liammóir's *Put Money in Thy Purse*, an hilarious account of the disaster-riddled making of Orson Welles' *Othello*.

This anthology does not claim to be definitive, in the same way that no one person's sense of humour can claim to embrace or appreciate every form of comedy. I willingly admit that I made no attempt to be fair to anyone except myself. The stories are arranged chronologically, both for convenience and to high-light the consistency of the Irish comic vision and of its deploy-ment in a variety of unique, highly engaging ways. I have stuck to prose for reasons of convenience and space but primarily because it is the form I am interested in. I have no doubt that equally valid and engaging anthologies of Irish comic theatre or Irish comic verse, not to mention comic journalism or essays, are long overdue for compilation.

Finally, a wish. Should an Irish university – or any university for that matter – by some miracle decide to inaugurate a chair of Irish Comic Writing in the near future, I hope they will appoint a professor who has a good and highly-developed sense of humour. I would hate to see some dry old stick getting the job and driving everyone mad deconstructing the works of Flann O'Brien and Samuel Beckett and squeezing the laughter and joy out of the writing until it lies there limp, dead from over-analysis. Perhaps the professor could introduce joke-telling seminars or oral examinations in ribald humour, or even mock wakes complete with obscene party games. I hope that whoever gets the job will bear in mind George Bernard Shaw's famous line from *John Bull's Other Island* which is as close to a definition of Irish comic writing as I can find, 'My way of joking is to tell the truth. It's the funniest joke in the world.'

In the meantime, enjoy.

FERDIA MAC ANNA

JAMES JOYCE
From *Ulysses*

James Joyce (1882–1941) is one of Ireland's most celebrated writers.
Ulysses was published in Paris in 1922 (on Joyce's fortieth birthday)
and had a long and turbulent publishing history before establishing itself
as one of the great works of world literature. In this extract from the
'Cyclops' episode, an unnamed narrator enters Barney Kiernan's pub
where the fearsome Irish Nationalist known as 'The Citizen' is holding
court.

I was just passing the time of day with old Troy of the DMP
at the corner of Arbour hill there and be damned but a bloody
sweep came along and he near drove his gear into my eye. I
turned around to let him have the weight of my tongue when
who should I see dodging along Stony Batter only Joe Hynes.

 – Lo, Joe, says I. How are you blowing? Did you see that
bloody chimneysweep near shove my eye out with his brush?

 – Soot's luck, says Joe. Who's the old ballocks you were
talking to?

 – Old Troy, says I, was in the force. I'm on two minds not to
give that fellow in charge for obstructing the thoroughfare with
his brooms and ladders.

 – What are you doing round those parts? says Joe.

 – Devil a much, says I. There is a bloody big foxy thief
beyond by the garrison church at the corner of Chicken Lane –
old Troy was just giving me a wrinkle about him – lifted any
God's quantity of tea and sugar to pay three bob a week said he
had a farm in the county Down off a hop of my thumb by the
name of Moses Herzog over there near Heytesbury street.

 – Circumcised! says Joe.

 – Ay, says I. A bit off the top. An old plumber named
Geraghty. I'm hanging on to his taw now for the past fortnight
and I can't get a penny out of him.

– That the lay you're on now? says Joe.

– Ay says I. How are the mighty fallen! Collector of bad and doubtful debts. But that's the most notorious bloody robber you'd meet in a day's walk and the face on him all pockmarks would hold a shower of rain. *Tell him*, says he, *I dare him*, says he, *and I doubledare him to send you round here again or if he does*, says he, *I'll have him summonsed up before the court, so will I, for trading without a licence.* And he after stuffing himself till he's fit to burst! Jesus, I had to laugh at the little jewy getting his shirt out. *He drink me my teas. He eat me my sugars. Because he no pay me my moneys?*

For nonperishable goods bought of Moses Herzog, of 13 Saint Kevin's parade, Wood quay ward, merchant, hereinafter called the vendor, and sold and delivered to Michael E. Geraghty, Esquire, of 29 Arbour Hill in the city of Dublin, Arran quay ward, gentleman, hereinafter called the purchaser, videlicet, five pounds avoirdupois of first choice tea at three shillings per pound avoirdupois and three stone avoirdupois of sugar, crushed crystal, at three pence per pound avoirdupois, the said purchaser debtor to the said vendor of one pound five shillings and six pence sterling for value received which amount shall be paid by said purchaser to said vendor in weekly instalments every seven calendar days of three shillings and no pence sterling: and the said nonperishable goods shall not be pawned or pledged or sold or otherwise alienated by the said purchaser but shall be and remain and be held to be the sole and exclusive property of the said vendor to be disposed of at his good will and pleasure until the said amount shall have been duly paid by the said purchaser to the said vendor in the manner herein set forth as this day hereby agreed between the said vendor his heirs, successors, trustees and assigns of the one part and the said purchaser, his heirs, successors, trustees and assigns of the other part.

– Are you a strict t. t.? says Joe.

– Not taking anything between drinks, says I.

– What about paying our respects to our friend? says Joe.

– Who? says I. Sure, he's in John of God's off his head, poor man.

– Drinking his own stuff? says Joe.

– Ay, says I. Whisky and water on the brain.

– Come around to Barney Kiernan's, says Joe. I want to see the citizen.

– Barney mavourneen's be it, says I. Anything strange or wonderful, Joe?

– Not a word, says Joe. I was up at that meeting in the City Arms.

– What was that, Joe? says I.

– Cattle traders, says Joe, about the foot and mouth disease. I want to give the citizen the hard word about it.

So we went around by the Linenhall barracks and the back of the courthouse talking of one thing or another. Decent fellow Joe when he has it but sure like that he never has it. Jesus, I couldn't get over that bloody foxy Geraghty, the daylight robber. For trading without a licence, says he.

In Inisfail the fair there lies a land, the land of holy Michan. There rises a watchtower beheld of men afar. There sleep the mighty dead as in life they slept, warriors and princes of high renown. A pleasant land it is in sooth of murmuring waters, fishful streams where sport the gunnard, the plaice, the roach, the halibut, the gibbed haddock, the grilse, the dab, the brill, the flounder, the mixed coarse fish generally and other denizens of the aqueous kingdom too numerous to be enumerated. In the mild breezes of the west and of the east the lofty trees wave in different directions their first class foliage, the wafty sycamore, the Lebanonian cedar, the exalted planetree, the eugenic eucalyptus and other ornaments of the arboreal world with which that region is thoroughly well supplied. Lovely maidens sit in close proximity to the roots of the lovely trees singing the most lovely songs while they play with all kinds of lovely objects as for example golden ingots, silvery fishes, crans of herrings, drafts of eels, codlings, creels of fingerlings, purple seagems and playful insects. And heroes voyage from afar to woo them, from Eblana to Slievemargy, the peerless princes of unfettered Munster and of Connacht the just and of smooth sleek Leinster and of Cruachan's land and of Armagh the splendid and of the noble district of Boyle, princes, the sons of kings.

And there rises a shining palace whose crystal glittering roof is seen by mariners who traverse the extensive sea in barks built expressly for that purpose and thither come all herds and fatlings and first fruits of that land for O'Connell Fitzsimon takes toll of them, a chieftain descended from chieftains. Thither the extremely large wains bring foison of the fields, flaskets of cauliflowers, floats of spinach, pineapple chunks, Rangoon beans, strikes of tomatoes, drums of figs, drills of Swedes, spherical potatoes and tallies of iridescent kale, York and Savoy, and trays of onions, pearls of the earth, and punnets of mushrooms and custard marrows and fat vetches and bere and rape and red green yellow brown russet sweet big bitter ripe pomellated apples and chips of strawberries and sieves of gooseberries, pulpy and pelurious, and strawberries fit for princes and raspberries from their canes.

I dare him, says he, and I doubledare him. Come out here, Geraghty, you notorious bloody hill and dale robber!

And by that way wend the herds innumerable of bellwethers and flushed ewes and shearling rams and lambs and stubble geese and medium steers and roaring mares and polled calves and longwools and storesheep and Cuffe's prime springers and culls and sowpigs and baconhogs and the various different varieties of highly distinguished swine and Angus heifers and polly bullocks of immaculate pedigree together with prime premiated milchcows and beeves: and there is ever heard a trampling, cackling, roaring, lowing, bleating, bellowing, rumbling, grunting, champing, chewing, of sheep and pigs and heavyhooved kine from pasturelands of Lush and Rush and Carrickmines and from the streamy vales of Thomond, from

M'Gillicuddy's reeks the inaccessible and lordly Shannon the unfathomable, and from the gentle declivities of the place of the race of Kiar, their udders distended with superabundance of milk and butts of butter and rennets of cheese and farmer's firkins and targets of lamb and crannocks of corn and oblong eggs, in great hundreds, various in size, the agate with the dun.

So we turned into Barney Kiernan's and there sure enough was the citizen up in the corner having a great confab with himself and that bloody mangy mongrel, Garryowen, and he waiting for what the sky would drop in the way of drink.

– There he is, says I, in his gloryhole, with his cruiskeen lawn and his load of papers, working for the cause.

The bloody mongrel let a grouse out of him would give you the creeps. Be a corporal work of mercy if someone would take the life of that bloody dog. I'm told for a fact he ate a good part of the breeches off a constabulary man in Santry that came round one time with a blue paper about a licence.

– Stand and deliver, says he.

– That's all right, citizen, says Joe. Friends here.

– Pass, friends, says he.

Then he rubs his hand in his eye and says he:

– What's your opinion of the times?

Doing the rapparee and Rory of the hill. But, begob, Joe was equal to the occasion.

– I think the markets are on a rise, says he, sliding his hand down his fork.

So begob the citizen claps his paw on his knee and he says:

– Foreign wars is the cause of it.

And says Joe, sticking his thumb in his pocket:

– It's the Russians wish to tyrannize.

– Arrah, give over your bloody codding, Joe, says I, I've a thirst on me I wouldn't sell for half a crown.

– Give it a name, citizen, says Joe.

– Wine of the country, says he.

– What's yours? says Joe.

– Ditto MacAnaspey, says I.

– Three pints, Terry, says Joe. And how's the old heart, citizen? says he.

– Never better, *a chara*, says he. What Garry? Are we going to win? Eh?

And with that he took the bloody old towser by the scruff of the neck and, by Jesus, he near throttled him.

The figure seated on a large boulder at the foot of a round tower was that of a broadshouldered deepchested stronglimbed frankeyed redhaired freely freckled shaggybearded widemouthed largenosed longheaded deepvoiced barekneed brawnyhanded hairylegged ruddyfaced sinewyarmed hero. From shoulder to shoulder he measured several ells and his rocklike mountainous knees were covered, as was likewise the rest of his body wherever visible, with a strong growth of tawny prickly hair in hue and toughness similar to the mountain gorse (*Ulex Europeus*). The widewinged nostrils, from which bristles of the same tawny hue projected, were of such capaciousness that within their cavernous obscurity the fieldlark might easily have lodged her nest. The eyes in which a tear and a smile strove ever for the mastery were of the dimensions of a goodsized cauliflower. A powerful current of warm breath issued at regular intervals from the profound cavity of his mouth while in rhythmic resonance the loud strong hale reverberations of his formidable heart thundered rumblingly causing the ground, the summit of the lofty tower and the still loftier walls of the cave to vibrate and tremble.

He wore a long unsleeved garment of recently flayed oxhide reaching to the knees in a loose kilt and this was bound about his middle by a girdle of plaited straw and rushes. Beneath this he wore trews of deerskin, roughly stitched with gut. His nether extremities were encased in high Balbriggan buskins dyed in lichen purple, the feet being shod with brogues of salted cowhide laced with the windpipe of the same beast. From his girdle hung a row of seastones which dangled at every movement of his portentous frame and on these were graven with rude yet striking art the tribal images of many Irish heroes and heroines of antiquity, Cuchulin, Conn of hundred battles, Niall of nine hostages, Brian of Kincora, the Ardri Malachi, Art MacMurragh, Shane O'Neill, Father John Murphy, Owen Roe, Patrick Sarsfield, Red Hugh O'Donnell, Red Jim MacDermott, Soggarth Eoghan O'Growney, Michael Dwyer, Francy Higgins, Henry Joy M'Cracken, Goliath, Horace Wheatley, Thomas Conneff, Peg Woffington, the Village Blacksmith, Captain Moonlight, Captain Boycott, Dante Alighieri, Christopher Columbus, S. Fursa, S. Brendan, Marshall MacMahon, Charlemagne, Theobald Wolfe Tone, the Mother of the Maccabees, the Last of the Mohicans, the Rose of Castille, the Man for Galway, The Man that Broke the Bank at Monte Carlo, The Man in the Gap, The Woman Who Didn't, Benjamin Franklin, Napoleon Bonaparte, John L. Sullivan, Cleopatra, Savourneen Deelish, Julius Caesar, Paracelsus, Sir Thomas Lipton, William Tell, Michelangelo, Hayes, Muhammad, the Bride of Lammermoor, Peter the Hermit, Peter the Packer, Dark Rosaleen, Patrick W. Shakespeare, Brian Confucius, Murtagh Gutenberg, Patricio Velasquez, Captain Nemo, Tristan and Isolde, the first Prince of Wales, Thomas Cook and Son, the Bold Soldier Boy, Arrah na Pogue, Dick Turpin, Ludwig Beethoven, the Colleen Bawn, Waddler Healy, Angus the Culdee, Dolly Mount, Sidney Parade, Ben Howth, Valentine Greatrakes, Adam and Eve, Arthur Wellesley, Boss Croker, Herodotus, Jack the Giantkiller, Gautama Buddha, Lady Godiva, The Lily of Killarney, Balor of the Evil Eye, the Queen of Sheba, Acky Nagle, Joe Nagle, Alessandro Volta, Jeremiah O'Donovan Rossa, Don Philip O'Sullivan Beare. A couched spear of acuminated granite rested by him while at his feet reposed a savage animal of the canine tribe whose stertorous gasps announced that he was sunk in uneasy slumber, a supposition confirmed by hoarse growls and spasmodic movements which his master repressed from time to time by tranquillizing blows of a mighty cudgel rudely fashioned out of paleolithic stone.

So anyhow Terry brought the three pints Joe was standing and begob the sight nearly left my eyes when I saw him hand out a quid. O, as true as I'm telling you. A goodlooking sovereign.

– And there's more where that came from, says he.

– Were you robbing the poorbox, Joe? says I.

– Sweat of my brow, says Joe. 'Twas the prudent member gave me the wheeze.

– I saw him before I met you, says I, sloping around by Pill lane and Greek street with his cod's eye counting up all the guts of the fish.

Who comes through Michan's land, bedight in sable armour? O'Bloom, the son of Rory: it is he. Impervious to fear is Rory's son: he of the prudent soul.

– For the old woman of Prince's street, says the citizen, the subsidized organ. The pledgebound party on the floor of the house. And look at this blasted rag, says he. Look at this, says he. The *Irish Independent*, if you please, founded by Parnell to be the workingman's friend. Listen to the births and deaths in the *Irish all for Ireland Independent* and i'll thank you and the marriages.

And he starts reading them out:

– Gordon, Barnfield Crescent, Exeter; Redmayne of Iffley, Saint Anne's on Sea, the wife of William T. Redmayne, of a son. How's that eh? Wright and Flint, Vincent and Gillett to Rotha Marion daughter of Rosa and the late George Alfred Gillett, 179 Clapham Road, Stockwell, Playwood and Risdale at Saint Jude's Kensington by the very reverend Dr Forrest, Dean of Worcester, eh? Deaths. Bristow, at Whitehall lane, London: Carr, Stoke Newington, of gastritis and heart disease: Cockburn, at the Moat house, Chepstow . . .

– I know that fellow, says Joe, from bitter experience.

– Cockburn. Dimsey, wife of David Dimsey, late of the admiralty: Miller, Tottenham, aged eightyfive: Welsh, June 12, at 35 Canning Street, Liverpool, Isabella Helen. How's that for a national press, eh, my brown son? How's that for Martin Murphy, the Bantry jobber?

– Ah, well, says Joe, handing round the boose. Thanks be to God they had the start of us. Drink that, citizen.

– I will, says he, honourable person.

– Health, Joe, says I. And all down the form.

Ah! Ow! Don't be talking! I was blue mouldy for the want of that pint. Declare to God I could hear it hit the pit of my stomach with a click.

And lo, as they quaffed their cup of joy, a godlike messenger came swiftly in, radiant as the eye of heaven, a comely youth, and behind him there passed an elder of noble gait and countenance, bearing the sacred scrolls of law, and with him his lady wife, a dame of peerless lineage, fairest of her race.

Little Alf Bergan popped in round the door and hid behind Barney's snug, squeezed up with the laughing, and who was sitting up there in the corner that I hadn't seen snoring drunk, blind to the world, only Bob Doran. I didn't know what was up and Alf kept making signs out of the door. And begob what was it only that bloody old pantaloon Denis Breen in his bath slippers with two bloody big books tucked under his oxter and the wife hotfoot after him, unfortunate wretched woman trotting like a poodle. I thought Alf would split.

– Look at him, says he. Breen. He's traipsing all round Dublin with a postcard someone sent him with u. p.: up on it to take a li . . .

And he doubled up.

– Take a what? says I.

– Libel action, says he, for ten thousand pounds.

– O hell! says I.

The bloody mongrel began to growl that'd put the fear of God in you seeing something was up but the citizen gave him a kick in the ribs.

– *Bi i dho husht*, says he.

– Who? says Joe.

– Breen, says Alf. He was in John Henry Menton's and then he went round to Collis and Ward's and then Tom Rochford met him and sent him round to the subsheriff's for a lark. O God, I've a pain laughing. U. p.: up. The long fellow gave him an eye as good as a process and now the bloody old lunatic is gone round to Green Street to look for a G. man.

– When is long John going to hang that fellow in Mountjoy? says Joe.

– Bergan, says Bob Doran, waking up. Is that Alf Bergan?

– Yes, says Alf. Hanging? Wait till I show you. Here, Terry, give us a pony. That bloody old fool! Ten thousand pounds. You should have seen long John's eye. U. p . . .

And he started laughing.

– Who are you laughing at? says Bob Doran. Is that Bergan?

– Hurry up, Terry boy, says Alf.

Terence O'Ryan heard him and straightway brought him a crystal cup full of the foaming ebon ale which the noble twin brothers Bungiveagh and Bungardilaun brew ever in their divine alevats, cunning as the sons of deathless Leda. For they garner the succulent berries of the hop and mass and sift and bruise and brew them and they mix therewith sour juices and bring the must to the sacred fire and cease not night or day from their toil, those cunning brothers, lords of the vat.

Then did you, chivalrous Terence, hand forth, as to the manner born, that nectarous beverage and you offered the crystal cup to him that thirsted, the soul of chivalry, in beauty akin to the immortals.

But he, the young chief of the O'Bergan's, could ill brook to be outdone in generous deeds but gave therefor with gracious gesture a testoon of costliest bronze. Thereon embossed in excellent smithwork was seen the image of a queen of regal port, scion of the house of Brunswick, Victoria her name, Her Most Excellent Majesty, by grace of God of the United Kingdom of Great Britain and Ireland and of the British dominions beyond the sea, queen, defender of the faith, Empress of India, even she,

who bore rule, a victress over many peoples, the wellbeloved,
for they knew and loved her from the rising of the sun to the
going down thereof, the pale, the dark, the ruddy and the
ethiop.

– What's that bloody freemason doing, says the citizen, prowl-
ing up and down outside?

– What's that? says Joe.

– Here you are, says Alf, chucking out the rhino. Talking
about hanging. I'll show you something you never saw. Hang-
men's letters. Look at here.

So he took a bundle of wisps of letters and envelopes out of
his pocket.

– Are you codding? says I.

– Honest injun, says Alf. Read them.

So Joe took up the letters.

– Who are you laughing at? says Bob Doran.

So I saw there was going to be bit of a dust. Bob's a queer
chap when the porter's up in him so says I just to make talk:

– How's Willy Murray those times, Alf?

– I don't know, says Alf. I saw him just now in Capel Street
with Paddy Dignam. Only I was running after that . . .

– You what? says Joe, throwing down the letters. With who?

– With Dignam, says Alf.

– Is it Paddy? says Joe.

– Yes, says Alf. Why?

– Don't you know he's dead? says Joe.

– Paddy Dignam dead? says Alf.

– Ay, says Joe.

– Sure I'm after seeing him not five minutes ago, says Alf, as
plain as a pikestaff.

– Who's dead? says Bob Doran.

– You saw his ghost then, says Joe, God between us and harm.

– What? says Alf. Good Christ, only five . . . What? . . . and
Willy Murray with him, the two of them there near whatdoyou-
callhim's . . . What? Dignam dead?

    – What about Dignam? says Bob Doran. Who's talking about . . .?

    – Dead! says Alf. He is no more dead than you are.

    – Maybe so, says Joe. They took the liberty of burying him this morning anyhow.

    – Paddy? says Alf.

    – Ay, says Joe. He paid the debt. of nature, God be merciful to him.

    – Good Christ! says Alf.

Begob he was what you might call flabbergasted.

JAMES STEPHENS
A Rhinoceros, Some Ladies and A Horse

James Stephens (1882–1950) was born in Dublin. Best known for his fantasy novels, The Crock of Gold *and* The Charwoman's Daughter, *Stephens also wrote poetry and memoirs and was one of the major figures of the Irish Literary Renaissance. He had the distinction of being nominated by James Joyce as the man to complete* Finnegans Wake *should he, Joyce, die in the attempt. 'A Rhinoceros, Some Ladies and A Horse', originally intended as the first chapter of an autobiography, has become one of Stephens' most celebrated short stories.*

One day, in my first job, a lady fell in love with me. It was quite unreasonable, of course, for I wasn't wonderful: I was small and thin, and I weighed much the same as a largish duck-egg. I didn't fall in love with her, or anything like that. I got under the table, and stayed there until she had to go wherever she had to go to.

I had seen an advertisement – 'Smart boy wanted', it said. My legs were the smartest things about me, so I went there on the run. I got the job.

At that time there was nothing on God's earth that I could do, except run. I had no brains, and I had no memory. When I was told to do anything I got into such an enthusiasm about it that I couldn't remember anything else about it. I just ran as hard as I could, and then I ran back, proud and panting. And when they asked me for the whatever-it-was that I had run for, I started, right on the instant, and ran some more.

The place I was working at was, amongst other things, a theatrical agency. I used to be sitting in a corner of the office floor, waiting to be told to run somewhere and back. A lady would come in – a music-hall lady that is – and, in about five minutes, howls of joy would start coming from the inner office. Then, peacefully enough, the lady and my two bosses would

come out, and the lady always said, 'Splits! I can do splits like
no one.' And one of my bosses would say, 'I'm keeping your
splits in mind.' And the other would add, gallantly – 'No one
who ever saw your splits could ever forget 'em.'

One of my bosses was thin, and the other one was fat. My fat
boss was composed entirely of stomachs. He had three baby-
stomachs under his chin: then he had three more descending in
even larger englobings nearly to the ground: but, just before
reaching the ground, the final stomach bifurcated into a pair of
boots. He was very light on these and could bounce about in the
neatest way.

He was the fattest thing I had ever seen, except a rhinoceros
that I had met in the Zoo the Sunday before I got the job. That
rhino was *very* fat, and it had a smell like twenty-five pigs. I was
standing outside its palisade, wondering what it could possibly
feel like to be a rhinoceros, when two larger boys passed by.
Suddenly they caught hold of me, and pushed me through the
bars of the palisade. I was very skinny, and in about two
seconds I was right inside, and the rhinoceros was looking at
me.

It was very fat, but it wasn't fat like stomachs, it was fat like
barrels of cement, and when it moved it creaked a lot, like a
woman I used to know who creaked like an old bedstead. The
rhinoceros swaggled over to me with a bunch of cabbage
sticking out of its mouth. It wasn't angry, or anything like that,
it just wanted to see who I was. Rhinos are blindish: they mainly
see by smelling, and they smell in snorts. This one started at my
left shoe, and snorted right up that side of me to my ear. He
smelt that very carefully: then he switched over to my right ear,
and snorted right down that side of me to my right shoe: then
he fell in love with my shoes and began to lick them. I,
naturally, wriggled my feet at that, and the big chap was so
astonished that he did the strangest step-dance backwards to his
pile of cabbages, and began to eat them.

I squeezed myself out of his cage and walked away. In a

couple of minutes I saw the two boys. They were very frightened, and they asked me what I had done to the rhinoceros. I
answered, a bit grandly, perhaps, that I had seized it in both
hands, ripped it limb from limb, and tossed its carcase to the
crows. But when they began shouting to people that I had just
murdered a rhinoceros I took to my heels, for I didn't want to
be arrested and hanged for a murder that I hadn't committed.

Still, a man can't be as fat as a rhinoceros, but my boss was as
fat as a man can be. One day a great lady of the halls came in,
and was received on the knee. She was very great. Her name
was Maudie Darling, or thereabouts. My bosses called her
nothing but 'Darling,' and she called them the same. When the
time came for her to arrive the whole building got palpitations
of the heart. After waiting a while my thin boss got angry, and
said – 'Who does the woman think she is? If she isn't here in
two twos I'll go down to the entry, and when she does come I'll
boot her out.' The fat boss said – 'She's only two hours late,
she'll be here before the week's out.'

Within a few minutes there came great clamours from the
courtyard. Patriotic cheers, such as Parnell himself never got,
were thundering. My bosses ran instantly to the inner office.
Then the door opened, and the lady appeared.

She was very wide, and deep, and magnificent. She was
dressed in camels and zebras and goats: she had two peacocks in
her hat and a rabbit muff in her hand, and she strode among
these with prancings.

But when she got right into the room and saw herself being
looked at by three men and a boy she became adorably shy: one
could see that she had never been looked at before.

'O,' said she, with a smile that made three and a half hearts
beat like one, 'O,' said she, very modestly, 'is Mr Which-of-'em-
is-it really in? Please tell him that Little-Miss-Me would be so
glad to see and to be –'

Then the inner door opened, and the large lady was surrounded by my fat boss and my thin boss. She crooned to them

– 'O, you dear boys, you'll never know how much I've thought of you and longed to see you.'

That remark left me stupefied. The first day I got to the office I heard that it was the fat boss's birthday, and that he was thirty years of age: and the thin boss didn't look a day younger than the fat one. How the lady could mistake these old men for boys seemed to me the strangest fact that had ever come my way. My own bet was that they'd both die of old age in about a month.

After a while they all came out again. The lady was helpless with laughter: she had to be supported by my two bosses – 'O,' she cried, 'you boys will kill me.' And the bosses laughed and laughed, and the fat one said – 'Darling, you're a scream,' and the thin one said – 'Darling, you're a riot.'

And then . . . she saw me! I saw her seeing me the very way I had seen the rhinoceros seeing me: I wondered for an instant would she smell me down one leg and up the other. She swept my two bosses right away from her, and she became a kind of queen, very glorious to behold: but sad, startled. She stretched a long, slow arm out and out and then she unfolded a long, slow finger, and pointed it at me – 'Who is THAT??' she whispered in a strange whisper that could be heard two miles off.

My fat boss was an awful liar – 'The cat brought that in,' said he.

But the thin boss rebuked him: 'No,' he said, 'it was not the cat. Let me introduce you; darling, this is James. James, this is the darling of the gods.'

'And of the pit,' said she, sternly.

She looked at me again. Then she sank to her knees and spread out both arms to me –

'Come to my boozalum, angel,' said she in a tender kind of way.

I knew what she meant, and I knew that she didn't know how to pronounce that word. I took a rapid glance at the area indicated. The lady had a boozalum you could graze a cow on. I didn't wait one second, but slid, in one swift, silent slide, under the table. Then she came forward and said a whole lot of poems to me under the table, imploring me, among a lot of odd things, to 'come forth, and gild the morning with my eyes,' but at last she was reduced to whistling at me with two fingers in her mouth, the way you whistle for a cab.

I learned after she had gone that most of the things she said to me were written by a poet fellow named Spokeshave. They were very complimentary, but I couldn't love a woman who mistook my old bosses for boys, and had a boozalum that it would take an Arab chieftain a week to trot across on a camel.

The thin boss pulled me from under the table by my leg, and said that my way was the proper way to treat a rip, but my fat boss said, very gravely – 'James, when a lady invites a gentleman to her boozalum a real gentleman hops there as pronto as possible, and I'll have none but real gentlemen in this office.'

'Tell me,' he went on, 'what made that wad of Turkish Delight fall in love with you?'

'She didn't love me at all, sir,' I answered.

'No?' he inquired.

'She was making fun of me,' I explained.

'There's something in that,' said he seriously, and went back to his office.

I had been expecting to be sacked that day. I was sacked the next day, but that was about a horse.

I had been given three letters to post, and told to run or they'd be too late. So I ran to the post office and round it and back, with, naturally, the three letters in my pocket. As I came to our door a nice, solid, red-faced man rode up on a horse. He thrust the reins into my hand –

'Hold the horse for a minute,' said he.

'I can't,' I replied, 'my boss is waiting for me.'

'I'll only be a minute,' said he angrily, and he walked off.

Well, there was I, saddled, as it were, with a horse. I looked at it, and it looked at me. Then it blew a pint of soap-suds out of its nose and took another look at me, and then the horse fell in love with me as if he had just found his long-lost foal. He started to lean against me and to woo me with small whinneys, and I responded and replied as best I could.

'Don't move a toe,' said I to the horse, 'I'll be back in a minute.'

He understood exactly what I said, and the only move he made was to swing his head and watch me as I darted up the street. I was less than half a minute away anyhow, and never out of his sight.

Up the street there was a man, and sometimes a woman, with a barrow, thick-piled with cabbages and oranges and apples. As I raced round the barrow I pinched an apple off it at full speed, and in ten seconds I was back at the horse. The good nag had watched every move I made, and when I got back his eyes were wide open, his mouth was wide open, and he had his legs all splayed out so that he couldn't possibly slip. I broke the apple in halves and popped one half into his mouth. He ate it in slow crunches, and then he looked diligently at the other half. I gave him the other half, and, as he ate it, he gurgled with cidery gargles of pure joy. He then swung his head round from me and pointed his nose up the street, right at the apple-barrow.

I raced up the street again, and was back within the half-minute with another apple. The horse had nigh finished the first half of it when a man who had come up said, thoughtfully –

'He seems to like apples, bedad!'

'He loves them,' said I.

And then, exactly at the speed of lightning, the man became angry, and invented bristles all over himself like a porcupine.

'What the hell do you mean,' he hissed, and then he bawled, 'by stealing my apples?'

I retreated a bit into the horse.

'I didn't steal your apples,' I said.

'You didn't!' he roared and then he hissed, 'I saw you,' he hissed.

'I didn't steal them,' I explained, 'I pinched them.'

'Tell me that one again,' said he.

'If,' said I patiently, 'if I took the apples for myself that would be stealing.'

'So it would,' he agreed.

'But as I took them for the horse that's pinching.'

'Be dam, but!' said he. ''Tis a real argument,' he went on, staring at the sky. 'Answer me that one,' he demanded of himself, and he is a very stupor of intellection. 'I give it up,' he roared, 'you give me back my apples.'

I placed the half apple that was left into his hand, and he looked at it as if it was a dead frog.

'What'll I do with that?' he asked earnestly.

'Give it to the horse,' said I.

The horse was now prancing at him, and mincing at him, and making love at him. He pushed the half apple into the horse's mouth, and the horse mumbled it and watched him, and chewed it and watched him, and gurgled it and watched him.

'He does like his bit of apple,' said the man.

'He likes you too,' said I. 'I think he loves you.'

'It looks like it,' he agreed, for the horse was yearning at him, and its eyes were soulful.

'Let's get him another apple,' said I, and, without another word, we both pounded back to his barrow and each of us pinched an apple off it. We got one apple into the horse, and were breaking the second one when a woman said gently –

'Nice, kind, Christian gentlemen, feeding dumb animals – with my apples,' she yelled suddenly.

The man with me jumped as if he had been hit by a train.

'Mary,' said he humbly.

'Joseph,' said she in a completely unloving voice.

But the woman transformed herself into nothing else but woman –

'What about my apples?' said she. 'How many have we lost?'

'Three,' said Joseph.

'Four,' said I, 'I pinched three and you pinched one.'

'That's true,' said he. 'That's exact, Mary. I only pinched one of our apples.'

'You only,' she squealed.

And I, hoping to be useful, broke in –

'Joseph,' said I, 'is the nice lady your boss?'

He halted for a dreadful second, and made up his mind.

'You bet she's my boss,' said he, 'and she's better than that, for she's the very wife of my bosum.'

She turned to me.

'Child of Grace –' said she –

Now, when I was a child, and did something that a woman didn't like she always expostulated in the same way. If I tramped on her foot, or jabbed her in the stomach – the way women have multitudes of feet and stomachs is always astonishing to a child – the remark such a woman made was always the same. She would grab her toe or her stomach, and say – 'Childagrace, what the hell are you doing?' After a while I worked it out that Childagrace was one word, and was my name. When any woman in agony yelled Childagrace I ran right up prepared to be punished, and the woman always said tenderly, 'What are you yowling about, Childagrace.'

'Childagrace,' said Mary earnestly, 'how's my family to live if you steal our apples? You take my livelihood away from me! Very good, but will you feed and clothe and educate my children in,' she continued proudly, 'the condition to which they are accustomed?'

I answered that question cautiously.

'How many kids have you, ma'am?' said I.

'We'll leave that alone for a while,' she went on. 'You owe me two and six for the apples.'

'Mary!' said Joseph, in a pained voice.

'And you,' she snarled at him, 'owe me three shillings. I'll take it out of you in pints.' She turned to me.

'What do you do with all the money you get from the office here?'

'I give it to my landlady.'

'Does she stick to the lot of it?'

'Oh, no,' I answered, 'she always gives me back threepence.'

'Well, you come and live with me and I'll give you back fourpence.'

'All right,' said I.

'By gum,' said Joseph, enthusiastically, 'that'll be fine. We'll go out every night and we won't steal a thing. We'll just pinch legs of beef, and pig's feet, and barrels of beer —'

'Wait now,' said Mary. 'You stick to your own landlady. I've trouble enough of my own. You needn't pay me the two and six.'

'Good for you,' said Joseph heartily, and then, to me —

'You just get a wife of your bosum half as kind as my wife of my bosum and you'll be set up for life. 'Mary,' he cried joyfully, 'let's go and have a pint on the strength of it.'

'You shut up,' said she.

'Joseph,' I interrupted, 'knows how to pronounce the word properly.'

'What word?'

'The one he used when he said you were the wife of his what-you-may-call-it.'

'I'm not the wife of any man's what-you-may-call-it,' said she, indignantly — 'Oh, I see what you mean! So he pronounced it well, did he?'

'Yes, ma'am.'

She looked at me very sternly —

'How does it come you know about all these kinds of words?'

'Yes,' said Joseph, and he was even sterner than she was, 'when I was your age I didn't know any bad words.'

'You shut up,' said she, and continued, 'what made you say that to me?'

'A woman came into our office yesterday, and she mispronounced it.'

'What did she say now?'

'Oh, she said it all wrong.'

'Do you tell me so? We're all friends here: what way did she say it, son?'

'Well, ma'am, she called it boozalum.'

'She said it wrong all right,' said Joseph, 'but 'tis a good, round, fat kind of a word all the same.'

'You shut up,' said Mary. 'Who did she say the word to?'

'She said it to me, ma'am.'

'She must have been a rip,' said Joseph.

'Was she a rip, now?'

'I don't know, ma'am. I never met a rip.'

'You're too young yet,' said Joseph, 'but you'll meet them later on. I never met a rip myself until I got married – I mean,' he added hastily, 'that they were all rips except the wife of my what-do-you-call-ems, and that's why I married her.'

'I expect you've got a barrel-full of rips in your past,' said she bleakly, 'you must tell me about some of them tonight.' And then, to me, 'tell us about the woman,' said she.

So I told them all about her, and how she held out her arms to me, and said, 'Come to my boozalum, angel.'

'What did you do when she shoved out the old arms at you?' said Joseph.

'I got under the table,' I answered.

'That's not a bad place at all, but,' he continued earnestly, 'never get under the bed when there's an old girl chasing you, for that's the worst spot you could pick on. What was the strap's name?'

'Maudie Darling, she called herself.'

'You're a blooming lunatic,' said Joseph, 'she's the loveliest thing in the world, barring,' he added hastily, 'the wife of my blast-the-bloody-word.'

'We saw her last night,' said Mary, 'at Dan Lowrey's Theatre, and she's just lovely.'

'She isn't as nice as you, ma'am,' I asserted.

'Do you tell me that now?' said she.

'You are twice as nice as she is, and twenty times nicer.'

'There you are,' said Joseph, 'the very words I said to you last night.'

'You shut up,' said Mary scornfully, 'you were trying to knock a pint out of me! Listen, son,' she went on, 'we'll take all that back about your landlady. You come and live with me, and I'll give you back sixpence a week out of your wages.'

'All right, ma'am,' I crowed in a perfectly monstrous joy.

'Mary,' said Joseph, in a reluctant voice –

'You shut up,' said she.

'He can't come to live with us,' said Joseph. 'He's a bloody Prodestan,' he added sadly.

'Why –' she began –

'He'd keep me and the childer up all night, pinching apples for horses and asses, and reading the Bible, and up to every kind of devilment.'

Mary made up her mind quickly.

'You stick to your own landlady,' said she, 'tell her that I said she was to give you sixpence.' She whirled about. 'There won't be a thing left on that barrow,' said she to Joseph.

'Damn the scrap,' said Joseph violently.

'Listen,' said Mary to me very earnestly, 'am I nicer than Maudie Darling?'

'You are ma'am,' said I.

Mary went down on the road on her knees: she stretched out both arms to me, and said –

'Come to my boozalum, angel.'

I looked at her, and I looked at Joseph, and I looked at the horse. Then I turned from them all and ran into the building and into the office. My fat boss met me –

'Here's your five bob,' said he. 'Get to hell out of here,' said he.

And I ran out.

I went to the horse, and leaned my head against the thick end of his neck, and the horse leaned as much of himself against me as he could manage. Then the man who owned the horse came up and climbed into his saddle. He fumbled in his pocket –

'You were too long,' said I. 'I've been sacked for minding your horse.'

'That's too bad,' said he: 'that's too damn bad,' and he tossed me a penny.

I caught it, and lobbed it back into his lap, and I strode down the street the most outraged human being then living in the world.

PADRAIG O'SIOCHFHRADHA
Death to the Master

*Padraig O'Siochfhradha (1883–1964) was born in Dingle, County Kerry.
In 1913 he joined the Irish Volunteers and was jailed three times for
Republican activities. From 1927–1964 he was president of the Irish
Folklore Society and from 1946–1964 he was a member of the Irish
senate. His Jimeen books are still popular in Ireland. Translated from
the Irish by Patricia Egan.*

If only I were big! More than anything else in the world I'd like
to be grown up – then everyone wouldn't be at me the way they
are now. Boys have a very hard time of it. We can't do a single
thing but someone gives out to us. The other day I hit Big-
Betty's gander on the side of the head with a stone, and Betty
complained to my Mam.

When Betty went, Mam quizzed me about it. I did my best to
explain that I wasn't aiming at the gander at all, but at
Mickileen-Owen, and the gander just happened to get in the
way. Mam grabbed me and gave me a beating for throwing
stones, anyway. Did you ever hear the like of that? I tell you I
paid for that gander.

At home they're after me until my heart is broken. I have to
bring in the turf and the water; and I have to go to the outhouse
for potatoes for the dinner. Then, if I'm out there playing a
game of jackstones or throwing buttons, they're shouting and
roaring at me that the cow has broken into the cabbage, and off
I have to go again.

You know, I think they're not satisfied if that cow isn't
straying into the cabbage patch – just to torment poor Jimeen. I
can't imagine why boys are afflicted with mothers and fathers at
all.

But when I'm grown up, not a cow or a calf will I herd. Nor
will I help wind wool. Nor will I go to my aunt's house with

the clocking hen. And I won't sit at the top of the table and do my lessons.

Nothing ever bothered me as much as those wretched lessons. There's no escaping them.

– Jimeen, says Mam, every night, did you do your lessons yet?

Once I chanced saying that the master hadn't given any. But she questioned Mickileen-Owen, and the good-for-nothing squealed on me. I didn't know a thing about it until Mam took the stick from the back loft and gave it to me across the shins. There was nothing I could do but escape through the side window. Off I went, looking for Mickileen-Owen, but he was afraid to face me. I asked him to come out so I could break his face, but he wouldn't.

Then I began calling him 'pet' and 'eejit' and 'tell-tale', and he said back 'poor little boy, did your Mammy beat you? Oh! bold Mammy!' and he went on like that mocking me until I was in a right temper. I stayed a good while daring him to come out the door. But that was my mistake. His father was inside and when he heard me, out he came and warned me to be off.

Worse was to follow, because Mam was at the gable of the cowhouse and she heard him. She didn't rest until she had all the details of my doings. After he made his complaint, Owen went off, and when he was gone Mam started in on me. I wouldn't like to say what happened after that – I'd be ashamed. Mickileen-Owen told the other boys that Mam took down my britches – whoever told him – and that she beat me. I'm not saying she did. But I have to admit I wasn't able to sit down for three whole days – I was so sore in a certain spot.

Oh! indeed I'd rather be grown up, any day. But Mam's no worse than the master. He's always asking us to answer tricky questions – questions no one would bother with because they're not real at all. He's at his wits' end thinking up problems that will put us all in a fix: If a person had four pigs at a fair and got sixty-five pounds for them, how much each is that?

That's the kind of question the master gives us. Why should he, or anyone else, want to know how much each is that? If someone got sixty-five pounds for four pigs, shouldn't the master leave it at that and not be bothering us? But no, he won't; he's not that type.

One day he said to us – he was reading from a book: If a horse trotted ten miles in one hour, how far from home would he be in twenty-four hours?

Well, I didn't know and I gave up. Some of the others did it. When the master came as far as me, he stopped.

– Is it that you don't know?

– I don't, master, said I.

Then he put the figures on the blackboard.

– Four times ten? said he.

– That's forty, said I.

– Twice ten? said he.

– That's twenty.

– And four?

– That's twenty-four, said I. He wrote down 240.

– Now, how many miles from home would he be?

– Who knows? said I.

– You and your wooden head, said the master. Don't you understand that a horse travelling at ten miles an hour would do 240 miles in twenty-four hours?

– He would not, said I, he'd have to stop, or he'd fall with the hunger, or lose a shoe, or get a stone in his hoof, or . . .

– Enough of that! said the master, and he really had it in for me. Hold out your hand.

He slapped me twice, two strokes of the stick that went right through me, and he put me down to the back of the school. I started crying.

I sat down there for a long time, vexed and full of spite. I was thinking about the kind of death I'd like to give the master. It would give me great pleasure to run up to him, punch him, a right and a left, and choke him, and dump his body in a bog-hole, with a big stone tied around his neck.

When I remembered the horse in his book that travelled 240 miles a day, I thought I'd tie the master to him and let him off without reins or harness, at 240 miles every five minutes, forever and ever, until he came to the edge of a cliff, where they'd fall down, down, down, and be smashed into smithereens on the stones – and no one would know which was which, a piece of the master or a piece of the horse. That gave me great satisfaction – to finish off the master like that.

After that I started writing questions that would put him in a fix! If there was a horse that could travel 240 miles in one day, how many miles could the same horse travel in 300 years. If Big-Tim got fifty-nine pounds sixteen shillings and elevenpence three farthings for three sheep at the fair in Dingle, what would the master get for the horse that went 240 miles in twenty-four hours? How many ricks of turf would make a bag of soot?

I was laughing away to myself, I was so pleased, and I never noticed a thing until the master was behind me. He let out a big guffaw and took my piece of paper and read it out to the whole school!

They all roared laughing and I thought I'd go down through the floor with shame. Mickileen made a mocking face at me. I told him to wait until after school.

The master stuck my miserable page on the wall – for fun. I tell you, I was glad I hadn't written down the death I'd given him!

MICHÁEL MAC LIAMMÓIR
From *Put Money in Thy Purse*

Michéal Mac Liammóir (1889–1978) was one of Ireland's most renowned actors and raconteurs. His association with Hilton Edwards at Dublin's Gate Theatre established him as a powerful influence in Irish theatre. A one-man show based on the writings of Oscar Wilde, The Importance of Being Oscar *opened in Dublin in 1960 and went on to tour the world. Mac Liammóir also wrote plays, of which the best known is* Ill Met by Moonlight. *He first met Orson Welles at The Gate in the 1930s, and established a long and stormy relationship with him. In 1949, Welles cast Mac Liammóir as Iago in the film version of* Othello. Put Money in Thy Purse *is an acerbic and hilarious account of the troubled making of the film.*

FEBRUARY 4TH

Loathesome weather. Old Pal Johnny Sheridan arrived and walked me to doctor's house, where I was assured I was twice the man I was. Quelled with difficulty all sorts of sub-acid witticisms that came welling up in reply to this ridiculous sally, but must admit that I now remain calm at sight of clouds blowing over the sky, child playing at open doorway on corner of canal, Hilton turning from Sartre to Spenser with remote contented sigh, rain coming down from the mountains, tabby-kitten running stiff-tailed across the street, and that these and other innocent spectacles no longer fill me with panic-stricken desire to die and go to heaven, hell, or wherever it is one is sent.

At door of our house Johnny departed and I walked round blackened garden through the damp, dream-soggy air muttering lines for test (definitely decided by dear friends and self that I go to Paris): 'First I must tell thee this: Desdemona is directly in love with him.'

Hilton, smoking gigantic cigar, said film acting will be good for me as I'll be forced to *think* rather than *frame about*, a phrase I do not find in good taste.

Drove to my old aunt Craven's to say goodbye. She remarked with truth that we are now an excessively scattered family, what with Mac, beloved brother-in-law, and Mana, beloved sister, on Australian tour, and other sisters in England and Ceylon. Mac's daughter, Mary Rose, the only one of us left at home. I point out that I am only going for a week and only to Paris, where I go at least once every year; Aunt C. looked prophetic and said she didn't fancy all this travelling by air. Came away feeling apprehensive.

FEBRUARY 6TH

Arthur, looking determined, has begun to pack. Hilton inserts bottle of Power's Whiskey for Orson between suits and loads me with messages. Winnie Menary and her two boys to supper: feel depressed saying goodbye, but Winnie, H., and entire army of friends combined to remind me how lucky I am to leave Dublin for delirious week in Paris. Have never thought of film test as delirious experience but am doubtless wrong.

PARIS. FEBRUARY 7TH

Direct flight Dublin–Paris allowed no glimpse but vast ectoplasmic blanket of fog which occasionally gave nauseous heaving movement as though the earth below were turning from side to side in uneasy sleep. Fog slowly gave way to dim landscape seemingly miles below and peppered with snow, but could judge from slim oblongs of fields that France had been achieved.

Sat next to bony Australian gentleman, who said in tones of echoing corrugated iron that he admired my acting but couldn't remember what the plays he'd seen it in were called. Asked me whether like himself I was an internationalist, and went on to say he couldn't speak French or any other foreign tongue as he didn't like foreigners and failed to see why everyone couldn't speak the same way. Felt more convinced than ever that internationalism exists only as fancy-dress disguise for uniformity, and that chiefly in the minds of those who are familiar with one nation only and with language and mode of thought of that nation. Also that probabilities of friendship between nations speaking same language are slight. Alliance perfectly feasible, friendship unlikely, as they are bound to pronounce words in a manner not merely different but irritating to each other's taste; one set calling it *Luv* and the other *Laav*, whereas if one of them calls it *Love* and the other *Amour* all is well. They then seem neither popinjays nor outsiders, merely intriguingly incomprehensible.

Aer Lingus crew very friendly and had drinks with them on arrival at Le Bourget with immediate results of dizziness. No one to meet me but suddenly heard my name announced followed by request to repair to telephone.

This found to be situated in remote wooden tower, approached by rickety wooden ladder swaying in heavy gale and filled with bickering officials who gave brief business-like smile, politely indicated telephone, and proceeded with bickering. Long silence punctuated with baritone buzzings finally gave way to unknown (female) voice with apparently Viennese accent that said Was I Me? Said, after brief hesitation, Yes, and was asked in agitated tone was I *sure* of this? Said Absolutely in spite of sudden hideous doubt (owing to memories of N.B-D.) and voice cried 'Gott sei Dank!', and would I wait until she could contact the sheep's-head of a chauffeur at airport of Orly where he had insisted I was to alight. Said Yes again and repaired to bar.

All this had taken a long time and friends from Aer Lingus had now vanished. Sat alone and read *Invitation au Château* in great contentment, and after an hour and a half was collected by small man in leather coat and beret with strong Belgian accent and driven to the Hotel Lancaster in the Rue de Berri. Tall sprays of lilac in the hall, groups of apéritif drinkers, and a glowing warmth, and I found myself suddenly confronted by tall and striking lady, very smart, black hair-do, wearing horn-rimmed glasses and harassed expression and speaking effortless English. Viennese accent, so remarkable on the phone, only detectable in certain words. She introduced herself as Mme Rita Ribolla, 'the secretary of Mr Velles,' she added, then sneezed violently and muttered 'Pfui Teufel'. I said 'Gesundheit' and she 'Danke' as the lift took us to sixth floor, and there was Orson in the doorway, huge, expansive, round-headed, almond-eyed, clad apparently in dungarees, and miraculously unchanged.

Indulged in much hugging and dancing round discreet olive-green and dull-gold suite, then settled down to some *fine à l'eau* by log fire. No bridging of the years seemed necessary: exactly as he used to be, perhaps larger and more, as it were, tropically Byzantine still, but essentially the same old darkly waltzing *tree*, half banyan, half oak, the Jungle and the Forest lazily pawing each other for mastery. I said incredulously that most people changed some way or another as life flowed by, and he said that only applied to *nice* people, and that lousers like us never changed at all whether it was 1934 or 1949 or Dublin or Chicago or Paris.

Room filled with people: I can only remember Lou Lindsay, an American who Cuts, and Maurice Bessi, a Frenchman who Edits and Publicizes; both agreeable. Where should we all dine? Felt dizzy at the very thought, arranged to meet O. for lunch the next day, and am going to eat in my room, which is in red and white and has colossal jar of parrot tulips to welcome me.

FEBRUARY 8TH

No work today as O., looking profoundly Baronial, said I ought to relax. So we relaxed together at Méditerranée in Place de l'Odéon for lunch, relaxed in the car all afternoon (driver as Belgian as ever and the Bois superbly arranged in seven hundred shades of grey at lowest estimate), relaxed alone for tea in red and white room, where O.'s doctor visited me and relaxed me more than ever by putting me on a diet of all the things I like best, also on much air, not too much exercise, and massage once daily.

Masseur recommended duly arrived, an uncommunicative giant with an obliterated nose, hands like muffins, and the name of Moïse; I now feel equal to, if not anxious for, several rounds of boxing if only I knew the rules: can this be correct state of affairs from relaxation viewpoint?

Charlie Lederer turned up at seven, known to the world and to Hollywood in particular as Wit and Scriptwriter, Champion of his Race, and Practical Joker. Found him entirely sympathetic and was struck by intense almost dazzling blueness of eyes not as a rule associated with Jewish faces: Lou Lindsay made vigorous reappearance, and atmosphere of relaxation continued with sense of stimulus and well-being, a combination one meets occasionally but rarely except among Americans and which is one of their greatest achievements. Dinner, which was at Tour d'Argent, hilarious. Claude Térrail, the genius of the place, and forever associated in the mind with its dimly coloured impeccability, panelled lift, perfume of wine-dabbled rose-leaves and sour cream, curving glass wall with panorama of Paris reclining at one's feet, Claude Térrail, in spite of sleek and burnished appearance as of ambiguous hero in some *madrigal de Provence*, proves in conversation full of humanity and has a store of curious stories reflecting – is it unconsciously? – great plainness and sincerity of temperament. This, with Lou's blond, bluff blackguardism, Charles's sympathetic skipping-rope form of wit, and Orson's thunderous chortling, made a good party. Orson contributed mood of thirteenth-century pirate (if there were any in the thirteenth century) and entire Renaissance was dealt with and practically exploded by him before coffee was reached.

No reaction of dizziness followed, but was promptly replaced, on return to red and white room, by unsuitable and morbid pangs of homesickness.

FEBRUARY 9TH

We did some scenes today, 'First I must tell thee this' and some others; O. sitting with a script in his hand against a window past which rain fell in slanting sheets, and self alternately sitting and pacing up and down past log fire. Overhead some workmen hammered fitfully at something or other. Not relaxed at all. O., however, enthusiastic at intervals that grew shorter and proclaimed loudly that he would now not hear of my making test, as he knew definitely already that Iago and I were just made for each other, and waxed so prophetic of triumph that my mind, grown suspicious through long years spent, however brokenly, in native land, thought this was probably tactful if roundabout way of getting me back to Dublin. Contract, however, immediately discussed in detail, and small army of business men summoned for cocktails and duly warned I was to be treated with care.

Rita Ribolla, summoned from her lair where she spends her days and nights, she tells me, either in waiting for Mr Velles to ring her or in telling others who *do* ring her that he, Mr Velles, is not at home, arrived in smart grey slacks, and, armed with note-book, took down impressive particulars on separate piece of paper, looking patient as she did it. Slacks and patient expression did not escape critical comment from O.

Discovered during the evening that certain scenes of proposed *Othello* film had already been shot in Venice last September with Lea Padovani as Desdemona, and another Italian artist as Iago. Name, though he was found unsuitable, escapes me (Freud? Probably). Remember Padovani — a beautiful creature — very well in Italian part in English film made two years ago at Taormina in which Hilton played with her, John Clements and Kay Hammond, but could not recall that she spoke any English. Nor, said O., did she, but she was learning it with great application, and had, moreover, dyed her superb dark hair to required Venetian blonde.

But could she learn enough English to play Desdemona in time for film? If not, said O., she could be dubbed (this indeed a revelation, though on second thoughts I must have known that such a process would be possible).

Fell to brooding on Padovani's English and on time required for all there was to do if I really was going to make the film with him, and put some leading questions to O., reminding him that Hilton and I wanted to re-open in Dublin in October; that illness and film combined had kept me out of present season, and that if I was to be of any use to my partner or to our theatre –

Nothing easier, cried O., as film undoubtedly over by August at latest, which would give me time not only for Irish season but for short holiday with himself beforehand. Felt delightfully reassured.

FEBRUARY IITH

Relaxation treatment continues in the guise of frantic whirl of luncheon and dinner parties with Charlie Lederer and Lou Lindsay, also with dear Virginia, Orson's first wife, who has skipped through Paris like a gay little thrush *en route* for some-where else, Orson presiding over these feasts with dark and cataclysmic gaiety that suggests old English word, now regretta-bly fallen into disuse, Wassail, Wassail.

Also there are repeated rehearsals of various passages concern-ing Othello and Iago (Orson still apparently pleased) inter-spersed with lengthy discussions with Trauner, who is doing the sets.

Trauner is a stocky Hungarian-Parisian of sober yet twinkling intelligence and charm, whose pale auburn hair and skin and pale, restless eyes make him look as if he were carved out of fresh gingerbread, also as if he had a moustache, though he is clean-shaven. Cannot explain these impressions, but there they are. He made the décor for *Enfants du Paradis* and many other good things; I find his designs for *Othello* impressively virile and evocative.

All is to be Carpaccio, says Orson, lumbering round the room and waving his arms about. (Why do directors always walk about rooms? Is this their only way of getting exercise, or do they expect, on principle of African witch doctor, to find solution hidden somewhere in the furniture? Hilton also has this distracting habit, but he pounds up and down and O. floats, though lumberingly, round and round.) Carpaccio; which means hair falling wispishly to shoulders, small round hats of plummy red felt (though film not to be in colour), very short belted jackets, undershirt pulled in puffs through apertures in sleeves laced with ribbons and leather thongs, long hose, and laced boots. Females also laced, bunched, puffed, slashed, and rib-boned and with rather calculating curly hair-do; they won't like any of this if I know them, but like true actresses will, I am convinced, endeavour to look as unlike period as possible and brilliantly succeed.

Shooting, they think, will be in Rome, Venice, and Nice; this will be pleasant, I imagine, though a more adventurous nature might hanker after regions less familiar, but I'm feeling battered and am content with people and places I know.

Had tea today with Seán Murphy, our Minister in Paris, and with his wife, both of them charming to me, and a lovely house. Missed for a moment the car driven by Belgian, who had changed parking position while waiting for me, and, overcome by sudden dizziness, fell flat on my back in middle of the Rue Georges V (so glad it wasn't Place Blanche). Explained to officer and wife who assisted me with great helpfulness to my feet that I wasn't drunk, merely *surmené*, which did not however appear to impress Madame, who gave the national chortle and said 'Ah sans blague,' which might have meant anything and probably did.

Orson, perturbed at my vivid recounting of this incident, made me lie flat (this time on olive-green sofa) while he diverted me with stories of his first arrival in Galway on his way to act with us at the Gate in 1930: this also revived unpleasing memories of my portrait of him in my autobiography *All for Hecuba*, at which he nearly lost control and admitted to having read the book with pleasure until reaching the Ghastly Parody of himself, at which he had thrown it several times across the room (presumably to and fro, or would it be in same direction on different occasions?).

I made stirring defence, thus banishing last remains of dizziness, and mentioned that everyone I knew had felt the same, from Lady Headfort to my sister Mana, all agreeing that everyone but themselves was painted with sympathy and even skill, and it was only when I got to *them* that I showed a disappointing lack of perception, even of common decency; and O. then said the truth was that I was sweet to my acquaintances and mean to my friends.

Some desultory brooding over this ever since has led me to think it may be true.

FEBRUARY 13TH

Sunday. Pearl-grey morning, all the colours dimmed and blurred; one of those French Sundays to be interpreted only by Seurat or Debussy. Walked alone to Cité and wandered through bird and flower markets; indescribably delicate light. Best of all on return was sight of elderly gentleman in black bicycling slowly round Place de l'Étoile through mother-of-pearl atmosphere with basket on the front handles containing beautifully shaved French poodle, its paws on front of the basket and a large Heliotrope Bow round its neck. Orson says I made up the Heliotrope Bow but I didn't.

Well-known English actor called Robert Coote suddenly appeared tonight, having flown from Hollywood in order to play Roderigo, for which O. says he should be perfect. Long session began; we read through many scenes and I perceived O.'s judgement to be right. Coote very agreeable, with that mixture of jumpy seriousness and abrupt good humour that makes the English so different from all other people; also first-rate comedy sense. He vanished however as suddenly as he had arrived, leaving O. pleased with the cast so far. Found myself alone with Rita and Orson in olive-green suite illumined by leaping flames from log fire. Rain, still audible, now invisible owing to darkness having fallen. O. began to dab away at picture-book written and illustrated by him for his daughter Christopher, while I continued reading of enchanting book by Colette called *Prisons et Paradis*.

Rita filed her nails pensively and sighed, and the workmen began again to hammer at something overhead.

O., still dabbing brilliantly but looking disturbed, said those workmen followed him all over the world and had disturbed him in places as far apart as Brazil, Austria, Great Britain, and USA. He was sure they were the same ones.

Rita, muttering *fantastisch*, *fantastisch*!, continued with her nails.

O. said would she shut up and throw that file out of the window, she sounded like a chipmunk having lunch.

Rita put away file into discreet grey and gold bag and sat demurely with folded hands.

O. asked her severely, Had she no amusing anecdotes to relate?

Rita said No; amusing things seldom happened to those whose lot in life was to sit in a small room waiting for der telephone to ring.

O., moistening brush and eyeing her with abstract scientific interest, said why, in that case, not get herself a larger room?

Rita, with faultless logic, said she could not see how a larger room would necessarily supply her mit amusing anecdotes.

Was he, Orson, to take it then that, she, Rita, was not contented with her lot in life? (Sullen are you, Mme Ribolla? Eh? Mutinous are you, eh, Madam Glum?)

Ach, not at all, Mr Velles.

Then why was she wearing expression of second contralto in minor operatic work? And why did she always have to carry that God-awful note-book around?

To make notes in, said Rita.

Then who, said O., as she was so clever, was expected to arrive that night?

No von at all, except a Dutchman who vished to play Roderigo, said Rita, after elaborate glance at book.

What about Miss Padovani, said O., throwing down his brush.

That was for tomorrow night, Mr Velles.

What! wasn't today Monday?

No, Mr Velles, today we are Sunday.

In that case what was she, Mme Ribolla, thinking of to appear in slacks?

Na wirklich, Mr Velles, what is then wrong mit the Schlacks?

It is *Sunday*, Mme Ribolla. Perhaps you don't quite realize what *Sunday* means to us plain folks from the Middle West? No? Well, that's just too bad. But one of the things it *doesn't* mean is mutinous women in slacks.

Madam Glum and self then invited by O. to dine at the Taillevent in the Rue St Georges. (What about der Dutchman? said Madam G. Der Dutchman, said O., could come another time, and added that she, Rebellious Rita, must leave word mit dem porter. At any rate, Roderigo, like Iago, was now cast.)

Talked during dinner (Rebellious Rita's slacks now replaced by irreproachable black skirt) about Othello, New England, the Bible, Al. Jolson, and the Inequality of Woman, latter topic directed entirely by O., who reveals himself as implacable reactionary and says they can't even cook. (Faint protests from Rita quelled by his popping lumps of lobster into her mouth.)

On return to hotel we were confronted by spectacle of der Dutchman, immensely lanky youth with flapping overcoat, flowing scarf, fluttering tie, and flying blond locks, who, in spite of porter's suggestions, had waited for audition for four hours, much of that time it would appear having been spent in the bar. Rita flew to her room.

Dutchman, in spite of Orson's Ivan the Terrible expression and brief stop-press mode of address, pursued us to suite, and endless reading of Roderigo scenes ensued. Dutchman (looking like Jane, Jane tall as a Crane) now began to fly unsteadily round the room throwing cushions and books about, tearing off his tie and opening his shirt to ensure what he called 'den batter breading, esn't et?' He then announced in hearty Rotterdam accent that his conception of Roderigo was, perhaps, unorthodox (could he please heff en liddle drink, *ja*, en liddle, diny visky?) but if Mr Velles would listen for en moment he would see: (ah! tankoo, Mr Velles, glug, glug, glug). Now! Lazzen to thass, Mr Velles,

> Vot en full fortune dott de tack-laps owe
> Eff he can cahrry et dhoos!

Ha ha ha! You understand now, I tank, esn't et? Sach en fool, this poor Roderigo – as Iago has explicked of him, one Poor Trash of Vaynice. And mit den eyes, when he tries to be intalligent, exprassion somesing *so*. (Demonstration of demented smile and of violent squint now offered as *pièce de résistance*.) For en Close Up, esn't it? Wery amusing! Ow yes, dear Chappies! *dess* wass how he *feels* it must be! So has somesing already to his anspiration spoke, and Lazzen!

A good deal more then followed, interspersed with more liddle diny viskies, language growing less and less easy to understand and more and more reminiscent of Beowulf.

He left us at unidentified hour – my watch had stopped and O. never wears one – but loud crowing of cocks would undoubtedly have accompanied his tottering exit had we been in the country – and after this O. lay flat on his back in front of (now lifeless) remains of log fire and said that admittedly we had been in the presence of genius but probably *talent* was what was required for the part of Roderigo, and he still thought Coote was good.

Morning now creeps greyly over Champs-Élysées and rain still patters down. Unearthly energy, which invades and deserts me at alternate and unsuitable moments, would easily enable me to continue writing this blather from now till Doomsday, but one must sleep sometimes.

EIMAR O'DUFFY

From *King Goshawk and the Birds*

Eimar O'Duffy (1893–1935) was born in Dublin, the eldest son of a prosperous dentist. He joined the Irish Republican Brotherhood and eventually became a captain in the Irish Volunteers but he grew disillusioned with the Republican movement after the 1916 Rising. In 1920, he married Kathleen Cruise O'Brien, aunt of the later well-known statesman and writer Conor Cruise O'Brien. Perhaps the most neglected of modern Irish writers, his Cuanduine trilogy, King Goshawk and the Birds *(1926),* The Spacious Adventures of the Man in the Street *(1928) and* Asses in Clover *(1933) reveals O'Duffy as one of Ireland's best satiric fantasists.* King Goshawk and the Birds *is set in the near future when the world is under the control of a few King Capitalists. One of these Kings, Goshawk, decides to buy up all the birds and flowers in the world to please his wife, Guzelinda. To combat this, an old Dublin philosopher brings the legendary hero Cuchulain back to earth in the body of a scrawny shop assistant. In this chapter, Cuchulain attempts to woo a young woman.*

HOW CUCHULAIN COURTED A GIRL OF DRUMCONDRA

The new geasa that were laid upon Cuchulain were that he should not again go forth alone until, by the Philosopher's instruction, he should have become thoroughly acquainted with the manners and customs of the people. So for the next two days the hero applied himself diligently to this course of study. But when the third day dawned, because of a prick and urge of the flesh, together with a dancing of the blood and a singing of the spirit, that could no longer brook such inaction, with the temerity that had once brought dark disaster and woe upon Conaire Mor, he broke his geasa and sallied forth by himself till he came to the district of Drumcondra.

There he beheld a young girl leaning over the garden gate of her father's house, watching the people go by in the sunshine. When she saw the young man looking at her, she blushed and smiled; for the spirit of Cuchulain had imparted to the smug features of Robert Emmett Aloysius O'Kennedy a moiety of the beauty and the fire that in the olden times had won the love of Aoife, and Emer, and Fand, and Blanadh, and Niamh, and of three times fifty queens that came to Emain Macha from the four quarters of the earth to look upon the Hound of Ulster. Cuchulain, turning to the maiden, saw that she was fair: for though she was pasty-faced and lanky of figure, yet was she pleasing to the eyes of Robert Emmett Aloysius O'Kennedy, through which he looked upon the world. O'Kennedy's body was thus smitten with a yearning for the damsel which infected even the soul of Cuchulain, so that he stopped and spoke to her, saying:

'Fair maiden, you are beautiful as a morn of spring when the cherries are in bloom.'

'Galong out o' that,' answered the girl, smirking.

'Nay,' said Cuchulain, 'send me not away from your gracious presence, for truly your voice is like the love-song of birds on a musky evening, and the Twin Stars shed not sweeter light than your wondrous eyes.'

The girl blushed fiery red, and kicked the gate nervously with her shabby toe; but she made no answer. Then Cuchulain said:

'Bid me again to go, and like the lightning I will be gone: for no woman yet asked me a boon that I refused her. Nevertheless, bid me not; for bitter is the air that is not sweetened by your breath. Speak, therefore: shall I go or stay?'

'Sure, why would you go?' said the girl. 'I was only joking.'

Then Cuchulain kissed with his ambrosial lip the grubby finger-tips of the maiden; and he said:

'In the gardens of Paradise the winds play a melody as of silver flutes over the golden heads of the swaying asphodels. But now my desire is for a cool spot by a woodland stream, amid odours of fern and damp earth, with wild hyacinths, maybe, in the long grass, or wood anemones, and yourself stretched beside me, plashing your white feet in the water.'

The girl, playing with a faded ribbon on her blouse, thrust it between her teeth and giggled. Cuchulain, watching her, said:

'My thirst is for the honey that is gathered from a bed of scarlet flowers.'

'I don't care for the kind you get in them combs,' said the girl. 'I prefer the bottled stuff. But I like jam best.'

Silence fell between them at that; but presently the girl, thinking he would have invited her for a walk or to the pictures but had been prevented by shyness, said: 'What was it you wanted to ask me about?'

Cuchulain answered: 'My desire is for two snowy mountains, rose-crowned, that are fenced about with thorns and barriers of ice. What shall I do to melt the ice and turn aside the menace of the thorns?'

'What do you mean?' asked the maiden.

Then said Cuchulain: 'It is your fair bosom that is the fruit of my desiring, and your red lips ripe for kissing, and your warm white body to be pressed to mine in the clasp of love.'

'O you dirty fellow!' cried the girl, and turning, she fled into her house.

Cuchulain would have pursued her, but a tap on the shoulder made him turn round, and he found himself confronted by two men of singular aspect. Their clothing was all white, though somewhat soiled, with buttons of ivory and facings of swansdown. On their heads they wore helmets in the likeness of a sitting dove; and they carried batons of some white metal wrought in the shape of a lily. On their collars were these words in letters of ivory: CENSOR MORUM.

The official who had tapped him addressed Cuchulain, saying: 'What were you wanting with that girl?'

Cuchulain, mindful of his geasa, restraining his desire to
smite him, answered: 'That, sir, is a matter between her and
me.'

'Now, then,' said the Censor, 'none of your lip. I've reason to
suspect that you were asking her more than the time of day; and
I've power to put you under arrest unless you can give me a
satisfactory explanation.'

'I can tell you nothing of what passed between us,' said
Cuchulain, 'without the consent of the lady.'

'Tush, sir,' said the Censor. 'You must be one of these
foreigners if you think we would so outrage the modesty of our
Womanhood by questioning them on such a subject. Come,
now. What is your explanation?'

More difficult was Cuchulain's task to bridle his wrath at
that moment than once had been the feat of bridling the
Grey of Macha by the dark lake near Sliabh Fuaith. The veins of
his forehead stood out like black and knotted cords; his collar
at his neck was scorched deep brown; his heart missed
seven beats; but calling to mind the calm visage of the Philosopher, he put constraint on his voice and said: 'I was making
love.'

'With matrimonial intent?' asked the Censor, entering the
reply in his lambskin-covered notebook.

'I do not understand you,' said Cuchulain.

'Do you want to marry the girl?' explained the other Censor.

'Indeed, no,' said Cuchulain. 'There are no marriages in
heaven.'

'Then you must come with us,' said the Censors, laying hands
on him.

'Whither?' asked Cuchulain.

'To the Lothario Asylum,' said the Censors, and began to
haul him away between them.

'Dogs!' cried Cuchulain. 'Let me be'; and he put forth his
strength so that his feet dug deep holes in the stone pathway, and
the Censors could not move him. Thereupon these raised their

lily-shaped truncheons to beat purity into the son of Lugh:
but he, taking them up one in each hand, entwined the right
leg of the one with the left leg of the other in a truelove
knot, and left them there on the pavement for the gathering
throngs to admire.

SEÁN O'FAOLAIN
The Confessional

Seán O'Faolain (1900–1991) published many collections of short stories including Midsummer Night Madness, A Purse of Coppers *and* Foreign Affairs. *He found fame and notoriety as an outspoken critic of the Irish clergy and as editor of* The Bell *magazine which provided a forum for like-minded young writers in the 1940s. He also wrote a biography of Daniel O'Connell,* King of the Beggars *and an autobiography,* Vive Moi, *which was re-published in 1994. 'The Confessional' is taken from* A Purse of Coppers.

In the wide navé the wintry evening light was faint as gloom and in the shadows of the aisle it was like early night. There was no sound in the chapel but the wind blowing up from the river-valley, or an occasional tiny noise when a brass socket creaked under the great heat of a dying flame. To the three small boys crouched together in a bench in the farther aisle, holding each other's hands, listening timidly to the crying wind, staring wide-eyed at the candles, it seemed odd that in such a storm the bright flames never moved.

Suddenly the eldest of the three, a red-headed little ruffian, whispered loudly; but the other two, staring at the distant face of the statue, silenced him with a great hiss like a breaking wave. In another moment the lad in the centre, crouching down in fear and gripping the hand on each side of him, whispered so quietly that they barely heard: 'She's moving.'

For a second or two they did not even breathe. Then all three expelled a deep sigh of disappointment.

It was Monday afternoon, and every Monday as they had each heard tell over and over again in their homes, Father Hanafin spoke with the Blessed Virgin in the grotto. Some said she came late at night; some said in the early morning before the chapel was opened; some said it was at the time when the sun goes

down, but until now nobody had dared to watch. To be sure
Father Hanafin was not in the chapel now, but for all that the
three little spies had come filled with high hope. The eldest
spoke their bitter disappointment aloud.

'It's all my eye,' he said angrily. The other two felt that what
he said was true, but they pretended to be deeply shocked.

'That's an awful thing you said, Foxer,' whispered the boy in
the middle.

'Go away, you, Philpot!' said Foxer.

'God! I think it's a cause for confession, Foxer!' whispered
Philpot again.

'It's a mortal sin, Foxer!' said the third, leaning over to say it.

'Don't try to cod me, Cooney, or I'd bust yer jaw!' cried
Foxer angrily.

Philpot hushed them sternly and swiftly, but the spell was
broken. They all leaned back in the bench.

Beside them was Father Hanafin's confession-box, its worn
purple curtain partly drawn back, his worn purple stole hanging
on a crook on the wall inside, and as Foxer gazed into the box
with curiosity the Adversary tempted him in his heart.

'Come on, Cooney!' he invited at last, 'come on, and I'll hear
yer confession.'

'Gor! Come on,' said Cooney, rising.

'That's a sin,' said Philpot, though secretly eager to sit in the
priest's chair.

'You're an awful ould Aunt Mary!' jeered Foxer, whereupon
all Philpot's scruples vanished and the three scrambled for the
confessor's seat. But Foxer was there before either of them, and
at once he swished the curtains together as he had seen Father
Hanafin do, and put the long stole about his neck. It was so nice
in there in the dark that he forgot his two penitents waiting
beyond the closed grilles on either side, and he was putting
imaginary snuff into his nostrils and flicking imaginary specks
of snuff from his chest when Cooney's angry face appeared
between the curtains.

'Are you going to hear me confession, Foxer, or are yeh not?' he cried in a rage, eager for his turn to be priest.

'Go back, my child,' said Foxer crossly, and he swished the curtains together again. Then, as if in spite, he leaned over to the opposite grille and slowly and solemnly he drew the slide and peered into the frightened eyes of Philpot.

'Tell me how long since your last confession, my child,' he said gravely.

'Twenty years,' whispered Philpot in awe.

'What have you done since then?' intoned Foxer sadly.

'I stole sweets, father. And I forgot my prayers. And I cursed, father.'

'You cursed!' thundered Foxer. 'What curse did you say?'

'I said that our master was an ould sod, father,' murmured Philpot timidly.

'So he is, my child. Is there anything else?'

'No, father.'

'For your penance say two hundred and forty-nine rosaries, and four hundred and seventy Our Fathers, and three hundred and thirty-two Hail Marys. And now be a good obedient boy. And pray for me, won't you? Gawd bless you, my child.'

And with that Foxer drew the slide slowly before the small astonished face.

As he turned to the other side his hand fell on a little box – it was Father Hanafin's consolation during the long hours spent in that stuffy confessional listening to the sins and sorrows of his parishioners. Foxer's awkward fingers lifted the cover and the sweet scent rose powerfully through the darkness as he coaxed the loose snuff down from the cover. Then drawing the slide on Cooney, he gravely inhaled a pinch and leaned his ear to the cool iron of the grille.

Outside a footstep sounded on the marble floor, and peering out Foxer saw the priest walk slowly up the farther aisle, turn and walk slowly down again, his breviary held high to the slanting radiance of the Virgin's altar.

'It's Father Hanafin,' whispered Foxer to Cooney; and to Philpot – 'Keep quiet or we're all ruined.'

Up and down the solemn footsteps went, and high above their heads in the windows of the clerestory and along the lath and plaster of the roof the wind moaned and fingered the loose slates, and now and again they heard the priest murmur aloud the deep, open vowels of his prayer, Gaudiamus Domine, or Domine, Domine meo, in a long breathing sigh.

'He's talking to the Virgin,' breathed Cooney to Foxer.

'He's talking to the Virgin,' breathed Foxer in turn to Philpot.

'Amen,' sighed the priest, and went on his knees before the candles that shone steadily and were reflected brilliantly in the burnished brass.

The three spies had begun to peep from their hiding-place when the snuff fell on Foxer's lap and the grains began to titillate his nose. In agony he held his mouth for a full minute and then burst into a furious sneeze. In astonishment the priest gazed about him and once again Foxer held his breath and once again he sneezed. At the third sneeze the priest gazed straight at the box.

'Come out!' he said in a loud voice. 'Come out of that box!'

And as the three guilty forms crept from the three portals he commanded again, 'Come here!'

Awkwardly they stumbled forward through the seats, trying to hide behind one another, pushing and upbraiding one another until they stood before him.

'What were you doing in there?' he asked Foxer.

'I was hearing their confession, father,' trembled Foxer, and half raised his arm as if to ward off a blow.

For a moment the priest glared at him and then he asked, 'And what penance did you give?'

'I – I gave three hundred and thirty Hail Marys, father, and I think it was four hundred Our Fathers, father, and two hundred and forty-nine rosaries, father.'

'Well!' pronounced the priest in a solemn voice, 'go home and let each one of ye say that penance three times over before nine o'clock tomorrow morning.'

Stumbling over one another's heels the three crept down the dark aisle and crushed out through the green baize door and into the falling night that was torn by the storm. The street-lamps were lit and under one of these they halted and looked at each other, angry and crestfallen.

'Nine hundred and ninety Hail Marys!' wailed Philpot, and Cooney squared up to Foxer with clenched fists.

'Yerrah!' said Foxer. 'It's all a cod!'

And he raced suddenly away to his supper, followed by the shouts and feet of the other two.

FRANK O'CONNOR
First Confession

Frank O'Connor (1903–1966) was the pseudonym of Michael O'Donovan who wrote in many forms, including short stories, novels, criticism, drama, history and autobiography and translations of early Irish poetry. It is as a master of the short story, though, that O'Connor has found enduring fame. His collections include Guests of the Nation, The Collected Stories of Frank O'Connor *and* Collection Two. *'The First Confession' is taken from* The Collected Stories of Frank O'Connor.

All the trouble began when my grandfather died and my grandmother – my father's mother – came to live with us. Relations in the one house are a strain at the best of times, but, to make matters worse, my grandmother was a real old countrywoman and quite unsuited to the life in town. She had a fat, wrinkled old face, and, to Mother's great indignation, went round the house in bare feet – the boots had her crippled, she said. For dinner she had a jug of porter and a pot of potatoes with – sometimes – a bit of salt fish, and she poured out the potatoes on the table and ate them slowly, with great relish, using her fingers by way of a fork.

Now, girls are supposed to be fastidious, but I was the one who suffered most from this. Nora, my sister, just sucked up to the old woman for the penny she got every Friday out of the old-age pension, a thing I could not do. I was too honest, that was my trouble; and when I was playing with Bill Connell, the sergeant major's son, and saw my grandmother steering up the path with the jug of porter sticking out from beneath her shawl I was mortified. I made excuses not to let him come into the house, because I could never be sure what she would be up to when we went in.

When Mother was at work and my grandmother made the

dinner I wouldn't touch it. Nora once tried to make me, but I hid under the table from her and took the bread-knife with me for protection. Nora let on to be very indignant (she wasn't, of course, but she knew Mother saw through her, so she sided with Gran) and came after me. I lashed out at her with the breadknife, and after that she left me alone. I stayed there till Mother came in from work and made my dinner, but when Father came in later Nora said in a shocked voice: 'Oh, Dadda, do you know what Jackie did at dinnertime?' Then, of course, it all came out; Father gave me a flaking; Mother interfered, and for days after that he didn't speak to me and Mother barely spoke to Nora. And all because of that old woman! God knows, I was heart-scalded.

Then, to crown my misfortunes, I had to make my first confession and communion. It was an old woman called Ryan who prepared us for these. She was about the one age with Gran; she was well-to-do, lived in a big house on Montenotte, wore a black cloak and bonnet, and came every day to school at three o'clock when we should have been going home, and talked to us of hell. She may have mentioned the other place as well, but that could only have been by accident, for hell had the first place in her heart.

She lit a candle, took out a new half-crown, and offered it to the first boy who would hold one finger – only one finger! – in the flame for five minutes by the school clock. Being always very ambitious I was tempted to volunteer, but I thought it might look greedy. Then she asked were we afraid of holding one finger – only one finger! – in a little candle flame for five minutes and not afraid of burning all over in roasting hot furnaces for all eternity. 'All eternity! Just think of that! A whole lifetime goes by and it's nothing, not even a drop in the ocean of your sufferings.' The woman was really interesting about hell, but my attention was all fixed on the half-crown. At the end of the lesson she put it back in her purse. It was a great disappointment; a religious woman like that, you wouldn't think she'd bother about a thing like a half-crown.

Another day she said she knew a priest who woke one night to find a fellow he didn't recognize leaning over the end of his bed. The priest was a bit frightened – naturally enough – but he asked the fellow what he wanted, and the fellow said in a deep, husky voice that he wanted to go to confession. The priest said it was an awkward time and wouldn't it do in the morning, but the fellow said that last time he went to confession, there was one sin he kept back, being ashamed to mention it, and now it was always on his mind. Then the priest knew it was a bad case, because the fellow was after making a bad confession and committing a mortal sin. He got up to dress, and just then the cock crew in the yard outside, and – lo and behold! – when the priest looked round there was no sign of the fellow, only a smell of burning timber, and when the priest looked at his bed didn't he see the print of two hands burned in it? That was because the fellow had made a bad confession. This story made a shocking impression on me.

But the worst of all was when she showed us how to examine our conscience. Did we take the name of the Lord, our God, in vain? Did we honour our father and our mother? (I asked her did this include grandmothers and she said it did.) Did we love our neighbours as ourselves? Did we covet our neighbour's goods? (I thought of the way I felt about the penny that Nora got every Friday.) I decided that, between one thing and another, I must have broken the whole ten commandments, all on account of that old woman, and so far as I could see, so long as she remained in the house I had no hope of ever doing anything else.

I was scared to death of confession. The day the whole class went I let on to have a toothache, hoping my absence wouldn't be noticed; but at three o'clock, just as I was feeling safe, along comes a chap with a message from Mrs Ryan that I was to go to confession myself on Saturday and be at the chapel for communion with the rest. To make it worse, Mother couldn't come with me and sent Nora instead.

Now, that girl had ways of tormenting me that Mother never knew of. She held my hand as we went down the hill, smiling sadly and saying how sorry she was for me, as if she were bringing me to the hospital for an operation.

'Oh, God help us!' she moaned. 'Isn't it a terrible pity you weren't a good boy? Oh, Jackie, my heart bleeds for you! How will you ever think of all your sins? Don't forget you have to tell him about the time you kicked Gran on the shin.'

'Lemme go!' I said, trying to drag myself free of her. 'I don't want to go to confession at all.'

'But sure, you'll have to go to confession, Jackie,' she replied in the same regretful tone. 'Sure, if you didn't, the parish priest would be up to the house, looking for you. 'Tisn't, God knows, that I'm not sorry for you. Do you remember the time you tried to kill me with the bread-knife under the table? And the language you used to me? I don't know what he'll do with you at all, Jackie. He might have to send you up to the bishop.'

I remember thinking bitterly that she didn't know the half of what I had to tell − if I told it. I knew I couldn't tell it, and understood perfectly why the fellow in Mrs Ryan's story made a bad confession; it seemed to me a great shame that people wouldn't stop criticizing him. I remember that steep hill down to the church, and the sunlit hillsides beyond the valley of the river, which I saw in the gaps between the houses like Adam's last glimpse of Paradise.

Then, when she had manoeuvred me down the long flight of steps to the chapel yard, Nora suddenly changed her tone. She became the raging malicious devil she really was.

'There you are!' she said with a yelp of triumph, hurling me through the church door. 'And I hope he'll give you the penitential psalms, you dirty little caffler.'

I knew then I was lost, given up to eternal justice. The door with the coloured-glass panels swung shut behind me, the sunlight went out and gave place to deep shadow, and the wind whistled outside so that the silence within seemed to crackle like ice under my feet. Nora sat in front of me by the confession box. There were a couple of old women ahead of her, and then a miserable-looking poor devil came and wedged me in at the other side, so that I couldn't escape even if I had the courage. He joined his hands and rolled his eyes in the direction of the roof, muttering aspirations in an anguished tone, and I wondered had he a grandmother too. Only a grandmother could account for a fellow behaving in that heartbroken way, but he was better off than I, for he at least could go and confess his sins; while I would make a bad confession and then die in the night and be continually coming back and burning people's furniture.

Nora's turn came, and I heard the sound of something slamming, and then her voice as if butter wouldn't melt in her mouth, and then another slam, and out she came. God, the hypocrisy of women! Her eyes were lowered, her head was bowed, and her hands were joined very low down on her stomach, and she walked up the aisle to the side altar looking like a saint. You never saw such an exhibition of devotion; and I remembered the devilish malice with which she had tormented me all the way from our door, and wondered were all religious people like that, really. It was my turn now. With the fear of damnation in my soul I went in, and the confessional door closed of itself behind me.

It was pitch-dark and I couldn't see priest or anything else. Then I really began to be frightened. In the darkness it was a matter between God and me, and He had all the odds. He knew what my intentions were before I even started; I had no chance. All I had ever been told about confession got mixed up in my mind, and I knelt to one wall and said: 'Bless me, father, for I have sinned; this is my first confession.' I waited for a few minutes, but nothing happened, so I tried it on the other wall. Nothing happened there either. He had me spotted all right.

It must have been then that I noticed the shelf at about one height with my head. It was really a place for grown-up people to rest their elbows, but in my distracted state I thought it was probably the place you were supposed to kneel. Of course, it was on the high side and not very deep, but I was always good at climbing and managed to get up all right. Staying, up was the trouble. There was room only for my knees, and nothing you could get a grip on but a sort of wooden moulding a bit above it. I held on to the moulding and repeated the words a little louder, and this time something happened all right. A slide was slammed back; a little light entered the box, and a man's voice said: 'Who's there?'

''Tis me, father,' I said for fear he mightn't see me and go away again. I couldn't see him at all. The place the voice came from was under the moulding, about level with my knees, so I took a good grip of the moulding and swung myself down till I saw the astonished face of a young priest looking up at me. He had to put his head on one side to see me, and I had to put mine on one side to see him, so we were more or less talking to one another upside-down. It struck me as a queer way of hearing confessions, but I didn't feel it my place to criticize.

'Bless me, father, for I have sinned; this is my first confession,' I rattled off all in one breath, and swung myself down the least shade more to make it easier for him.

'What are you doing up there?' he shouted in an angry voice, and the strain the politeness was putting on my hold of the moulding, and the shock of being addressed in such an uncivil tone, were too much for me. I lost my grip, tumbled, and hit the door an unmerciful wallop before I found myself flat on my back in the middle of the aisle. The people who had been waiting stood up with their mouths open. The priest opened the door of the middle box and came out, pushing his biretta back from his forehead; he looked something terrible. Then Nora came scampering down the aisle.

'Oh, you dirty little caffler!' she said. 'I might have known you'd do it. I might have known you'd disgrace me. I can't leave you out of my sight for one minute.'

Before I could even get to my feet to defend myself she bent down and gave me a clip across the ear. This reminded me that I was so stunned I had even forgotten to cry, so that people might think I wasn't hurt at all, when in fact I was probably maimed for life. I gave a roar out of me.

'What's all this about?' the priest hissed, getting angrier than ever and pushing Nora off me. 'How dare you hit the child like that, you little vixen?'

'But I can't do my penance with him, father,' Nora cried, cocking an outraged eye up at him.

'Well, go and do it, or I'll give you some more to do,' he said, giving me a hand up. 'Was it coming to confession you were, my poor man?' he asked me.

''Twas, father,' said I with a sob.

'Oh,' he said respectfully, 'a big hefty fellow like you must have terrible sins. Is this your first?'

''Tis, father,' said I.

'Worse and worse,' he said gloomily. 'The crimes of a lifetime. I don't know will I get rid of you at all today. You'd better wait now till I'm finished with these old ones. You can see by the looks of them they haven't much to tell.'

'I will, father,' I said with something approaching joy.

The relief of it was really enormous. Nora stuck out her tongue at me from behind his back, but I couldn't even be bothered retorting. I knew from the very moment that man opened his mouth that he was intelligent above the ordinary. When I had time to think, I saw how right I was. It only stood to reason that a fellow confessing after seven years would have more to tell than people that went every week. The crimes of a lifetime, exactly as he said. It was only what he expected, and the rest was the cackle of old women and girls with their talk of hell, the bishop, and the penitential psalms. That was all they knew. I started to make my examination of conscience, and barring the one bad business of my grandmother it didn't seem so bad.

The next time, the priest steered me into the confession box himself and left the shutter back the way I could see him get in and sit down at the further side of the grille from me.

'Well, now,' he said, 'what do they call you?'

'Jackie, father,' said I.

'And what's a-trouble to you, Jackie?'

'Father,' I said, feeling I might as well get it over while I had him in good humour, 'I had it all arranged to kill my grandmother.'

He seemed a bit shaken by that, all right, because he said nothing for quite a while.

'My goodness,' he said at last, 'that'd be a shocking thing to do. What put that into your head?'

'Father,' I said, feeling very sorry for myself, 'she's an awful woman.'

'Is she?' he asked. 'What way is she awful?'

'She takes porter, father,' I said, knowing well from the way Mother talked of it that this was a mortal sin, and hoping it would make the priest take a more favourable view of my case.

'Oh, my!' he said, and I could see he was impressed.

'And snuff, father,' said I.

'That's a bad case, sure enough, Jackie,' he said.

'And she goes round in her bare feet, father,' I went on in a rush of self-pity, 'and she know I don't like her, and she gives pennies to Nora and none to me, and my da sides with her and flakes me, and one night I was so heart-scalded I made up my mind I'd have to kill her.'

'And what would you do with the body?' he asked with great interest.

'I was thinking I could chop that up and carry it away in a barrow I have,' I said.

'Begor, Jackie,' he said, 'do you know you're a terrible child?'

'I know, father,' I said, for I was just thinking the same thing myself. 'I tried to kill Nora too with a bread-knife under the table, only I missed her.'

'Is that the little girl that was beating you just now?' he asked.

''Tis, father.'

'Someone will go for her with a bread-knife one day, and he won't miss her,' he said rather cryptically. 'You must have great courage. Between ourselves, there's a lot of people I'd like to do the same to but I'd never have the nerve. Hanging is an awful death.'

'Is it, father?' I asked with the deepest interest – I was always very keen on hanging. 'Did you ever see a fellow hanged?'

'Dozens of them,' he said solemnly. 'And they all died roaring.'

'Jay!' I said.

'Oh, a horrible death!' he said with great satisfaction. 'Lots of the fellows I saw killed their grandmothers too, but they all said 'twas never worth it.'

He had me there for a full ten minutes talking, and then walked out the chapel yard with me. I was genuinely sorry to part with him, because he was the most entertaining character I'd ever met in the religious line. Outside, after the shadow of the church, the sunlight was like the roaring of waves on a beach; it dazzled me; and when the frozen silence melted and I heard the screech of trams on the road my heart soared. I knew now I wouldn't die in the night and come back, leaving marks on my mother's furniture. It would be a great worry to her, and the poor soul had enough.

Nora was sitting on the railing, waiting for me, and she put on a very sour puss when she saw the priest with me. She was mad jealous because a priest had never come out of the church with her.

'Well,' she asked coldly, after he left me, 'what did he give you?'

'Three Hail Marys,' I said.

'Three Hail Marys,' she repeated incredulously. 'You mustn't have told him anything.'

'I told him everything,' I said confidently.

'About Gran and all?'

'About Gran and all.'

(All she wanted was to be able to go home and say I'd made a bad confession.)

'Did you tell him you went for me with the bread-knife?' she asked with a frown.

'I did to be sure.'

'And he only gave you three Hail Marys?'

'That's all.'

She slowly got down from the railing with a baffled air. Clearly, this was beyond her. As we mounted the steps back to the main road she looked at me suspiciously.

'What are you sucking?' she asked.

'Bullseyes.'

'Was it the priest gave them to you?'

''Twas.'

'Lord God,' she wailed bitterly, 'some people have all the luck! 'Tis no advantage to anybody trying to be good. I might just as well be a sinner like you.'

MOLLY KEANE
From *Good Behaviour*

Molly Keane (1904–) wrote her first novels under the pseudonym M.J. Farrell (taken from the name of a pub) because she feared the disapproval of her aristocratic Anglo-Irish family. In 1981, under her own name, she published Good Behaviour *which was nominated for the Booker Prize. Her other novels include* Time After Time *and* Loving and Giving. *She has also written a book of recipes for those who hanker after nanny's cooking.*

When Hubert and I were children and after we grew up we lived at Temple Alice. Temple Alice had been built by Mummie's ancestor, before he inherited his title and estates. He built the house for his bride, and he gave it her name. Now, the title extinct and the estates entirely dissipated, Temple Alice, after several generations as a dower house, came to Mummie when her mother died. Papa farmed the miserably few hundred acres that remained of the property. Mummie loved gardening. On fine days she would work in the woodland garden, taking the gardener away from his proper duties among the vegetables. On wet days she spent hours of time in the endless, heatless, tumbling-down greenhouses, which had once sheltered peaches and nectarines and stephanotis. One vine survived – she knew how to prune it and thin its grapes, muscatels. Papa loved them.

Her painting was another interest to take the place of the social life she loathed. A pity for herself that she was so withdrawn a character. *Recluse* would be a truer word to describe her. She could have had such a lovely time gadding round with Papa – hunting and race meetings and all those shoots. But she was really frightened of horses, and if she did go to a race-meeting, in Papa's riding days, she would shut her eyes during his race, and once when he was to ride a bad jumper she got drunk in the bar and fell down in the Owners and Trainers. She simply could not endure the anxiety about him.

I don't understand what it was that held them together – they never had much to say to each other. He had no more understanding of her painting or gardening than she had of horses or fishing or shooting – so what can they have had to talk about?

Once she had a show of her pictures in a London gallery. During a whole year she painted for it. No art critic noticed it. Hardly anybody came in to look – one picture was sold. Even that disastrous experience did not stop her painting. She went on with it, making almost anything she painted look preposterous and curiously hideous too. Give her a bunch of roses to paint – lovely June roses with tear-drops of morning rain on their petals – and she reproduced them as angular, airified shapes in a graveyard atmosphere, unimaginably ugly; but in a crude way you could not forget roses as you looked at this picture in speechless dislike. She would laugh and rub her little hands and shiver – it was deathly cold in her studio.

Nowhere was it possible to sit down in her studio, once a stone-flagged storeroom in the depths of the house. Pyramids of cardboard boxes full of old letters, stacks of newspapers and photographs, old hunting boots, leather boxes that might hold hats or again might be full of letters, all hovered to a fall. A stuffed hedgehog, the dust of years solid between its spines, sat on top of a bird's egg cabinet, empty of eggs, its little drawers full only of dented cottonwool and the smell of camphor. Polo sticks hanging in a bunch and obsolete fishing rods in dusty canvas cases, tied with neat, rotten tapes, showed this house to have been lived in by gentlemen of leisure – my mother's family.

Leisure they may have enjoyed but they knew little about comfort. Our water supply was meagre and my grandfather had deflected a considerable quantity of it to a pond on which, in the shelter of a grove of rhododendrons, he loved to row himself about. It was his escape from the land agent and other buzzing tormentors of a leisured life.

I think, now, that Mummie looked at her studio as her escape from responsibility. She had an enormous distaste for housekeeping. The sort of food we ate then owed nothing to the splendid Elizabeth Davids of the present day. I think Papa would have fainted at the very breath of garlic. It was for his sake only that Mummie expended some extreme essence of herself in bullying and inspiring her treasured cook, Mrs Lennon. I have seen her tremble and go green as she faced the slate on the kitchen table and the deadly quietness of the cook who stood so cheerlessly beside her. While longing only to put on her gauntlets, pick up her trug and trowel and get into the garden or into the blessed isolation of her studio, Mummie would penetrate her cook's mind – praising just a little, demanding always more effort, a higher standard of perfection for the Captain.

When we were children the food in the nursery was quite poisonously disgusting. None of the fruit juice and vitamins of today for us – oranges only at Christmastime and porridge every morning, variable porridge slung together by the kitchen maid, followed by white bread and butter and Golden Syrup. Boiled eggs were for Sundays and sausages for birthdays. I don't think Mummie gave us a thought – she left the ordering of nursery meals to the cook, who sent up whatever came easiest, mostly rabbit stews and custard puddings riddled with holes. No wonder the nannies left in quick succession.

Why do I hate the word 'crusted'? Because I feel with my lips the boiled milk, crusted since the night before, round the rim of the mug out of which I must finish my breakfast milk. . . . I am again in the darkness of the nursery, the curtains drawn against the winter morning outside. Nannie is dragging on her corsets under her great nightdress. Baby Hubert is walking up and down his cot in a dirty nightdress. The nursery maid is pouring paraffin on a sulky nursery fire. I fix my eyes on the strip of morning light where wooden rings join curtains to curtain pole and think about my bantams. . . . Even then I knew how to ignore things. I knew how to behave.

I don't blame Mummie for all this. She simply did not want

to know what was going on in the nursery. She had had us and she longed to forget the horror of it once and for all. She engaged nannie after nannie with excellent references, and if they could not be trusted to look after us, she was even less able to compete. She didn't really like children; she didn't like dogs either, and she had no enjoyment of food, for she ate almost nothing.

She was sincerely shocked and appalled on the day when the housemaid came to tell her that our final nannie was lying on her bed in a drunken stupor with my brother Hubert beside her in another drunken stupor, while I was lighting a fire in the day nursery with the help of a tin of paraffin. The nannie was sacked, but given quite a good reference with no mention of her drinking; that would have been too unkind and unnecessary, since she promised to reform. Her next charge (only a Dublin baby) almost died of drink and its mother wrote a very common, hysterical letter, which Mummie naturally put in the fire and forgot about. Exhausted, bored, and disgusted by nannies, she engaged a governess who would begin my education and at the same time keep an eye on the nursery maid who was to be in charge of Hubert's more menial four-year-old necessities.

SAMUEL BECKETT
From *Murphy*

Samuel Beckett (1906–1989) spent much of his early literary career in obscurity. In 1953, his play Waiting for Godot *became an international success, transforming the author into a literary giant. The success served to refocus attention on Beckett's early neglected works, including the novels,* Murphy, Watt *and* Molloy. *Reviewing* Murphy *on its first appearance in 1938, the novelist Kate O'Brien called it 'a sweeping bold adventure of the soul'. Beckett was awarded the Nobel prize for Literature in 1969. This extract occurs towards the end of* Murphy *when the protagonist's friends gather to carry out his final wishes.*

Forenoon, Wednesday, October the 23rd. Not a cloud left in the sky.

Cooper sat – *sat!* – beside the driver, Wylie between Celia and Miss Counihan, Neary on one bracket-seat with his legs on the other and his back against the door, a very perilous position for Neary. Neary considered himself better off than Wylie because he could see Celia's face, which was turned to the window. And Wylie considered himself better off than Neary, especially when they came to a cobbled surface or turned a corner. Faces held up Neary a little longer than they did Wylie.

Miss Counihan's face was also turned to the window, but in vain, as she read there unmistakably. This did not greatly trouble her. They would never get any more than they were getting now, which she did not do them the credit of assessing at a very large amount. Indeed, they would never again get as much as the little that would shortly be withdrawn. Then they would come ramping to her again.

Miss Couniham could think ill of her partners, past, present and prospective, without prejudice to herself. This is a faculty that no young man or woman, stepping down into the sexpit, should be without.

For all except Celia, whose affective mechanisms seemed to be arrested, it was like being in the chief mourners' cab, so strong was the feeling of getaway. Indeed, Brewery Road had become intolerable. The old endless chain of love, tolerance, indifference, aversion and disgust.

Miss Counihan would not have minded going up to Wylie if Celia had not minded Neary coming down to her. Nor would Wylie have objected in the least going down to Celia if Miss Counihan had not objected most strongly to going up to Neary. Nor would Neary have been less than delighted to go down to either, or have either come up to him, if both had not been more than averse to his attentions, whether on the first floor or the second.

Accordingly Celia and Miss Counihan continued to share the bed in the big room, the latter shedding lights on Murphy that were no credit to herself and no news to the former; and Neary and Wylie to take spells in the bed in the old boy's room, each evoking Celia according to disposition.

So Neary and Celia cease slowly to need Murphy. He, that he may need her; she, that she may rest from need.

To cap all Cooper was given a shakedown in the kitchen. Through the keyhole Miss Carridge watched him, settling down for the night in his socks, moleskins, shirt and hat. A dull coucher for Miss Carridge.

For two days and three nights they did not leave the house. Neary, because distrusting his associates singly and as a pair he feared lest Murphy should arrive while he was absent; Wylie and Miss Counihan, for the same reason; Cooper, because he was forbidden; Celia, because it did not occur to her; Miss Carridge, because she had no time. It seemed as though none of them would ever go out again, when relief arrived in the shape of an assurance from Dr Angus Killiecrankie that so far as the fear of missing Murphy was concerned, they might all take the air without the least anxiety.

Nothing was said on the way down. For the little they knew

of the little they felt could with no more propriety be acknowledged than denied. Celia leaning back with her face to the window was aware only of all the colours of light streaming back into the past and the seat thrusting her forward. Miss Counihan pressed her bosom with vague relish against the lesser of two evils that had befallen her. So long as she had not lost Murphy thus beyond recall, the risk subsisted of his setting her simply aside without more, which would have been bad, or in favour of Celia, which would have been awful, or of some other slut, which would have been pretty bad also. In a somewhat similar way Neary, for whom the sight of Celia had restored Murphy from being an end in himself to his initial condition of obstacle (or key), had cause to be pleased with the turn events had taken. And to Wylie, between jolts and corners, the only phrase to propose itself was: 'Didn't I tell you she would lead us to him?' But politeness and candour run together, when one is not fitting neither is the other. Then the occasion calls for silence, that frail partition between the ill-concealed and the ill-revealed, the clumsily false and the unavoidably so.

They were received at the Mercyseat by Dr Angus Killie-crankie, the Outer Hebridean RMS, an eminescent home county authority and devout Mottist. He was a large, bony, stooping, ruddy man, bluff but morose, with an antiquary's cowl whiskers, mottled market-gardener's hands thickly overlaid with pink lanugo, and eyes red with straining for degenerative changes. He tucked up his whiskers and said:

'Mrs Murrphy?'

'I fear we were just his very dear friends,' said Miss Counihan.

Dr Killiecrankie drew a singed envelope from his pocket and held it up with the air of a conjuror displaying the ace. It bore the name of Mrs Murphy and the address in Brewery Road, pencilled in laborious capitals.

'This was all we had to go on,' he said. 'If he had any other papers, they were consoomed.'

Neary, Wylie and Miss Counihan flung out their hands with one accord.

'I'll see she gets it,' said Neary.

'Without fail,' said Wylie.

'His very dear friends,' said Miss Counihan.

Dr Killiecrankie put up the envelope and led the way.

The mortuary was at its bungaloidest, the traveller's joy gleamed wanly with its pale old wood, the scarlet ampelopsis quenched the brick. Bim and Ticklepenny were sitting cheek by jowl on the dazzling granite step, and out in the middle of the forecourt of lawn a short but willowy male figure, dressed wearily in black and striped, his lithe bowler laid crown downwards on the grass beside him, was making violent golfing movements with his umbrella. Appearances were not deceptive, it was the county coroner.

They entered the mortuary, when the little duel between RMS and coroner as to which would pass second had been amicably settled without dishonour, in the following order: RMS and coroner, twined together; Neary; Miss Counihan; Celia; Wylie; Cooper; Ticklepenny and Bim, wreathed together. They proceeded directly along a short passage, flanked on either hand with immense double-decker refrigerators, six in all, to the post-mortem room, a sudden lancination of white and silver, to the north an unbroken bay of glass frosted to a height of five feet from the floor and reaching to the ceiling. Outside the horns of yew had the hopeless harbour-mouth look, the arms of two that can reach no farther, or of one in supplication, the patient impotence of charity or prayer.

Bim and Ticklepenny paused in the passage to collect Murphy. They slid him out on his aluminium tray, they carried him into the pm room, they laid him out on the slab of ruin marble in the key of the bay. In the narrow space to the north of the slab Dr Killiecrankie and the coroner took up the demonstrative attitude. Bim and Ticklepenny awaited the signal at the head and foot of the tray, the four corners of the sheet gathered in their hands. The rest drooped in a crescent near the door. Celia watched a brown stain on the shroud where the iron had scorched it. Wylie supported Miss Counihan, mistress of the graded swoon, who closed her eyes and murmured, 'Tell me when to look.' Neary remarking with a shock that Cooper had taken off his hat and that his head was apparently quite normal, except that the hair was perhaps rather more abundant than is usual in men of Cooper's age, and horribly matted, suddenly realized that Cooper had sat all the way from Brewery Road.

'These remains,' said the coroner in his nancy soprano, 'were deposited just within my county, my county, I am most heartily sorry to say. Another long putt and I would be sinking them now.'

He closed his eyes and struck a long putt. The ball left the club with the sweet sound of a flute, flowed across the green, struck the back of the tin, spouted a foot into the air, fell plumb into the hole, bubbled and was still. He sighed and hurried on:

'My function perhaps it is part of my duty to inform you is to determine, one, who is dead, and, two, how. With regard to the latter matter, the latter matter, happily it need not detain us, thanks to the, how shall I say –?'

'The irrefragable post-mortem appearance,' said Dr Killiecrankie. 'Mr Clinch, please.'

Bim and Ticklepenny lifted the sheet. Celia started forward.

'One moment,' said Dr Killiecrankie. 'Thank you, Mr Clinch.'

Bim and Ticklepenny lowered the sheet. Celia remained standing a little in advance of the others.

'I say shock following burns,' said the coroner, 'without the slightest hesitation.'

'Not the slightest,' said Dr Killiecrankie.

'Death by burns,' said the coroner, 'perhaps I am expected to add, is a wholly unscientific condition. Burns always shocks, I beg your pardon, my dear Angus, always shock, sometimes more, sometimes less, according to their strength, their locus and the shockability of the burner. The same is true of scalds.'

'Sepsis does not arise,' said Dr Killiecrankie.

'My physiology is rather rusty,' said the coroner, 'but no doubt it was not required.'

'We arrived too late for sepsis to arise,' said Dr Killiecrankie. 'The shock was ample.'

'Then suppose we say severe shock following burns,' said the coroner, 'to be absolutely clear.'

'Yes,' said Dr Killiecrankie, 'or severe shock following severe burns. I do not think that is too strong.'

'By all means,' said the coroner, 'severe burns let it be, followed by severe shock. So much for the *modus morendi*, the *modus morendi*.'

'An accident?' said Neary.

The coroner stood quite still for a moment with the stupefied, almost idiot, expression of one who is not quite sure if a joke has been made, nor, if so, in what it consists. Then he said:

'I beg your pardon.'

Neary repeated his question, on a rising note. The coroner opened and closed his mouth a number of times, threw up his arms and turned aside. But words never failed Dr Killiecrankie, that for him would have been tantamount to loose thinking, so up went the whiskers.

'A classical case of misadventure.'

Unromantic to the last, thought Miss Counihan. She had taken out her leaving certificate.

'Before we get completely out of our depth,' said the coroner, 'perhaps there is something else the gentleman here would like to know. Whether for example it was a Brymay safety that exploded the mixture, or a wax vesta. Such poor lights as I possess are his to extinguish.'

Neary attended to his nose with studied insolence. Wylie felt proud of his acquaintance, for the first time.

'Then perhaps I may venture to proceed,' said the coroner, 'to the other matter, the identity of the ac – the deceased. Here I need hardly say we find ourselves embarrassed by that very feature of the – the –'

'Tragic occurrence,' said Dr Killiecrankie.

'Very feature of the tragic occurrence that stood us in such good stead in the matter of the manner of death. The matter of the manner of death. Still we must not complain. What does the poet say, Angus, perhaps you remember?'

'What poet?' said Dr Killiecrankie.

'"Never the rose without the thorn",' said the coroner. 'I quote from memory, bitter memory.'

'Mr Clinch, please,' said Dr Killiecrankie.

Bim and Ticklepenny reached forward with their corners, Bim received the shroud in folio, converted it deftly into octavo, and both stood back. The very dear friends moved up to the slab, Celia in the centre and still a little to the fore.

'By all accounts,' said the coroner, 'if I may say so without prejudice, it was a person abounding in distinctive marks, both mental and physical. But –'

'You forget the moral,' sneered Dr Killiecrankie, 'and the spiritual, or as some say, functional.'

'But whether –'

'Remarkable for the pertinacity,' said Dr Killiecrankie, 'with which they elude the closest autopsy.'

'But whether any of these have survived the conflagration,' continued the coroner, 'is a question that I for one, and I should imagine all those who were not of the inner circle, cannot presume to decide. It is here that you may help us.'

Such a silence followed these words that the faint hum of the refrigerators could be heard. The eyes of all, seventeen in all, strayed and mingled among the remains.

How various are the ways of looking away! Bim and Ticklepenny raised their heads together, their eyes met in a look both tender and ardent, they were alive and well and had each other. Dr Killiecrankie slowly sunk his head, till he was nothing but legs, skull and whiskers. He owed not a little of his reputation to this gift of seeming to brood when in fact his mind was entirely blank. The coroner did not move his head, he simply let go the focus and ceased to see. Neary and Wylie diverted their attention calmly to other things, the appointments of the room, beyond the glass the bright green and the dark green, leaning on the blue of heaven. The disclaimer was evident. One rapid glance from his solitary eye was enough for Cooper, whom the least little thing upset. Miss Counihan looked away and back, away and back, surprised and pleased to find she was of such stern stuff, annoyed that no trace remained of what she had known, chagrined that she could not exclaim, before them all, pointing to her justification: 'This is Murphy, whose very dear friend I was.' Celia alone seemed capable of giving her undivided attention to the matter in hand, her eyes continued to move patiently, gravely and intently among the remains long after the others had ceased to look, long after Miss Counihan herself had despaired of establishing the closeness of her acquaintance.

From his dream of pins split and bunkers set at nought the coroner came to with a start and said:

'Any luck?'

'Could you turn him over?' said Celia, her first words for fully sixty hours, her first request for longer than she could have remembered.

'By all means,' said the coroner, 'though I fancy you have seen the best of him.'

'Mr Clinch,' said Dr Killiecrankie.

The remains having been turned over. Celia addressed herself with a suddenly confident air to the farther of the charred buttocks and found at once what she sought. She put her finger lightly on the spot and said:

'Here he had a big birthmark.'

Coroner and RMS pounced on the find.

'Beyond the slightest doubt,' said Dr Killiecrankie, 'an extensive capillary angioma of most unusual situation.'

'A proper port-winer,' said the coroner. 'The afterglow is unmistakable.'

Miss Counihan burst into tears.

'I knew of no such mark,' she cried, 'I don't believe he ever had a horrid mark like that, I don't believe it's my Murphy at all, it doesn't look at *all* like him, I don't believe –'

'There there,' said Neary. 'There there. There there.'

'How beautiful in a way,' said the coroner, 'birthmark death-mark, I mean, rounding off the life somehow, don't you think, full circle, you know, eh, Angus?'

'There there,' said Neary. 'No man is without blemish.'

'Well,' said the coroner, 'now that we know who is dead, who is?'

'Mr Murphy,' said Neary, 'native of the city of Dublin.'

'Dear old indelible Dublin,' said the coroner. 'Our only female link passed peacefully away in the Coombe, a month and a half before her time, under the second George. Christian name. Next-of-kin.'

'None,' said Neary. 'A Dutch uncle.'

'Who the devil are you?' said the coroner.

'His very dear friends,' said Miss Counihan. 'His dearest friends.'

'How often have you to be told?' said Wylie.

'Was it to Murphy he answered,' said the coroner, 'or only to Mr Murphy?'

'Mr Clinch,' said Dr Killiecrankie.

They covered the tray and carried it out to the refrigerators. Neary saw Clonmachnois on the slab, the castle of the O'Melagh-lins, meadow, eskers, thatch on white, something red, the wide bright water, Connaught.

'And this young lady,' said the coroner, 'who knew him in such detail, such opportune detail –'

'Miss Celia Kelly,' said Neary.

'Did Miss Kelly murmur Murphy,' said the coroner, 'or Mr Murphy?'

'Damn you and blast you,' said Neary, 'the man was unbaptized. What the bloody hell more do you want?'

'And this Mrs Murrrphy,' said Dr Killiecrankie, 'who was she? The Dutch uncle?'

'There is no Mrs Murphy,' said Neary.

'An epigram,' said the coroner, 'has been attempted.'

'Miss Kelly would have been Mrs Murphy,' said Neary 'if Mr Murphy had been spared a little longer.'

'One would have thought so,' said the coroner.

Cooper and Wylie supported Miss Counihan.

'No,' said Celia.

With a bow Dr Killiecrankie handed the letter to Celia, who handed it to Neary, who opened it, read, reread, hesitated, read again and said at last:

'With Miss Kelly's permission . . .'

'Is there anything more?' said Celia. 'I should like to go.'

'This may concern you,' said Dr Killiecrankie, 'since it appears to be addressed to you.'

Neary read out:

> 'With regard to the disposal of these my body, mind and soul, I desire that they be burnt and placed in a paper bag and brought to the Abbey Theatre, Lr Abbey Street, Dublin, and without pause into what the great and good Lord Chesterfield calls the necessary house, where their happiest hours have been spent, on the right as one goes down into the pit, and I desire that the chain be there pulled upon them, if possible during the performance of a piece, the whole to be executed without ceremony or show of grief.'

Neary continued to gaze on the sheet for some time after he had ceased to read. At last he put it back in the envelope and handed it to Celia, who grasped it to tear it across, remembered her solitude was not without witnesses and contented herself for the time being with crumpling it in the palm of her hand.

'The necessary house,' said the coroner, catching up his hat and umbrella.

'Their happiest hours,' groaned Miss Counihan. 'When is it dated?'

'Burnt,' said Wylie.

'Body and all,' said Dr Killiecrankie.

Bim and Ticklepenny had gone, already they were far away, behind a tree, in the sun.

'Leave me among the slops,' begged Ticklepenny, 'do not send me back to the wards.'

'Darling,' said Bim, 'that is entirely up to you.'

The coroner had gone, he unbuttoned his black and striped with one hand and drove with the other, sweater and slacks would soon enfold him.

Celia was going.

'Just one moment,' said Dr Killiecrankie. 'What arrangements do you wish to make?'

'Arrangements?' said Neary.

'The essence of all cold storage,' said Dr Killiecrankie, 'is a free turrnover. I need every refrigerator.'

'I shall be outside,' said Celia.

Neary and Wylie listened for the sound of the outer door opened and closed. It did not come and Neary stopped listening. Then it came, neither loudly nor softly, and Wylie stopped listening.

'Surely his last wish is sacred,' said Miss Counihan. 'Surely we are bound to honour it.'

'Hardly his last, I fancy,' said Wylie, 'all things considered.'

'Do you incinerate here?' said Neary.

Dr Killiecrankie confessed to a small close furnace of the reverberatory type, in which the toughest body, mind and soul could be relied on to revert, in under an hour, for the negligible sum of thirty shillings, to an ash of an eminently portable quantity.

Neary slapped down his cheque-book on the slab, wrote four cheques and handed them round. To Miss Counihan and Wylie he said goodbye, to Cooper 'Wait', to Dr Killiecrankie, 'I trust you will accept my cheque.'

'Accompanied by your card,' said Dr Killiecrankie. 'Thank you.'

'When it is ready,' said Neary, 'give it to this man, and to no one else.'

'This is all rather irregular,' said Dr Killiecrankie.

'Life is all rather irregular,' said Neary.

Miss Counihan and Wylie had gone. The scarlet leaves drooped over them, they consulted together. Neary had not distinguished between their services, or their sexes, but had been not ungenerous with an even hand. She, in obedience to an impulse of long standing, seized him passionately by the Fifty Shilling lapels and cried:

'Do not leave me, oh do not walk out on me at this unspeakable juncture.'

She impeded his view, he caught her by the wrists, she tightened her hold and continued.

'Oh hand in hand let us return to the dear land of our birth, the bays, the bogs, the moors, the glens, the lakes, the rivers, the streams, the brooks, the mists, the – er – fens, the – er – glens, by tonight's mail-train.'

Not only was there no sign of Celia, but in an hour the banks would close. Wylie squeezed open the hands and hastened away. He had indeed to leave her, but not for long, for his tastes were expensive and Cooper had whispered that the Cox was dead. Miss Counihan followed slowly.

The Cox had swallowed 110 aspirins following the breaking off of a friendship with a Mr Sacha Few, an anti-vivisection worker.

Neary and Cooper came out, closely followed by Dr Killiecrankie, who locked the mortuary, fixed Cooper with his eye, pointed to the ground at his feet, said, 'Be here in an hour', and was gone.

Neary seeing Wylie afar off, Miss Counihan following slowly and no sign of Celia, said, 'Dump it anywhere', and hastened away.

Cooper called after him:

'She is dead.'

Neary stopped but did not turn. He thought for a second that Celia was meant. Then he corrected himself and exulted.

'Some time,' said Cooper.

Neary went on, Cooper stood looking after him. Wylie having travelled twice as fast as Miss Counihan, disappeared round the corner of the main block. Miss Counihan turned, saw Neary coming up behind her at a great pace, stopped, then advanced slowly to meet him. Neary tacked sharply, straightened up when she made no move to cut him off and passed her rapidly at a comfortable remove, his hat raised in salute and his head averted. Miss Counihan followed slowly.

Cooper did not know what had happened to set him free of those feelings that for so many years had forbidden him to take a seat or uncover his head, nor did he pause to inquire. He placed his ancient bowler crown upward on the step, squatted high above it, took careful aim through his crutch, closed his eye, set his teeth, flung his feet forward into space and came down on his buttocks with the force of a pile ram. No second blow was necessary.

The furnace would not draw, it was past five o'clock before Cooper got away from the Mercyseat with the parcel of ash under his arm. It must have weighed well on four pounds. Various ways of getting rid of it suggested themselves to him on the way to the station. Finally he decided that the most convenient and inconspicuous was to drop it in the first considerable receptacle for refuse that he came to. In Dublin he need only have sat down on the nearest bench and waited. Soon one of the gloomy dustmen would have come, wheeling his cart marked, 'Post your litter here.' But London was less conscious of her garbage, she had not given her scavenging to aliens.

He was turning into the station, without having met any considerable receptacle for refuse, when a burst of music made him halt and turn. It was the pub across the way, opening for the evening session. The lights sprang up in the saloon, the doors burst open, the radio struck up. He crossed the street and stood on the threshold. The floor was palest ochre, the pintables shone like silver, the quoits board had a net, the stools the high rungs that he loved, the whisky was in glass tanks, a slow cascando of pellucid yellows. A man brushed past him into the saloon, one of the millions that had been waiting for a drink for the past two hours. Cooper followed slowly and sat down at the bar, for the first time in more than twenty years.

'What are you taking, friend?' said the man.

'The first is mine,' said Cooper, his voice trembling.

Some hours later Cooper took the packet of ash from his pocket, where earlier in the evening he had put it for greater security, and threw it angrily at a man who had given him great offence. It bounced, burst, off the wall on to the floor, where at once it became the object of much dribbling, passing, trapping, shooting, punching, heading and even some recognition from the gentleman's code. By closing time the body, mind and soul of Murphy were freely distributed over the floor of the saloon; and before another dayspring greyened the earth had been swept away with the sand, the beer, the butts, the glass, the matches, the spits, the vomit.

MERVYN WALL
From *The Unfortunate Fursey*

*Mervyn Wall (1908–) was born in Dublin. A playwright, novelist and
radio broadcaster, Wall has been one of Ireland's outstanding satirists.
Among his best-known works are the plays,* Alarm Among the Clerks
and The Lady in Twilight, *the novels,* Leaves For the Burning,
The Unfortunate Fursey *and* The Return of Fursey *and a collection
of stories,* A Flutter of Wings.

Brother Fursey possessed the virtue of Holy Simplicity in such a
high degree that he was considered unfit for any work other
than paring edible roots in the monastery kitchen, and even at
that, it could not be truthfully claimed that he excelled. The
cook, a man of many responsibilities, was known on occasion to
have been so wrought upon by Brother Fursey's simplicity as to
threaten him with a ladle. The lay brother never answered back,
partly because in the excess of his humility he believed himself
to be the least of men, and partly because of an impediment in
his speech which rendered him tongue-tied when in a state of
excitement or fright. So it came to pass that for three whole days
the wretched lay brother kept his alarming knowledge to himself
through sheer terror at the thought of having to face the Abbot.
While all Clonmacnoise believed that the satanic hordes had
taken their departure, one man alone knew that they had not.

When the settlement had first been plagued by demons,
Brother Fursey, in common with everyone else, had been
strongly moved to perturbation and alarm, but when night after
night had passed, and the first week had crept into the second,
without his having been maltreated or belaboured, or even
seeing a demon in the shape of beast or bird, he happily
concluded that his soul was too mean to excite the avarice of
Hell. So while the rest of the community sweated and prayed,
Brother Fursey, convinced of his own worthlessness, slept bliss-

fully beneath his blankets; but on the very first night during which the others were untroubled by devilish manifestations, the door of Brother Fursey's cell was suddenly and violently flung open. The lay brother started into a sitting position and fixed his eyes on the open doorway with some misgiving, for he knew that it was unlucky for the door of a chamber to open of its own accord and nobody to enter. He had been sitting thus for some time when an ungainly creature of the gryphon family ambled in from the corridor and, casting a disdainful glance at the startled monk, sat down in the centre of the floor. It wheezed once or twice as if its wind were broken, and gloomily contemplated the resultant shower of sparks which fell in every corner of the cell. Appalled at such a foul sight, Brother Fursey fell back against his pillows. When he roused himself again, he felt that he was like to lose his wits, for a seemingly endless procession of four- and six-legged creatures of most uninviting aspect was shuffling in through the doorway and disposing themselves about the cell. An incubus followed, and clambering on to the bed, seated itself without much apparent enthusiasm astride on Brother Fursey's chest. The lay brother was by this time so nigh driven frantic by fear that he scarcely noticed the galaxy of undraped females of surpassing loveliness who assembled in a corner and appeared to be exchanging gossip while they tidied up their hair. Lastly there entered a black gentleman who walked with a slight limp. He carefully closed the door behind him and, advancing to the head of the bed, saluted the lay brother politely. Brother Fursey's brain simmered in his head as he tried to remember the form of adjuration, but the only words that he could bring to mind were those of the Abbot's injunction: 'Be not over-confident in yourself and presumptuously daring.' The sable gentleman signed to the incubus to give place, whereupon, grunting horri- bly, it slid off Brother Fursey's chest and, waddling across the room on its bandy legs, seated itself astride the prie-dieu. The dark stranger sat on the side of the bed and addressed the monk with affability.

'You have no occasion to be alarmed,' he said. 'You must regard this as a friendly visit.'

Brother Fursey's eyes rolled agonizingly towards the stoup of holy water on the adjoining table.

'Now, now,' said the Devil, shaking his head reprovingly, 'you mustn't do that. Even if you can nerve your arm to stretch it forth from beneath the bedclothes, I would point out that in the past fortnight myself and the children have acquired considerable dexterity in skipping out of the way of a slash of that nasty, disagreeable stuff, especially when it is cast by a shaky hand. Now,' he continued, 'I expect that you are mildly exercised as to the reason for this seemingly discourteous interruption of your sleeping hours. We had no choice, Brother Fursey, we had no choice. Never in all my experience as a devil have I encountered such obstinate sanctity as exists in this monastery. The boys are half-blinded with holy water and completely worn out. They need a rest, a little while to recuperate before returning to the fight, newly armed with the experience they have gained, the next time to succeed and to wipe out forever this sickly plague-spot of womanish men and chanting monkdom.' Here the archfiend grated his teeth horribly, and lightenings danced in his eyes; but he glanced down in a manner by no means unfriendly at the wisp of hair and the two button-like eyes above the quilt, which was all that could be seen of Brother Fursey.

'To compress the matter into a nutshell,' continued His Highness, 'I admit that my forces have been worsted in the first encounter, but I am not the sort of demon to retire with my tail between my legs and meekly allow the victory to my opponents. My troops are in need of rest and re-armament, that is all. What with the smell of incense, the splashing of holy water and the sound of the Latin language, there is no safety for any of us in this settlement elsewhere than in your cell, where due to the happy chance of your having an impediment in your speech, we are in no danger of being suddenly ejected, by a string of Latin or a shrewd adjuration, into the outer air, which is a different sort of place entirely. If I were to withdraw my legions altogether for recuperation to a clime more salubrious and more welcome to their natures, that dull fellow you have for abbot, would be up to some game such as the sevenfold circuit of the bounds of the settlement with chantings and bells so as to render our return difficult, if not altogether impossible. I intend keeping a foothold in Clonmacnoise until I clear it of its pale inhabitants. Your cell is our sanctuary. You, my dear Fursey, are our bridgehead.'

For a few moments there was silence broken only by the chattering of the monk's teeth. Then a choking sound became audible from beneath the quilt. The black gentleman withdrew a pace with some distaste.

'I beg of you,' he said coldly, 'to give over your attempts at prayer. You know well that your fright is such as to render you incapable of the formation of a single syllable. We are both men of the world, and a ready acceptance of the position will do much credit to your commonsense and make for mutual respect. And now, to show you that I am not ungenerous, but am willing to repay your hospitality, I should like to do something for you. Purely as a matter of accounting and to keep my books straight, I shall, of course, require your soul in exchange. It's not a very valuable soul, its market value would be small; but you won't find me haggling over the price. Are you perhaps a lover of beauty?'

The demon waved his hand, and a queue of desirable females began to move monotonously across the cell from the door to the far wall, where they disappeared through the plaster. The monk gave vent to a deep groan and closed his eyes tightly. When he re-opened them with due caution his visitor was regarding him with professional interest.

'You have been a long time in a world of wattled huts and whitewashed cells,' he said. 'Do you never long for the freedom you once had, to climb the hills and move through the woods just as you please? The breeze was pleasant when you were a boy, the forests were full of mystery, and you had a great liking for paddling your feet in the fords of rivers. All the length of a summer day you had to yourself, with no one to say "Fursey, do this," or "Fursey, do that".'

Immediately a bird call was heard and the gurgling of streams. A silvan sounded a few hesitant notes on a rustic pipe, and the cell became full of heavenly fragrance and sweet odours. The demon studied the lay brother's reactions in his staring eyes and twitching forehead. It was all he could see of the monk, who had the bedclothes drawn up to the bridge of his nose.

'I'm afraid your tastes are vulgar,' said the fiend with some disappointment. 'What about a mighty reputation as a warrior?'

Brother Fursey became aware of the clash and clamour of battle, the heartening burst of trumpets, and the brave flash of coloured cloaks as swords were wielded. At this point the lay-brother lost consciousness, for his was a timorous nature, and he had always been adverse to violence.

For three days the wretched Fursey crept about the monastery as in a trance. He spoiled hundreds of edible roots and pared large slices of flesh from his thumbs. He would certainly have fallen foul of Brother Cook but for the latter's exceeding good humour resultant on the departure of a poltergeist which had made itself at home in his cell and whose least prank had been to heave him out of bed several times during the night. It was only at the close of the third day that Brother Fursey gathered together his wits and the remnants of his courage. He came faltering into the Abbot's presence and knelt at his feet. It took the lay-brother a long time to stammer out his story. The Abbot heard him in silence sitting brooding in his great chair. At length he arose, uttered a sigh; and raising Fursey, bade him return to the kitchen. Then he summoned the elder fathers to council and when they had assembled, he went down on his knees before them.

'I accuse myself,' he said, 'of spiritual pride. In my foolish presumption I imagined that my wretched prayers had been efficacious. The clearance of the greater part of the settlement from fiendish visitants has, in fact, been due to the stalwart piety of you, my fathers, and of the rest of the community.' Then not wishing to cause his monks further embarrassment by the sight of their abbot so humbling himself before them, he got to his feet and resumed the abbatical chair. Alarm, and then consternation, manifested itself on every face as he related the lay-brother's story. There was some toothless whispering among the fathers and a great nodding of bald heads, then Father Crustaceous spoke.

'None of us is without sin,' he said, 'and a man's sins concern only himself and Heaven. Let us proceed at once to consider how Brother Fursey may best be relieved of this intolerable burden, and these execrable fiends be dispersed and scattered for once and for all. No doubt your lordship can now make arrangements to surround and lead them into captivity, preparatory to binding them securely to the bottom of Lough Ree.'

The Abbot coughed.

'I am but a poor sinner,' he said, 'in sanctity the least among you. Many a man excelling me by far in piety has in the course of such an operation been torn into small pieces, and the pieces dispersed no man knows where.'

'If such should be your fate,' said Father Placidus, 'you would be assured of a martyr's crown. Your saintly successor would certainly not omit to plead at Rome the cause for your canonization.'

'These matters are not easily put into execution,' remarked the Abbot diffidently.

'It should at least be attempted,' said Father Crustaceous.

'But how will the monastery benefit by my demise and subsequent canonization, if the suggested operation be not efficacious in scattering the dread sprites that infest it? My saintly successor would be in an even worse plight with the horrid example of my failure before him.'

The Master of Novices rose to his feet. 'Fathers,' he said, 'this discussion is getting us nowhere. I am responsible for the spiritual care and well-being of our novices and students. I cannot but rejoice that the female demons who have displayed themselves with such disregard for decency in the cells of our impressionable youth, now restrict their disgraceful activities to one cell only, and that cell the cell of a lay-brother so grounded in piety as to be indifferent to their hellish charms. Let us leave well alone. Brother Fursey is winning for himself a celestial seat. Would you deprive him of it? Who knows but that the sufferings which he is at present enduring, may not result in his speedy demise and assumption to his Heavenly reward? He seems to me to be a man of poor constitution. With Fursey's happy translation Heavenwards, the Archfiend will no longer have a foothold in Clonmacnoise.'

'Is there not a danger,' asked Father Placidus, 'that Brother Fursey, being subjected to such an assembly of the batteries of Hell, may before his constitution fails him, succumb to the unhallowed suggestions of the Evil One, and even form a compact with him detrimental to this holy foundation?'

'But,' said the Novice Master, 'I understand from our lord the Abbot that this lay-brother is a man of such resolution and so charged with the seven virtues, that he laughs to scorn the most insidious temptations that Hell has been able to devise.'

'That is generally true,' said the Abbot. 'According to what Brother Fursey has related to me, only one suggestion of the Fiend appeared to him to have been even sensible. With more than diabolical cunning the Father of Lies represented to Brother Fursey the attractiveness of murdering Brother Cook by creeping on him unawares and tipping him into the cauldron of Tuesday soup. But as soon as this devilish suggestion was insinuated into Fursey's mind, his mental agony was such that he for once succeeded in bursting the bonds which impede his speech, and he called aloud on the blessed Kieran for aid, which aid was forthcoming with such little delay that the desire to kill faded instantly from Fursey's mind beneath the outpouring of grace which drowned and overwhelmed his soul. I think we may safely assume that now that Brother Fursey is aware of this chink in his armour, he will be forearmed to resist any infernal promptings in this regard to which he may be subjected.'

'Nevertheless,' said Father Placidus 'a word to Brother Cook would perhaps be not amiss. He should not turn his back to Brother Fursey, and it would be no harm to remove any choppers that may be lying around the kitchen.'

'A good cook is hard to come by,' muttered Father Crustaceous.

'It is agreed then,' said the Master of Novices, 'that the heroic Fursey continue to hold at bay the powers of darkness until his happy demise (which will deprive the Archfiend of his only foothold in Clonmacnoise) or until the blessed Kieran intervenes powerfully on our behalf, whichever be the shorter. In the meantime the community should address itself urgently to prayer.'

'And,' added Father Crustaceous, 'our lord the Abbot will no doubt make every effort to increase in sanctity, and in the intervals of his fastings and scourgings he will continue in his studies as to how demons are best fastened to the bottoms of lakes. Is that the position?'

'That is the position,' said the Abbot shortly, and he dismissed the council.

When Brother Cook was informed of the grievous temptation to which his helpmate was exposed, he generously urged that it was not fitting that a man of Fursey's piety should be called upon to perform the menial tasks of the kitchen. The Abbot, however, insisted that Brother Fursey continue his offices among the edible roots, whereupon the Cook respectfully petitioned for a transfer to the poultry house, where Father Killian, who had never fully recovered from his grim experience, was not doing as well as might be desired. The Abbot curtly refused, and there was much grumbling in the monastery at the deterioration in the cooking, due to Brother Cook's difficulty in keeping his mind on his work, and the fact that he spent most of his time with his back to the wall watching Brother Fursey.

MYLES NA GOPALEEN
From *The Best of Myles*

Myles na Gopaleen was the journalistic persona of Brian O'Nolan (1911–1966). O'Nolan borrowed the name from a character in Gerald Griffin's novel, The Collegians *(1829). It means Myles of the ponies. For over twenty years, Myles na Gopaleen's hilarious, irreverent Cruiskeen Lawn columns delighted readers of the* Irish Times. (*Cruiskeen Lawn was an Irish drinking song, the title means 'Little Full Jug'.*)

OUR NEW SERVICE

That, however, is by the way. A lot of the letters we receive are from well-off people *who have no books*. Nevertheless, they want to be thought educated. Can we help them, they ask?

Of course. Let nobody think that only book-owners can be smart. The Myles na Gopaleen Escort Service is the answer.

Why be a dumb dud? Do your friends shun you? Do people cross the street when they see you approaching? Do they run up the steps of strange houses, pretend they live there and force their way into the hall while you are passing by? If this is the sort of a person you are, you must avail yourself today of this new service. Otherwise, you might as well be dead.

OUR SERVICE EXPLAINED

Here is how it happened. The WAAMA League has had on its hands for some time past a horde of unemployed ventriloquists who have been beseeching us to get them work. These gentlemen have now been carefully trained and formed in a corps to operate this new escort service.

Supposing you are a lady and so completely dumb that the dogs in the street do not think you are worth growling at. You ring up the WAAMA League and explain your trouble. You are pleased by the patient and sympathetic hearing you get. You are instructed to be in attendance at the foyer of the Gate Theatre that evening, and to look out for a tall, distinguished-looking gentleman of military bearing attired in immaculate evening dress. You go. You meet him. He advances towards you smiling, ignoring all the other handsome baggages that litter the place. In an instant his moustaches are brushing your lips.

'I trust I have not kept you waiting, Lady Charlotte,' he says pleasantly. What a delightfully low, manly voice!

'Not at all, Count,' you answer, your voice being the tinkle of silver bells. 'And what a night it is for Ibsen. One is in the mood, somehow. Yet a translation can never be quite the same. Do you remember that night . . . in Stockholm . . . long ago?'

THE SECRET

The fact of the matter is, of course, that you have taken good care to say nothing. Your only worry throughout the evening is to shut up and keep shut up completely. The trained escort answers his own manly questions in a voice far pleasanter than your own unfeminine quack, and gives answers that will astonish the people behind for their brilliance and sparkle.

There are escorts and escorts according to the number of potatoes you are prepared to pay. Would you like to score off your escort in a literary argument during an interlude? Look out for further information on this absorbing new service.

'Well, well, Godfrey, how awfully wizard being at the theatre with you!'

'Yes, it *is* fun.'

'What have you been doing with yourself?'

'Been trying to catch up with my reading, actually.'

'Ow, good show, keep in touch and all that.'

'Yes, I've been studying a lot of books on Bali. You know?'

'Ballet is terribly bewitching, isn't it? D'you like Petipa?'

'I'm not terribly sure that I do, but they seem to have developed a complete art of their own, you know. Their sense of décor and their general feeling for the plastic is quite marvellous.'

'Yes, old Dérain did some frightfully good work for them; for the Spectre, I think it was, actually. Sort of grisaille, you know.'

'But their feeling for matière is so profound and . . . almost brooding. One thinks of Courbet.'

'Yes, or Ingres.'

'Or Delacroix, don't you think?'

'Definitely. Have you read Karsavina?'

'Of course.'

'Of course, how stupid of me. I saw her, you know.'

'Ow, I hadn't realized that she herself was a Balinese.'

'Balinese? What *are* you driving at?'

'But –'

'But –'

EXPLANATION

This ridiculous conversation took place recently in an Irish theatre. The stuff was spoken in loud voices so that everybody could hear. It was only one of the many fine things that have been done by the Dublin WAAMA League's Escort Service. The League's horde of trained ventriloquists can now be heard carrying out their single-handed conversations all over the city and in the drawing-rooms of people who are very important and equally ignorant. You know the system? If you are very dumb, you hire one of our ventriloquists to accompany you in public places, and he does absolutely all the talking. The smart replies which you appear to make will astonish yourself as much as the people around you.

The conversation I have quoted is one of the most expensive on the menu. You will note that it contains a serious misunderstanding. This makes the thing appear extraordinarily genuine. Imagine my shrewdness in making the ventriloquist misunderstand what he is saying himself! Conceive my guile, my duplicate duplicity, my play on ignorance and gullibility! Is it any wonder that I have gone into the banking business?

SUFFERERS HELPED

I want now to turn to something rather more important. Some ladies have approached me for advice. They are in trouble with their ballet. They are too fat to lep the requisite six feet and have been sternly warned that they will be expelled from the corps unless they can show better 'altitude' – the latter a technical term that is used by Dublin teachers. Could I help them?

Yes, yes, yes. The "Myles" Patent Ballet Pumps meet and demolish this difficulty. Each shoe is fitted with three diminutive land mines, one in the heel and one in each side of the front foot. If you give a little hop and take care to land on one mine (e.g., land with the full weight on the ball of the foot or the heel) the mine will go off and you will be sent flying through the air with the greatest of ease. When you land, there is another explosion and away up with you again. If you don't want a second super-lep, you simply take care to land on the spent or exploded mine, and there you are. The pumps ensure at least six terrific jumps in the one performance and refills, of course, can be had very cheaply. The audience may think it strange that a dancing piece should be punctuated by loud detonations followed by smoke and the acrid stench of dynamite and gun-powder, but they will not mind if they are assured that it is the usual thing in Russia. Your foot, of course, is protected by a steel shield, but I am afraid the stage –

The Plain People of Ireland: That's a fine looking lump of a girl. What's her address?

Myself: I was wondering how long I'd have to wait for that question. Her address is none of your business.

But I am afraid the stage will be full of holes. I have for

disposal a limited number of cork bungs suitable for stopping up the holes, price four shillings per dozen while they last. Bungs, pumps and all in a presentation casket with a suitable greeting card, twenty-eight bob, post free.

Remind me to come back to this subject.

'Hear you were at old Lebensold's bottle do the other night. How was it, sticky and all that?'

'Pretty average grim, actually. Old Peter Piper was there.'

'Not that intoxicatingly witty painter person?'

'Sorry, one hadn't thought of him as a painter, actually. His work irritates one, you know, so derivative and all that.'

'I do quite definitely agree, but personally I trace his influences more in sorrow than in anger.'

'You do mean more in Seurat than in Ingres, old thing, I s'ppowse.'

This is just a sample of the very special dialogues that our WAAMA League ventriloquist escorts have prepared for the round of Christmas parties. The extra charge is paltry.

And do not think that an escort will humiliate you by making you crack smart jokes like the one above after it has already been cracked at several other parties. Each service is exclusive. The same build-up will be retained (you can't have everything different) but the names in the last line will be changed. For instance, if the 'conversation' is on a philosophic topic, the names will be Suarez and Engels. If on a literary topic, Thoreau and Béranger. And so on, until every reference book and guide to this and that has been ransacked.

Mark your envelope 'Christmas Escort' and enclose two pounds.

SERIOUS SITUATION

Desperate is the only word that will do when it comes to describing the latest developments of the WAAMA League Escort

Service. Several 'incidents' (using the word practically in the Japanese sense) have occurred in recent weeks, and it is now practically certain that we may expect unsavoury court sequels. Such a prospect makes me shudder, because the presence of even one small Escort in the High Court could lead to unheard of complications. Soon the nation may be faced with a vast constitutional crisis arising from pronouncements made (or, at all events, distinctly heard to have been made) by the princes of the bench and all sorts of lesser judicial dignitaries. I am afraid the astonishment on His Honour's own face will not be accepted as evidence to the contrary. Nor will a plea of gross-feasaunce be valid either.

Briefly, the ranks of my respectable and loyal Escorts have been infiltrated by cheats and disaffected elements who have, however, surpassing competence at the game of voice-throw. Extraordinary utterances have been made in public places, but nobody knows for certain who made them. Worse, intelligent and perfectly genuine remarks made by dowdy young women have been completely ignored by the person to whom they were addressed, whose first instinct is to turn round and search the faces of inoffensive strangers to find the 'genuine' speaker.

I will have more to say on this matter in a day or two.

THE ESCORT MESS

The trouble I referred to the other day began like this. A lady dumb-bell hired out what she took to be a genuine WAAMA League Escort, and went with him to the Gate Theatre. Before the play and during the first interval dozens of eavesdroppers were astounded at the brittle cut and thrust of the one-man conversation. The lady herself, who barely knew how to ask for her porridge, was pleased at the extraordinary silence that was won by her companion's conversational transports. Quite suddenly he said loudly:

'By the way, old girl, is that your old woman's dress you are wearing tonight?'

Simultaneously, the unfortunate client found a printed card shoved under her nose. It read:

'Don't look round, don't move, and don't scream for the police. Unless you sign on the dotted line promising to pay me an extra fiver for tonight, I will answer in the affirmative, and then go on to talk about your wretched tinker-woman's blouse. Play ball and nobody will be hurt. Beware! Signed, The Black Shadow.'

The poor girl, of course, had no alternative but to accept the proffered pencil and scrawl her name. Instantly she was heard to say in her merry twinkling voice:

'Really, Godfrey, it's the first time I ever wore the same gown twice, why must you be so quaint! One must make forty guineas go a bit further nowadays, you know, tightening the belt and all that.'

WORSE TO COME

After the show there was an extraordinary scene in the foyer. The lady's husband called to fetch her home, and was immediately presented with her IOU by the 'Escort'. The demand for £5 out of the blue made his face the colour of war-time bread. He roared at his wife for an explanation. Floods of tears and mutterings was the best she could do. Then the husband rounded on the escort and denounced him as one who preyed on women, an extortionist, and a blackmailer of the deepest dye.

'And you over there with the whiskey face on you,' he added, apparently addressing a well-known and respected member of the justiciary, 'I don't like you either, and I've a damn good mind to break your red neck!'

The flabbergasted jurist (not that he was one whit less flabbergasted than the excited husband) turned the colour of cigar-ash and ran out into the street in search of a Guard. In his absence the husband began to insult the wife of another bystander and to 'dar and double-dar' her companion to hit him. This favour was no sooner asked for than received. The unobtrusive 'Black Shadow' gallantly ran forward and picked up the prostrate figure, adroitly extracting in the process every item of silver and notes in his pockets. It was a chastened warrior that was delivered in due course into the arms of the rain-glistening Guard.

All this, I need hardly say, is only a beginning. Horrible slurs on our civilization were to follow.

THOSE ESCORTS

Let me give some further details of the Escort mess I mentioned the other day. When it became generally known that a non-union man had succeeded in extracting a five-pound note from a client by menaces, hordes of unscrupulous ventriloquists descended upon the scene and made our theatre foyers a wilderness of false voices, unsaid remarks, anonymous insults, speakerless speeches and scandalous utterances which had no known utterer. Every second person wore a blank flabbergasted expression, having just offered some gratuitous insult to a stranger, or, perhaps, received one. Of course, blows were exchanged. Innocent country visitors coming to the theatre for the first time, and unaware of the situation could scarcely be expected to accept the savage jeers of some inoffensive bystander. Nor was the boot always on the same foot. The visitor's first impression of our intellectual theatres was all too frequently a haymaker in the belly, the price of some terrible remark he was heard to have made as he pushed in through the door.

Practised theatre-goers have trained themselves to listen for the almost imperceptible little pause between the genuine answer to a question and the bogus addendum of some ill-disposed ventriloquist. Thus:

'Have a cigarette?'

'No, thanks (pause), you parrot-clawed, thrush-beaked, pigeon-chested clown!'

'Do you like the play, Miss Plug? (pause) I'm only asking for politeness, because how an illiterate slut like you would presume to have an opinion on anything is more than I can understand!'

'The first act was wizard, actually. (Pause.) There's egg on your tie, you pig!'

And so on, I regret to say.

MOREOVER

Several people prefer to remain inside at intervals nowadays. They are afraid of their lives of what they might blurt out if they ventured forth for a little air. This means, of course, putting up with the quieter and more deadly snake-bites of the seated malcontents, living in a phantom world of menacing mumble, ghost-whisper, and anonymous articulations of the most scandalous character, not to mention floods of threatening postcards. This sort of thing:

> 'Slip me a pound or I will see that you ask the gentleman beside you where he got the money to pay for his seat. Beware! Do not attempt to call for help! Signed, The Grey Spider.'

> 'Empty everything in your handbag into my right-hand coat pocket and make sure that nobody sees you doing it! Otherwise you will spend the evening plying strangers with salacious conundrums, even in the middle of the play. Don't think too hard of me, we all have to live. I have a wife and ten children. I do this because I have to. Signed, The Firefly.'

> 'Pay me 25s instantly or I will make a holy show of you. Be quick or you're for it. No monkey work! Signed, The Hooded Hawk.'

> 'This is a stick-up. Slip off that ring and drop it in the fold of my trousers. Otherwise you are going to heckle the players in the next act and think of what Hilton will have to say. Signed, The Mikado.'

This is merely the background of this ramp. What happened afterwards is another day's story. Just imagine Lord Longford saying: 'Has anybody here got a handball? I challenge any man here to a moonlight game above in the gardens, against the gable of the Nurses' Home!'

> 'Put five single bank-notes in an envelope and stick the envelope under your seat with chewing gum before you leave the theatre for the first interval. Stay out for at least ten minutes. No monkey-work, mind. Fail me in this and I will fix your hash for you. Signed, The Green Mikado.'

The somewhat scared lady who showed me this mysterious missive at the Abbey the other night asked me what she was to do. Naturally, I counselled courage and no truck with the evil voices that were infesting the national theatre like plague-nits in a rat's back. I promised her the assistance of my genuine WAAMA League Escorts, in ever-growing volume, until the stream became a torrent. Grievous and sombre as the prospect was, I assured her, our mighty and illimitable resources would be marshalled towards the common-end. I then telephoned for my ace-escort. His wife said that he was out, but that she would send a message to him. I knew that he had no wife. He arrived just as the curtain was going up.

DRAMATIC INCIDENT

My lady friend had bravely ignored the threat and all of us sat down for the second act with some little trepidation. Just how would the dread Mikado strike? What did he mean by his threat to settle my friend's hash? I was waiting every moment to hear her make some horrible remark, of which she would be as innocent as the child unborn.

Quite suddenly the blow fell. It happened that there was a lengthy pause in the play where the story had reached a stage of crisis. A pause, but not silence. A player standing on the left of the stage electrified the audience by saying:

'Do you know, I have been wondering all night who in the name of Pete that fat cow in the fur coat is. The one second from the left in the third row!'

I turned to my own escort, thunderstruck.

'It's all right,' he whispered. 'Your lady friend is fifth from the right. The addendum was mine. I was expecting this. It is common Leipzig practice.'

Meanwhile, the unknown victim was being assisted out, the theatre was in uproar, the curtain had been rung down and the livid husband was already on his way behind the scenes to ask the reason why.

Horrible developments have taken place in the Escort scandal. One particular theatre has become a bedlam of 'voices' and coarse badinage, notwithstanding the foolish rule of the management that 'no one who looks like a ventriloquist is to be admitted.' If you say something, no one will believe that you said it. Even a simple 'what-time-is-it?' simply evokes a knowing smile and an involuntary search of the nearest bystander's countenance; that or some extraordinary reply like 'Pie-face!' 'Who wants to know?' or 'Time we were rid of a hook like you!'

Meanwhile, decent people are taking steps to protect their interests. I was at a play the other night and could not help overhearing a scandalous monologue that was apparently being recited by my neighbour on the right, a very respectable-looking elderly man. I watched him through the corner of my eye and saw the hand go into an inside pocket. Was he searching for his card? Was he The Black Dragon about to shove some printed threat under my nose? Yes, yes, the small white card was in his claw! In a second it was held adroitly for my gaze. Imagine my astonishment when I read it:

> 'I give you my solemn word of honour that I am a civil servant and that the appalling language that you hear coming from me is being uttered by some other person. Signed, JUST A MINOR STAFF OFFICER.'

You see the point? He was afraid to *say* this. Because if he did, his explanation would be instantly followed up with a coarse insult to my wife, who was sitting beside me.

EACH WITH HIS OWN CARD

I had further evidence of this later in the foyer. I was standing smoking when a small gentleman said to me: 'Excuse me for addressing a stranger, but I cannot help assuring you that it is only with the greatest difficulty that I restrain myself from letting you have a pile-driver in your grilled steak and chips, me bucko?' Instantly he produced a card and handed it to me:

> 'So help me, I am a crane-driver from Drogheda, and I have not opened my beak since I came in tonight. Cough twice if you believe me. Signed, NED THE DRIVER.'

I coughed and walked away. Just for fun I said to a lady who was standing near: 'Hello, hag! How's yer ould one?' Her reply was the sweet patient smile that might be exchanged between two fellow-sufferers from night starvation. What a world!

FLANN O'BRIEN
From *The Third Policeman*

Flann O'Brien was one of two famous pseudonyms of Brian O'Nolan (1911–1966) – the other being Myles na Gopaleen. Flann O'Brien wrote four novels in English – The Hard Life, The Dalkey Archive, At Swim-Two Birds *and* The Third Policeman *– as well as a novel in Irish,* An Beal Bocht, *now translated as* The Poor Mouth.

Of all the many striking statements made by de Selby, I do not think that any of them can rival his assertion that 'a journey is an hallucination'. The phrase may be found in the *Country Album*[1] cheek by jowl with the well-known treatise on 'tent-suits', those egregious canvas garments which he designed as a substitute alike for the hated houses and ordinary clothing. His theory, insofar as I can understand it, seems to discount the testimony of human experience and is at variance with everything I have learnt myself on many a country walk. Human existence de Selby has defined as 'a succession of static experiences each infinitely brief', a conception which he is thought to have arrived at from examining some old cinematograph films which belonged probably to his nephew.[2] From this premise he discounts the reality or truth of any progression or serialism in life, denies that time can pass as such in the accepted sense and attributes to hallucinations the commonly experienced sensation of progression as, for instance, in journeying from one place to another or even 'living'. If one is resting at A, he explains, and desires to rest in a distant place B, one can only do so by resting

1. Page 822.
2. These are evidently the same films which he mentions in *Golden Hours* (p. 155) as having 'a strong repetitive element' and as being 'tedious'. Apparently he had examined them patiently picture by picture and imagined that they would be screened in the same way, failing at that time to grasp the principle of the cinematograph.

for infinitely brief intervals in innumerable intermediate places. Thus there is no difference essentially between what happens when one is resting at A before the start of the 'journey' and what happens when one is 'en route', i.e., resting in one or other of the intermediate places. He treats of these 'intermediate places' in a lengthy footnote. They are not, he warns us, to be taken as arbitrarily-determined points on the A-B axis so many inches or feet apart. They are rather to be regarded as points infinitely near each other yet sufficiently far apart to admit of the insertion between them of a series of other 'intermediate' places, between each of which must be imagined a chain of other resting-places – not, of course, strictly adjacent but arranged so as to admit of the application of this principle indefinitely. The illusion of progression he attributes to the inability of the human brain – 'as at present developed' – to appreciate the reality of these separate 'rests', preferring to group many millions of them together and calling the result motion, an entirely indefensible and impossible procedure since even two separate positions cannot obtain simultaneously of the same body. Thus motion is also an illusion. He mentions that almost any photograph is conclusive proof of his teachings.

Whatever about the soundness of de Selby's theories, there is ample evidence that they were honestly held and that several attempts were made to put them into practice. During his stay in England, he happened at one time to be living in Bath and found it necessary to go from there to Folkestone on pressing business.[3] His method of doing so was far from conventional. Instead of going to the railway station and inquiring about trains, he shut himself up in a room in his lodgings with a supply of picture postcards of the areas which would be traversed on such a journey, together with an elaborate arrangement of clocks and barometric instruments and a device for regulating the gaslight in conformity with the changing light of the outside

3. See Hatchjaw's *De Selby's Life and Times*.

day. What happened in the room or how precisely the clocks and other machines were manipulated will never be known. It seems that he emerged after a lapse of seven hours convinced that he was in Folkestone and possibly that he had evolved a formula for travellers which would be extremely distasteful to railway and shipping companies. There is no record of the extent of his disillusionment when he found himself still in the familiar surroundings of Bath but one authority[4] relates that he claimed without turning a hair to have been to Folkestone and back again. Reference is made to a man (unnamed) declaring to have actually seen the savant coming out of a Folkestone bank on the material date.

Like most of de Selby's theories, the ultimate outcome is inconclusive. It is a curious enigma that so great a mind would question the most obvious realities and object even to things scientifically demonstrated (such as the sequence of day and night) while believing absolutely in his own fantastic explanations of the same phenomena.

Of my own journey to the police-barracks I need only say that it was no hallucination. The heat of the sun played incontrovertibly on every inch of me, the hardness of the road was uncompromising and the country changed slowly but surely as I made my way through it. To the left was brown bogland scarred with dark cuttings and strewn with rugged clumps of bushes, white streaks of boulder and here and there a distant house half-hiding in an assembly of little trees. Far beyond was another region sheltering in the haze, purple and mysterious. The right-hand side was a greener country with the small turbulent river accompanying the road at a respectful distance and on the other side of it hills of rocky pasture stretching away into the distance up and down. Tiny sheep could be discerned near the sky far away and crooked lanes ran hither and thither. There was no sign whatever of human life. It was still early morning, perhaps. If I had not

4. Bassett: *Lux Mundi: A Memoir of de Selby.*

lost my American gold watch it would be possible for me to tell the time.

You have no American gold watch.

Something strange then happened to me suddenly. The road before me was turning gently to the left and as I approached the bend my heart began to behave irregularly and an unaccountable excitement took complete possession of me. There was nothing to see and no change of any kind had come upon the scene to explain what was taking place within me. I continued walking with wild eyes.

As I came round the bend of the road an extraordinary spectacle was presented to me. About a hundred yards away on the left-hand side was a house which astonished me. It looked as if it were painted like an advertisement on a board on the roadside and indeed very poorly painted. It looked completely false and unconvincing. It did not seem to have any depth or breadth and looked as if it would not deceive a child. That was not in itself sufficient to surprise me because I had seen pictures and notices by the roadside before. What bewildered me was the sure knowledge deeply-rooted in my mind, that this was the house I was searching for and that there were people inside it. I had no doubt at all that it was the barracks of the policemen. I had never seen with my eyes ever in my life before anything so unnatural and appalling and my gaze faltered about the thing uncomprehendingly as if at least one of the customary dimensions was missing, leaving no meaning in the remainder. The appearance of the house was the greatest surprise I had encountered since I had seen the old man in the chair and I felt afraid of it.

I kept on walking, but walked more slowly. As I approached, the house seemed to change its appearance. At first, it did nothing to reconcile itself with the shape of an ordinary house but it became uncertain in outline like a thing glimpsed under ruffled water. Then it became clear again and I saw that it began to have some back to it, some small space for rooms behind the frontage. I gathered this from the fact that I seemed to see the front and the back of the 'building' simultaneously from my position approaching what should have been the side. As there was no side that I could see I thought the house must be triangular with its apex pointing towards me but when I was only fifteen yards away I saw a small window apparently facing me and I knew from that that there must be *some* side to it. Then I found myself almost in the shadow of the structure, dry-throated and timorous from wonder and anxiety. It seemed ordinary enough at close quarters except that it was very white and still. It was momentous and frightening; the whole morning and the whole world seemed to have no purpose at all save to frame it and give it some magnitude and position so that I could find it with my simple senses and pretend to myself that I understood it. A constabulary crest above the door told me that it was a police station. I had never seen a police station like it.

I cannot say why I did not stop to think or why my nervousness did not make me halt and sit down weakly by the roadside. Instead I walked straight up to the door and looked in. I saw, standing with his back to me, an enormous policeman. His back appearance was unusual. He was standing behind a little counter in a neat whitewashed day-room; his mouth was open and he was looking into a mirror which hung upon the wall. Again, I find it difficult to convey the precise reason why my eyes found his shape unprecedented and unfamiliar. He was very big and fat and the hair which strayed abundantly about the back of his bulging neck was a pale straw-colour; all that was striking but not unheard of. My glance ran over his great back, the thick arms and legs encased in the rough blue uniform. Ordinary enough as each part of him looked by itself, they all seemed to create together, by some undetectable discrepancy in association or proportion, a very disquieting impression of unnaturalness, amounting almost to what was horrible and monstrous. His hands were red, swollen and enormous and he appeared to have one of them halfway into his mouth as he gazed into the mirror.

'It's my teeth,' I heard him say, abstractedly and half-aloud. His voice was heavy and slightly muffled, reminding me of a thick winter quilt. I must have made some sound at the door or possibly he had seen my reflection in the glass for he turned slowly round, shifting his stance with leisurely and heavy majesty, his fingers still working at his teeth; and as he turned I heard him murmuring to himself:

'Nearly every sickness is from the teeth.'

His face gave me one more surprise. It was enormously fat, red and widespread, sitting squarely on the neck of his tunic with a clumsy weightiness that reminded me of a sack of flour. The lower half of it was hidden by a violent red moustache which shot out from his skin far into the air like the antennae of some unusual animal. His cheeks were red and chubby and his eyes were nearly invisible, hidden from above by the obstruction of his tufted brows and from below by the fat foldings of his skin. He came over ponderously to the inside of the counter and I advanced meekly from the door until we were face to face.

'Is it about a bicycle?' he asked.

His expression when I encountered it was unexpectedly reassuring. His face was gross and far from beautiful but he had modified and assembled his various unpleasant features in some skilful way so that they expressed to me good nature, politeness and infinite patience. In the front of his peaked official cap was an important-looking badge and over it in golden letters was the word SERGEANT. It was Sergeant Pluck himself.

'No,' I answered, stretching forth my hand to lean with it against the counter. The Sergeant looked at me incredulously.

'Are you sure?' he asked.

'Certain.'

'Not about a motor-cycle?'

'No.'

'One with overhead valves and a dynamo for light? Or with racing handle-bars?'

'No.'

'In that circumstantial eventuality there can be no question
of a motor-bicycle,' he said. He looked surprised and puzzled
and leaned sideways on the counter on the prop of his left
elbow, putting the knuckles of his right hand between his
yellow teeth and raising three enormous wrinkles of perplexity
on his forehead. I decided now that he was a simple man and
that I would have no difficulty in dealing with him exactly as I
desired and finding out from him what had happened to the
black box. I did not understand clearly the reason for his
questions about bicycles but I made up my mind to answer
everything carefully, to bide my time and to be cunning in all
my dealings with him. He moved away abstractedly, came back
and handed me a bundle of differently-coloured papers which
looked like application forms for bull-licences and dog-licences
and the like.

'It would be no harm if you filled up these forms,' he said.
'Tell me,' he continued, 'would it be true that you are an
itinerant dentist and that you came on a tricycle?'

'It would not,' I replied.

'On a patent tandem?'

'No.'

'Dentists are an unpredictable coterie of people,' he said. 'Do
you tell me it was a velocipede or a penny-farthing?'

'I do not,' I said evenly. He gave me a long searching look as
if to see whether I was serious in what I was saying, again
wrinkling up his brow.

'Then maybe you are no dentist at all,' he said, 'but only a
man after a dog licence or papers for a bull?'

'I did not say I was a dentist,' I said sharply, 'and I did not
say anything about a bull.'

The Sergeant looked at me incredulously.

'That is a great curiosity,' he said, 'a very difficult piece of
puzzledom, a snorter.'

He sat down by the turf fire and began jawing his knuckles
and giving me sharp glances from under his bushy brows. If I

had horns upon my head or a tail behind me he could not have
looked at me with more interest. I was unwilling to give any
lead to the direction of the talk and there was complete silence
for five minutes. Then his expression eased a bit and he spoke to
me again.

'What is your pronoun?' he inquired.

'I have no pronoun,' I answered, hoping I knew his meaning.

'What is your cog?'

'My cog?'

'Your surnoun?'

'I have not got that either.'

My reply again surprised him and also seemed to please him.
He raised his thick eyebrows and changed his face into what
could be described as a smile. He came back to the counter, put
out his enormous hand, took mine in it and shook it warmly.

'No name or no idea of your originality at all?'

'None.'

'Well, by the holy Hokey!'

Signor Bari, the eminent one-leggèd tenor!

'By the holy Irish-American Powers,' he said again, 'by the
Dad! Well carry me back to old Kentucky!'

He then retreated from the counter to his chair by the fire and
sat silently bent in thought as if examining one by one the bygone years stored up in his memory.

'I was once acquainted with a tall man,' he said to me at last,
'that had no name either and you are certain to be his son and the
heir to his nullity and all his nothings. What way is your pop
today and where is he?'

It was not, I thought, entirely unreasonable that the son of a man
who had no name should have no name also but it was clear that
the Sergeant was confusing me with somebody else. This was no
harm and I decided to encourage him. I considered it desirable that
he should know nothing about me but it was even better if he knew
several things which were quite wrong. It would help me in using
him for my own purposes and ultimately in finding the black box.

'He is gone to America,' I replied.

'Is that where,' said the sergeant. 'Do you tell me that? He was a true family husband. The last time I interviewed him it was about a missing pump and he had a wife and ten sonnies and at that time he had the wife again in a very advanced state of sexuality.'

'That was me,' I said, smiling.

'That was you,' he agreed. 'What way are the ten strong sons?'

'All gone to America.'

'That is a great conundrum of a country,' said the Sergeant, 'a very wide territory, a place occupied by black men and strangers. I am told they are very fond of shooting-matches in that quarter.'

'It is a queer land,' I said.

At this stage there were footsteps at the door and in marched a heavy policeman carrying a small constabulary lamp. He had a dark Jewish face and hooky nose and masses of black curly hair. He was blue-jowled and black-jowled and looked as if he shaved twice a day. He had white enamelled teeth which came, I had no doubt, from Manchester, two rows of them arranged in the interior of his mouth and when he smiled it was a fine sight to see, like delph on a neat country dresser. He was heavy-fleshed and gross in body like the Sergeant but his face looked far more intelligent. It was unexpectedly lean and the eyes in it were penetrating and observant. If his face alone were in question he would look more like a poet than a policeman but the rest of his body looked anything but poetical.

'Policeman MacCruiskeen,' said Sergeant Pluck.

Policeman MacCruiskeen put the lamp on the table, shook hands with me and gave me the time of day with great gravity. His voice was high, almost feminine, and he spoke with a delicate careful intonation. Then he put the little lamp on the counter and surveyed the two of us.

'Is it about a bicycle?' he asked.

'Not that,' said the Sergeant. 'This is a private visitor who says he did not arrive in the townland upon a bicycle. He has no personal name at all. His dadda is in far Amurikey.'

'Which of the two Amurikeys?' asked MacCruiskeen.

'The Unified Stations,' said the Sergeant.

'Likely he is rich by now if he is in that quarter,' said MacCruiskeen, 'because there's dollars there, dollars and bucks and nuggets in the ground and any amount of rackets and golf games and musical instruments. It is a free country too by all accounts.'

'Free for all,' said the Sergeant. 'Tell me this,' he said to the policeman, 'Did you take any readings today?'

'I did,' said MacCruiskeen.

'Take out your black book and tell me what it was, like a good man,' said the Sergeant. 'Give me the gist of it till I see what I see,' he added.

MacCruiskeen fished a small black notebook from his breast pocket.

'Ten point six,' he said.

'Ten point six,' said the Sergeant. 'And what reading did you notice on the beam?'

'Seven point four.'

'How much on the lever?'

'One point five.'

There was a pause here. The Sergeant put on an expression of great intricacy as if he were doing far-from-simple sums and calculations in his head. After a time his face cleared and he spoke again to his companion.

'Was there a fall?'

'A heavy fall at half-past three.'

'Very understandable and commendably satisfactory,' said the Sergeant. 'Your supper is on the hob inside and be sure to stir the milk before you take any of it, the way the rest of us after you will have our share of the fats of it, the health and the heart of it.'

Policeman MacCruiskeen smiled at the mention of food and went into the back room loosening his belt as he went; after a moment we heard the sounds of coarse slobbering as if he was eating porridge without the assistance of spoon or hand. The Sergeant invited me to sit at the fire in his company and gave me a wrinkled cigarette from his pocket.

'It is lucky for your pop that he is situated in Amurikey,' he remarked, 'if it is a thing that he is having trouble with the old teeth. It is very few sicknesses that are not from the teeth.'

'Yes,' I said. I was determined to say as little as possible and let these unusual policemen first show their hand. Then I would know how to deal with them.

'Because a man can have more disease and germination in his gob than you'll find in a rat's coat and Amurikey is a country where the population do have grand teeth like shaving-lather or like bits of delph when you break a plate.'

'Quite true,' I said.

'Or like eggs under a black crow.'

'Like eggs,' I said.

'Did you ever happen to visit the cinematograph in your travels?'

'Never,' I answered humbly, 'but I believe it is a dark quarter and little can be seen at all except the photographs on the wall.'

'Well it is there you see the fine teeth they do have in Amurikey,' said the Sergeant.

He gave the fire a hard look and took to handling absently his yellow stumps of teeth. I had been wondering about his mysterious conversation with MacCruiskeen.

'Tell me this much,' I ventured. 'What sort of readings were those in the policeman's black book?'

The Sergeant gave me a keen look which felt almost hot from being on the fire previously.

'The first beginnings of wisdom,' he said, 'is to ask questions but never to answer any. *You* get wisdom from asking and *I* from not answering. Would you believe that there is a great

increase in crime in this locality? Last year we had sixty-nine
cases of no lights and four stolen. This year we have eighty-two
cases of no lights, thirteen cases of riding on the footpath and
four stolen. There was one case of wanton damage to a three-
speed gear, there is sure to be a claim at the next Court and the
area of charge will be the parish. Before the year is out there is
certain to be a pump stolen, a very depraved and despicable
manifestation of criminality and a blot on the county.'

'Indeed,' I said.

'Five years ago we had a case of loose handlebars. Now there
is a rarity for you. It took the three of us a week to frame the
charge.'

'Loose handlebars,' I muttered. I could not clearly see the
reason for such talk about bicycles.

'And then there is the question of bad brakes. The country is
honeycombed with bad brakes, half of the accidents are due to
it, it runs in families.'

I thought it would be better to try to change the conversation
from bicycles.

'You told me what the first rule of wisdom is,' I said. 'What
is the second rule?'

'That can be answered,' he said. 'There are five in all. Always
ask any questions that are to be asked and never answer any.
Turn everything you hear to your own advantage. Always carry
a repair outfit. Take left turns as much as possible. Never apply
your front brake first.'

'These are interesting rules,' I said dryly.

'If you follow them,' said the Sergeant, 'you will save your
soul and you will never get a fall on a slippery road.'

'I would be obliged to you,' I said, 'if you would explain to
me which of these rules covers the difficulty I have come here
today to put before you.'

'This is not today, this is yesterday,' he said, 'but which of the
difficulties is it? What is the *crux rei*?'

Yesterday? I decided without any hesitation that it was a

waste of time trying to understand the half of what he said. I persevered with my inquiry.

'I came here to inform you officially about the theft of my American gold watch.'

He looked at me through an atmosphere of great surprise and incredulity and raised his eyebrows almost to his hair.

'That is an astonishing statement,' he said at last.

'Why?'

'Why should anybody steal a watch when they can steal a bicycle?'

Hark to his cold inexorable logic.

'Search me,' I said.

'Who ever heard of a man riding a watch down the road or bringing a sack of turf up to his house on the crossbar of a watch?'

'I did not say the thief wanted my watch to ride it,' I expostulated. 'Very likely he had a bicycle of his own and that is how he got away quietly in the middle of the night.'

'Never in my puff did I hear of any man stealing anything but a bicycle when he was in his sane senses,' said the Sergeant, '—except pumps and clips and lamps and the like of that. Surely you are not going to tell me at my time of life that the world is changing?'

'I am only saying that my watch was stolen,' I said crossly.

'Very well,' the Sergeant said with finality, 'we will have to institute a search.'

He smiled brightly at me. It was quite clear that he did not believe any part of my story, and that he thought I was in delicate mental health. He was humouring me as if I were a child.

'Thank you,' I muttered.

'But the trouble will only be beginning when we find it,' he said severely.

'How is that?'

'When we find it we will have to start searching for the owner.'

'But I am the owner.'

Here the Sergeant laughed indulgently and shook his head.

'I know what you mean,' he said. 'But the law is an extremely intricate phenomenon. If you have no name you cannot own a watch and the watch that has been stolen does not exist and when it is found it will have to be restored to its rightful owner. If you have no name you possess nothing and you do not exist and even your trousers are not on you although they look as if they were from where I am sitting. On the other separate hand you can do what you like and the law cannot touch you.'

'It had fifteen jewels,' I said despairingly.

'And on the first hand again you might be charged with theft or common larceny if you were mistaken for somebody else when wearing the watch.'

'I feel extremely puzzled,' I said, speaking nothing less than the truth. The Sergeant gave his laugh of good humour.

'If we ever find the watch,' he smiled, 'I have a feeling that there will be a bell and a pump on it.'

I considered my position with some misgiving. It seemed to be impossible to make the Sergeant take cognizance of anything in the world except bicycles. I thought I would make a last effort.

'You appear to be under the impression,' I said coldly and courteously, 'that I have lost a golden bicycle of American manufacture with fifteen jewels. I have lost a watch and there is no bell on it. Bells are only on alarm clocks and I have never in my life seen a watch with a pump attached to it.'

The Sergeant smiled at me again.

'There was a man in this room a fortnight ago,' he said, 'telling me that he was at the loss of his mother, a lady of eighty-two. When I asked him for a description – just to fill up the blanks in the official form we get for half-nothing from the Stationery Office – he said she had rust on her rims and that her back brakes were subject to the jerks.'

This speech made my position quite clear to me. When I was

about to say something else, a man put his face in and looked at us and then came in completely and shut the door carefully and came over to the counter. He was a bluff red man in a burly coat with twine binding his trousers at the knees. I discovered afterwards that his name was Michael Gilhaney. Instead of standing at the counter as he would in a public house, he went to the wall, put his arms akimbo and leaned against it, balancing his weight on the point of one elbow.

'Well, Michael,' said the Sergeant pleasantly.

'That is a cold one,' said Mr Gilhaney.

Sounds of shouting came to the three of us from the inner room where Policeman MacCruiskeen was engaged in the task of his early dinner.

'Hand me in a fag,' he called.

The Sergeant gave me another wrinkled cigarette from his pocket and jerked his thumb in the direction of the back room. As I went in with the cigarette I heard the Sergeant opening an enormous ledger and putting questions to the red-faced visitor.

'What was the make,' he was saying, 'and the number of the frame and was there a lamp and a pump on it into the same bargain?'

PATRICK CAMPBELL
The Hot Box

Patrick Campbell (1913–1980), 3rd Baron of Glenavy, was a well-known columnist for the Irish Times *and the* Sunday Times. *He was also famous for his stammer which, along with his wit, made him a favourite of millions on BBC television's* Call My Bluff. *This story is taken from* The Campbell Companion.

Once upon a time I was given an assignment to write an article about a load of archaeological remains, dug up by some fool on the outskirts of Waterford.

This was in the days when the newsprint situation allowed us to devote whole columns to fossils, rubbings, or even the Franciscan method of illuminating manuscripts.

Caught by the Waterford job, I made a demur. No knowledge of archaeological remains – very busy at the moment with an article about badminton . . .

'Round about 1,200 words,' said the news editor. 'Riordan, in the public library, knows all about it.'

He measured me for a moment. 'You two ought to get on,' he said, 'like a house on fire. Or an ammunition dump exploding,' he added.

I asked him what he meant.

'You mind your own business,' he said.

I went along to the library, already rehearsing 'Riordan', and 'archaeological remains'. It had, of course, to be Riordan and archaeological remains just at a time when my intermittent stammer was passing through a cycle which left me incapable of dealing with these initial letters.

There were two elderly gentlemen in subdued suits at the desk, both reading.

I chose the one on the right.

'Excuse me,' I said, 'are you Mr M'Reer – M'Reer – M'Reer . . .'

I was full of air, and putting in the intrusive 'm' – a stratagem which often worked – but this time nothing happened.

The librarian looked up. He wore half-moon, gold-rimmed glasses, and a black woollen cardigan. He nodded towards his colleague. He also put down his book and prepared to listen – with what seemed to be a disproportionate measure of interest.

I saw why a moment later.

'I'm A'Rah – A'Rah – A'Rah . . .' began the second librarian, with his eyes tightly shut.

I'd walked into another one.

I should, of course, have given it up at once – gone back to the office, and said Riordan was on holiday.

But then the fighting instinct arose in me. My intrusive 'm' against his intrusive 'a'. I'd tried the intrusive 'a' myself, and knew that in careless hands it could bring on strangulation.

I scanned the sentence that lay before me. It contained only a number of minor obstacles.

I shot it out very quickly.

'I believe you know something abow-abow-abowbow – could you tell me what you know of the Waterford arkie-arkie-arkie – the Waterford find?'

It turned out to be rather rougher than I'd expected.

Riordan sat back. 'What was that?' he said.

I looked at him coldly. He knew perfectly well what we'd got ourselves into. It was up to him to pull his weight.

'Man found some flints in Wafa – in Wafa – in Wafa –' – Even Waterford seemed to have collapsed. I took another breath. 'Man found some flints or something down south and I was told you knew something abah-abah . . . You knew something,' I said.

The other librarian had now abandoned all interest in his book, and was leaning forward intently.

'Ah, yes,' said Riordan easily. 'The archaeological remains

discovered in Waterford.' You could hear every syllable, clear as a bell.

He stood up. 'I think I can find you the reference. I have aboo-aboo-aboo-aboo . . .'

I let him have it. It was sheer joy.

He'd nearly torn his memo pad in half by the time that I released him.

'You have a book,' I said, 'which will help us.'

'Downstairs,' said Riordan. He loosened his collar. 'Come this way,' he said.

The other librarian half rose in his seat, watching us right to the door. He'd taken his glasses off, and his mouth was open.

We went down into the basement, and along a passage lined with pipes.

'By the way,' I said, 'what's your first name? I think I know a friend of yours.'

I'd seen the card on his desk, in a brass slot: BRIAN RIORDAN. The chances were if he couldn't say book he couldn't say Brian either.

He stopped, as if shot. Convulsively, he gripped the handle of a low, barred door which had appeared in front of us. His neck began to swell. He drew a couple of long, shuddering breaths.

I watched him with interest. One foot came off the ground, and writhed about.

Suddenly, he got it. It came out like a tyre bursting.

'Jack!' said Brian Riordan.

'Can't be the same person,' I said easily. 'The Riordan I was thinking of is —' Everything shut down. I fought it blindly for a second. 'Someone else,' I said.

We went into the cellar with honours approximately even. It was a tiny room, brilliantly whitewashed, about six feet by six. A bare electric light bulb hung from the ceiling at eye level. It was very hot. Pipes ran all round the walls.

Riordan turned round. The light hung between us, very bright and dazzling.

'Where was this find made?' he said.

The stuff had been dug up in a place called Rathally. But as far as I was concerned, what with the heat, and the glare, and the congestion, it might well just have been Czrcbrno, a hamlet in the Balkans.

I tried everything – the finger tapping, the coughing, the intrusive 'm', even a short whistle. Nothing happened. The light, agitated by some truant blast, swayed gently backwards and forwards. Riordan waited, leaning forward politely – exultant.

I thought I was going to faint. I had ceased to breathe. I half-turned my head – intending, perhaps, to jump upon Rathally from the rear – and then I saw Theodore Blake. He was peering through the bars, and from the look of deep peace upon his face, I knew that he, too, was engaged with the priceless gift of speech.

Theodore – of all people!

Riordan opened the gate. 'Well,' he said, 'Mr Bla – Mr Bla – Bla . . .' He gave it up. Theodore came in. We moved back a little to give him room.

Theodore had lately been using an old method of my own. No sound emerged. No hint of expression ever crossed his face. He seemed to be lost in meditation. But it was then you knew that he was really on the griddle.

The three of us, tightly pressed together, the bulb hanging between us, stood there, waiting.

A full minute later Theo said, 'Hello.'

I'd better luck than Riordan. I said, 'What are *you* doing here?'

Riordan tried to say, 'What can I do for you, Mr Blake?' and nearly made it, until the 'b', as usual, beat him all ends up. He actually struck his head against the books behind him.

All this time Theodore was quietly at work. Suddenly, he got it out. 'Can I have that book on Roman coins?' he said, so careful and expressionlessly that it sounded like Roger, the talking Robot.

'Certainly,' said Riordan, and turned to the bookshelves.

It was certainly unfair. He must have known quite well where the book was, but he began fiddling about, pretending he couldn't find it.

Theo and I looked at one another. It was up to someone to say something. We got down to it together.

Theo won. 'What are *you* doing here?' he said.

I lowered my voice an octave. 'I'm gathering material on the arkie-arkie –' I couldn't go on. I simply couldn't face 'archaeological' again.

'On coins,' I said. 'M'Roh – M'Roh – the same kind of coins as yourself.'

Riordan swung round from the bookcase. I'd forgotten about him.

'You said you wanted the Waterford archaeological remains!' he exclaimed.

'You've got it wrong,' I said. 'I'm doing a story abah – a story on coins.' I was going to add – 'through the ages' – and then abandoned it. 'Just coins,' I said.

The awful look of unearthly peace came over Theo's face. I knew what he was going to say. He was going to say that he'd been commissioned to write an article about coins and couldn't understand why I was doing one, too.

We waited for Theodore. It was difficult not to look at him, because we were jammed cheek to cheek, but we did our best.

Theodore looked straight ahead, motionless, carved out of stone.

'But,' he said, three minutes later, 'I'm doing an article about coins. Why are you doing one, too?'

Riordan opened his mouth.

'Ubu-ubu-ubu –' he began, harping on my commitment to archaeological remains.

'It doesn't matter,' I said. 'There has been some confusion. I can easily switch over to the arkie-arkie-arkie –'

'Ubu-ubu –' gasped Riordan, 'you asked me for that boo – boo-boo – that in the first pip-pip –'

It was absolutely indescribable. And suddenly Theodore joined in. On the very first word he slipped right back into his old habit – the wurr-wurr-wurr. God alone knows what he was trying to say. He simply wurred.

I don't know how long it went on for – me busy with arkie-arkie, Riordan pip-pipping, and Theo lost in the throes of wurr.

Steam seemed to be running down the walls. Once the electric light bulb bounced off my forehead with a sharp 'Ponk!'

Something snapped. 'Here,' I said, 'Let me –' I couldn't say 'out'. I let it go. I pushed past them, fled along the passage, and a moment later was in the open air.

In my hand was Theo's book about coins.

I sent it back next day, by registered post.

SPIKE MILLIGAN
From *Puckoon*

Spike Milligan (1918–) was born in Ahmegnagar in India, the son of an Irish father. He began his career as a band musician but became famous as the principal scriptwriter and performer of the infamous Goon Show *on BBC radio. He is the author of numerous prose works and collections of poetry, as well as six incomparable volumes of war memoirs, including* Adolf Hitler: My Part in His Downfall, Mussolini: His Part in My Downfall *and* Where Have All the Bullets Gone? Puckoon *is his best-known comic novel.*

The Dan Milligan cycled tremendously towards the Church of St Theresa of the Little Flowers. Since leaving the area known as his wife he had brightened up a little. 'Man alive! The *size* of her though, she's a danger to shipping, I mean, every time I put me key in the front door I'll wonder what I'm lettin' meself in for.' Away down a lumpy road he pedalled, his right trouser leg being substantially chewed to pulp in the chain. His voice was raised in that high nasal Irish tenor, known and hated the world over.

> 'Ohhhhhhhhhhhhhhh IIIIIIIIIIIIIII
> *Once* knew a judy in Dubleen Town
> Her eyes were blue and her hair was brown,
> One night on the grass I got her down
> And I . . .'

The rest of the words were lost to view as he turned a bend in the road. Farther along, from an overhanging branch, a pure-blooded Irish crow watched the Milligan approach. It also watched him hit the pothole, leave the bike, strike the ground, clutch the shin, scream the agony, swear the word. 'Caw!' said the crow. 'Balls!' said the Milligan. Peering intently from behind a wall was something that Milligan could only hope was a face.

The fact that it was hanging from a hat gave credulity to his belief.

'Are you all right, Milligan?' said the face in the hat.

'Oh ho!' Milligan's voice showed recognition. 'It's Murphy. Tell me, why are you wearing dat terrible lookin' trilby?'

'We sold der hat stand, an' dere's no place ter hang it.' Murphy's face was a replica of the King Edwards he grew. He did in fact look like King Edward the Seventh. He also resembled King Edward the Third, Fifth and Second, making a grand total of King Edward the Seventeenth. He had a mobile face, that is, he always took it with him. His nose was what the French call retroussé, or as we say, like a pig; his nostrils were so acutely angled, in stormy weather the rain got in and forced him indoors. His eyebrows grew from his head like Giant Coypu rats, but dear friends, when you and I talk of eyebrows, we know not what eyebrows be until we come face to face with the *Murphy's* eyebrows! The man's head was a veritable plague of eyebrows, black, grey, brown and red they grew, thick as thieves. They covered two-thirds of his skull, both his temples and the entire bridge of his nose. In dry weather they bristled from his head like the spears of an avenging army and careless flies were impaled by the score. In winter they glistened with hoar-frost and steamed by the fire. When wet they hung down over his eyes and he was put to shaking himself like a Cocker Spaniel before he could proceed. For all their size dose eyebrows were as mobile as piglets, and in moments of acute agitation had been seen as far south as his chin. At the first sight of Milligan they had wagged up and down, agitati ma non troppo. As he spoke they both began to revolve round his head at speed.

'I heeerd a crash,' said Murphy. 'I examined meself, and I knew it wasn't me.'

'It was me,' said Milligan. 'I felled off me bi-cycle. Tank heaven the ground broke me fall.'

'Oh yes, it's very handy like dat,' said Murphy, settling his arms along the wall.

'Oh dear, dear!' said Milligan, getting to his feet. 'I've scratched all the paint off the toe of me boot.'

'Is dat right den, you paint yer boots?'

'True, it's the most economical way. Sometimes I paints 'em brown, when I had enough o' dat I paints 'em black again. Dat way people tink you got more than one pair, see? Once when I played the cricket I painted 'em white, you should try dat.'

'Oh no,' said Murphy solemnly. 'Oh no, I don't like intefering wid nature. Der natural colour of boots is black as God ordained, any udder colour and a man is askin' fer trouble.'

'Oh, and what I may ask is wrong wid brown boots?'

'How do I know? I never had a pair.'

'Take my tip, Murphy, you got to move wid der times man. The rich people in Dublin are all wearin' the brown boots; when scientists spend a lifetime inventin' a thing like the brown boots, we should take advantage of the fact.'

'No, thank you,' said Murphy's eyebrows, 'I'll stick along wid the inventor of the black boots. After all they don't show the dirt.'

'Dat's my argument, black don't show the dirt, brown ones don't show the mud and a good pair of green boots won't show the grass.'

'By Gor', you got something dere,' said the Murphy. 'But wait, when you was wearing dem white boots, what didn't dey show?'

'They didn't show me feet,' said Milligan, throwing himself on to the bike and crashing down on the other side.

'Caw!' said the crow.

'BALLS!' said Milligan. 'I'll be on me way.' He remounted and pedalled off.

'No, stay and have a little more chat,' called Murphy across the widening gap. 'Parts round here are lonely and sparse populated.'

'Well it's not for the want of you tryin',' came the fading reply.

*

The day brewed hotter now, it was coming noon. The hedgerows hummed with small things that buzzed and bumbled in the near heat. From the cool woods came a babel of chirruping birds. The greenacious daisy-spattled fields spread out before Milligan, the bayonets of grass shining bravely in the sun, above him the sky was an exaltation of larks. Slowfully Milligan pedalled on his way. Great billy bollers of perspiration were running down his knees knose and kneck, the torrents ran down his shins into his boots where they escaped through the lace holes as steam. 'Now,' thought the Milligan, 'why are me legs goin' round and round? eh? I don't tink it's me doin' it, in fact, if I had me way dey wouldn't be doin' it at all. But dere dey are goin' round and round; what den was der drivin' force behind dose legs? Me wife! *That's* what's drivin' 'em round and round, dat's the truth, dese legs are terrified of me wife, terrified of bein' kicked in the soles of the feet again.' It was a disgrace how a fine mind like his should be taken along by a pair of terrified legs. If only his mind had a pair of legs of its own they'd be back at the cottage being bronzed in the Celtic sun.

The Milligan had suffered from his legs terribly. During the war in Italy. While his mind was full of great heroisms under shell fire, his legs were carrying the idea, at speed, in the opposite direction. The Battery Major had not understood.

'Gunner Milligan? You have been acting like a coward.'

'No sir, not true. I'm a hero wid coward's legs, I'm a hero from the waist up.'

'Silence! Why did you leave your post?'

'It had woodworm in it, sir, the roof of the trench was falling in.'

'Silence! You acted like a coward!'

'I wasn't acting sir!'

'I could have you shot!'

'Shot? Why didn't they shoot me in peacetime? I was still the same coward.'

'Men like you are a waste of time in war. Understand?'

'Oh? Well den! Men like *you* are a waste of time in peace.'

'Silence when you speak to an officer,' shouted the Sgt. Major at Milligan's neck.

All his arguments were of no avail in the face of military authority. He was court martialled, surrounded by clanking top brass who were not cowards and therefore biased.

'I may be a coward, I'm not denying dat sir,' Milligan told the prosecution. 'But you can't really *blame* me for being a coward. If I am, then you might as well hold me responsible for the shape of me nose, the colour of me hair and the size of me feet.'

'Gunner Milligan,' Captain Martin stroked a cavalry moustache on an infantry face. 'Gunner Milligan,' he said. 'Your personal evaluations of cowardice do not concern the court. To refresh your memory I will read the precise military definition of the word.'

He took a book of King's Regulations, opened a marked page and read 'Cowardice'. Here he paused and gave Milligan a look.

He continued: 'Defection in the face of the enemy. Running away.'

'I was not running away sir, I was retreating.'

'The whole of your Regiment were advancing, and you decided to retreat?'

'Isn't dat what you calls personal initiative?'

'Your action might have caused your comrades to panic and retreat.'

'Oh, I see! One man retreating is called running away, but a whole Regiment running away is called a retreat? I demand to be tried by cowards!'

A light, commissioned-ranks-only laugh passed around the court. But this was no laughing matter. These lunatics could have him shot.

'Have you anything further to add?' asked Captain Martin.

'Yes,' said Milligan. 'Plenty. For one ting I had no desire to partake in dis war. I was dragged in. I warned the Medical Officer, I told him I was a coward, and he marked me A1 for Active Service. I gave everyone fair warning! I told me Battery Major before it started, I even wrote to Field Marshal Montgomery. Yes, I warned everybody, and now you're all acting surprised?'

Even as Milligan spoke his mind, three non-cowardly judges made a mental note of Guilty.

'Is that all?' queried Martin with all the assurance of a conviction. Milligan nodded. What was the use? After all, if Albert Einstein stood for a thousand years in front of fifty monkeys explaining the theory of relativity, at the end, they'd still be just monkeys.

Anyhow it was all over now, but he still had these cowardly legs which, he observed, were still going round and round. 'Oh dear, dis weather, I niver knowed it so hot.' It felt as though he could have grabbed a handful of air and squeezed the sweat out of it. 'I wonder,' he mused, 'how long can I go on losin' me body fluids at dis rate before I'm struck down with the dehydration? Ha ha! The answer to me problems,' he said, gleefully drawing level with the front door of the 'Holy Drunkard' pub.

'Hello! Hi-lee, Ho-la, Hup-la!' he shouted through the letter box.

Upstairs, a window flew up like a gun port, and a pig-of-a-face stuck itself out.

'What do you want, Milligan?' said the pig-of-a-face. Milligan doffed his cap.

'Ah, Missis O'Toole, you're looking more lovely dan ever. Is there any chance of a cool libation for a tirsty traveller?'

'Piss off!' said the lovely Mrs O'Toole.

'Oh what a witty tongue you have today,' said Milligan, gallant in defeat. Well, he thought, you can fool some of the people all the time and all the people some of the time, which is just long enough to be President of the United States, and on that useless profundity, Milligan himself pedalled on, himself, himself.

'Caw!' said a crow.

'Balls!' said Milligan.

BRENDAN BEHAN
The Confirmation Suit

Brendan Behan (1923–1964) wrote in Irish and English. His prison experiences (for Republican activities) inspired his book Borstal Boy *and the play,* The Quare Fellow. *The success of his play* The Hostage (An Giall) *and his often boisterous appearances on television made him an international figure. Among his prose works are* Brendan Behan's Island, Hold Your Hour and Have Another *and a novel,* The Scarperer.

For weeks it was nothing but simony and sacrilege, and the sins crying to heaven for vengeance, the big green Catechism in our hands, walking home along the North Circular Road. And after tea, at the back of the brewery wall, with a butt too to help our wits, what is a pure spirit, and don't kill that, Billser has to get a drag out of it yet, what do I mean by apostate, and hell and heaven and despair and presumption and hope. The big fellows, who were now thirteen and the veterans of last year's Confirmation, frightened us, and said the Bishop would fire us out of the Chapel if we didn't answer his questions, and we'd be left wandering around the streets, in a new suit and top-coat with nothing to show for it, all dressed up and nowhere to go. The big people said not to mind them; they were only getting it up for us, jealous because they were over their Confirmation, and could never make it again. At school we were in a special room to ourselves, for the last few days, and went round, a special class of people. There were worrying times too, that the Bishop would light on you, and you wouldn't be able to answer his questions. Or you might hear the women complaining about the price of boys' clothes.

'Twenty-two and sixpence for tweed, I'd expect a share in the shop for that. I've a good mind to let him go in jersey and pants for that.'

'Quite right, ma'am', says one to another, backing one another up, 'I always say what matter if they are good and pure'. What had that got to do with it, if you had to go into the Chapel in a jersey and pants, and every other kid in a new suit, kid gloves and tan shoes and a *scoil* cap. The Cowan brothers were terrified. They were twins, and twelve years old, and every old one in the street seemed to be wishing a jersey and pants on them, and saying their poor mother couldn't be expected to do for two in the one year, and she ought to go down to Sister Monica and tell her to put one back. If it came to that, the Cowans agreed to fight it out, at the back of the brewery wall; whoever got best, the other would be put back.

I wasn't so worried about this. My old fellow was a tradesman, and made money most of the time. Besides, my grandmother, who lived at the top of the next house, was a lady of capernosity and function. She had money and lay in bed all day, drinking porter or malt, and taking pinches of snuff, and talking to the neighbours that would call up to tell her the news of the day. She only left her bed to go down one flight of stairs and visit the lady in the back drawing-room, Miss McCann.

Miss McCann worked a sewing-machine, making habits for the dead. Sometimes girls from our quarter got her to make dresses and costumes, but mostly she stuck to the habits. They were a steady line, she said, and you didn't have to be always buying patterns, for the fashions didn't change, not even from summer to winter. They were like a long brown shirt, and a hood attached, that was closed over the person's face before the coffin lid was screwn down. A sort of little banner hung out of one arm, made of the same material, and four silk rosettes in each corner, and in the middle, the letters IHS, which mean, Miss McCann said, 'I Have Suffered'.

My grandmother and Miss McCann liked me more than any other kid they knew. I like being liked, and could only admire their taste.

My Aunt Jack, who was my father's aunt as well as mine,

sometimes came down from where she lived, up near the Basin, where the water came from before they started getting it from Wicklow. My Aunt Jack said it was much better water, at that. Miss McCann said she ought to be a good judge. For Aunt Jack was funny. She didn't drink porter or malt, or take snuff, and my father said she never thought much about men either. She was also very strict about washing yourself very often. My grandmother took a bath every year, whether she was dirty or not, but she was in no way bigoted in the washing line in between times.

Aunt Jack made terrible raids on us now and again, to stop snuff and drink, and make my grandmother get up in the morning, and wash herself, and cook meals and take food with them. My grandmother was a gilder by trade, and served her time in one of the best shops in the city, and was getting a man's wages at sixteen. She liked stuff out of the pork butchers, and out of cans, but didn't like boiling potatoes, for she said she was no skivvy, and the chip man was better at it. When she was left alone it was a pleasure to eat with her. She always had cans of lovely things and spicy meat and brawn, and plenty of seasoning, fresh out of the German man's shop up the road. But after a visit from Aunt Jack, she would have to get up and wash for a week, and she would have to go and make stews and boil cabbage and pig's cheeks. Aunt Jack was very much up for sheep's heads too. They were so cheap and nourishing.

But my grandmother only tried it once. She had been a first-class gilder in Eustace Street, but never had anything to do with sheep's heads before. When she took it out of the pot, and laid it on the plate, she and I sat looking at it, in fear and trembling. It was bad enough going into the pot, but with the soup streaming from its eyes, and its big teeth clenched in a very bad temper, it would put the heart crossways in you. My grandmother asked me, in a whisper, if I ever thought sheep could look so vindictive, but that it was more like the head of an old man, and would I for God's sake take it up and throw it out of the window. The sheep kept glaring at us, but I came the far side of it, and rushed over to the window and threw it out in a flash. My grandmother had to drink a Baby Power whiskey, for she wasn't the better of herself.

Afterwards she kept what she called her stock-pot on the gas. A heap of bones and, as she said herself, any old muck that would come in handy, to have boiling there, night and day, on a glimmer. She and I ate happily of cooked ham and California pineapple and sock-eyed salmon, and the pot of good nourishing soup was always on the gas even if Aunt Jack came down the chimney, like the Holy Souls at midnight. My grandmother said she didn't begrudge the money for the gas. Not when she remembered the looks that sheep's head was giving her. And all she had to do with the stock-pot was throw in another sup of water, now and again, and a handful of old rubbish the pork butcher would send over, in the way of lights or bones. My Aunt Jack thought a lot about barley, too, so we had a package of that lying beside the gas, and threw a sprinkle in any time her foot was heard on the stairs. The stock-pot bubbled away on the gas for years after, and only when my grandmother was dead did someone notice it. They tasted it, and spat it out just as quick, and wondered what it was. Some said it was paste, and more that it was gold size, and there were other people and they maintained that it was glue. They all agreed on one thing, that it was dangerous tack to leave lying around where there might be young children, and in the heel of the reel, it went out the same window as the sheep's head.

Miss McCann told my grandmother not to mind Aunt Jack but to sleep as long as she liked in the morning. They came to an arrangement that Miss McCann would cover the landing and keep an eye out. She would call Aunt Jack in for a minute, and give the signal by banging the grate, letting on to poke the fire, and have a bit of a conversation with Aunt Jack about dresses and costumes, and hats and habits. One of these mornings, and Miss McCann delaying a fighting action, to give my grandmother

time to hurl herself out of bed and into her clothes and give her
face the rub of a towel, the chat between Miss McCann and
Aunt Jack came to my Confirmation suit.

When I made my first Communion, my grandmother dug
deep under the mattress, and myself and Aunt Jack were sent
round expensive shops, and I came back with a rig that would
take the sight of your eye. This time, however, Miss McCann
said there wasn't much stirring in the habit line, on account of
the mild winter, and she would be delighted to make the suit, if
Aunt Jack would get the material. I nearly wept, for terror of
what these old women would have me got up in, but I had to let
on to be delighted, Miss McCann was so set on it. She asked
Aunt Jack did she remember my father's Confirmation suit. *He*
did. He said he would never forget it. They sent him out in a
velvet suit, of plum colour, with a lace collar. My blood ran cold
when he told me.

The stuff they got for my suit was blue serge, and that was
not so bad. They got as far as the pants, and that passed off very
civil. You can't do much to a boy's pants, one pair is like the
next, though I had to ask them not to trouble themselves
putting three little buttons on either side of the legs. The
waistcoat was all right, and anyway the coat would cover it. But
the coat itself, that was where Aughrim was lost.

The lapels were little wee things, like what you'd see in
pictures like Ring magazine of John L. Sullivan, or Gentleman
Jim, and the buttons were the size of saucers, or within the bawl
of an ass of it, and I nearly cried when I saw them being put on,
and ran down to my mother, and begged her to get me any sort
of a suit, even a jersey and pants, than have me set up before the
people in this get-up. My mother said it was very kind of Aunt
Jack and Miss McCann to go to all this trouble and expense, and
I was very ungrateful not to appreciate it. My father said that
Miss McCann was such a good tailor that people were dying to
get into her creations, and her handiwork was to be found in all
the best cemeteries. He laughed himself sick at this, and said if it

was good enough for him to be sent down to North William
Street in plum-coloured velvet and lace, I needn't be getting the
needle over a couple of big buttons and little lapels. He asked
me not to forget to get up early the morning of my Confirmation,
and let him see me, before he went to work: a bit of a laugh
started the day well. My mother told him to give over and let
me alone, and said she was sure it would be a lovely suit, and
that Aunt Jack would never buy poor material, but stuff that
would last forever. That nearly finished me altogether, and I ran
through the hall up to the corner, fit to cry my eyes out, only I
wasn't much of a hand at crying. I went more for cursing, and I
cursed all belonging to me, and was hard at it on my father, and
wondering why his lace collar hadn't choked him, when I
remembered that it was a sin to go on like that, and I going up
for Confirmation, and I had to simmer down, and live in fear of
the day I'd put on that jacket.

The days passed, and I was fitted and refitted, and every old
one in the house came up to look at the suit, and took a pinch of
snuff, and a sup out of the jug, and wished me long life and the
health to wear and tear it, and they spent that much time
viewing it round, back, belly and sides, that Miss McCann
hadn't time to make the overcoat, and like an answer to a
prayer, I was brought down to Talbot Street, and dressed out in
a dinging overcoat, belted, like a grown-up man's. And my
shoes and gloves were dear and dandy, and I said to myself that
there was no need to let anyone see the suit with its little lapels
and big buttons. I could keep the topcoat on all day, in the
chapel and going round afterwards.

The night before Confirmation day, Miss McCann handed
over the suit to my mother, and kissed me, and said not to
bother thanking her. She would do more than that for me, and
she and my grandmother cried and had a drink on the strength
of my having grown to be a big fellow, in the space of twelve
years, which they didn't seem to consider a great deal of time.
My father said to my mother, and I getting bathed before the

fire, that since I was born Miss McCann thought the world of me. When my mother was in hospital, she took me into her place till my mother came out, and it near broke her heart to give me back.

In the morning I got up, and Mrs Rooney in the next room shouted in to my mother that her Liam was still stalling, and not making any move to get out of it, and she thought she was cursed; Christmas or Easter, Communion or Confirmation, it would drive a body into Riddleys, which is the mad part of Grangegorman, and she wondered she wasn't driven out of her mind, and above in the puzzle factory years ago. So she shouted again at Liam to get up and washed and dressed. And my mother shouted at me, though I was already knotting my tie, but you might as well be out of the world as out of fashion, and they kept it up like a pair of mad women, until at last Liam and I were ready and he came in to show my mother his clothes. She hanselled him a tanner which he put in his pocket and Mrs Rooney called me in to show her my clothes. I just stood at her door, and didn't open my coat, but just grabbed the sixpence out of her hand, and ran up the stairs like the hammers of hell. She shouted at me to hold on a minute, she hadn't seen my suit, but I muttered something about it not being lucky to keep a Bishop waiting, and ran on.

The Church was crowded, boys on one side and the girls on the other, and the altar ablaze with lights and flowers, and a throne for the Bishop to sit on when he wasn't confirming. There was a cheering crowd outside, drums rolled, trumpeters from Jim Larkin's band sounded the Salute. The Bishop came in and the doors were shut. In short order I joined the queue to the rails, knelt and was whispered over, and touched on the cheek. I had my overcoat on the whole time, though it was warm, and I was in a lather of sweat waiting for the hymns and the sermon.

The lights grew brighter and I got warmer, was carried out fainting. But though I didn't mind them loosening my tie, I

clenched firmly my overcoat, and nobody saw the jacket with
the big buttons and the little lapels. When I went home I got
into bed, and my father said I went into a sickness just as the
Bishop was giving us the pledge. He said this was a master
stroke and showed real presence of mind.

Sunday after Sunday, my mother fought over the suit. She
said I was a liar and a hypocrite, putting it on for a few minutes
every week, and running into Miss McCann's and out again,
letting her think I wore it every weekend. In a passionate
temper my mother said she would show me up, and tell Miss
McCann, and up like a shot with her, for my mother was always
slim and light on her feet as a feather, and in next door. When
she came back she said nothing, but sat at the fire looking into
it. I didn't really believe she would tell Miss McCann. And I put
on the suit and thought I would go in and tell her I was wearing
it this week-night, because I was going to the Queen's with
my brothers. I ran next door and upstairs, and every step was
more certain and easy that my mother hadn't told her. I ran,
shoved in the door, saying: 'Miss Mc., Miss Mc., Rory and Sean
and I are going to the Queen's . . .' She was bent over the
sewing-machine and all I could see was the top of her old grey
head, and the rest of her shaking with crying, and her arms
folded under her head, on a bit of habit where she had been
finishing the IHS. I ran down the stairs and back into our place,
and my mother was sitting at the fire, sad and sorry, but saying
nothing.

I needn't have worried about the suit lasting forever. Miss
McCann didn't. The next winter was not so mild, and she was
whipped before the year was out. At her wake people said how
she was in a habit of her own making, and my father said she
would look queer in anything else, seeing as she supplied the
dead of the whole quarter for forty years, without one complaint
from a customer.

At the funeral, I left my topcoat in the carriage and got out
and walked in the spills of rain after her coffin. People said I

would get my end, but I went on till we reached the graveside, and I stood in my Confirmation suit drenched to the skin. I thought this was the least I could do.

J.P. DONLEAVY
From *The Ginger Man*

J.P. Donleavy (1926–) was born in New York and came to Dublin in
1946 to study at Trinity College. The Ginger Man, *his first novel,*
was published in 1955 and made Donleavy an international name. Since
then, he has published a number of bawdy novels with alliterative titles
such as The Saddest Summer of Samuel S, The Beastly Beati-
tudes of Balthazar B, The Destinies of Darcy Dancer, Gentleman, *and a collection of short stories* Meet My Maker, The Mad
Molicule. *In 1986, he published a memoir,* J.P. Donleavy's Ireland
in All of Her Sins and Some of Her Graces.

With two tomes under the arm walking out the back gate of
Trinity College. Bright warm evening to catch the train. These
business people are bent for their summer gardens and maybe a
swim by Booterstown. On these evenings Dublin is such an
empty city. But not around the parks or pubs. It would be a
good idea to pop onto the Peace Street and buy a bit of meat.
I'm looking forward to a nice dinner and bottle of stout and
then I'll go out and walk along the strand and see some fine
builds. For such a puritan country as this, there is a great deal to
be seen in the way of flesh if one is aware and watching when
some of them are changing on the beach.

'Good evening, sir.'

'Good evening.'

'And how can I help you, sir?'

'To be quite honest with you, I think I would like a nice piece
of calf's liver.'

'Now, sir, I think I can see you with a lovely bit, fresh and
steaming. Now I'll only be a minute.'

'Bang on. Wizard.'

'Now here we are, sir. It's a fine bit. On a bit of a holiday, sir?
Nice to have a bit of fresh meat.'

'Yes, a holiday.'

'Ah England's a great country, now isn't it sir?'

'Fine little country you have here.'

'Ah it's got its points. Good and bad. And hasn't everything now. And here we are, sir, enjoy your holiday. It's a nice evening, now.'

'A great evening.'

'I see you're a man of learning and good-sized books they are too.'

'They're that. Bye bye, now.'

'Grand evening. Good luck, sir.'

Wow, what conversation. Doctor of Platitudes. Holiday, my painful arse. But a nice bit of liver.

Into the gloom of Westland Row Station. He bought the papers, rolled them and beat his thigh up the stairs. Sitting on the iron bench, could see the people pouring in the gate. Where are the slim ankles on you women. None of you. All drays. Well what's in the paper. Dreariness. The Adventures of Felix the Cat. Put it away. I must to the lavatory. So big in here. Dribbling water. Good God, the train.

Rumbling, pounding, black dirty toy. Whistling by with the whole gang of these evening faces peeking and pouting out the windows. Must find a first class compartment. Jesus jammed, the whole damn train. O me, try the third. Pulling himself up. Pushing his meat onto the rack, squeezing around, sitting down.

Across from him the people who lived in the semi-detached houses of Glenageary and Sandycove, all buried in the paper reading madly. Why don't some of you look out the window at the nice sights. See the canal and gardens and flowers. It's free, you know. No use getting meself upset by the crut. I say there, you, you little pinched bastard, what are you staring at. That little man staring at me. Go away, please.

Chug, chug, chug.
Choo, choo, choo.
Woo, woo, woo.

We're away. Mustn't mind these damn people. Getting me upset. Mustn't get upset. Still staring at me. If he keeps it up I swear by Christ I'll lash his head right through that window. Expect rudeness like this in the third class.

The girl sitting across from him gave a startled gasp. What is this. Must be I've gotten in a train going to Grangegorman. What's the matter with her. That pinched bastard must be up to something, feeling her thigh. Lecher. Perhaps it's my place to take measures against this sneak. O but mind my own business. Things bad enough as they are already. Well look at them all. Whole seat is writhing, wriggling. What are they looking at. This is the end. I look forward to a nice evening of my liver and a walk and what's that girl pressing the book up to her face for. Is she blind. Get a pair of glasses you silly bitch. Maybe that bastard is embarrassing her, she's blushing. The damn sexual privation in this city. That's it. Root of it all. Distraction. I need distraction. Read the In Memoriams.

Donoghue – (Second Anniversary) – In sad and loving memory of our dear father, Alex (Rexy) Donoghue, taken away July 25, 1946, late of Fitzwilliam Square (Butcher's porter in the Dublin abattoir) on whose soul, sweet Jesus, have mercy.

Masses offered. RIP.

Gone forever, the smiling face,
The kindly, cheerful heart
Loved so dearly through the years
Whose memory shall never depart.

Coming upon his ears like goblets of hot lead.

'I say, I say there. There are women present.'

Absolute silence in the compartment as the little train clicked past the Grand Canal and the slovenly back gardens of Ringsend.

Sebastian glued to the print, paper pressed up to his eyes. Again, like an obscenity uttered in church.

'Sir. I say. There are ladies present in the carriage.'

Who would be the first to jump on him. Must let someone else make the first move, I'll grab his legs when trouble starts. O this so worries me. I hate this kind of thing. Why in the name of the suffering Jesus did I have to get into this damn car. Will I ever be delivered. No doubt about it, this man was a sexual maniac. Start using obscene language any second. There's just so much I can take. It's like that old woman saying her rosary and after every decade screaming out a mouthful of utter, horrible foulness. And I can't bear foulness. Look at them, all behaving as if nothing had happened. Better keep my eyes up, he may try to level me with a surprise blow. That man in the corner with the red nose. He's laughing, holding his stomach. For hell, deliver me. Never again ride third class.

'I say there. Must I repeat. There are ladies present.'

Sebastian levelled his face at him, lips shearing the words from his mouth.

'I beg your pardon.'

'Well, I say, haven't you forgotten something?'

'I beg your pardon.'

'I repeat, there are ladies present. You ought to inspect yourself.'

'Are you addressing me?'

'Yes.'

This conversation is too much. Should have ignored the fool. This is most embarrassing. I ought to take a clout at that bastard in the corner who seems to be enjoying it so much. He'll enjoy it if I break his jaw for him. Why don't they lock these people up in Ireland. The whole city full of them. If I'm attacked, by God, I'll sue the corporation for selling this madman a ticket. Those two girls are very upset. This damn train an express all the way to the Rock. My God. Sit and bear it. Control. Absolute and complete control at all costs.

'Sir, this is abdominable behavior. I must caution you.

Frightfully serious matter, this. Shocking on a public conveyance. Part of you, sir, is showing.'

'I beg your pardon, but would you please mind your own business or I'll break your jaw.'

'It is my business to discourage this sort of thing when there are ladies present. Shameful. There are other people in the car you know.'

No hope. Don't let him suck me into conversation like that. Must employ me brain. We're coming into the Booterstown. Get out in a minute. Showing? Yes. My fingers are out. Holy Catholic Ireland, have to wear gloves. Don't want to be indecent with uncovered fingers. And my face too. This is the last time positively that I appear without wearing a mask. There's a breaking point. But I'll not break not for any of them and certainly not for this insane lout.

Avoiding the red, pinched, insistent, maniacal face. Look out the window. There's the park and where I first saw my dear Chris to speak to me. O deliverance. That laughing monster in the corner, I'll drag him out of the car and belt him from one end of the station to the other. What's he doing. Pointing into his lap. Me? Lap? Good Christ. It's out. Every inch of it.

Leaping for the door. Get out. Fast. Behind him, a voice.

'Haven't you forgotten something else?'

Wheeling, wrenching the blood-stained parcel from the rack. Behind him.

'You can't remember your meat at all today.'

HUGH LEONARD

From *Home Before Night*

Hugh Leonard (1926–) is the pseudonym of John Keyes Byrne. One of Ireland's most successful writers, Leonard's plays include the Tony award-winning Da (*now also a film*), Time Was *and* A Life. *He has written television screenplays such as adaptations of* Strumpet City *and* Good Behaviour *and the original script* Parnell and the English-woman. *Leonard also writes a celebrated and very funny column for the* Sunday Independent. Home Before Night *is his acclaimed autobiography.*

The sun was splitting the trees and he had the front door on the hinge when his ma said not to go out until he had written the letter to Mrs Pim.

His da had been given a pension of ten shillings a week when Mrs Jacob died, and every three months there would come the cheque for six pounds ten and a letter written on blue paper with wording of a darker blue that said *Annegrove, Mountmellick, Co. Westmeath.* The letter hoped that they were all keeping well and was signed *Winifred R. Pim.* Mrs Pim was the Jacob's daughter, and sometimes when she came to Dublin for the day she would call to the house and sit in the baldy armchair by the range, saying: 'How are you, Keyes, and how is our dear Enderley?' His da was still working there, for the new owners who were Catholics, and the name of the house was Santa Maria now, but of course to him it was Enderley for ever more. The new people and himself were oil and water: for one thing, they had an ordinary way of talking – not like the quality at all; for another, they followed him around the garden to make certain that he earned his four pounds ten a week and was not idling in the greenhouse or the stable loft. 'Never work for your own,' he would tell Jack, 'for they'd skin you.' And with Mrs Pim forenenst him, holding a cup of tea in one hand and a cut of buttered brack in the other, he would go rawmayshing about the old days, a sob rising in his throat when he mentioned the Master and the Mistress, sure God be good to them. She said 'Indeed' or 'Dear me' every now and again to keep him happy, letting him talk the way you would let a dog run free in a park for a while. She wore a knitted cap with a tassel the size of your fist, and her brown lisle stockings were stretched at the knees when she sat, so that the skin showed through. There was a scent off her you could not place, a smell of gardens. When she spoke, every word was kept distinct and on its own, the way you would divide a bar of chocolate into fair shares. She had never stuttered or whispered in her life.

When she had given his da his say for long enough, she would interrupt him, turning to Jack. 'I hope,' she said, 'that when you find employment and make your own way in the world, you will be good to this old man.'

'Oh, Jack's the lad won't see us stuck,' his da said, and the thought of Jack being good to him brought a second lump into his throat, clattering against the first one like a hacking chestnut.

Jack's ma did not say yes, aye or no to this, but her eyes went darker and her mouth smaller. She had never forgiven Mrs Pim for the spectacle frames from the San Francisco earthquake or for the twenty-five pounds lump sum. Later, when their visitor had taken herself off to Mountmellick, leaving a whiff of lavender in the kitchen and the scent of verbena in the hall, Jack's da would be skewered with a look for letting himself be called an old man.

'The cheek of her,' his ma would say, 'with her ten shillings a week and then coming in here and being pass-remarkable. Her and her "old man" out of her. I wouldn't like to be hanging since she passed fifty.'

A week before the cheque was due, she would be on the lookout for Dick Cullen, the postman, and if the first of the month went by and it had not come there would be a face on her like a plateful of mortal sins. 'Bad scran to her, that money is dead,' she would say angrily, meaning that it was already spent or as good as, on shoes for Jack or a winter coat for his da or new wallpaper for the kitchen, for she was the devil for style. Then, just when she was about to call Dick Cullen a robber to his face, the envelope was slid under the weatherboard of the door.

'There now, Mag,' his da would say, and now of course she would pretend that it was no matter to her whether the money had ever been sent or no. 'We've been so long waiting for it,' she would grumble, 'that all the good has been took out of it.'

It was Jack's job to write to Mrs Pim to thank her, if only, his ma said, to show her that they were in the land of the living and had manners every bit as good as her own. Today was Sunday, when he and his friend Oliver would go down the sea front in Dun Laoghaire, so when she called him back he sat at the kitchen table in a temper, waiting while she put the notepad and the blue-black ink in front of him.

'Tell her that you're done with school,' she said, 'and please God she might find you something.'

She meant work. He had had a job only the once, two years ago when he was sixteen, as a French soldier in *Henry V* the time it was filmed above in Powerscourt. It was the Battle of Agincourt: he lay down and was a corpse one week and ran into a swamp and was drowned the next. Later, when he saw the film at the Pavilion, there were so many soldiers packed together and drowning that you could not see the swamp. It had been a great gas, except for getting your legs painted yellow or red to look like tights, but now of course he needed something steadier. He wrote: 'I am out of Presentation College this month past and like Mr Micawber am waiting for something to turn up.'

'What sort of codology is that?' his ma said when she read it.

'How?'

'*Who* is it you're like?'

'It's a character out of a book.'

The way he said it, short and sweet, told her she would not understand and that it would be a waste of his time to explain. It told her that she read books by Ruby M. Ayres and Nat Gould and that he was cleverer than she was. More than that, it told her that there was a foreign language he could speak that would be understood by Mrs Pim and not by her.

She said: 'Write it out again and do it proper.'

'What for?'

'Because I tell you to.'

He looked across at his da, who had the *Sunday Dispatch* open at the racing page and was wondering what ailed the pair of them. His mad aunt Mary was sitting at the kitchen table with her eyes turned up. 'Because he's told to, Mag,' she said.

'You dry up,' he said. Then, to his ma: 'There's this character who's an optimist –'

'I won't tell you a second time.'

'It's my letter. You're not writing it: I am.'

'Then do it proper.'

'Properly,' he said.

The old look came on her face: the one that said it was the price of her for rearing him. 'Don't you pull *me* up,' she said. 'Don't you act the gent with *me*, not in this house. They all said I'd rue the day, and gawm that I was I didn't believe them. Me own mother, me good neighbours –'

'Oh, play another record.'

'Don't you back-answer me, you cur. Showing off for the Pims, setting yourself up to be what you're not, no, and never will be . . . they must have a right laugh at you.'

His face told her that if she had not hit the mark she had staggered it. 'A nice article to be let go to the Presentation, acting the man-een, letting on he's the quality, and the whole pack of them making a jeer of him.'

'Ah, Mag,' his da said.

'Sure you're not good enough for him either, no more nor I

am.' Her small round body was shaking. She leaned against the table so that the edge of it cut into her. Her fists, pressed down on yesterday's *Irish Press* that was the tablecloth, were bunched and white. 'Well, thanks be to God,' she said, 'there's them in this house that knows where they were got and how they were got.'

It would be years before he learned that love turned upside-down is love for all that. Now, his hate was too much for her alone: it ran past her like a flood tide: it took in his da and Mary: it swallowed the room itself, the row of cracked jugs filled with betting slips and spools of thread, the bakelite grotto, turning from white to yellow, that said 'A Present from Lourdes', the old coats behind the door that were used as blankets on winter nights, the clock on the dresser, lying on its back like an invalid. Most of all, as the sea had done on the day his da tried to drown the dog, the hate filled his own eyes and mouth. He got up from the table, but his ma was at the door before him. 'You're not going from here until that letter is wrote.'

She had moved at such a lick of speed for her size that to his dismay he felt a grin come out of nowhere and he shot it for its treachery. He said: 'There's nothing wrong with it, and I'm not doing it again.'

'Oh, are you not?' She looked past him. 'Nick.'

'Ah, son,' his da said. 'Write it out again the way she wants you to.'

'Don't beg him,' she said. 'Tell him.'

At this, his da let a roar out of him that made Mary jump and say 'Jesus'. 'Will you do as you're bloody well told,' he said, 'and not be putting the woman into a passion? Can we not have peace in the house on a shaggin' Sunday without you and your curse-o'-God jack-actin'?'

The upshot was that he wrote the letter again, getting his own back by ending it with 'Yours, and oblige', as if it was a note to Toole's shop looking for tick. His da, beaming now, his temper gone like smoke from his pipe, stood over him and said: 'Begod, son, you always made a great fist of writing a letter.' His ma, coffined in her sulks, was limping around the kitchen to show how much he had taken out of her. He went to the door again, unhindered this time, and gave her daggers' looks. 'Mag, he's makin' faces,' said Mary the informer.

By the back road that dipped down into Glasthule and climbed out again as if policemen were chasing it, it was a mile and a bit to where Oliver lived in Crosthwaite Park. The sky burned and made his eyes ache; along Eden Road the tar shone and smelled new again. The trees were a tired August yellow-green, standing heavy as a glutton might, afraid to breathe until the fullness went. It was still dinner time: the roads were dozing. He whistled under his breath as he walked, thinking about the film *Lifeboat* he had seen last week at the Astoria. He had not forgotten the row with his ma: it had come with him like a dog to the corner of Begnet's Villas and would be waiting there when the last tram brought him home. *Lifeboat* had been brutal, a washout, but he remembered the bit where a man held up a newspaper and there was this advertisement for slimming, with one picture of Alfred Hitchcock real fat as 'before' and another one of him not so fat as 'after'. It was his way of getting into the film somehow, even though it all took place in this lifeboat. Jack had nudged the man sitting next to him. 'That's Alfred Hitchcock,' he said. 'Feck off,' the man said.

Oliver lived in the hall flat of the end house where, from the bay window, you looked across tennis courts. His mother was a fierce woman for moving. Previously, they had lived in Monks-town, and before that in Dalkey, on the Barrack Road. There, they played chess on the landing under the gap lamp and listened to the noises from the back room. They could see the door of this room from the stairs: it was kept shut and there were iron bars on the windows because it had once been part of the old police barracks next door. It was bare of furniture except for an iron bedstead, and yet every night there came these crashings, scrapings and thumpings, like from ten peluthered handymen.

'What is it?' Jack had asked the first time he heard it.

'Oh-there-you-have-me,' Oliver said in the loud, jolly, every-word-the-same voice he had used ever since he took the elocution lessons, and went on setting out the pieces on the chessboard.

Jack's first thought was that Oliver's da, Mr Mongan, was in the room, cod-acting to take a rise out of him. 'Do you see the green in me eye?' he said and ran up the half-flight, throwing open the door; but there was only the room, now quiet, with the shadows of the window bars flung slantwise across the floor by the street lamp on Railway Road. In time, he became as used to the noises as Oliver was: they would yell out 'This is Funf speaking' or sing 'Open the door, Richard!'; but whenever the gas light began to blink and die they would be down the stairs and out of the house like whippets, not coming back until someone – Oliver's mother or his da or his aunt who lived with them – put a shilling in the meter. One night, there was a noise worse than any knockings or bangings. They heard music and singing: far off, muffled and crackling, like an old gramophone.

Whatever was in the room or was not, people said that Oliver's mother was the cause of it. She had won a mint of money – five hundred pounds – in a crossword competition, and it had turned her peculiar: talking your head off one day and biting it off the next. She would queen it into the pork shop or Findlater's or the Leinster House as if she was the quality calling upon tinkers, and tell them they were robbers trying to diddle her, and, sign's on it, she was having them deported. Once, she pushed Oliver's aunt half-way out of an upstairs window, and all that saved the poor woman was that Mrs Mongan let go of her while she went to look for a hatchet. If you asked how any of this could connect her with the nightly concert in the back room, you would be smiled at for your innocence and told that the devil's children have the devil's luck and if you want to know me come and live with me. In the heel of the hunt, howsomever, the know-it-alls were wrong, for when the Mongans moved to a flat in Monkstown the noises still went on. In fact, after a night in the back room one of the new tenants swore a hole in an iron pot that he had seen an old woman stepping over his bed, and before that week was out the whole town turned up to see Father Creedon saying prayers over the house.

'Ah, yass, a grand and glorious Irish evening,' he said to anyone who saluted him as he sailed down Castle Street at the head of a procession of no one. He had a holy water bucket in one hand, a sprinkler, shaped like a drumstick, in the other and prayer book under his oxter. The crowd around the front door made way for him and a woman said 'God protect you, Father.' He gave her his blessing, forgetting that he was holding the sprinkler, and in a second she looked like a watered fuchsia. He hung the holy water bucket on the crook of his arm as if it was a handbag and opened his prayer book. The way he blessed himself made the people next to him step back for fear of being hit, treading on the feet of whoever was behind them, and his voice sang out over the slate roofs: 'In NOMiNe PAAHtrie et FILii et SPIRituuus SAHNCTi . . . AHHHmen.' Then, dipping the sprinkler and waving it, he made a bull's rush through the doorway of Number 28 and was gone from sight. He was wearing his altar slippers and the only sound was the smack of the holy water hitting the stairs. There was silence then, except, now and again, for the far-off thunder of his praying. A few of the old ones in the crowd had their beads out and were wading through the Sorrowful Mysteries; the others were quiet, hoping for something to happen and afraid that it might. After a while, a young lad in a red gansy – a little gouger from White's Villas up the town – edged to the open front door and slipped inside. Before anyone could make a move to go in after him, he was out again with a face that would frighten you. 'Jasus, run,' he said. 'It's comin' out.'

It was the 'it' that did the damage. He could have shouted 'He's comin' out' or 'She's comin' out'; but no, the little gett said 'it', and where there was a crowd one minute there was a stampede the next. Johnny Quinn, who was sitting on the window sill of the Foresters' Hall, that used to be the police barracks, was butted in the chest and fell backwards into the committee room, taking the window with him, and poor old Winnie Carthy that kept the sweetshop was knocked down and stepped on. When Father Creedon came out of the house after doing his praying and having a cup of tea in his hand to be sociable, there was not a cricket stirring except for the young lad that had started the rush, and Johnny Quinn, who was crying in the Foresters' Hall. He looked up and down the empty road and patted the young lad on the head and gave him sixpence. 'Couldst thou,' he said to the crowd, even though it was a mile away by now and still travelling, 'not watch with me one hour?'

The only noises from the back room of the flat where Oliver lived now, in Crosthwaite Park, were of his father snoring. He was a bus driver and because he talked through his nose like a black he was nicknamed Sammy. Himself and Mrs Mongan did not get on. Between him and Oliver there was never a cross word, but he was like a man who kept from tricking with what he did not understand, and believed that even God Almighty would draw the line at trying to understand Oliver. Now, while Jack was still on the front steps, he opened the door. He was wearing his busman's uniform with the silver watch-chain. 'Ollie,' he shouted down the hall. 'Kokomoko is here.' He gave Jack a wink to show that there was no harm in the name and went down the steps, singing through his nose and happy to be away from the person he could not understand, as well as from the other person that he could.

Oliver came into the hall in his shirt sleeves and fastening his tartan tie. 'Sappy days,' he said.

'Sappy days,' Jack said. It was a saying they had.

He told Oliver that it was roasting out and there would be a mob on the pier. 'Oh-jolly-good,' Oliver said and went off again to get ready. Because Jack was not invited into the flat he knew that Mrs Mongan was either as cross as two sticks or in one of her silences where if you talked to her she would turn her head away as if the wall made more sense to her than you did. He sat on the front step, bursting the blisters of green paint on the hall door and listening to the slow pock of a tennis ball from across the way.

When it came to getting ready to go out, you might as well order the sun to set early as try and hurry Oliver. He would take twenty minutes to wash himself, another ten foosthering with the knot in his tie and five more tugging at the handkerchief in his breast pocket until it sprouted like a flower. He had two handkerchiefs: for show and blow. 'Always look after your appearance,' he said once, 'and pronounce properly. That's how you get on.' His suit never had a speck on it, and there was a crease in his trousers you could pare a pencil on. He filed his nails, then polished them. He rubbed Silvikrin into his hair, which was dark and in neat waves except for one strand he left hanging loose on purpose, as if he was Charles Starrett, maybe, after a fight with the bully.

The time his mother won the five hundred pounds she had taken him out of the national school, meaning to send him to the Christian Brothers' secondary; then, the contrary sort she was, she changed her mind. That was when he was twelve and he had not been to school since. He was not worried: you would never be stuck, he said, as long as you developed your personality. Learn to be masterful and there would be no stopping you. So he sent off for the Charles Atlas course and did the exercises, even giving himself cold friction rubs, whatever *they* were. He went to Potter's College to learn elocution, and now he talked like a bacon slicer, using the same voice to let you know you had won the Sweep as he would to tell you your dog was run over. He was teaching himself psychology out of books you would strain yourself lifting. '"I think, therefore I am",' he said to Jack. 'That's from Des Carty.' His favourite book of all was called *How to Win Friends and Influence*

People, and he could spout screeds from it. He was doing
Pelmanism so as to be magnetic, and lately he had joined the
Rosicrucians, which brought out your hidden powers. This was
secret stuff, but he told Jack about the Cathedral of the Soul
and how he had meditated and lit rose-scented candles in front
of a looking glass and had seen his face changing to what it had
been like in previous existences. 'Oh-very-frightening-you-
know,' he said.

The lads on the sea front thought that Oliver was a howl.
'The guy has flipped his lid.' Dan Cleary said, throwing a piece
of invisible popcorn into the air, catching it in his mouth like
Alan Ladd did in *The Blue Dahlia* and giving a sad Richard
Conte smile out of his Glenn Ford face. Joe Byrne agreed with
him, saying that Oliver was a proper head-the-ball, but Liam
Cooney said no, that he was more of a harmless gobshite.
Whichever he was, eejit or head case, they were careful not to
laugh too loud or too long. Dan and Liam were apprentices, one
to a watchmaker, the other to an electrician, and Joe helped his
cousin Pat, who mended shoes. They could see their lives
running straight in front of them, cut and dried, and knew that
they could no more change direction now than the Dalkey tram
could turn and go up the mountains. But Oliver was still at the
starting gate, biding his hour so quiet and calm that you half-
expected him to make a leap and maybe go haring past the lot of
them. Then it would be they who would be the gobshites.

You could not ask for better company. He would laugh, nod
and be agreeable, never arguing the toss, but saying: 'By-Jove-
you're-right-you-know', and then, so gently that you had to think
twice to notice it, go his own sweet way. He would share out his
cigs, lend you a bob till Friday for the pictures or a table in the
billiard hall and listen to your troubles with never a yawn: and
yet, the more obliging he was, the more you felt a grudge against
him that swelled and turned white like a boil. You could endure a
messer or a hook or a bollix, even, but what you could not forgive
in Oliver was the worst lousiness of all – he had no need of you.

It was true. You could put him in your pocket but never own him. The lads and Jack were like a row of cottages, each one held up by the next and with one wall shared, but Oliver was a house standing off on its own, and whether he was too clever to need people or too thick, you could never be sure. If you found an excuse to have a row with him he would give his high-voiced laugh and remember he had a heavy date with Betty Brady or Maureen O'Reilly, saying: 'Must-be-hitting-the-old-trail . . . the-wife-you-know.' Then he was off along the sea front with that half-dancing walk of his, as if he had a spring in him. He was like a bubble in a piece of oil cloth: push on him and he went someplace else.

He was a desperate man for the women. Betty Brady, who had come over from England on account of the war, was mad about him and so jealous that she could hear a wink. She was sixteen years old, but you would give her another three, and from the way she linked him into the Pavilion or the Picture House you knew she was a red-hot coort. Still and all, one evening she moaned to Jack about how Oliver had put his hand on her chest during Maria Montez in *Cobra Woman*. She was not worth her salt from the shock of it, and the part of her Oliver was supposed to have touched was pumping like a bellows.

'Oh, Jack,' she said. 'I thought he had respect for me. And I just sat there and let him. I was petrified. Oh, God, where will it stop, now that I've encouraged him?'

Jack could not answer. He was staring bug-eyed at her chest, trying to imagine it without the fawn-coloured coat, the pullover, the blouse, the woolly vest and whatever else. The only dynamite coort he had ever had was off a dark girl with the nickname of Sticky Taite, and that was in a laneway near York Road. He had walked her home, then chanced his arm, rushing at her like a bull at a gate and landing a kiss that barked his nose off hers. It was over before he realized that her lips were different from other girls': instead of being soldered together, with the teeth clamped shut like iron bars behind red curtains, they had given way to him. As he drew back from her she smiled, reached out and said: 'C'm'ere to me.' Her arms went slowly around him, her legs opened and fastened on his thigh, her mouth ate him. It occurred to him where she had got her nickname, for between him and her from the knees up you could not have stuck a page from a penny copybook. Half an hour later, he went to meet the lads in the Roman Cafe, his heart thudding, the legs buckling under him and the sweet heavy taste of lipstick in his mouth.

When he told Liam Cooney about how Oliver had put his hand on Betty Brady's chest, Liam laughed and said: 'Will you go 'long out of that. He wouldn't know what to do with a diddy if she took it out and waved it at him.'

'No, honest. She was shaking.'

'Yeah, from wanting it and not getting it. There's more goes on inside that one's head than ever went on further down. If Mongan laid a finger on her he'd be in Lourdes now, praying for his hand to drop off. And you, you sap, you believed her.'

It made sense. Oliver was a great man for self-control: according to the Rosicrucians, he said, to be master of others you must first be master of yourself. Often, the lads would come the heavy, nudging him and winking: 'Eh, Ollie, did you ever get a bit? Come on, tell us . . . did-ja, wha'?' Oliver would take it in good part. 'Oh-now,' he would say, 'that would be telling. Ho-ho.' He believed that the greatest quality you could find in a girl was to be sincere, and he and Jack had made a list of all the sincere girls in the town, or at least on the sea front. Besides, he modelled himself on Tyrone Power, who was married to Annabella, and *Picturegoer* said they were Hollywood's happiest couple, preferring to spend their evenings in their cosy Bel Air home instead of becoming part of the studio colony's glamorous social whirl. Even in films. Tyrone Power might start off as a right louser, like in *Johnny Apollo* or *Crash Dive*, but he always redeemed himself in the end, and the most he gave Anne Baxter or Betty Grable was an old kiss and no messing. 'Of course, I know it's not true to life.'

Oliver would say, 'but the thing is, it gives you ideals-you-
know.'

Jack had punctured every blister on the hall door before
Oliver was done titivating himself. They walked down into the
town, talking about films the length of Mulgrave Terrace and
Marine Road until the pier came in sight. It was bright with
the colours of summer frocks: what you noticed most were the
reds and yellows, either moving towards the bandstand or like
quiet bunting on the benches or the folding chairs you paid
fourpence for. Along the sea front there were the smells of
scent and sea-wrack. Today, the pier seemed to have a light-
house at each end, for where it began the sun flashed off a
great hill of bicycles – a hundred near enough – thrown tangled
together after the journey out from Dublin, crawling the hot
winding length of the Merrion Road while the trams sang past
them.

Jack and Oliver walked down the pier along the lower level.
Among the people on the chairs above them, a woman was
sitting with her ankles crossed and knees spread wide, her long
pale-green knickers saluting the day. Jack looked away quickly
and nudged Oliver, who turned in time to see the knickers
vanishing as her knees shut like a trap. 'Oh-now,' he said, going
red, and went on about the film censor and what a louser he was
to cut out all the bits of *Reveille with Beverly* where Ann Miller
showed her legs. The mention of legs reminded them of the
women in the passion killers and they went into kinks. 'No-it's-
too-blooming-hot,' Oliver said, and that only made it worse, for
it was another saying of theirs, which they had heard William
Lundigan say in *The Sea Hawk*.

Near the bandstand, they met Maureen O'Reilly and the
ugly girl she knocked around with. Maureen was plump, with
fair hair and nun's eyes, flirting with the ground she walked
on. She and Oliver had been doing a steady line ever since last
April when the war was nearly over and Betty Brady had been
dragged back to London bawling her eyes out. From her

permed hair down to her shiny dark nylons and high heels she
was as neat as a bandbox and out of the same pod as Oliver:
seeing them together, you would take them for two dummies
that had stepped down out of Lee's window to go for a walk.
Betty Brady had not been the worst of them: for all her
codology, you could give her a squeeze whenever Oliver was
at home learning how to be magnetic, and not only would she
squeeze back but not go carrying tales. As far as Maureen
O'Reilly was concerned, however, Jack and the lads were back
of the neck: a coarse element, she called them. One evening on
the pier, Liam had said: 'Hey, Maureen, is it true you're
Oliver's new wife-you-know?' She had walked on, then turned
back to them. 'Oliver is too soft,' she said. 'He lets your kind
make free with him, and the only reward he gets is to be
jeered at.'

They watched her heels typing a goodbye message to them
on the granite flags. She had given them a right lemoner and
it took Liam a minute to get over it. 'Talk about having a
smell of yourself,' he said. 'That one thinks she pees
lemonade.'

Dan Cleary flicked a finger at the snap brim of his hat and
smiled sleepily. 'The broad has lost her marbles,' he said.

Today, she was wearing a gipsy sort of blouse that showed
off her shoulders. 'Well-hell-o,' Oliver said with as much surprise
as if he thought she had been in Fiji.

She gave the turn-ups of his trousers a pleased pink smile.
'Hello,' she said to them, 'isn't it shocking hot?'

'Oh-don't-be-talking,' Oliver said, quick as a flash.

She threw Jack a hello that fell on the pier and rolled into the
harbour, then she and Oliver moved away and stood talking,
with him giving her his You-are-in-my-power-but-I-will-spare-
you-never-fear look and her whispering at him like in a confession box. Jack was left with her ugly friend, a girl called May
Something, who had frizzy hair and a sour torn purse of a
mouth. One day, he had been looking at her and thinking how

desperate you would want to be to go with her, and at that moment he realized she was thinking the exact same about him. Since then, there had been the hatred between them of two people who are not good enough for one another. She looked straight through him at the three church spires of the town, and he looked through her at the bandstand. The Number 1 Army Band was playing 'Take a Pair of Sparkling Eyes.' The tune itself was as lilting as the day and the crowds, but the softness of the brass was melancholy, as if in regret for happy things that were gone.

Oliver finished his conversation and waved goodbye to Maureen, who went off down the pier with her stop-the-clock friend. A bunch of hard chaws from the town had their eyes glued to her bare shoulders, as pink as two legs of lamb. 'Are you seeing her later?' Jack asked.

'Oh-now,' Oliver said.

They found room to sit on the steps, hot under them, between the two levels and listened to the band. Off beyond the mailboat pier you could make out part of Dublin, lying like an old dog too hot to move. Jack began to sort what was left of the day into suits. Oliver's 'Oh-now' meant that he would be taking Maureen to the Pavilion after tea; they would sit at the back in the one-and-fourpennies, where the lads, below in the shilling seats, would not be near enough to blackguard them with 'Get your hand off that girl' or 'Eh, Ollie, would you risk it for a biscuit?' In the meantime, Jack could not go home to Oliver's house for tea because Mrs Mongan was in the glooms, or to his own house on account of the row with his ma. In his pocket he had one and eleven pence. That was a shilling for the pictures and eightpence for a glass of milk and a ham sandwich, instead of a proper tea, at the Roman Cafe. Tonight, maybe he could touch his da for fivepence to go with the three d. that was over: that would be enough for *The Uninvited* tomorrow afternoon. He was okie-doke until Tuesday, so. He was steeped.

He looked at Oliver, who had spread a handkerchief – the one for blow – under him when he sat and was tapping one long forefinger, stained yellow from ciggies, in time with the band. Their time for being friends was nearly up. Maureen's pull on Oliver was stronger than Jack's: she would win the tug-o'-war – at least until the day came when she would pull at him too hard and find the rope hanging empty in her hand.

A stout woman named Miss McGuinness was on the bandstand singing 'I Dreamt that I Dwelt in Marble Halls', Jack grinned, remembering the time the lads had sung it in the queue for the Pavilion and had been turfed out by Fleming the usher because the words they used were:

> I dreamt that I tickled my grandfather's balls
> With a drop of sweet oil and a feather,
> My grand-da, poor bugger, didn't like it at all,
> For his balls they went slap-bang together.

It was too hot to worry about Oliver. He found himself wondering if he would ever learn to seize a day like this, to use it somehow or keep it, instead of watching it go brushing past him into evening.

JOHN B. KEANE
The Change

John B. Keane (1928–) was born in Listowel, County Kerry where he now runs a pub. After a stint on London's building sites he turned to writing, becoming the most popular and prolific of contemporary Irish dramatists. His plays include Sive, Big Maggie, Many Young Men of Twenty *and* The Field, *which was made into an acclaimed film. He has also written many short stories and several novels, including the bestselling* The Bodhran Makers.

The village slept. It was always half asleep. Now, because there was a flaming sun in the June sky, it was really asleep. It consisted of one long street with maybe forty to fifty houses on either side. There were shops, far too many of them, and there were three decaying public houses, the doors of which were closed as if they were ashamed to admit people. No, that isn't quite true. The truth is that passing strangers upset the tenor of normal life. The locals only drank at night, always sparingly, and were therefore reluctant to accept habits that conflicted with their own.

In the centre of the roadway a mangy Alsatian bitch sunned herself inconsiderately and that was all the life there was. The day was Friday. I remember it well because my uncle, with whom I was staying, had cycled down to the pier earlier that morning for two fresh mackerel. Mackerel always taste better when they are cooked fresh.

Anyhow, the bitch lay stretched in the sun. From where I sat inside the window of my uncle's kitchen I could see the street from one end to the other. At nights when he didn't go to the pub that's what we would do; sit and watch the neighbours from the window. It was his place to comment and I would listen, dodging away to my room sometimes to write down something of exceptional merit. He was a great commentator but I never complimented him. He might stop if I did. It was hard, at times, to keep back the laughter although on rare occasions I was unable to smother it sufficiently and he would look at me suspiciously.

Behind me I could hear him in the kitchen. He made more noise than was strictly necessary.

'What way do you want it,' he called, 'boiled or fried?'

'Fried. Naturally.'

At the far end of the village a smart green sportscar came into view. Its occupants were a boy and a girl. One minute the car was at the end of the street and the next it was braking furiously to avoid collision with the Alsatian bitch.

'What's happening out there?' But he didn't wait for my reply.

He was standing beside me with the frying pan in his hand. The car had stopped and the driver climbed out to remove the obstacle.

'Come on. Come on. Get up outa that, you lazy hound.'

Slowly the bitch turned over on her side and scratched the ranges of twin tits which covered her belly. She rose painfully and without looking at the driver slunk to the pavement where she immediately lay down again.

By this time a number of people stood in the doorways of their houses. The squeal of brakes had penetrated the entire village and they had come to investigate. I followed my uncle to the doorway where we both stood silently watching the girl. She had eased herself from her seat and was now standing with hands on hips. She was tall and blonde. The tight-fitting red dress she wore clung to her body the way a label sticks to a bottle.

'Very nice. Very nice indeed,' my uncle said.

'I think,' the girl told the driver, 'I'll take off this dress. I feel clammy.'

'Suit yourself,' he replied. With that he returned to his seat and lit a cigarette. The red dress was buttoned right down the front.

'What's the name of this place?' she asked as she ripped the topmost button. From the way she said it we knew that she couldn't care less.

'Don't know,' the driver said. Then, as an afterthought, 'Don't care.'

She shrugged her slender shoulders and set to work on the other buttons, oblivious of the wide eyes and partly open mouths of the villagers. A door banged a few houses away but it was the only protest. When she reached the bottom buttons she was forced to stoop but she didn't grunt the way the village women did. Another shrug and the dress flowed from her to the ground.

Underneath she wore chequered shorts and a red bra, no more. The driver didn't even look when she asked him to hand her the sweater which was underneath her seat. Fumbling, his hand located the garment and he tossed it to her. He did make a comment however.

'Godsake hurry up,' he said with some irritation.

'Did you ever see such a heartless ruffian?' My uncle folded his arms and there was a dark look on his face. The girl stood for a moment or two shaking dust or motes or some such things from the sweater. Her whole body rippled at every movement. She started to pull the sweater over her head and then an astonishing thing happened. Nobody was prepared for it and this is probably why no one ever spoke about it afterwards. Everybody thought about it afterwards. I'm pretty certain of that.

Quite accidentally, I'm sure of that too, while she was adjusting her neck and shoulders so that she could the better accommodate the sweater, one of her breasts popped out into the sunlight. There were gasps. More doors banged.

A woman's voice called, 'Hussy. Hussy.'

Obviously she didn't hear. It was a deliciously pink living thing, dun-nippled and vital.

'Do 'em good,' my uncle whispered. 'Give 'em something to think about.'

The sweater in place, the girl adjusted her close-cropped hair. It didn't need adjusting but girls always seem to adjust their hair when it least needs it.

She picked up the dress and with her fingers felt the bonnet of the car. It must have been hot because she took the fingers away quickly and covered the bonnet with the dress. She then sat on the bonnet and from nowhere produced a tube of lipstick. All the while the driver sat looking straight in front of him. He threw the cigarette away before it had burned to the halfway stage. Now he sat with folded arms and hooded eyes that saw nothing.

The girl, her lips glistening, neatly folded the dress, went round to the boot of the car, flicked a button and tucked in the dress. Closing the boot she looked up and down the street. Her eyes scanned the few remaining faces with interest. If she noticed any reaction she did not show it in the least. For an instant her eyes met those of my uncle. He winked almost imperceptibly but she must have noticed it because she permitted herself the faintest glimmer of a smile as she entered the car. She punched the driver playfully and to give him his due he caught her round the shoulders and planted a swift kiss on the side of her face. Gears growled throatily and the car leaped forward into sudden life. In an instant it was gone and I was old enough to know that it had gone forever.

Later when we had eaten our mackerel we went to drive in the cows for the evening milking. This was the part of the day I liked best. The morning and afternoon hours dragged slowly and lamely but as soon as the evening milking was done there was the prospect of some excitement. We could cycle down to the pier and watch the lobster boats arriving home or we could go to the pub and listen.

On that particular evening we decided on the pub. Earlier while we were eating he had said that things would never be the same again. 'At least,' he confided, 'not for a hell of a long time anyway.' I had pressed him for an explanation.

'Look,' he said, 'I don't know exactly how to put it but that girl we saw changed things.'

'In what way?' I asked.

'Oh, damn,' he said, not unkindly, 'you have me addled. How do I know in what way? Is this the thanks I get for cooking your mackerel?'

'Aren't you afraid I'll grow up in ignorance?' He was fond of saying this when I failed to show interest in things he considered to be important. But he didn't rise to it. Instead he said: 'Wait and see. Wait and see, that's all.'

We went to the pub earlier than usual. He shaved before we left the house which was unusual for him. Most men in the village shaved only on Saturday nights or on the eve of holy days.

The pub was cool. There was a long wooden seat just inside the door. We sat and he called for a pint of stout and a bottle of lemonade. There were two other customers. One was a farmer's boy I knew by sight and the other was the young assistant teacher in the local boys' school.

'There was a lot of hay knocked today,' the publican said when he had served the drinks and collected his money.

'There was indeed,' my uncle answered piously, 'and if this weather holds there will be a lot more knocked tomorrow.'

I gathered from this that he was at the top of his form. He was saying nothing out of the way. Nobody could possibly benefit from his words. He would go on all night like this, relishing the utterly meaningless conversation.

The young teacher, who was not a native of the place, finished his drink and called for another. There was an unmistakable belligerence about him.

'A chip-carrier,' the uncle whispered, 'if ever I saw one.'

'What about the strip-tease act today?' the teacher ventured. When no one answered him he went to the window and looked out.

'Nothing ever happens here,' he pouted.

'True for you,' said the uncle.

He joined the teacher at the window. The three of us looked out into the street.

'Deserted,' the teacher said.

'Terrible,' from the uncle.

A couple came sauntering up the street.

'Here's up Flatface,' the teacher complained. Flatface was the name given to Mrs O'Brien. She had the largest number of children in the village. She wasn't an attractive woman. Neither was her husband an attractive man. But tonight Mrs O'Brien looked different. She wore make-up and her hair was freshly washed and combed.

'That's a change,' my uncle said.

'He'll have her pregnant again,' the teacher protested.

Other couples appeared on the street, husbands and wives who were never seen out together. Some were linking arms. All the pairs walked ingratiatingly close to one another.

'What is this?' the teacher asked anxiously. 'What's happening?'

'Strange,' said the uncle.

Later when the pub closed we walked down the street together. At the doorway of the house next to ours a man and his wife were standing. She wore her Sundays and he leaned heavily on her shoulder.

'I know he's leaning on her,' said the uncle, 'but for him that's a lot.'

Two girls were sitting on the window ledge of the house at the other side.

'Come in for a cup of tea, Jack,' one said. My uncle hesitated.

'Ah, come on, Jack,' said the other, 'it's early yet.'

The young teacher stood at the other side of the street, legs crossed, back propped against the wall. He looked gangly, wretched and lost.

'Care for a drop of tea?' the uncle called across. Suddenly the teacher sprang into action. He checked first by looking up and down to confirm that it was really he who was being invited. Then fully assured he bounded across the roadway, a mad hunger for companionship in his eyes.

The uncle explained to the girls how he would have to see me safely indoors but promised he would be back in a matter of moments. He suggested that meanwhile they start the proceedings without him. Courteously, or rather gallantly, the teacher stood aside to allow the ladies first passage indoors. One giggled but covered her mouth in atonement when the other nudged her to stop. In our own house the uncle poured me a glass of milk and we sat at the table for a spell.

'See what I mean?' he said. 'I told you things would never be the same.'

I nodded that I fully understood.

'Was that why you shaved tonight?' I asked.

'No,' he answered, 'but I can see now it was a good job I did.'

SEÁN MAC MATHÚNA
The Queen of Killiney

Seán Mac Mathúna (1936–) was born in County Kerry. He has worked as a schoolteacher at both primary and secondary levels. His short stories in Irish have garnered him a cult following. The Atheist, from which this story is taken is his first collection of stories in English.

Dinny Long, TD, was too wise to get married and too young to recognize the pain of loneliness. At forty-four, his name was as familiar to his constituents as was their brand of cornflakes, Land Rover, or cure for scour in cattle. He had an intense feeling for geography. He lived within thirty yards of his constituency boundary, and he knew that if he lived any closer, his constituents would accuse him of trying to escape. He lived close enough to Dublin to visit his mistress twice a week and far away enough to be safe from the marauding hordes of scavengers when the country had a debt of 40 billion and the dole would be stopped.

He was busy; but sometimes busy became hectic and hectic became insane. Then he withdrew to Bowlawling House, Georgian Residence, c. 300 acres plus eight loose boxes – home. And his housekeeper, Kitty, who could charm away callers as well as she could jug a hare. But they still pursued him up the gravel drive, on foot, bikes, mercs and now and again an oddity on a horse. 'Mercs are the worst, they walk down on you,' said Kitty. They almost did, pushing past her, saying firmly, 'Tell Mr Long it's only a minute.'

It never was. It was an eternity of 'Swing this for me and I'll canvass for you' or worse, 'Swing this for me for I canvassed for you'. It was all a litany of supplication that dulled his mind, and which he barely acknowledged by nodding at the pauses. Humanity had become transparent. In an ironic moment he had the idea of getting a badge with 'Support your local swinger' written on it, but Sambo said no, it would only draw them on. When things really got bad, Dinny sought out the damp quiet of the cellars in Bowlawling. They were filled with the remnants of former occupants. In such moments he leafed through old diaries, fingered books spotted with mould, and closing his eyes drew their antique fragrance deep within him. If ever he were free he would bottle the smell of old books and hawk it through the world to lost romantics. And photographs. A woman, a parasol, in the doorway of Bowlawling, smiling, all washed in the sepia of eternity. Scrawled on the back with surging flourish 'Remember Ballskarney! Love for ever, Rodney'. In such moments he would press the object to his heart and whisper 'Maybe I do love humanity after all'.

But out of the cellars he had to come, into the bright insanity of day. And that meant Sambo. Dinny walked into the clinic in Rathgrew. Sambo had his kinky snakeskin boots on the desk. 'Howdy Pal, just havin' me some shut-eye. Git off your feet and have a seat.' 'Sambo,' said Dinny, standing in the middle of the clinic, 'this place is looking more and more like the O.K. Corral.' Sambo drew on a large Havana and blew a smoke-ring towards the ceiling. 'Gawd damn, Dinny, you're real hornery, guess it's gonna be one o' them days.'

Dinny eyed the walls of the clinic – a paradox of posters advertising Sambo Reilly as a Bronco Buster, a cowpoke, a gambler on a Mississippi sternwheeler, a laster of nine seconds on a Texas Longhorn, all set against the posters of the Pro-life campaign. Nowhere did the name Dinny Long appear; more and more Sambo was taking over the clinic. This suited Dinny. 'Sambo, I don't mind you wearing a stetson because you have a face only a mother could love. It adds a bit of class – the cigar some flavour, but the spurs I object to. You're my election agent, secretary, fender-offer of *gaeilgeoirí*. I need you but you're trying to escape into a western. Spurs out.' Sambo didn't move. He pulled the brim of his stetson down to the half-moons of his eyes and lay back farther on the swivel. 'Folks agettin' kinda nasty about mah face. Waal, ah guess there must be sumpin to it – guy rode into town yistahday, said I got a face like a corduroy trousers – gal way down Tucson way tells me ah got a face like an unmade bed.' Slowly he eased his boots onto the ground and removed the spurs. 'Dollar ninety-five – Maceys – only plastic.'

Sambo filled him in on the goings on. Dinny was president, secretary, patron, committee member of so many bodies that he needed help. Sambo told him what funerals should be attended, weddings, christenings. But above all, he'd have to go down to the Rathgrew Community School, where he was chairman of the Board of Management. Detta Hearne, the Principal, needed him fast. 'The old gal's in a flap.'

And then the Amendment Campaign. Dinny eyed a number of placards that Sambo had made with markers. There was no 'double M' in amendment. It didn't matter, said Sambo, folks didn't care whether he was illiterate or not, they were all raring to vote against abortion. It was important that Dinny be associated with that response. The whole constituency was ninety-five percent Catholic farmers. But Dinny looked after everybody – Catholic, Protestant and Atheist. The Atheist's name was Tom Ruddy and he snarled about God, Ethiopia and the price of drink.

Dinny felt dynamic and grabbed a hammer and nails and began to nail placards to the battens. Suddenly he stopped and said 'Sambo, this is the way Christianity started.' 'How boss?' 'With a hammer and nails.' He paused in thought for a moment and then continued to hammer. Manual labour of the monotonous kind eased his mind.

'Boss waddya think o' this abortion business?' Dinny paused again. 'Sambo my father told me once – in this politics business you don't think, you interpret. If I start thinking, I'm out of a job in the morning.' Sambo wanted to know what he meant. Dinny was a thinker. Things stuck in his throat, especially in the

Dáil. But they always vanished, not into thin air but into his thin blood. Thinner and thinner.

The typewriter clicked; it was time to leave. Sambo had recently discovered its magic. Any moment the questions would start – spell this, spell that, a nicotined finger waiting for the answers. Dinny needed Sambo's flamboyance to flood him with votes and that was all. But sometimes Sambo went too far. If he was caught personating again, Dinny would have to give him a dressing down. Anyone in the constituency would know that face boiled in porridge.

Click, click. Dinny headed for the door. 'I'm going to need you Sunday night at the concert, bound to be a gaeilgeoir problem.' Dinny didn't hate Irish. He even had one sentence – *Vótáil Donncha Ó Longaigh, Uimh. 1.* He knew that in Irish all the four-lettered words were three-lettered – fifteen in German – and that there were only three ways to have Irish. One, to be born into it; two, to pretend to have it; three, to have a ventriloquist. As he wasn't a hypocrite he rejected the second, but sometimes toyed with the third. Sambo had a way of putting a pint into a gaeilgeoir's hand, and a way of talking pure Cowpoke without subjunctives that stilled all linguistic differences. On his way out, he picked from a shelf a copy of the Irish Constitution, *Bunreacht na hÉireann*, and stuffed it into his pocket. Seeing as they were going to amend the Constitution, he might as well read the damn thing.

Down at the community school, Detta Hearne ruled with an iron fist. Her office was decorated with posters of babies and tiny tots, all proclaiming the sanctity of life. On the wall behind her was a huge replica of a voting paper. VOTE X TÁ/YES TO PROTECT LIFE. She explained rapidly that he would be chairing the appointments board – and that there was a certain young lady part-time on the staff who had a good chance of getting the job. Detta wanted her stopped; out. She had recently been to England. Her health had improved immensely since that visit. Did Dinny understand? He nodded. She was also a member of the following organizations: Well-Woman's Centre, AIM, Women's Right to Choose, Rape Crisis Centre, Women's Political Association and the AFMFW. 'No way is she wanted here. She is trouble with a big T.' It was important that it happen today, because the girl was not beyond using influence.

Dinny tried to argue, but it was no use. Who else would be on the Board? Old political friends – Joe Heaslip, Cecil Falvey, Tadhg MacCarthy. And Seosamh O Mianain. He was just one of the staff. She'd take care of him. She ranted on about the Fight, the Glory. Dinny found himself twisting *Bunreacht na hÉireann* in his hands. She was going to have a great school. There were the Brothers up the road and the convent down the road and by God she'd drive both of them to the wall yet. Her lips snipped the words like scissors.

Dinny did what he was told. It was easy. The girl in question was in temperament identical to Detta. She had enough fire in her soul to set any school ablaze. She'd get a job somewhere else, he felt, as he crossed her name off the list. Afterwards, as he walked the gravel with Tadhg Mac to the car, their footsteps sounding like chewing horses, Tadhg said: 'Did you get the irony? If the girl aborts – no job. If she has the baby – still no job.' At the door of his car Dinny paused. 'The structure of society is a flimsy thing – it is vulnerable, a stand must be made.' He fell into the seat.

Things lingered on – wrong things in his mind. It was time for Jenny. Jenny was his favourite person, a roan Irish hunter who never answered him back. Although, once she had thrown him on the lawn, and the Chief standing on the steps of Bowlawling. He had raged at her: 'Jenny, you thundering fart, you whore out of the knackers' yard, may you never foal again.' But the Chief had said it was alright, he fell off his horse too. Today, he allowed her to take him all the way across the fields to Faarness Wood. He threw himself upon the ground, listening to Jenny champ stray grass among the shadows. He watched the trees release the clouds one by one, by one. He searched his pockets for *Bunreacht na hÉireann*. He must have left it in the school.

Dinny loved Dublin, the freedom of a city where you could drink a pint without having your hand pumped by someone on the take, get a hamburger without being set upon by swingsters. He avoided the Stroke Triangle between Mount Street, Stephen's Green and Dublin Castle like the plague. Even Sambo agreed: 'Only Billy the Kid would go in there and come out with his hat on.' Sometimes when the whip was on, he had to go to the Dáil. He disliked it. He had made his maiden speech there a long time ago, on sewerage schemes. He had worn a blue pinstripe mohair suit with a rose in his buttonhole. Sealy, the political correspondent, who made TDs crawl all the way to Slea Head, had seen some irony in this and dubbed him 'Dinny the Swank'. It had stuck. His opponent in Rathgrew, Jack Halloran, who, according to polls, was narrowing the gap between them, had dubbed him 'Swing-along Dinny'. It was Jack Halloran that Dinny feared. Jack had beaten him to the Rathlickey disaster, where 40 pigs were drowned. Jack Halloran was shown in *The Post*, standing, hat off, beside the trailer of dead pigs, a solemn look on his face. 'Halloran is as slow as the second coming of Christ,' was Sambo's verdict, however.

The freedom of Neasa's flat always overwhelmed Dinny. It was home not just because he paid for it; it was a safe house in good or bad times. And Neasa a beauty – he only went for beautiful women. She was also vivacious. 'Do you like me in this, should I wear pink – will the blue go with this? How about black? Are we going to the Dáil restaurant? Will Jamsey be there, and Finnegan. They're great crack. How's Sambo, I have cigars for him. Who's this Kitty? Why is she always gone when I go down? I could do Kitty's job better. I'm great with people.' Dinny told her that with a face like hers, she'd only draw them on. She should see Kitty's face. Would he like to have dinner or did he want to go to bed now? She had chilli with red and green peppers

– she had wine. He wasn't drinking. The blinds killed the sunshine and turned her bed to rose. He didn't just love her, he needed her. Only he knew that. And he'd have to marry her. Only she knew that.

He crossed Killiney Hill to his brother, Paddy, parish priest of Tigraskin. They were in his sitting room. 'Why can't you have a brandy, just one?' Dinny wouldn't. 'This place reminds me of my clinic – no sign of God in it.' He glanced around the room, strewn with spears, flints, skulls and photographs of digs. 'This room is for me brother, and as for God, God is everywhere. No need to remind him,' said Paddy, cupping his brandy in his hánds. 'You'd have made a great politician,' said Dinny. 'There's very little difference' was the reply. And then, 'Come up to Killiney Hill with me before it gets dark.'

'You still rootin' up there?'

Paddy said he was. He had discovered something. His eyes twinkled. But it had to be before it got dark.

They stood in the wood of Killiney Hill. It was a tangle of light and leafy shadows. Paddy stood in a glade and pointed out the three large stones. They were boundaries. 'Of what?' asked Dinny. 'Come,' said Paddy, 'look!' He pressed a spade into the turf and levered it back to reveal a widening crack. Dinny peered in. 'What is it, a bone some dog buried?' 'No, it's an infant's skull.' Dinny felt a shiver pass through him, going somewhere fast. Paddy told him it was a *Cillíneach*, a graveyard for unbaptized infants and aborted foetuses. In Irish they said 'as lonely as a *Cillíneach*'. No man could go in at night. Women were free. The dead had their power and the underprivileged dead the greatest power of all. 'To the people who live near here, Killiney Hill is but some rocks, some trees and a place for the dog to piss – they holiday in Spain, work in the city and drink in Dalkey – the media has swamped their souls – but the magic of Killiney waits – woe to those who tread on the magic of Killiney.' The shadows were getting too long. They would have to go.

Back in the sitting room they talked some more. 'You talk like a pagan,' said Dinny. 'God loves pagans too,' replied Paddy. 'Superstition is wrong, it doubts the love of God,' said Dinny.

'You'd have made a good priest,' said Paddy.

They talked into the night. Dinny decided to walk over the hill to Neasa's flat. The night was dark. Late closers had cleared. The night was still. He could barely make out the path through the trees. Then he lost it and stumbled on. Suddenly he was in the glade. He stood at the boundary and looked in. He did not believe. He walked into the middle. Nothing, just the moon and all the stars. He pressed on until he saw a light through the trees. It was some kind of hotel. The moon shone on its sign-board: 'The Queen of Killiney. Open to Non-Residents'. He had never heard of it. Curiosity made him mount the steps. He stopped and listened. Something was wrong. He couldn't hear the city traffic. He pushed the door and entered a bar foyer. It was tasteful. 'Just like I'd design it myself,' he muttered.

'Were you talking to me?' said a voice full of laughter. In the shadow he saw a woman. As she moved into the light, he thought there was something familiar about her. But when she came up close, he knew.

'Incredible!' he said, '– you're the spitting image of Jean Simmons.'

She stopped in front of him, her eyes glassy with pleasure. 'Is that good or bad?' she asked, wetting her lips.

'The best,' he said. 'She was always my favourite actress, even more than Ursula Andress.'

'What was *she* like?' she asked, with fluttering eyelashes.

He looked into eyes that were the colour of faded jeans. She blushed slightly under his gaze, dropped her eyes, raised them again quizically, brushed a lock of hair and smiled. 'Ursula Andress is magnetic in an animal kind of way – sullen, demanding.'

'Go on,' said the girl.

'She radiates desire but never peace. She'd need a lion-tamer or weight-lifter or something.'

'I know what you mean,' she said, 'I'm not like that.'

'Not in a million years,' he said, looking into her sky-blue wells. He thought of Jean Simmons, gorgeously frail, helpless and alone, always waiting to be rescued. Dependent beautiful Jean who couldn't buy a drink for herself or cross the road. If he were married to her, he would gladly spend his life buttering her bread and peeling her potatoes.

Suddenly he was aware that he was still staring into her eyes. He thought of Neasa and excused himself. 'I've got to go.' She looked at him with disappointment, her fingers twisting the corner of her blouse. 'Please don't go yet. Stay and have a drink. It's lonely here, the hotel hasn't opened yet.'

'By Christ, I *will* have a drink – a big brandy and fast,' he heard himself saying. The girl radiated so much well-being that he felt himself re-charging.

She brought a huge drink to the fireplace and taking his arm, led him to a chair. Her hand excited him so much she could have pushed him off a cliff. She placed a pillow behind his head, and this made his toes open and shut. He began to relax so much he could hear the hiss. She sat beside him on a foot stool. He looked down at her dress and could have sworn it was the one she wore in *The Big Country*. 'Do you go to films?' he asked. No, she said, she was an orphan and knew nobody. Her name was Macha. It was lonely on the hill at night. She leaned over and whispered into his ear that twigs snapping in the scrub frightened her at night.

The glow of her breath in his ear and the proximity of her mouth made springs go twang within him. He looked down at the curve of her firm thigh very much at home in her *Big Country* dress. When he had finished his drink and she asked him to see her as far as her door, which was down at the end of a long corridor, it seemed natural to say yes.

At the door she paused and said, 'Come in a minute.' All he noticed was the black bedsheets trimmed in scarlet, colours he had once seen on his cousin's panties and which remained in his mind as symbols of carnality. But there was no need for symbols, for the real thing was in his arms and the ancient heritage of man ruled.

One morning a month later, Dinny Long got sick in the clinic. Sambo said, 'Boss, you been hittin' the booze again.' Dinny looked as frail as a shadow in a bottle. He just shook his head at Sambo and said, 'Christ.' After a week of his getting sick, Sambo was convinced it wasn't booze. 'You gotta see Doc Holiday, Dinny, fast.'

Séamus Cridden listened to the symptoms: 44 years old, sick, would like to be young again. 'Male menopause – classic symptoms,' said Séamus. He prescribed a track suit and a tonic and to send Kitty up to him. As he departed, Séamus called after him, 'If it isn't that, you're pregnant!' His laughter followed Dinny all the way to the car.

He looked fine in his plum track suit, except for the middle-age spread the doctor had mentioned. Once while jogging in Killiney, he searched for The Queen of Killiney. Nothing but briars, heather and rocks. He stood at the Obelisk looking out to sea, his eyes clouded, seagulls drifting through his dreams.

One night he awoke. He called for Kitty. 'Have we any blackberry jam in the house?' 'No, but we have gooseberry, lemon curd and pear flan.' 'I want some blackberry jam and I want it now.' Kitty put on her coat and went looking for blackberry jam. Nothing surprised her.

Dinny asked Paddy about the hotel. 'No such hotel – Heights, Castle and Court, but no Queen.'

'Even in the past?'

'Negative. You look in poor shape, you should see a doctor.'

'Has there ever been a Queen of Killiney in this dark world and wide?' he wailed. 'No sir, never been — I'm the historian — you sure you won't have a drink? No, never been a place like that. Only Queen of Killiney I ever heard about was Macha.'

Dinny Long bundled himself out of the sofa and stood bolt upright so fast that Paddy was taken aback. 'You either take a drink or I call a doctor.' He poured the drink carefully and passed it to Dinny. 'Fella called Léinín, sixth century. Had five daughters: Druigan, Euigen, Luicill, Riomthach and Macha — five saints, feast day 6th of March. They built the old church in Killiney which still stands — hence the name Killiney, which means the church of the daughters of Léinín. The awful people who live around here never spare a thought for those girls. Macha was beautiful and called the Queen.'

'Did she look like Jean Simmons?'

Paddy smiled. 'You should drink more often. See — you're getting your sense of humour back. No, we haven't a snap of her. All I know is she's the patron saint of stillborn, unbaptized and aborted children.' He looked at his brother, a frail thing in the embrace of a wing chair. He was pale and remote.

'Do you believe in magic?' Dinny asked.

'God is magic.'

'I thought magic was the dark end of the spectrum.'

'God created the spectrum.'

'But —'

Dinny pulled the cord over his bed. He had never done it before. Kitty came in a nightdress. 'Any peaches in the house?' he asked. 'I'm dying for a spoon of peaches.' 'No —' she said, 'but you never ate the blackberry jam. Will you have a spoonful of that?'

He grew fatter and depressed. One morning as he was shaving, something kicked him in the belly. He dropped the razor and backed all the way into the shower. He placed his hand on his stomach; then it kicked again. 'Crucified Jesus! Kitty, come up here fast!' he roared. She came tearing in. 'Jesus – I'm terrified, something is moving in my stomach.' She made him sit on the bath and ran her hand expertly over the swelling. 'Get down on your knees and throw your head back.' He did so, and all the while, the hand on his stomach. She made him go on all fours, take a deep breath and hold it. He did. Shortly, she told him to get up. 'What's wrong with me?' he whined. 'It's only the baby,' she said.

For a long time he stared at her, and then he began to fall like a tree. She caught him in time and dragged him to his bed. When he was tucked in he began to wail. 'I'm a man – how could I have a baby?' She fussed around the room. 'Look,' she said, 'I was midwife in this parish for twenty years. That's what they all said. "How could I be pregnant?" From the way it's sitting, I'd say it's a girl.'

'I love God,' said Dinny. 'Why would he do this to me? If it's a baby, how do we get it out?'

Kitty was hanging his clothes in the wardrobe. 'No problem getting it out. What I'd like to know is how did it get in. Do you want those peaches? The place below is filling up with stuff. Do you want them?' 'No. But I want the bottle of Redbreast, and I want it fast.'

'No drink, bad for the baby, no pills, aspros, or tobacco.' Suddenly he sat up. 'You wouldn't tell Sambo or Séamus Cridden? If word gets out, I'm ruined. I can make you rich. I'm in the agri business. I have shares in pubs and hotels from here to Helvick Head. Sure you won't tell anyone?'

'Nobody would believe it,' she said as she closed the door quietly.

He took to his bed, refused to go out, refused visitors. Word got out that he was dying. His opponent Jack Halloran called the whole thing 'Long D's journey into night' in *The Post*. The throng at the door kept Kitty going all day. Every second hour he called her up to make sure that it wasn't a phantom, air, something he ate, or a baby. When she pronounced it a baby, he wailed and thumped the pillows. On the way downstairs, she'd mutter about having two babies on her hands. All this fuss over a perfect pregnancy.

Kitty brought him every medical book she could find. He spent days going over the reproductive system. The whole thing was a mess. From the fallopian tubes to the vulva was a crazy plumbing system of nooks and crannies. He thanked the Lord he was a man. Then he remembered the baby and he sank into the pillows. Kitty stuck her head in the door. 'Do you want those apricots?'

Paddy brought the bishop, who put his hand on the bulge. 'Liver,' he said. 'French liver, gets very big, seen it in Avignon.' Dinny shook his head. 'Tell him Paddy.' Paddy said he didn't drink at all.

'Not a drop, at all, at all,' said the bishop. 'That's bad, makes a man mean and cranky. Then it's gluttony.' 'No, I hardly eat anything, not even blackberry jam or bloody apricots.' Paddy told the bishop it was true, that he had become quite ascetic.

'He's dying so,' said the bishop. 'Would you like to go to St Clement's?' Dinny shook his head vigorously. 'St Clement's is for the living dead,' he snarled. 'The living dead should be damn glad they're alive,' retorted the bishop. He gave Dinny his blessing and moved on to the next tragedy in the queue.

The Chief came to visit Dinny. Sambo waited outside the door, while they whispered inside. 'Sambo won't work for anybody 'cept you,' said the Chief, trying to persuade Dinny to change his mind.

'Then let Sambo work for himself – he'll do it hands down,' said Dinny. The Chief gulped, looked at the door and thought aloud, 'Jesus, Sambo?' Dinny felt himself laughing, but the baby stirred. Sambo would head the poll. His maiden speech would be a eulogy on Jesse James. Buswell's would stock his favourite cigars.

'Who can I turn to for help Kitty?' he begged. 'Try these –' and she dropped some women's magazines on a tray. Knitting patterns; 'Is your husband jealous of your baby?'; 'Knit your own babygro'; 'Diet for Mums'.

Neasa came. Dinny sank into the blankets. 'Don't come near me, stay five yards away from me.' Neasa stood three yards away. 'Is it one of these transmitted diseases?' 'No –' said Dinny, 'just contagious. Stay away from me.'

It was Neasa's visit that did it. The courage and immorality of desperation brought him in a taxi to the Liberties in Dublin. He knocked at a house in Protestant Row. An old woman answered. 'I've got business for you,' said Dinny, as he pushed his way in, '– a girl in trouble.'

'If it's that kind of trouble, forget it, after what they did to that poor nurse.'

Dinny remembered. They had hanged her.

'This girl is rich.'

The woman hesitated. 'How rich?'

'Three thousand pounds.'

'For that kind of money, we'd do an elephant. I'll send for Mena.'

'Who's Mena?'

'Mena's for special tricks. Have your girl here at seven o'clock tonight.'

He spent the day around Camden Street, Wexford Street and in the back streets off St Patrick's Cathedral. He noted the shabbiness of the houses – the poverty of the people – and yet their happiness. He was no longer a man. Nor a woman. He was a hunted animal. Yet he was discovering himself, discovering humanity.

He was at the door at 7 pm sharp. 'Where's the girl?' 'She'll be along – she's shy.' Cold sweat was breaking out on his forehead. 'I want to see the place first.' They took him into a room in which there was a large tub in the middle of the floor. Beside it was a large electric boiler, bubbling. He eyed it suspiciously. On the table was a large bottle of CDC gin. He looked from the bath to the gin. He had read *Saturday Night and Sunday Morning*. And the revulsion returned. 'How much gin?' he asked. 'The lot,' they said. 'That way boiling water might move it.' He hated gin. 'What's the sawdust on the floor for?' Mena came forward to the table and opened a large box. She took out a needle as big and curved as a coat hanger. She held it up, gleaming in the light.

'How?' he asked.

'How do you think?' she said.

He felt his sphincter muscle close like a door in a storm. Quickly he dug into his pockets and pulled out a fistful of notes and flung them on the table. 'She changed her mind,' he said leaving quickly and escaping into the clamour of Dublin's streets.

All night he spent walking the back streets off the Quays – Lotts, Great Strand Street, Liffey Street – there nobody knew him. The depressed and defeated found comfort in back streets. At twelve o'clock, black Liffey waters swelling from Ringsend, many, many mouthfuls. A ship, a man, somebody's newspaper flapping at his feet, unlit stores. Three more inches to eternity. He couldn't swim – it would be fast. But his body washed up in Sandymount – the autopsy would find the child. Christ, he'd be in the Guinness Book of Records. His relatives would curse his name. He staggered back into a dock-side doorway. If only he were a woman, he would gladly drown himself, herself.

'You okay?' It was an elderly garda.

'Yeah – just looking for a parishioner of mine.' He passed himself off as a priest effortlessly. 'A girl.'

'She on the make – sailors?'

'No, just pregnant.'

'They all go to England now 'cept the very young and frightened.' He stamped his feet against the chill. 'Time was we hauled out three a week from Alexandra Basin – poor little drowned rags of things.' He stamped his feet again and left.

He took the boat to Liverpool. It took some time with directories before he found the expensive private clinic, east of the city, that he knew would do. He slunk in for the appointment like a thieving dog.

The room was opulent, more like a film set for a period drama, and the consultant's cultured mildness matched the scene. He wasn't in the least perturbed that the patient was male. Such genetic quirks were quite fascinating, but of course it would cost double. Or would he like to have the child perhaps, and put it up for adoption? And give it a name. Most Irish girls called them either Patrick or Mary. Dinny took fright at the suggestion. Such a thing would damage his career. And then he remembered he didn't have a career. He was finished with all that sordidness.

'I'm afraid I shall have to ask you to proceed with the, th –'

'Abortion?'

'The operation.'

'Yes, there's a great comfort in words.'

They offered him a local anaesthetic but he asked to be knocked out, as it was a caesarian. When he awoke, there was group of white-coated surgeons all around his bed.

'Is it over –?' he croaked.

'Yes.' They said.

'Is it –?'

'Dead?' said one. 'Alive?' said another.

'No, it is not alive,' said somebody.

He felt a lump in his throat. The enormity of it all got to him. He felt loss.

'Who'd want to be a woman?'

'In Ireland.' They added.

'Was it a boy or girl?'

They looked at him for a long time in silence. Then one of them beckoned to a nurse. She came forward, pushing a trolley to the bedside. This sent him under the bedclothes in terror. But they insisted that he look. He raised his head and looked at the trolley for a long time. It was a copy of the Irish Constitution, greatly enlarged. The doctors pointed to the words on the cover – *Bunreacht na hÉireann* – and asked what it meant.

'It is meaningless,' he answered in a far away voice.

MAEVE BINCHY
Holland Park

Maeve Binchy (1940–) is a bestselling novelist and a noted columnist for the Irish Times. *Her first books were collections of her journalism. In 1977 she published a collection of short stories,* Central Line. *This was followed by* Victoria Line, *and* Dublin 4 *and her novel,* Light A Penny Candle, *which shot to the top of the bestseller charts. Since then she has remained at the top with novels such as* Echoes, Circle of Friends *and* The Glass Lake. *'Holland Park' is from* Central Line.

Everyone hated Malcolm and Melissa out in Greece last summer. They pretended they thought they were marvellous, but deep down we really hated them. They were too perfect, too bright, intelligent, witty and aware. They never monopolized conversations in the taverna, they never seemed to impose their will on anyone else, but somehow we all ended up doing what they wanted to do. They didn't seem lovey-dovey with each other, but they had a companionship which drove us all to a frenzy of rage.

I nearly fainted when I got a note from them six months later. I thought they were the kind of people who wrote down addresses as a matter of courtesy, and you never heard from them again.

'I hate trying to recreate summer madness,' wrote Melissa. 'So I won't gather everyone from the Hellenic scene, but Malcolm and I would be thrilled if you could come to supper on the 20th. Around eightish, very informal and everything. We've been so long out of touch that I don't know if there's anyone I should ask you to bring along; if so, of course the invitation is for two. Give me a ring sometime so that I'll know how many strands of spaghetti to put in the pot. It will be super to see you again.'

I felt that deep down she knew there was nobody she should ask me to bring along. She wouldn't need to hire a private detective for that, Melissa would know. The wild notion of hiring someone splendid from an escort agency came and went. In three artless questions Melissa would find out where he was from, and think it was a marvellous fun thing to have done.

I didn't believe her about the spaghetti, either. It would be something that looked effortless but would be magnificent and unusual at the same time. Perhaps a perfect Greek meal for nostalgia, where she would have made all the hard things like pitta and humus and fetta herself, and laugh away the idea that it was difficult. Or it would be a dinner around a mahogany table with lots of cut-glass decanters, and a Swiss darling to serve it and wash up.

But if I didn't go, Alice would kill me, and Alice and I often had a laugh over the perfection of Malcolm and Melissa. She said I had made them up, and that the people in the photos were in fact models who had been hired by the Greek Tourist Board to make the place look more glamorous. Their names had passed into our private short-hand. Alice would describe a restaurant as a 'Malcolm and Melissa sort of place', meaning that it was perfect, understated and somehow irritating at the same time. I would say that I had handled a situation in a 'Malcolm and Melissa way', meaning that I had scored without seeming to have done so at all.

So I rang the number and Melissa was delighted to hear from me. Yes, didn't Greece all seem like a dream nowadays, and wouldn't it be foolish to go to the same place next year in case it wasn't as good, and no, they hadn't really decided where to go next year, but Malcolm had seen this advertisement about a yacht party which wanted a few more people to make up the numbers, and it might be fun, but one never knew and one was a bit trapped on a yacht if it was all terrible. And super that I could come on the 20th, and then with the voice politely questioning, would I be bringing anyone else?

In one swift moment I made a decision. 'Well, if it's not going to make it too many I would like to bring this friend of mine, Alice,' I said, and felt a roaring in my ears as I said it. Melissa was equal to anything.

'Of course, of course, that's lovely, we look forward to meeting her. See you both about eightish then. It's not far from the tube, but maybe you want to get a bus, I'm not sure . . .'

'Alice has a car,' I said proudly.

'Oh, better still. Tell her there's no problem about parking, we have a bit of waste land around the steps. It makes life heavenly in London not to have to worry about friends parking.'

Alice was delighted. She said she hoped they wouldn't turn out to have terrible feet of clay and that we would have to find new names for them. I was suddenly taken with a great desire to impress her with them, and an equal hope that they would find her as funny and witty as I did. Alice can be eccentric at times, she can go into deep silences. We giggled a lot about what we'd wear. Alice said that we should go in full evening dress, with capes, and embroidered handbags, and cigarette-holders, but I said that would be ridiculous.

'It would make her uneasy,' said Alice with an evil face.

'But she's not horrible, she's nice. She's asked us to dinner, she'll be very nice,' I pleaded.

'I thought you couldn't stand her,' said Alice, disappointed.

'It's hard to explain. She doesn't mean any harm, she just does everything too well.' I felt immediately that I was taking the myth away from Malcolm and Melissa and wished I'd never thought of asking Alice.

Between then and the 20th, Alice thought that we should go in boiler suits, in tennis gear, dressed as Greek peasants, and at one stage that we should dress up as nuns and tell her that this was what we were in real life. With difficulty I managed to persuade her that we were not to look on the evening as some kind of search-and-destroy mission, and Alice reluctantly agreed.

I don't really know why we had allowed the beautiful couple to become so much part of our fantasy life. It wasn't as if we had nothing else to think about. Alice was a solicitor with a busy practice consisting mainly of battered wives, worried one-parent families faced with eviction, and a large vocal section of the female population who felt that they had been discriminated against in their jobs. She had an unsatisfactory love-life going on with one of the partners in the firm, usually when his wife was in hospital, which didn't make her feel at all guilty, she saw it more as a kind of service that she was offering. I work in a theatre writing publicity-handouts and arranging newspaper interviews for the stars, and in my own way I meet plenty of glittering people. I sort of love a hopeless man who is a good writer but a bad person to love, since he loves too many people, but it doesn't break my heart.

I don't suppose that deep down Alice and I want to live in a big house in Holland Park, and be very beautiful and charming, and have a worthy job like Melissa raising money for a good cause, and be married to a very bright, sunny-looking man like Malcolm, who runs a left-wing bookshop that somehow has made him a great deal of money. I don't *suppose* we could have been directly envious. More indirectly irritated, I would have thought.

I was very irritated with myself on the night of the 20th because I changed five times before Alice came to collect me. The black sweater and skirt looked too severe, the gingham dress mutton dressed as lamb, the yellow too garish, the pink too virginal. I settled for a tapestry skirt and a cheap cotton top.

'Christ, you look like a suite of furniture,' said Alice when she arrived.

'Do I? Is it terrible?' I asked, anxious as a sixteen-year-old before a first dance.

'No, of course it isn't,' said Alice. 'It's fine, it's just a bit sort of sofa-coverish if you know what I mean. Let's hope it clashes with her décor.'

Tears of rage in my eyes, I rushed into the bedroom and put on the severe black again. Safe, is what magazines call black. Safe I would be.

Alice was very contrite.

'I'm sorry, I really am. I don't know why I said that, it looked fine. I've never given two minutes' thought to clothes, you know that. Oh for God's sake wear it, please. Take off the mourning gear and put on what you were wearing.'

'Does this look like mourning then?' I asked, riddled with anxiety.

'Give me a drink,' said Alice firmly. 'In ten years of knowing each other we have never had to waste three minutes talking about clothes. Why are we doing it tonight?'

I poured her a large Scotch and one for me, and put on a jokey necklace which took the severe look away from the black. Alice said it looked smashing.

Alice told me about a client whose husband had put Vim in her tin of tooth powder and she had tried to convince herself that he still wasn't too bad. I told Alice about an ageing actress who was opening next week in a play, and nobody, not even the man I half love, would do an interview with her for any paper because they said, quite rightly, that she was an old bore. We had another Scotch to reflect on all that.

I told Alice about the man I half loved having asked me to go to Paris with him next weekend, and Alice said I should tell him to get stuffed, unless, of course, he was going to pay for the trip, in which case I must bring a whole lot of different judgements to bear. She said she was going to withdraw part of her own services from her unsatisfactory partner, because the last night they had spent together had been a perusal of *The Home Doctor* to try and identify the nature of his wife's illness. I said I thought his wife's illness might be deeply rooted in drink, and Alice said I could be right but it wasn't the kind of thing you said to someone's husband. Talking about drink reminded us to have another and then we grudgingly agreed it was time to go.

There were four cars in what Melissa had described as a bit of waste land, an elegantly paved semi-circular courtyard in front of the twelve steps up to the door. Alice commented that they were all this year's models, and none of them cost a penny under three thousand. She parked her battered 1969 Volkswagen in the middle, where it looked like a small child between a group of elegant adults.

Malcolm opened the door, glass in hand. He was so pleased to see us that I wondered how he had lived six months without the experience. Oh come on, I told myself, that's being unfair, if he wasn't nice and welcoming I would have more complaints. The whole place looked like the film set for a trendy frothy movie on gracious modern living. Melissa rushed out in a tapestry skirt, and I nearly cried with relief that I hadn't worn mine. Melissa is shaped like a pencil rather than a sofa; the contrast would have been mind-blowing.

We were wafted into a sitting-room, and wafted is the word. Nobody said 'come this way' or 'let me introduce you' but somehow there we were with drinks in our hands, sitting between other people, whose names had been said clearly, a Melissa would never mutter. The drinks were good and strong, a Malcolm would never be mean. Low in the background a record-player had some nostalgic songs from the Sixties, the time when we had all been young and impressionable, none of your classical music, nor your songs of the moment. Malcolm and Melissa couldn't be obvious if they tried.

And it was like being back in Andrea's Taverna again. Everyone felt more witty and relaxed because Malcolm and Melissa were there, sort of in charge of things without appearing to be. They sat and chatted, they didn't fuss, they never tried to drag anyone into the conversation or to force some grounds of common interest. Just because we were all there together under their roof . . . that was enough.

And it seemed to be enough for everyone. A great glow came over the group in the sunset, and the glow deepened when a huge plate of spaghetti was served. It was spaghetti, damn her. But not the kind that you and I would ever make. Melissa seemed to be out of the room only three minutes, and I know it takes at least eight to cook the pasta. But there it was, excellent, mountainous, with garlic bread, fresh and garlicky, not the kind that breaks your teeth on the outside and then is soggy within. The salad was like an exotic still-life, it had everything in it except lettuce. People moved as if in a dance to the table. There were no cries of praise and screams of disclaimer from the hostess. Why then should I have been so resentful of it all?

Alice seemed to be loving every minute of her evening, she had already fought with Malcolm about the kind of women's literature he sold, but it was a happy fight where she listened to the points he was making and answered them. If she didn't like someone she wouldn't bother to do this. She had been talking to Melissa about some famous woman whom they both knew through work, and they were giggling about the famous woman's shortcomings. Alice was forgetting her role, she was breaking the rules. She had come to understand more about the Melissa and Malcolm people so that we could laugh at them. Instead, she looked in grave danger of getting on with them.

I barely heard what someone called Keith was saying to me about my theatre. I realized with a great shock that I was jealous. Jealous that Alice was having such a nice time, and impressing Melissa and Malcolm just because she was obviously not trying to.

This shock was so physical that a piece of something exotic, avocado maybe, anyway something that shouldn't be in a salad, got stuck in my throat. No amount of clearing and hurrumphing could get rid of it and I stood up in a slight panic.

Alice grasped at once.

'Relax and it will go down,' she called. 'Just force your limbs to relax, and your throat will stop constricting. No, don't bang her, there's no need.'

She spoke with such confidence that I tried to make my hands and knees feel heavy, and miracles it worked.

'That's a good technique,' said Malcolm admiringly, when I

had been patted down and, scarlet with rage, assured everyone I was fine.

'It's very unscientific,' said the doctor amongst us, who would have liked the chance to slit my throat and remove the object to cries of admiration.

'It worked,' said Alice simply.

The choking had gone away but not the reason for it. Why did I suddenly feel so possessive about Alice, so hurt when she hadn't liked my dress, so jealous and envious that she was accepted here on her own terms and not as my friend? It was ridiculous. Sometimes I didn't hear from Alice for a couple of weeks; we weren't soul mates over everything, just long-standing friends.

'. . . have you had this flat in the City long?' asked Keith politely.

'Oh that's not my flat, that's Alice's,' I said. Alice was always unusual. She had thought that since the City would be deserted at weekends, the time she wanted a bit of peace, that's where she should live. And of course it worked. Not a dog barked, not a child cried, not a car revved up when Alice was sleeping till noon on a Sunday.

'No, I live in Fulham,' I said, thinking how dull and predictable it sounded.

'Oh I thought . . .' Keith didn't say what he thought but he didn't ask about my flat in Fulham.

Malcolm was saying that Alice and I should think about the yachting holiday. Keith and Rosemary were thinking about it, weren't they? They were, and it would be great fun if we went as a six, then we could sort of take over in case the other people were ghastly.

'It sounds great,' I said dishonestly and politely. 'Yes, you must tell me more about it.'

'Weren't you meant to be going on holiday with old Thing?' said Alice practically.

'That was very vague,' I snapped. 'The weekend in Paris was

definite but the holiday . . . nothing was fixed. Anyway weren't you meant to be going to a cottage with your Thing . . .?'

Everyone looked at me, it was as if I had belched loudly or taken off my blouse unexpectedly. They were waiting for me to finish and in a well-bred way rather hoping that I wouldn't. Their eyes were like shouts of encouragement.

'You said that if his wife was put away for another couple of weeks you might go to their very unsocialistic second home? Didn't you?'

Alice laughed, everyone else looked stunned.

Melissa spooned out huge helpings of a ten thousand calorie ice-cream with no appearance of having noticed a social gaffe.

'Well, when the two of you make up your minds, do tell us,' she said. 'It would be great fun, and we have to let these guys know by the end of the month, apparently. They sound very nice actually. Jeremy and Jacky they're called, he makes jewellery and Jacky is an artist. They've lots of other friends going too, a couple of girls who work with Jeremy and their boy friends, I think. It's just Jeremy and Jacky who are . . . who are organizing it all.'

Like a flash I saw it. Melissa thought Alice and I were lesbians. She was being her usual tolerant liberated self over it all. If you like people, what they do in bed is none of your business. HOW could she be so crass as to think that about Alice and myself? My face burned with rage. Slowly like heavy flowers falling off a tree came all the reasons. I was dressed so severely, I had asked could I bring a woman not a man to her party, I had been manless in Greece when she met me the first time, I had just put on this appalling show of spitely spiteful dykey jealousy about Alice's relationship with a man. Oh God. Oh God.

I knew little or nothing about lesbians. Except that they were different. I never was friendly with anyone who was one. I knew they didn't wear bowler hats, but I thought that they did go in for this aggressive sort of picking on one another in public. Oh God.

Alice was talking away about the boat with interest. How much would it cost? Who decided where and when they would stop? Did Jeremy and Jacky sound madly camp and would they drive everyone mad looking for sprigs of tarragon in case the pot au feu was ruined?

Everyone was laughing, and Malcolm was being liberated and tolerant and left-wing.

'Come on Alice, nothing wrong with tarragon, nothing wrong with fussing about food, we all fuss about something. Anyway, they didn't say anything to make us think that they would fuss about food, stop typecasting.'

He said it in a knowing way. I felt with a sick dread that he could have gone on and said, 'After all, I don't typecast you and expect you to wear a hairnet and military jacket.'

I looked at Alice, her thin white face all lit up laughing. Of course I felt strongly about her, she was my friend. She was very important to me, I didn't need to act with Alice. I resented the way the awful man with his alcoholic wife treated her, but was never jealous of him because Alice didn't really give her mind to him. And as for giving anything else . . . well I suppose they made a lot of love together but so did I and the unsatisfactory journalist. I didn't want Alice in that way. I mean that was madness, we wouldn't even know what to do. We would laugh ourselves silly.

Kiss Alice?

Run and lay my head on Alice's breast?

Have Alice stroke my hair?

That's what people who were in love did. We didn't do that.

Did Alice need me? Yes, of course she did. She often told me that I was the only bit of sanity in her life, that I was safe. I had known her for ten years, hardly anyone else she knew nowadays went back that far.

Malcolm filled my coffee cup.

'Do persuade her to come with us,' he said gently to me. 'She's marvellous really, and I know you'd both enjoy yourselves.'

I looked at him like a wild animal. I saw us fitting into their lives, another splendid liberal concept, slightly racy, perfectly acceptable. 'We went on holiday with that super gay couple, most marvellous company, terribly entertaining.' Which of us would he refer to as the He? Would there be awful things like leaving us alone together, or nodding tolerantly over our little rows?

The evening and not only the evening stretched ahead in horror. Alice had been laying into the wine, would she be able to drive? If not, oh God, would they offer us a double bed in some spare room in this mansion? Would they suggest a taxi home to Fulham since my place was nearer? Would they speculate afterwards why we kept two separate establishments in the first place?

Worse, would I ever be able to laugh with Alice about it or was it too important? I might disgust her, alarm her, turn her against me. I might unleash all kinds of love that she had for me deep down, and how would I handle that?

Of course I loved Alice, I just didn't realize it. But what lover, what poor unfortunate lover in the history of the whole damn thing, ever had the tragedy of Coming Out in Malcolm and Melissa's lovely home in Holland Park?

PAT INGOLDSBY

Articles from the *Evening Press*

Pat Ingoldsby (1942–) is a poet, playwright, newspaper columnist and television performer. His plays include When Am I Gettin' Me Clothes *and* The Case Against the Full Shilling. *Among his collections of poetry are* You've Just Finished Reading This Title, Welcome to My Head *and* Up the Leg of Your Jacket. *He writes a weekly humorous column for the* Evening Press.

A CRISIS FOR THE CÉILÍ BANDS

It's easy for an orchestra. They watch the conductor and read their music and everybody stops playing at the same time. Nobody has any twiddley bits left over. But céilí bands are different. Everyone is belting away on their fiddles and some of them have reached 'Around The Kitchen And Don't Step On The Semi-Conscious Granny' while others are still blasting away at 'Maggots In The Minestrone'. The woman on the piano keeps playing the same binkedy bonk bit over and over again until everyone has safely reached 'Lord Kilfeather's Gallstones.'

And that's the part where Nathan Quixby sensed a very real need. That's where they all began to play speculative diddle dee idles and optimistic snatches of 'Biddy Brady's Bedlinen' until everyone found a bit where they could all stop together.

'There's no problem in getting started,' said Nathan Quixby to the World Commission on Consenting Céilí Bands. 'Four bonks on the piano and you're all away on a hack.' He even designated this 'Four Bonk Conditioned Response'. 'Unfortunately,' he continued, 'there is no way of building in a corresponding Four Bonk Stopping Signal without wrecking the spontanaeity.'

And that was when he suggested a system of coded shouts.

'You can arrange this in advance with a reliable person at the céilí. When they whoop "Me life on ye Seanie" the band knows that everyone should be lashing into "Mattie Mangan's Nervous Twitch." A sudden yell of "Your blood is worth bottling Bertie" means throttle back a bit boys – one of the fiddlers is still rampaging through "Six Nights in a Haystack With Consolata Gilligan's Second Cousin."' But it was pointed out to Quixby that so many people get carried away and shout so many different things at céilís that one unexpected roar of 'Get up the yard and take your piano with you' could cause musical chaos.

That was when Quixby hit on the notion of the Honda 50 motorbikes. Each member of the band sits up on a bike and plays the fiddle while steering with their feet. They form up in a perfectly straight line across a field while the pianist travels alongside on the back of a lorry.

A course is carefully measured out with marker posts to indicate when the band should be swinging out of their first reel and into the second. The course ends with a sheer fifty foot drop into a pit of bubbling volcanic lava. 'Unless you all finish together lads someone is in for the big drop' explained Quixby. The musicians indicated in a secret ballot that they would rather take their chances with the coded shouts.

Quixby now wants them to practice playing their music in a crouched position over six inch nails. 'This is in case you get to a venue and there are no chairs,' he said. 'It's called The Céilí Crouch.'

The man has clearly got hidden depths.

A MAMMY FOR EVERY MAN

There is nothing sordid about these full-sized inflatable women. They are specially designed for Irish men who have left home and are living in flats or bedsitters. Men who miss the steadying influence of the mother often seek a substitute. Now they can have the world's very first inflatable mammy. Full sized, yet when the Mammy is deflated she can be carried around in the pocket. Ready for any emergency. She can be whipped out at any time and pumped up.

One of them appeared suddenly on a number 30 bus last week and when the conductor tried to collect a fare for it, the son explained that his mammy has the free travel.

'If that yoke bursts,' said the conductor, 'it could blind somebody.' So he took its name and address and submitted a written report. CIE has not yet fully decided where it stands on the inflatable mammy question.

'We have no objection to them travelling for nothing in their owner's pocket,' said a spokesperson. 'But once inflated, she must go underneath the stairs with the luggage. We don't want her exploding and putting the heart across the driver.'

Inflatable mammies are now standing in the corner of many Dublin bedsitters. They are fitted with a miniature voice box which can be pre-set by a time switch. If the door to the flat is opened after two o'clock in the morning, the mammy's eyes light up and she rasps: 'Where were you till this hour, ye shameless pagan? Don't think I don't know what you were up to.' If the son says something like 'Aw mammy' – the voice is programmed to respond with: 'Don't you "aw mammy" me. What am I after rearin'? Will ye tell me that?'

The inflatable mammy also incorporates a light-sensor which reacts to any sudden change in the atmosphere. If somebody dims the lights or switches them off altogether, the mammy glows bright green and sings 'Faith of Our Fathers'.

A model is already in the planning stages which will react to the presence of a female in the room. The text for the voice box in this model has not yet been finalized. 'Put one foot near the bedroom and I'll paralyse you' has been suggested. This of course is not suitable for one room bedsitters.

'Remember what the nuns taught you and play scrabble for pennies' is the text most favoured.

The slightest trace of alcohol in the atmosphere activates a self-destruct mechanism in the rubber mammy. It begins to swell to an alarming size and a voice shrills: 'Son – would ye be the cause of your mammy exploding and blowing herself to pieces?' The swelling can only be arrested by pouring the drink down the sink.

There is the ever-present danger of sons going home for the weekend and attempting to deflate their real mammies. This is something that Irish mothers must learn to live with.

IF YOU HAVE A PET YOU'LL WANT TO KNOW THIS

It's widely accepted that after a while many persons who keep a pet start to resemble it in some way. Yet the growing body of evidence points in the other direction. It clearly indicates that pets take unto themselves many of their owners' characteristics.

Amanda Verity-Squires agrees with this theory. She has a keenly developed sense of right and wrong. And she kept a pet rabbit. Every night she included it in her prayers: 'God bless Twitcher and grant that he grows up to be an exemplary bunny.'

She knelt beside the cage and prayed daily for all rabbits everywhere, including the ones in Russia. The cage was always placed on top of the television during religious services.

When Amanda went to Lourdes she discovered a shop which sold sweets containing holy water. On her arrival home she hollowed out carrots and embedded one sweet in each. The rabbit never knew the difference.

One morning while Amanda was renewing the prayer wheels in her back garden, the rabbit escaped. It wandered off into the wild and was gradually accepted by the other rabbits.

Over the next few months an amazing phenomenon occurred. Whenever the wild rabbits raided somebody's vegetable garden, Amanda's pet was racked with guilt. It recalled those evenings on top of the television during 'Songs of Praise' and was tormented with remorse.

Very slowly this feeling communicated itself to the other rabbits. They formed an anguished circle and released their guilt feelings in the form of groans. Late that evening when the verger came to lock the parish church he found the rabbits groaning in the centre aisle. He crept up into the organ loft and softly played 'Abide With Me'. The rabbits went away happy.

Even more startling proof is afforded by the case of Verity Gageby's sheep. She bottle-fed it as a lamb. One afternoon it watched as Verity's husband sawed the legs off the bed. He suffered from a pathological fear of heights. This profoundly affected the lamb.

The following week it watched as local firemen talked Verity's husband down from a stepladder. The lamb was wide-eyed and trembling.

Two years later it was grazing on a craggy cliff. Suddenly the trembling started again. Moments later, the sheep overbalanced and hurtled downwards. A marquee in the grounds of the vicarage broke its fall and it shot through a stained glass window into the church on the rebound. At that precise moment the vicar was explaining how God's messages to mankind come in the form of subtle whispers. 'That was when the bloody sheep crashed in through the window', he said afterwards.

This was not the same church where the rabbits groaned. It's important for you to know that.

LUST FOR LEATHER!

No right thinking person can condone his behaviour. It is nothing short of systematic torture. Somebody must be told.

They're out there in the darkness every night. Their breath comes in shivery clouds. Groups of men in tracksuits and foot-ball boots. And the only thing any of them wants to do is kick a ball. Even a little kick will do. But the trainer won't allow it.

'Yez have to be hungry for the ball,' he tells them. 'Yez have to really lust after that lump of leather, lads.'

He makes them lie on their backs and pedal imaginary bikes. He makes them sprint and hop and leap. 'If I give yez the ball now lads yez won't fight for it on Sunday.'

All along the seafront in Dollymount are groups of grown men – ravenous for the ball. Some of them would kill with their bare hands for a glimpse of it. This is not a healthy situation.

A bank official was walking home shortly before Christmas. After dark. Under his arm was a parcelled-up football for his eldest son. A present from Daddy and Mammy. He sensed that something was wrong when a group of men lying on their backs suddenly stopped pedalling imaginary bikes. Several of them sniffed the air. Their eyes widened. Nostrils dilated.

'There's a ball somewhere in the offing lads!' one of them shouted.

'Aw now lads,' the trainer pleaded. 'Stay on your backs and pedal them bikes.'

But he was too late. The lads broke rank and took off after the bank official. He got the fright of his life. Thirty men in tracksuits were hot on his heels – all shouting and roaring and bagsing the first kick. The bank official tossed his parcel in the air and shinned up a tree. 'They ate it,' he told a garda. 'Me parcel . . . they ate it – paper and all. They tore me football into shreds and devoured them. Then they ate the laces.' These men were clearly much too hungry for the ball. The Football Association of Ireland are worried about this form of training. Too many teams are trotting out onto the pitch on Sundays in a dangerous state of frenzy. They haven't seen a ball for seven whole days.

Their blood is up. More and more games are being abandoned shortly after the kick-off. The referee's report is brief and to the point. 'Play suspended . . . ball eaten.'

Some sports shops are now steeping their footballs overnight in drinking chocolate. This sort of carry-on should not be encouraged. It will only perpetuate the lust for leather and then where will we be?

BERNARD MAC LAVERTY
A Time to Dance

Bernard Mac Laverty (1942–) was born in Belfast where he worked for a time as a laboratory technician at Queen's University. He has published four volumes of short stories, A Time to Dance, Secrets, The Great Profundo *and* Walking the Dog. *His two novels,* Cal *and* Lamb *have been made into films. Mac Laverty now lives in Scotland.*

Nelson, with a patch over one eye, stood looking idly into Mothercare's window. The sun was bright behind him and made a mirror out of the glass. He looked at his patch with distaste and felt it with his finger. The Elastoplast was rough and dry and he disliked the feel of it. Bracing himself for the pain, he ripped it off and let a yell out of him. A woman looked down at him curiously to see why he had made the noise, but by that time he had the patch in his pocket. He knew without looking that some of his eyebrow would be on it.

He had spent most of the morning in the Gardens avoiding distant uniforms, but now that it was coming up to lunch-time he braved it on to the street. He had kept his patch on longer than usual because his mother had told him the night before that if he didn't wear it he would go 'stark, staring blind'.

Nelson was worried because he knew what it was like to be blind. The doctor at the eye clinic had given him a box of patches that would last for most of his lifetime. Opticludes. One day Nelson had worn two and tried to get to the end of the street and back. It was a terrible feeling. He had to hold his head back in case it bumped into anything and keep waving his hands in front of him backwards and forwards like windscreen wipers. He kept tramping on tin cans and heard them trundle emptily away. Broken glass crackled under his feet and he could not figure out how close to the wall he was. Several times he heard footsteps approaching, slowing down as if they were going to attack him in his helplessness, then walking away. One of the foot-steps even laughed. Then he heard a voice he knew only too well.

'Jesus, Nelson, what are you up to this time?' It was his mother. She led him back to the house with her voice blaring in his ear.

She was always shouting. Last night, for instance, she had started into him for watching TV from the side. She had dragged him round to the chair in front of it.

'That's the way the manufacturers make the sets. They put the picture on the front. But oh no, that's not good enough for our Nelson. He has to watch it from the side. Squint, my arse, you'll just go blind – stark, staring blind.'

Nelson had then turned his head and watched it from the front. She had never mentioned the blindness before. Up until now all she had said was, 'If you don't wear them patches that eye of yours will turn in till it's looking at your brains. God knows, not that it'll have much to look at.'

His mother was Irish. That was why she had a name like Skelly. That was why she talked funny. But she was proud of the way she talked and nothing angered her more than to hear Nelson saying 'Ah ken' and 'What like is it?' She kept telling him that someday they were going back, when she had enough ha'pence scraped together. 'Until then I'll not let them make a Scotchman out of you.' But Nelson talked the way he talked.

His mother had called him Nelson because she said she thought that his father had been a seafaring man. The day the boy was born she had read an article in the *Reader's Digest* about Nelson Rockefeller, one of the richest men in the world. It seemed only right to give the boy a good start. She thought it also had the advantage that it couldn't be shortened, but she was wrong. Most of the boys in the scheme called him Nelly Skelly.

He wondered if he should sneak back to school for dinner then skive off again in the afternoon. They had good dinners at school – like a hotel, with choices. Chips and magic things like rhubarb crumble. There was one big dinner-woman who gave him extra every time she saw him. She told him he needed fattening. The only drawback to the whole system was that he was on free dinners. Other people in his class were given their dinner money and it was up to them whether they went without a dinner and bought Coke and sweets and stuff with the money. It was a choice Nelson didn't have, so he had to invent other things to get the money out of his mother. In Lent there were the Black Babies; library fines were worth the odd 10p, although, as yet, he had not taken a book from the school library – and anyway they didn't have to pay fines, even if they were late; the Home Economics Department asked them to bring in money to buy their ingredients and Nelson would always add 20p to it.

'What the hell are they teaching you to cook – sides of beef?' his mother would yell. Outdoor pursuits required extra money. But even though they had ended after the second term, Nelson went on asking for the 50p on a Friday – 'to go horse riding'. His mother would never part with money without a speech of some sort.

'Horse riding? Horse riding! Jesus, I don't know what sort of a school I've sent you to. Is Princess Anne in your class or something? Holy God, horse riding.'

Outdoor pursuits was mostly walking round museums on wet days and, when it was dry, the occasional trip to Portobello beach to write on a flapping piece of foolscap the signs of pollution you could see. Nelson felt that the best outdoor pursuit of the lot was what he was doing now. Skiving. At least that way you could do what you liked.

He groped in his pocket for the change out of his 50p and went into a shop. He bought a giant thing of bubble-gum and crammed it into his mouth. It was hard and dry at first and he couldn't answer the woman when she spoke to him.

'Whaaungh?'

'Pick the paper off the floor, son! Use the basket.'

He picked the paper up and screwed it into a ball. He aimed

to miss the basket, just to spite her, but it went in. By the time
he reached the bottom of the street the gum was chewy. He
thrust his tongue into the middle of it and blew. A small
disappointing bubble burst with a plip. It was not until the far
end of Princes Street that he managed to blow big ones, pink
and wobbling, that he could see at the end of his nose, which
burst well and had to be gathered in shreds from his chin.

Then suddenly the crowds of shoppers parted and he saw his
mother. In the same instant she saw him. She was on him before
he could even think of running. She grabbed him by the fur of
his parka and began screaming into his face.

'In the name of God, Nelson, what are you doing here? Why
aren't you at school?' She began shaking him. 'Do you realize
what this means? They'll put me in bloody jail. It'll be bloody
Saughton for me, and no mistake.' She had her teeth gritted
together and her mouth was slanting in her face. Then Nelson
started to shout.

'Help! Help!' he yelled.

A woman with an enormous chest like a pigeon stopped.
'What's happening?' she said.

Nelson's mother turned on her. 'It's none of your bloody
business.'

'I'm being kidnapped,' yelled Nelson.

'Young woman. Young woman . . .' said the lady with the large
chest, trying to tap Nelson's mother on the shoulder with her
umbrella, but Mrs Skelly turned with such a snarl that the woman
edged away hesitatingly and looked over her shoulder and tut-
tutted just loudly enough for the passing crowd to hear her.

'Help! I'm being kidnapped,' screamed Nelson, but everybody
walked past looking the other way. His mother squatted down
in front of him, still holding on to his jacket. She lowered her
voice and tried to make it sound reasonable.

'Look Nelson, love. Listen. If you're skiving school, do you
realize what'll happen to me? In Primary the Children's Panel
threatened to send me to court. You're only at that Secondary

and already that Sub-Attendance Committee thing wanted to fine me. Jesus, if you're caught again . . .'

Nelson stopped struggling. The change in her tone had quietened him down. She straightened up and looked wildly about her, wondering what to do.

'You've got to go straight back to school, do you hear me?'

'Yes.'

'Promise me you'll go.' The boy looked down at the ground. 'Promise?' The boy made no answer.

'I'll kill you if you don't go back. I'd take you myself only I've my work to go to. I'm late as it is.'

Again she looked around as if she would see someone who would suddenly help her. Still she held on to his jacket. She was biting her lip.

'Oh God, Nelson.'

The boy blew a flesh-pink bubble and snapped it between his teeth. She shook him.

'That bloody bubble-gum.'

There was a loud explosion as the one o'clock gun went off. They both leapt.

'Oh Jesus, that gun puts the heart sideways in me every time it goes off. Come on, son, you'll have to come with me. I'm late. I don't know what they'll say when they see you but I'm bloody taking you to school by the ear. You hear me?'

She began rushing along the street, Nelson's sleeve in one hand, her carrier bag in the other. The boy had to run to keep from being dragged.

'Don't you dare try a trick like that again. Kidnapped, my arse. Nelson, if I knew somebody who would kidnap you – I'd pay *him* the money. Embarrassing me on the street like that.'

They turned off the main road and went into a hallway and up carpeted stairs which had full-length mirrors along one side. Nelson stopped to make faces at himself but his mother chugged at his arm. At the head of the stairs stood a fat man in his shirtsleeves.

'What the hell is this?' he said. 'You're late, and what the hell is that?' He looked down from over his stomach at Nelson.

'I'll explain later,' she said. 'I'll make sure he stays in the room.'

'You should be on *now*,' said the fat man and turned and walked away through the swing doors. They followed him and Nelson saw, before his mother pushed him into the room, that it was a bar, plush and carpeted with crowds of men standing drinking.

'You sit here, Nelson, until I'm finished and then I'm taking you back to that school. You'll get nowhere if you don't do your lessons. I have to get changed now.'

She set her carrier bag on the floor and kicked off her shoes. Nelson sat down, watching her. She stopped and looked over her shoulder at him, biting her lip.

'Where's that bloody eyepatch you should be wearing?' Nelson indicated his pocket.

'Well, wear it then.' Nelson took the crumpled patch from his pocket, tugging bits of it unstuck to get it flat before he stuck it over his bad eye. His mother took out her handbag and began rooting about at the bottom of it. Nelson heard the rattle of her bottles of scent and tubes of lipstick.

'Ah,' she said and produced another eyepatch, flicking it clean. 'Put another one on till I get changed. I don't want you noseying at me.' She came to him, pulling away the white backing to the patch, and stuck it over his remaining eye. He imagined her concentrating, the tip of her tongue stuck out. She pressed his eyebrows with her thumbs, making sure that the patches were stuck.

'Now don't move, or you'll bump into something.'

Nelson heard the slither of her clothes and her small grunts as she hurriedly got changed. Then he heard her rustle in her bag, the soft pop and rattle as she opened her capsules. Her 'tantalizers' she called them, small black and red torpedoes. Then he heard her voice.

'Just you stay like that till I come back. That way you'll come to no harm. You hear me, Nelson? If I come back in here and you have those things off, I'll *kill* you. I'll not be long.'

Nelson nodded from his darkness.

'The door will be locked, so there's no running away.'

'Ah ken.'

Suddenly his darkness exploded with lights as he felt her bony hand strike his ear.

'You don't ken things, Nelson. You *know* them.'

He heard her go out and the key turn in the lock. His ear sang and he felt it was hot. He turned his face up to the ceiling. She had left the light on because he could see pinkish through the patches. He smelt the beer and stale smoke. Outside the room pop music had started up, very loudly. He heard the deep notes pound through to where he sat. He felt his ear with his hand and it *was* hot.

Making small *aww* sounds of excruciating pain, he slowly detached both eyepatches from the bridge of the nose outwards. In case his mother should come back he did not take them off completely, but left them hinged to the sides of his eyes. When he turned to look around him they flapped like blinkers.

It wasn't really a room, more a broom cupboard. Crates were stacked against one wall; brushes and mops and buckets stood near a very low sink; on a row of coat-hooks hung some limp raincoats and stained white jackets; his mother's stuff hung on the last hook. The floor was covered with tramped-flat cork tips. Nelson got up to look at what he was sitting on. It was a crate of empties. He went to the keyhole and looked out, but all he could see was a patch of wallpaper opposite. Above the door was a narrow window. He looked up at it, his eyepatches falling back to touch his ears. He went over to the sink and had a drink of water from the low tap, sucking noisily at the column of water as it splashed into the sink. He stopped and wiped his mouth. The water felt cold after the mint of the bubble-gum. He looked up at his mother's things, hanging on the hook; her tights and drawers were as she wore them, but inside out and hanging knock-kneed on top of everything. In her bag he found her blonde wig and tried it on, smelling the perfume of it as he did so. At home he liked noseying in his mother's room; smelling all her bottles of make-up; seeing her spangled things. He had to stand on the crate to see himself but the mirror was all brown measles under its surface and the eyepatches ruined the effect. He sat down again and began pulling at the bubble-gum, seeing how long he could make it stretch before it broke. Still the music pounded outside. It was so loud the vibrations tickled his feet. He sighed and looked up at the window again.

If his mother took him back to school, he could see problems. For starting St John the Baptist's she had bought him a brand new Adidas bag for his books. Over five pounds it had cost her, she said. On his first real skive he had dumped the bag in the bin at the bottom of his stair, every morning for a week, and travelled light into town. On the Friday he came home just in time to see the bin lorry driving away in a cloud of bluish smoke. He had told his mother that the bag had been stolen from the playground during break. She had threatened to phone the school about it but Nelson had hastily assured her that the whole matter was being investigated by none other than the Headmaster himself. This threat put the notion out of his head of asking her for the money to replace the books. At that point he had not decided on a figure. He could maybe try it again some time when all the fuss had died down. But now it was all going to be stirred if his mother took him to school.

He pulled two crates to the door and climbed up but they were not high enough. He put a third one on top, climbed on again, and gingerly straightened, balancing on its rim. On tip-toe he could see out. He couldn't see his mother anywhere. He saw a crowd of men standing in a semicircle. Behind them were some very bright lights, red, yellow and blue. They all had pints in their hands which they didn't seem to be drinking. They were all watching something which Nelson couldn't see. Suddenly the music stopped and the men all began drinking and talking. Standing on tip-toe for so long, Nelson's legs began to shake and he heard the bottles in the crate rattle. He rested for a moment. Then the music started again. He looked to see. The men now just stood looking. It was as if they were seeing a ghost. Then they all cheered louder than the music.

Nelson climbed down and put the crates away from the door so that his mother could get in. He closed his eyepatches over for a while, but still she didn't come. He listened to another record, this time a slow one. He decided to travel blind to get another drink of water. As he did so the music changed to fast. He heard the men cheering again, then the rattle of the key in the lock. Nelson, his arms rotating in front of him, tried to make his way back to the crate. His mother's voice said,

'Don't you dare take those eyepatches off.' Her voice was panting. Then his hand hit up against her. It was her bare stomach, hot and damp with sweat. She guided him to sit down, breathing heavily through her nose.

'I'll just get changed and then you're for school right away, boy.' Nelson nodded. He heard her light a cigarette as she dressed. When she had finished she ripped off his right eyepatch.

'There now, we're ready to go,' she said, ignoring Nelson's anguished yells.

'That's the wrong eye,' he said.

'Oh shit,' said his mother and ripped off the other one, turned it upside down and stuck it over his right eye. The smoke from the cigarette in her mouth trickled up into her eye and she held it half shut. Nelson could see the bright points of sweat shining through her make-up. She still hadn't got her breath back fully yet. She smelt of drink.

On the way out, the fat man with the rolled-up sleeves held out two fivers and Nelson's mother put them into her purse.

'The boy – never again,' he said, looking down at Nelson.

They took the Number Twelve to St John the Baptist's. It was the worst possible time because, just as they were going in, the bell rang for the end of a period and suddenly the quad was full of pupils, all looking at Nelson and his mother. Some sixth-year boys wolf-whistled after her and others stopped to stare. Nelson felt a flush of pride that she was causing a stir. She was dressed in black satiny jeans, very tight, and her pink blouse was knotted, leaving her tanned midriff bare. They went into the office and a secretary came to the window.

'Yes?' she said, looking Mrs Skelly up and down.

'I'd like to see the Head,' she said.

'I'm afraid he's at a meeting. What is it about?'

'About him.' She waved her thumb over her shoulder at Nelson.

'What year is he?'

'What year are you, son?' His mother turned to him.

'First.'

'First Year. Oh, then you'd best see Mr MacDermot, the First Year Housemaster.' The secretary directed them to Mr MacDermot's office. It was at the other side of the school and they had to walk what seemed miles of corridors before they found it. Mrs Skelly's stiletto heels clicked along the tiles.

'It's a wonder you don't get lost in here, son,' she said as she knocked on the Housemaster's door. Mr MacDermot opened it and invited them in. Nelson could see that he too was looking at her, his eyes wide and his face smiley.

'What can I do for you?' he said when they were seated.

'It's him,' said Mrs Skelly. 'He's been skiving again. I caught him this morning.'

'I see,' said Mr MacDermot. He was very young to be a Housemaster. He had a black moustache which he began to stroke with the back of his hand. He paused for a long time. Then he said,

'Remind me of your name, son.'

'– Oh, I'm sorry,' said Mrs Skelly. 'My name is Skelly and this is my boy Nelson.'

'Ah, yes, Skelly.' The Housemaster got up and produced a
yellow file from the filing cabinet. 'You must forgive me, but
we haven't seen a great deal of Nelson lately.'

'Do you mind if I smoke?' asked Mrs Skelly.

'Not at all,' said the Housemaster, getting up to open the
window.

'The trouble is, that the last time we were at that Sub-Attendance Committee thing they said they would take court action if
it happened again. And it has.'

'Well, it may not come to that with the Attendance Sub-
Committee. If we nip it in the bud. If Nelson makes an effort,
isn't that right, Nelson?' Nelson sat silent.

'Speak when the master's speaking to you,' yelled Mrs Skelly.

'Yes,' said Nelson, making it barely audible.

'You're Irish too,' said Mrs Skelly to the Housemaster,
smiling.

'That's right,' said Mr MacDermot. 'I thought your accent
was familiar. Where do you come from?'

'My family come from just outside Derry. And you?'

'Oh, that's funny. I'm just across the border from you.
Donegal.' As they talked, Nelson stared out the window. He
had never heard his mother so polite. He could just see a corner
of the playing fields and a class coming out with the Gym
teacher. Nelson hated Gym more than anything. It was crap. He
loathed the changing rooms, the getting stripped in front of
others, the stupidity he felt when he missed the ball. The smoke
from his mother's cigarette went in an arc towards the open
window. Distantly he could hear the class shouting as they
started a game of football.

'Nelson! Isn't that right?' said Mr MacDermot loudly.

'What?'

'That even when you are here you don't work hard enough.'

'Hmmm,' said Nelson.

'You don't have to tell me,' said his mother. 'It's not just his
eye that's lazy. If you ask me the whole bloody lot of him is.

I've never seen him washing a dish in his life and he leaves everything at his backside.'

'Yes,' said the Housemaster. Again he stroked his moustache. 'What is required from Nelson is a change of attitude. Attitude, Nelson. You understand a word like attitude?'

'Yes.'

'He's just not interested in school, Mrs Skelly.'

'I've no room to talk, of course. I had to leave at fifteen,' she said, rolling her eyes in Nelson's direction. 'You know what I mean? Otherwise I might have stayed on and got my exams.'

'I see,' said Mr MacDermot. 'Can we look forward to a change in attitude, Nelson?'

'Hm-hm.'

'Have you no friends in school?' asked the Housemaster.

'Naw.'

'And no interest. You see, you can't be interested in any subject unless you do some work at it. Work pays dividends with interest . . .' he paused and looked at Mrs Skelly. She was inhaling her cigarette. He went on, 'Have you considered the possibility that Nelson may be suffering from school phobia?'

Mrs Skelly looked at him. 'Phobia, my arse,' she said. 'He just doesn't like school.'

'I see. Does he do any work at home then?'

'Not since he had his bag with all his books in it stolen.'

'Stolen?'

Nelson leaned forward in his chair and said loudly and clearly, 'I'm going to try to be better from now on. I am. I am going to try, sir.'

'That's more like it,' said the Housemaster, also edging forward.

'I am not going to skive. I am going to try. Sir, I'm going to do my best.'

'Good boy. I think, Mrs Skelly, if I have a word with the right people and convey to them what we have spoken about, I think

there will be no court action. Leave it with me, will you? And I'll
see what I can do. Of course it all depends on Nelson. If he is as
good as his word. One more truancy and I'll be forced to report
it. And he must realize that he has three full years of school to do
before he leaves us. You must be aware of my position in this
matter. You understand what I'm saying, Nelson?'

'Ah ken,' he said. 'I know.'

'You go off to your class now. I have some more things to
say to your mother.'

Nelson rose to his feet and shuffled towards the door. He
stopped.

'Where do I go, sir?'

'Have you not got your timetable?'

'No sir. Lost it.'

The Housemaster, tut-tutting, dipped into another file, read a
card and told him that he should be at RK in Room 72. As he
left, Nelson noticed that his mother had put her knee up against
the Housemaster's desk and was swaying back in her chair, as
she took out another cigarette.

''Bye, love,' she said.

When he went into Room 72 there was a noise of oos and ahhs
from the others in the class. He said to the teacher that he had
been seeing Mr MacDermot. She gave him a Bible and told him
to sit down. He didn't know her name. He had her for English
as well as RK. She was always rabbiting on about poetry.

'You, boy, that just came in. For your benefit, we are talking
and reading about organization. Page 667. About how we
should divide our lives up with work and prayer. How we
should put each part of the day to use, and each part of the year.
This is one of the most beautiful passages in the whole of the
Bible. Listen to its rhythms as I read.' She lightly drummed her
closed fist on the desk in front of her.

'"There is an appointed time for everything, and a time for
every affair under the heavens. A time to be born and a time to
die; a time to plant and a time to uproot . . ."'

'What page did you say, Miss?' asked Nelson.

'Six-six-seven,' she snapped and read on, her voice trembling, '"A time to kill and a time to heal; a time to wear down and a time to build. A time to weep and a time to laugh; a time to mourn and a time to dance . . ."'

Nelson looked out of the window, at the tiny white H of the goal posts in the distance. He took his bubble-gum out and stuck it under the desk. The muscles of his jaw ached from chewing the now flavourless mass. He looked down at page 667 with its microscopic print, then put his face close to it. He tore off his eyepatch, thinking that if he was going to become blind then the sooner it happened the better.

CLARE BOYLAN
Not a Recommended Hobby For a Housewife

Clare Boylan (1948–) has worked for radio and television as well as newspapers and magazines. Her short stories have appeared in England, Denmark, America, Australia, South Africa and Norway. She has published four novels – Holy Pictures, Last Resorts, Black Baby *and* Home Rule *– as well as two collections of short stories,* A Nail on the Head *and* Concerning Virgins.

Poor Maria. She had gone to seed.

The girls kissed her, assessed her savagely and then bent with uniform delicacy to their meal of omelette with salad and a dry white wine. But the message had been transmitted, processed. She was late. She was getting fat. She was wearing, for God's sake, a fur coat with jeans.

The girls were all in their thirties; a good age, because their faces had not yet fallen apart; a bad age, because their dreams had. Twenty years ago they had been friends at school. They met once a year for lunch. They were conscientious about the reunion. It brought the years together and smoothed them over, keeping youth in view and disappointment in hand. Plotting one another's failings with monstrous efficiency, they could each tell that their own lives were not wholly unsuccessful.

Elizabeth had got herself a job. 'Well, I had to, damn it,' she said, defending herself against a lack of response. 'The truth is, my Morgan has become a stinge.'

Maria ordered herself a lobster whose death had been ritualized in cream and cheese and brandy, and then recklessly demanded a bottle of red wine.

'It isn't as if we're poor,' said Elizabeth, dragging back the attention of Helen and Joan who had been temporarily dazed by the sheer tastelessness of poor Maria. 'We've been doing frightfully well since Morgan got his award in Vienna. I mean, he buys me stuff all right.' She shook wrists weighted down with lumps of gold and surveyed her jewelled fingers. 'It's just that he won't actually give me money.'

It was impossible to ignore the stones on her hands. They were like traffic lights. She did not permit herself to look at her friends directly but concentrated on her fingers, hoping to catch in the gleaming gems a reflection of the precise moment when sympathy gave way to . . .

Cruelly, she cut short her own pleasure. 'I like working,' she pronounced. 'I like having my own money. And it isn't really like work, putting down names and dates in a diary and making occasional cups of coffee.' She laughed lightly. 'The hardest thing is getting used to another man's moods.'

The hardest thing, Maria had found, was getting used to another man's shape. Over ten years she had geared herself to an armful of hostile, nervous bones that had to be gathered together with perseverance and tamed with authority before they could be melted down for honey. Harry was so relaxed he covered her like a sauce and she needed his erection, not just for sex, but because she expected something aggressive in the shape of a man.

The other thing was the response. Searching for her orgasm in the smiling dark, Maria was totally unprepared for a strange man's voice in her ear. 'Is it good? Isn't it wonderful?' She had opened her eyes and the man moving over her seemed as remote as if she was looking out a window at a child skipping in the street.

Harry had never been married, of course. People who had been married for a time did not expect things to be wonderful. They were even irritated by wonder, like old folk blinking crossly in bright sunlight.

She herself was not totally innocent of wonder. That was in the past. She saw herself in her mind's eye, not just younger, but smaller, a scale model, working away at the orange Formica counter with the aid of a fiendish cookbook. Perfectly good pieces of rib steak had been buried in a snowstorm of coconut, curry-powder, tinned fruit — even dried prunes once. 'Is it good?' she would beg, as Ned obediently forked the sludge into his mouth.

Ned, in bed, had massaged all the wrong places and then speared her with the single-mindedness of a Kamikaze. 'Is it good?' he would demand.

'Wonderful, wonderful,' they each assented, as though wonder waited just around the corner and could be lured into their lives by mere encouragement.

'Wonderful! Simply wonderful!' Helen was talking about her hobby. She had taken up Origami. It sounded like an unnatural act, she admitted with a gay little giggle but was, in fact, the art of folding paper.

Elizabeth and Joan exchanged the briefest of glances. Definitely an unnatural act, signalled the demurely dancing lashes.

'The Japanese do it,' Helen explained.

'What *don't* the Japanese do?' Joan said.

'Just ordinary paper. John says that our town alone throws out two hundred tons of waste paper a year. He's into recycling now. He's such a vital person. He really keeps you on your toes. I don't mind admitting I had begun to mope a bit when Jeff — the baby — brought home a girl last year. "Get yourself a hobby, Helen," John said. "Don't get on my back."' Her lips shivered. She picked up a paper napkin and began tearing at it with such nervous determination that for an instant the others experienced compassion.

It was a paper bird, tiny and perfect, so thin that the yellow smoky light of the restaurant shone right through. Such a bird might perch on a Perilla tree to bathe in the curious hay scent and sing the praises of a smoky yellow Eastern dawn. The women were silent. They knew a redemption when they saw one.

The mood lasted a moment or two. Maria's meal arrived. The lobster seemed to throb with sensual energy although in fact it was just the cream and cheese still whispering from the grill. Maria gulped her wine like a mug of milk. She gouged out a piece of lobster and bit it. It was murderously delicious.

Joan watched her warily, her mouth a mere scar of invisible mending. Her eyes crept back to the bird, cradled in the branches of a hand that was unconsciously closing. 'Hobbies are fine in their own way,' she said like a ventriloquist, with no perceptible lip movement. 'But they don't fulfil you as a person.'

Of all of them, Joan had improved most over the years. She had changed from a plain girl into a stylish woman. She was marvellously thin and expensively beige and was sculpted into a pale grey suit from France and a cream cashmere sweater. She looked, Maria thought, like a tasteful piece of modern pottery. She did not look, they all thought, fulfilled as a person.

'Don't laugh now, girls, but I've been getting into charity work,' she said. They did not laugh. They beamed; Joan making stuffed dates for sales of work and buns for functions!

'Snacks on tracks — that sort of thing?' Helen scratched a piece of lettuce around in a pool of lemon dressing.

'Meals on wheels,' Joan corrected. 'That and visiting lonely old folk. I love it really and it's been *good* for me. It's only once a week. Wednesdays are my days.'

Wednesdays were Harry's days too. Ned had arranged that. 'Won't be home on Wednesdays from now on, my love,' he had said. Something about golf and a conference, she thought, but his voice had drowned in the depths of her boredom. She found Harry in an art gallery and went home with him.

She liked his brown bachelor flat with its full bottles of whisky and wine. She liked his short toenails and his exotic smell and how he didn't keep looking in ovens and fridges to check on what was there that had not been there before, like a husband. She liked not having to make the bed afterwards.

The women called for coffee and a truce. Year by year they became more uneasy in each other's company, more anxious to call the meeting to order. There was nothing that wouldn't keep for another year. Then Maria ordered Black Forest cake.

'What have you been doing with yourself, darling?' Elizabeth asked in tones that were unnecessarily harsh. Maria shrugged. 'Oh, this and that. Nothing much. I'm afraid I'm not energetic like the rest of you.' 'It's time you took your life in hand.' Elizabeth shook a fork at her. 'In no time at all the children will be gone and you'll be middle-aged. You have to think ahead.'

The cake was brought – damp brown sponge breathing fumes of Kirsch with slovenly piles of whipped cream sliding down the sides; big, wet, crimson cherries sank into the snowdrift under a hail of chocolate curls. Maria stuck her fork into the cake – a gesture that herded her friends to the edge of outrage. 'I hate to have to say it,' Elizabeth said, 'but you've let yourself go.'

Maria accepted the reproach and put it away like a precious gift. It was true. She had let herself go.

It had been Tuesday, not Wednesday. The doctor told her she had to have a hysterectomy and she stepped out of his surgery and into a downpour, letting the rain wash all over her so that she might weep unobserved. It wasn't that she wanted another baby but it seemed such a miserable thing, to have the middle torn out of one's body. She felt old and disposable. She phoned Ned and a girl said that he was in conference.

She stood in the rain for a full ten minutes until her flat leather, bad-weather shoes filled with water and her costly curls lay on her forehead like torpid worms. She thought of Harry. It was not Wednesday but surely he existed on other days. She knew that he painted his strange purple pictures at home and that home was comfortingly nearby.

Maria knocked on Harry's door. 'It's open,' he said. She stepped inside and stood there, passive and dismal, puddles of water hanging at her feet.

Harry was propped up in bed eating a cheese sandwich, toasted. He wore a vest which matched his greying sheets and

he hadn't shaved in days. 'What do you want?' he said. His look
was a mixture of accusation and horror, which hurt until she
realized she was looking at him in the same way. The thought
struck them mutually so that they each cringed as though naked,
although naked they had rather flaunted. 'You've never come
on Tuesday before,' he said. 'My cleaner comes on Wednesday
morning.' Maria wondered if the cleaner dumped him in the
tub, leaving him to soak while she set about changing the bed
and cleaning the flat.

Her own explanation, she realized as she said it, was just as
irrelevant. 'I've got to have a hysterectomy.' She was surprised
all the same when he started to laugh. It began as a slow,
unshaven-man's chuckle, deep in his belly. 'I'm sorry, lady,' he
finished up bellowing. 'I'm not a doctor.'

She marched over to the bed, still dripping, seized him by the
shoulder and hit him. His laughter stopped, cut off at the mains.
He pulled her on to the bed and pranced upon her, his body a
primitive implement of conquest. He kissed her. She bit his
mouth. He sank his teeth into her ear and then tore off her
clothes to find more vulnerable places upon which to put
punishment. He scrubbed down and up the length of her body
with his unshaven face and they glared into each other's eyes
with malice. There was no distance between them. No one else
existed in the world. Her condemned womb lurched defiantly. 'I
love you,' she said. 'I love you,' he said.

They never noticed part of a toasted cheese sandwich somewhere in there with them; never even noticed wonder when it
found them, limp and aimlessly optimistic amid the greying
sheets, like the cloth toys of a child.

Maria licked. The last morsels of cream and crumbs vanished
from her fork. The others hovered, solicitous in their awe, to
make sure it had all been eaten.

They were the only women in the restaurant who didn't
notice a handsome man walk in alone. When Harry reached the
table Maria already had an arm stretched outward to close the

gap between them. She looked at him with eyes that said it all. Her lover.

His full credentials could only be guessed: that he would sweep her face with his hair to dry her tears or bring tears to her eyes; that he would nourish her breasts with his kisses; that he was brave enough to enter the place that had been vandalized by children and was due to be demolished.

Maria stood, aided by her lover's hand. Harry signalled for a bill and took it. The girls gaped, ungainly and timid as the children they had once been together.

'Next year,' Maria said, smiling.

'Next year!' they echoed, grasping adjective and noun as they began to slide back into the chasm of their lives.

BILLY ROCHE
From *Tumbling Down*

*Billy Roche (1949–) was born in Wexford. As a musician he worked on
the cabaret and rock scene in Ireland and England. His plays,* Poor
Beast in the Rain, Belfry, A Handful of Stars *and* Cavalcaders
have been acclaimed in Ireland and England. Tumbling Down *is his
first novel, published in 1986.*

About two hours later Hickey staggered out onto the street.
It was dark now. The Rock was basking beneath a cone of
street light as a mournful 'Danny Boy' came spilling out into
the night. Two men were arguing and pointing threatening
fingers at each other. There was a woman in between them
and she was trying to get them to come back inside. Hickey
cocked an ear and, satisfied that nothing would come of it, he
went lurching into the bar, giving a little drunken skip as he
went.

It was a smoky scene that greeted him. Paddy Wolfe sat on
the soft seat, playing the accordion, the tiny scut of a cigarette
clinging to his sticky lower lip and the long grey ash growing
with every pull, threatening to fall any day now. A little rebel
sing-song had struck up down by the dart board and although it
jarred and vied with his session Paddy didn't seem to let it
bother him. He just carried on regardless.

I went striding by, carrying a tray of drinks, and never even
noticed Hickey grinning in the doorway.

'Hey Wolfe, are you not discovered yet,' Hickey joked and
tossed my hair.

'Hickey! I never saw you there,' I said. 'When did you get in?'

'Just there now. Well a few hours ago,' Hickey replied and
waved back to Johnny who was down in his favourite corner.

'Hickey, me auld segotia,' my father piped between lines and
without missing a beat.

'How are ye keepin' Paddy?' Hickey said as he sidled through the crowd.

'You're lookin' well, were you sick?' my father added as Hickey took the butt out of his mouth, stuck another fag in and lit it up for him.

'There Paddy, that'll keep ye goin' for a while,' Hickey said and moved down to join Johnny and Joe. 'I was just renewin' Paddy's battery there.'

'I see that,' Johnny said and shook his hand.

'What are ye drinkin'?' Joe wondered.

'A pint of stout,' Hickey answered and gave the sleeping Forty Winks a kind of a hug.

'Davy, give us another drink here please,' Joe called calmly, trying to hide the pleasure he felt at seeing Hickey again.

'Yeah right Joe, I'll be there in one minute,' I said, finishing off a few pints for somebody else.

My father moved from song to song with ease, feeling it in his bones that there was a whore of a session brewing. He smoked, sang and coughed all at the same time and eventually one by one they reluctantly joined in with him.

> When April showers will come your way
> They bring the flowers that bloom in May
> 'Cause when it's raining
> Have no regrets
> Because it isn't raining rain you know
> It's raining violets.

Johnny was down there beside him now, throwing in little bits of harmony and scatting like Louis Armstrong. The crowd loved him and obeyed to the letter the instructions that wafted from his invisible baton. Sometimes he let them soar. Other times he took them right down, squeezing all their voices into a tiny space between his hands, giving the whole thing cadence and rhythm. My father was delighted and winked up at him.

Joe Crofton was enjoying the session. He was a regal sybarite, straight-backed and smirking. He sang out of the corner of his mouth, hoping that somebody else would get the blame for it. I was running around like a blue-arsed fly, serving, collecting glasses and wiping tables, and maybe passing out somebody his change as I went. Forty Winks would come up for air every so often and mutter something like, 'Give the man a chance.'

When Johnny sang 'The Whiffinproof Song' the entire place fell silent. It told the story of a bunch of misfits who were about to go on a dangerous mission from which they would never return. Johnny looked real moody as he peered out from behind a cloud of climbing smoke and the way he sang the song made us all feel that we were those men who were about to die.

> We are poor little lambs
> Who have gone astray,
> Ba ba ba.
> Little black sheep who have lost our way,
> Ba ba ba.
> Gentlemen songsters out on a spree
> Doomed from here to eternity
> May the Lord have mercy on such as we,
> Ba ba ba.

During the last chorus Lar Lyons nearly ruined the whole thing by imitating a sheep and he was nearly crucified with daggers of looks for it. Forty Winks drowsily told him to 'Shut yer fuckin' auld mouth up,' and Lar Lyons was sorry he spoke.

Then Hickey asked my father to recite 'The Farting Competition' and seeing that there were no women present and that it was Hickey's homecoming he obliged. This was a vulgar recitation about a farting competition which took place in Stockton-on-Tees. It went on for ages and my father took off all the different accents and facial expressions of the people competing and the clergy who blessed the occasion.

The odds were on Mrs McClean
With her cheeks painted red
And her hole painted green
'Cause the news had leaked out in the noonday edition
That this lady's arse was in perfect condition.

Some of the people who had never heard it before were in stitches. One fellow nearly had a hernia. He was holding his side with the pain and the tears were streaming down his face. Then to make matters worse somebody did actually fart and the whole place exploded. 'Open that window Davy,' someone shouted and all the doors and windows were flung open.

'Hey Martin, take it off till we all shit in it,' Hickey said, fanning the air.

Then the fellow who was doing all the laughing in the first place, and was still breaking his heart laughing in fact, let out a fart himself and he was answered by somebody else over on the far side. For the next five minutes men seemed to be able to fart at will and the whole place was just quaking with laughter. Men were careened against each other, hugging one another and holding each other up. One fellow was sitting on the floor and another had to go down to the toilet to try and get away.

People passing outside stopped to have a look in at this laughing bar and soon a little crowd had gathered on the street and they started laughing too even though they hadn't a clue what was going on. Victor was there among them with a big idiotic smile on his face and I heard one old man remark as he walked away, 'That must be a great pub.'

When my father eventually finished the recitation he thanked the lads for the special effects and the whole thing, which had more or less died down, started up again. For the next half an hour or so people were tittering away to themselves and grinning like a crowd of Cheshire cats.

It was time for the grand finale so my father picked up the accordion again and guided us from 'Have You Ever Been

Lonely' into 'Marta', 'Carolina Moon', and finally slipped into
'Irene Goodnight'.

Everybody knew that their time was short in The Rock when
they heard 'Irene Goodnight' and I was inundated with last
orders.

'Davy, give us another drink here when you're ready.'

'Yeah right Hickey just one second. Tommy there's your
pint. What did you ask me for? A what? Two pints and a glass
. . . Thanks Tommy. Jem says he has enough.'

> Last Saturday night I got married,
> Me and my wife settled down;
> Now me and my wife we are parting,
> Gonna take a little stroll down town.

'Davy did ye get me a drink yet?'

'What did you ask me for?'

'I asked you for the same again.'

> Irene goodnight Irene,
> Irene goodnight.
> Goodnight Irene, goodnight Irene,
> I'll see you in my dreams.

'Hickey what did you say to me?'

'A pint of ale, a pint of stout and twenty fags. Oh and give
your da a large bottle as well.'

The smoke-filled pub was a battlefield now with dirty glasses
lining the bar and knocked-over bottles spilling froth onto the
floor, which was already littered with squashed fag-ends, scattered confetti and crinkled-up racing dockets.

I squeezed past the men in the snug to turn off the outside
light and close the front door.

'I'll tell ye one thing Nick, I wouldn't piss on him now if he
was on fire and that's a fact.'

'Aw now Brendan he's not that bad. I mean to say . . .'

'No no . . . you don't know him.'

'Don't serve any more drink now Davy,' my father said, laying down the accordion for the night and he launched into his usual routine of trying to clear the house. 'Right now children, devotions in the morning at the usual hour, followed by a short instruction.'

'He came up to my house one night, oh it was late, I'd say it must have been after twelve o'clock. And do ye know what that coileáin said to me . . .'

'Give us two more drinks here son will ye before ye close up shop. Two quick ones. A couple of half ones. Sorry Brendan for interruptin' ye there. Go ahead . . .'

A dribbling drunk who hadn't uttered a word all night started singing 'Carrig River'.

'Oh no,' my father complained, throwing his eyes to heaven. 'I wouldn't mind but he knows all twenty-seven verses.'

> The hawthorn and sweet briars
> They would your heart illume,
> And the rippling of the waters when
> The fraochals were in bloom.

Old Willy crawled from word to word as my father paraded through the crowd like a policeman, shouting at the top of his voice, 'Come on now gentlemen, have you no homes to go to?'

'Stop the noise Paddy will ye,' Hickey slurred.

'Are you goin' to drink that pint Hickey or make soup out of it or what?' my father said, putting his arm around Hickey's shoulder. 'When are you goin' back anyway?'

'Aw give us a chance, I'm only after gettin' here,' Hickey pleaded.

My father grinned and moved along saying to Johnny as he went, 'You'd better give Rip Van Winkle a shout,' and Johnny began shaking Forty Winks.

> 'Tis well I do remember when
> Together we did roam,

> Through the lonely dells of Carrig
> Where the woodcock makes his home.
> All nature it is smiling
> Upon each rocky side.

One by one they reluctantly departed, some of them taking little parcels of drink with them. My father stood at the door watching the exodus and making sure nobody sneaked back in again.

'Are you alright Johnny? Can you manage?'

'Yeah, game-ball Paddy,' Johnny replied as he helped Forty Winks to his feet and out the door and then stopped to whisper, 'The blind leadin' the blind.'

> And the silvery stream flows down between
> To join the Slaney tide.

'Willy, you can give us the second instalment tomorrow,' my father said, leaving his post and coming across to get the old singer out.

'What's it doin' out Paddy?' Joe wondered when the door was shut behind old Willy, who went singing up the street.

'It's a grand night,' my father answered and started sweeping the floor.

Joe lowered his pint, picked up his coat, which was draped across a high stool, and made for the door.

'Good night Paddy,' he said and peeped in at me and called, 'Good luck Davy.'

'All the best Joe,' we said and my father sighed to see the last of them leave.

When I had most of the glasses washed my father told me to go ahead home, saying that he would finish up, and being weary of the busy day I didn't argue with him. I grabbed my 'bum freezer' and vanished.

Joe Crofton was standing outside, buttoning up his top-coat and tucking himself snugly into it and acclimatizing himself to the sharp night air. Old Willy was still giving 'Carrig River' socks a few doors up.

'A grand night says he,' Joe Crofton complained when he saw me standing beside him. 'I wouldn't mind but it's freezin' brass friggin' monkeys.'

Lar Lyons flagged down a passing car and secured himself a lift home.

'There he goes. Rigor Mortis Junior,' Joe said, pointing him out with his head.

The quay was practically deserted now except for a boy and a girl kissing in a shop arcade and a perished young guard blowing into his hands. We crossed over onto the wooden-works to avoid getting tied up with old Willy and I slowed down my pace to suit Joe's tipsy swagger. The tide was high and the rain-swollen river waged war on the ocean. Behind us the bridge was just a shadowy spectre hiccuping to the other side and Useless Island seemed close enough to touch. The yellow moon was a shiny witch in the sky as Wexford tangled and twisted and jumbled itself into a town to tumble upside down into the sea.

When I said that it was a wonder someone wouldn't build a casino or something out on Useless Island Joe gave the idea some thought and kind of smiled at my ingenuity. He seemed neither contented nor agitated at the thought of spending the rest of his days in Wexford. He had been around and this was as good a place as any, better than some.

One day, when I had saved a little money and a whole lot of courage, I would run away from here. I would come back rich and famous and cock-sure of myself. I would buy Useless Island for my very own and then with the greatest of pleasure I'd blow it clean out of the water. I would have my revenge for all the years that I was forced to love this good-for-nothing monstrosity.

When I was a little boy I used to dream of Useless Island. In the event of war I would make a daring escape and swim out there. I would discover fruit trees and wildlife (not visible from the shore) and a hut that needed only a small amount of repair

to make it cosy, safe and warm. All I needed would be out there
and I would be king. Later on, when I got a little older, I used
to add things to my dream – things like naked women and
barrels of beer.

But right now I hated it and I didn't want to look. I
didn't want to see. It would only make it harder for me to break
away from here just like all those other poor eejits who sailed
broken-hearted over the horizon with this town clawing at their
hearts and in their minds Useless Island elevated to a planet of
gold.

'Will this casino have a whorehouse?' Joe inquired out of the
blue.

'Yeah. Upstairs,' I replied as if it was all planned.

Joe allowed himself another little regal smirk as we crossed
over into Cinema Lane and the pair of us were swallowed up by
the darkness.

MOY McCRORY
The Wrong Vocation

*Moy McCrory (1953–) was born in Liverpool of Irish parents. She has
published three collections of short stories,* Those Sailing Ships of His
Boyhood Dreams, The Water's Edge *and* Bleeding Sinners, *as
well as a novel,* The Fading Shrine.

'When God calls you, he is never denied' Sister Mercy told us
with a finality which struck terror into our hearts.

She stood at the front of the room with the window behind
her, so we were blinded and could not see her features but we
knew she smiled.

'He waits patiently until we hear his voice. When that happens,
you are never the same.'

It terrified me that this thing called a vocation might come
dropping in to my mind out of nowhere one day and wedge
there like a piece of grit.

'God is looking now, seeing who is pure of heart and ready to
be offered up.'

Every girl shifted uncomfortably. Sister looked at our up-
turned faces and seemed pleased with the effect she was
having. By way of illustration she told us about a young
woman from a rich home who was always laughing, with
young men waiting to escort her here, there and everywhere,
and a big family house with chandeliers in the rooms and a
lake in the garden.

'I've seen it. It was on the telly the other night,' Nancy Lyons
whispered to me.

'With all these good things in life, she was spoiled. Her
wealthy father indulged his daughter's every wish. And do you
think she was happy?'

'She damned well ought to be,' Nancy hissed while around us
the more pious members of the form shook their heads.

Sister placed her bony hands across her chest and stood up on her tiptoes as if reaching with her rib cage for something that would constantly evade it.

'Her heart was empty.'

Sister went on to tell us how the young woman resisted the call, but eventually realized she would never be happy until she devoted her life to Christ. Going out beside the lake, she asked him to enter her life.

'She is one of our very own nuns, right here in this convent. Of course I cannot tell you which sister she is, but when you imagine that we were all born as nuns, remember that we were once young girls like yourselves, without a thought in our heads that we should devote our lives to God.'

There was a silence. We all stared out past her head.

'Oh, Sister, it's beautiful,' said a voice. Nancy rolled her eyes to heaven. Lumpy, boring Beatrice who always sat at the front would like it. She was so slow-witted and so good. She was one of the least popular girls in the class, a reporter of bad news and always the first to give homework in. With mini skirts *de rigueur*, her uniform remained stoically unadapted. She must have been the only girl in the school that did not need to have her hemline checked at the end of the day. While we struggled to turn over our waistbands Beatrice always wore her skirt a good two inches below her plump knees and looked like one of the early photographs, all sepia and foggy, of the old girls in their heyday.

Nancy pulled a face.

'But wasn't her rich father angry?' someone asked, and Sister Mercy nodded.

'Mine would sodding kill me. They don't even want me to stay on at school. Me mother's always reminding me how much money they're losing because I'm not bringing any wages home.'

'Do you have something to say, Nancy Lyons?' Sister's stern voice rapped.

'No Sister, I was just saying what a great sacrifice it was to make.'

'Ah yes, a great sacrifice indeed.'

But the sacrifice was not just on the nun's part. Everyone else was made to suffer. There was a woman in our street who never recovered after her eldest daughter joined the Carmelites. Mrs Roddy's daughter was a teacher in the order. It was not the fact that she would never give her mother grandchildren that caused the greatest upset, but the economics of it. All a nun's earnings go straight back into the convent. Mrs Roddy used to wring her hands.

That money's mine,' she would shout, 'for feeding and clothing her all those years. The church has no right to it!'

Then her daughter went peculiar. We only noticed because they sent her home for a week on holiday, and we thought that was unusual, but it was around the time they were relaxing the rule. Nuns were appearing on the streets with skirts that let them walk easily, skimming their calves instead of the pavement.

During that week she got her cousin to perm her hair, on account of the new head-dress. She assured her that it was all right because even nuns had to look groomed now their hair showed at the front, and every night she continued to lead the family in the joyful mysteries.

'I'll tell you Mrs Mac, I'm worn out with all the praying since our Delcia's been back,' her mother would confide to mine as they passed quickly in the street, while her daughter muttered 'God bless you' to no one in particular and with a vague smile.

But indoors, she borrowed her mother's lipstick, deep red because Mrs Roddy still had the same one from before the war. That was when they thought she was going a bit far, when they saw her outmoded, crimson mouth chanting the rosary. She drove her family mad. She had tantrums and kept slamming doors. Then they saw her out in the street asking to be taken for rides on Nessie Moran's motorbike. Everyone said she had taken her vows too young. She crammed all those teenage things she never did into that week. By the end of it they were relieved to send her back.

Her mother hated nuns. She did not mind priests half as much.

'At least they're human' she would say. 'Well, half human. Nuns aren't people. They're not proper women. They don't know what it is to be a mother and they'll never be high up in the church. They'll never be the next pope. They can't even say mass. What good are they? They're stuck in the middle, not one thing or the other. Brides of Christ! They made me sick. Let them try cooking, cleaning and running a home on nothing. I'd have a damned easier life if I'd married Christ, instead of that lazy bugger inside.'

But she was fond of the young priest at her church, a good looking, fresh faced man from Antrim who would sit and have a drink with them at the parish club.

'At least you can have a laugh with him,' she'd say, 'but that stuck up lot, they're all po-faced up at Saint Ursula's. They're no better than any of us. I'm a woman, don't I know what their minds are like. They're no different. Gossipy, unnatural creatures, those ones are. Look what's happened to our poor Delcia after being with them.'

And then the convent sent Delcia home to be looked after by her family. An extended holiday they called it, on account of her stress and exhaustion.

'They've used her up, now they don't want what's left over, so I've got her again. What good is she to anyone now? She can't look after herself. She can't even make a bloody cup of tea. How will she fend for herself if the order won't have her back? I'm dying, Mrs Mac; I can't be doing with her.'

My mother would tut and nod and shut the door.

'It's a shame. What sort of a life has that poor girl had?' she would say indoors, shaking her head at the tragedy.

'I know she's gone soft now, but she was good at school. Her mam and dad thought she'd be something and now she's lit for nothing if the church can't keep her.'

In the evening we would hear Mrs Roddy shouting 'Get in off the street!'

Finally they took her into a hospice and we heard no more about it, but Mrs Roddy always crossed the road to avoid nuns. Once outside Lewis's a Poor Clare thrust a collection box at her and asked for a donation. Mrs Roddy tried to take it from her and the box was pulled back and forth like a bird tugging at a worm. It was not the nun's iron grip, but the bit of elastic which wrapped itself around her wrist that foiled Mrs Roddy's attempt to redistribute the church's wealth.

'They're just like vultures,' she would say, 'waiting to see what they can tear from your limbs. They're only happy when they've picked you clean. Better hide your purses!'

At the collection on Sundays she sat tight lipped and the servers knew better than to pass the collecting plate her way.

'A vocation gone wrong,' was what my father called Delcia Roddy. He would shake his head from side to side and murmur things like 'the shame' or 'the waste'. He had a great deal of sympathy for her tortured soul. It was about this time that I became tortured. He had none for me.

Sister Mercy's words had stung like gravel in a grazed knee. At night I could hear them as her voice insisted, 'You cannot fight God's plan,' and I would pray that God keep his plans to himself.

'You must pray for a vocation,' she told us.

I gritted my teeth and begged His Blessed Mother to intervene.

'I'll be worse than the Roddy girl,' I threatened, 'and look what a disgrace she was.' Then, echoing the epitaph of W.B. Yeats, I would point into the darkness and urge 'Horseman; Pass by!'

'We are instruments of God's will,' Sister Mercy told us and I did not want to be an instrument.

I knew if God had any sense he would not want me, but Sister Mercy frightened us. Beatrice was the one headed for a convent. She had made plain her intentions at the last retreat

when she stood up and announced to the study group that she
was thinking of devoting her life to Christ.

'She may as well, there's nothing else down for her,' Nancy
commented.

Yet Sister Mercy told us that often the ones we did not
suspect had vocations, and she looked around the room like a
mindreader scrutinizing the audience before pulling out likely
candidates.

The convent terrified me; the vocation stalked my shadow
like a store detective. One day it would pounce and I would be
dead-locked into a religious life, my will subsumed by one
greater than I. Up there was a rapacious appetite which con-
sumed whole lives, like chicken legs. I dreaded that I should end
up in a place where every day promised the same, the gates
locked behind me and all other escape sealed off. It wasn't that I
had any ambitions for what I might do, but I could not happily
reconcile myself to an existence where the main attraction was
death. I dreaded hearing God's call.

'He can wait for years. God is patient.'

I decided that I would have to exasperate him, and fast.

Down at the Pier Head, pigeons gathered in thousands. The Liver
Buildings were obscured as they all rose in unison like a blanket of
grey and down. I never knew where my fear came from, but I was
terrified of those birds. Harmless seagulls twice their size flew
about me, followed the ferry out across the water to Birkenhead
and landed flapping and breathless on the landing plank. Their
screech was piercing. They never disturbed me. Yet when I stepped
out into Hamilton Square and saw the tiny cluster of city birds
waiting, my heart would beat in panic. City birds who left slime
where they went, their excrement the colour of the new granite
buildings springing up. They nodded their heads and watched you
out of the corners of their eyes. They knocked smaller birds out of
the way and I had seen them taking bread away from each other.
They were a fighting, quarrelsome brood, an untidy shambling

army, with nothing to do all day but walk around the Pier Head or
follow me through Princess Park and make my life a misery.

Once I was crossing for a bus, just as a streak of them flew up
into the air. I put my hands over my head, the worst fear being
that one should touch my face, and I could think of nothing
more sickening than the feel of one of these ragged creatures,
bloated with disease, the flying vermin which flocked around
the Life Assurance building, to remind us we were mortal.

I had a nightmare at the time of being buried alive under
thousands of these birds. They would make that strange cooing
noise as they slowly suffocated me. Their fat greasy bodies
would pulsate and swell, as satiated, they nestled down onto me
for the heat my body could provide. Under this sweltering,
stinking mass I would be unable to scream. Each time I opened
my mouth it filled with dusty feathers.

Then my nightmare changed. Another element crept into my
dreams. Alongside the pigeons crept the awful shape that was a
vocation. It came in all colours, brown and white, black and
white, beige, mottled, grey and sandy, as the different robes of
each order clustered around me, knocking pigeons out of the
way. They muttered snatches of Latin, bits of psalms, and
rubbed their clawed hands together like banktellers. The big
change in the dream was that they, unlike the pigeons, did not
suffocate me, but slowly drew away, leaving me alone in a
great empty space, which at first I thought was the bus terminal,
but which Nancy Lyons assured me was the image of my life to
be.

Her older sister read tea leaves and was very interested in
dreams. Nancy borrowed a book from her.

'It says here, that dreaming about water means a birth.'

'I was dreaming about pigeons, and then nuns.'

'Yeah, but you said you were down at the Pier Head didn't
you, and that's water.'

'I don't know if I was at the Pier Head.'

'Oh you must have been. Where else would you get all them

pigeons?' Nancy was a realist. 'Water means a birth,' she repeated firmly. 'I bet your mam gets pregnant.'

I knew she was wrong. I was the last my mother would ever have, she told me often enough. But Nancy would not be put off. The book was lacking on nuns so she held out for the water and maintained that the big empty space was my future.

'There's nothing down for you unless you go with the sisters,' she said.

It was not because I lacked faith that I dreaded the vocation. I suffered from its excesses, it hung around me, watching every move, and passing judgement. I was a failed miserable sinner and I knew it, but I did not want to atone. I did not want the empty future I was sure it offered. Our interpretation of the dream differed.

Around this time I had a Saturday job in a delicatessen in town. I was on the cold-meat counter. None of the girls were allowed to touch the bacon slicer. Only Mister Calderbraith could do that. He wore a white coat and must have fancied himself as an engineer the way he carried on about the gauge of the blades. He would spend hours unscrewing the metal plates and cleaning out the bolts and screws with a look of extreme concentration on his face.

His balding head put out a few dark strands of hair which he grew to a ludicrous length and wore combed across his scalp to give the impression of growth. Some of the girls said he wore a toupee after work, and that if we were to meet him on a Sunday we would not know him.

He used to pretend he was the manager. He would come over and ask customers solicitously if everything was all right and remark that if the service was slow, it was because he was breaking in new staff.

'Who does he think he's kidding!' Elsie said after he had leaned across the counter one morning. 'He couldn't break in his shoes.'

Shoes were a problem. I was on my feet all day, and they would ache by the time we came to cash up. I used to catch the bus from the Pier Head at around five-thirty, if I could get the glass of the counter wiped down and the till cashed. The manager and seniors were obsessed with dishonesty. Cashing up had to be done in strict military formation. None of us were allowed to move until we heard a bell and the assistant manager would take the cash floats from us in silence.

Inside his glass office the manager sat on a high stool with mirrors all around him, surveying us. If any of the girls sneezed, or moved out of synch another bell would sound and we would all have to instantly shut our tills while the manager shouted over the loudspeaker system, 'Disturbance at counter number four' or wherever it was. Sometimes it took ages.

They never failed to inform us that staff were all dishonest. Not the management, Mister Calderbraith or senior staff, but the floor workers, and especially the temporary staff, the Saturday workers, because as they told us, we had the least to lose, and we were 'fly by nights' according to the manager, who grinned as he told us that.

I could not imagine anything there worth stealing. It was all continental meats and strange cheeses that smelt strongly, the mouldier the better.

'Have you seen that bread they're selling?' Elsie said to me one Saturday.

'The stuff that looks like it's got mouse droppings on top?'

But people came from all over the city and placed orders.

One Saturday evening I was waiting for the next bus having missed the five-thirty. My feet ached. The manager would not let you sit down. Even when there were no customers in sight you were supposed to stand to attention. I took it in turns with Elsie to duck beneath the wooden counter supports and sit on the floor when business was slack. Whenever Mister Calderbraith was about, we both stood rigidly. He loathed serving customers.

'See to that lady,' he would say if anyone asked him for a quarter of liver sausage.

I had worn the wrong shoes, they had heels. Throughout the week I wore comfortable brown lace-ups, but at the weekend I wanted to wear things that did not scream 'schoolgirl'. But my mother had been right. I was crippled.

After a few minutes I leant back on the rail and kicked one shoe off. My toes looked puffy and red. I put that one back and kicked off the other. It shot into the gutter. Before I had a chance to hop after it, a pigeon the size of a cat flapped down and stood between it and me. It looked at me, then slowly began to walk around the shoe. I was rigid, gripping the rail and keeping my foot off the pavement. Then the bird hopped inside the shoe and seemed to settle as a hen might in a nest. It began to coo. I was perspiring. I would never be able to take the shoe from it, and even if I managed to I would not be able to put my foot inside after that vile creature had sat in it. I was desperate. Suddenly, as if it sensed my fright, it flew up in the air towards me almost brushing my face with its wings, then it circled and landed squarely back inside the shoe. I did not wait. It could have it. I hopped away from the bus stop and limped towards the taxi stand. I reckoned I had just enough money to get a cab home. It would be all my pay for the Saturday, and I would not be able to go out that night, but I did not care. It would take me, shoeless, right to the front door and away from the pigeon.

Then, I thought it was my mind playing tricks, but I saw three shapes blowing in the breeze, veils flapping behind them. The Pier Head was so windy, I thought they might become airborne. They got bigger and bigger. I was certain that they flew. Soon they would be right on top of me. God was giving me a sign. The Vocation had decided to swoop after so long pecking into my dreams. Three silent figures, as mysterious as the Trinity, crossed the tarmac of the bus terminal. I could not

take my eyes from them. They seemed to swell the way a pigeon
puffs out its chest to make itself important. They were getting
fatter and rounder like brown and white balloons. Carmelites. I
could not stay where I was. I had to escape. Some people moved
to one side as I hobbled to a grass verge. I tripped on the
concrete rim of the grassy area and caught my ankle. As I put
my hand down to catch myself, several birds pecking on rubbish,
rose into the air just in front of me, and I thought for one
deluded second that I was flying with them as the white sky
span and I tumbled over. Only when my head came level with a
brown paper carrier bag did I smell the grossly familiar scent of
cold meats.

'Young lady, are you in some sort of difficulty?'

The voice of Mister Calderbraith pulled me out of my terrified
stupor. I lifted my head and came eye to quizzical eye.

'Whatever is wrong with you? Can't you walk properly?
Good heavens, what has happened to your shoe? Have you been
in some sort of incident?' He straightened up and looked around
desperately.

'Tell me who did it,' he insisted. 'Check that you still have
your front door keys.'

I raised myself up on one knee and obediently opened my
bag. Everything was intact. Mister Calderbraith's eyes opened
wide.

'I really don't understand . . .' he began.

Behind him I could see a triangle formation moving against
the empty sky. The three sisters seemed to glide inside its rigid
outline like characters in the medals people brought back from
Fatima. Behind them flapped wings, veils, patches of brown,
and feathers. Dark against the white sky they enveloped me, just
as my dream had forewarned. I could not speak. My hands
shook.

'What is it? Have you seen the culprit?'

I nodded, still struggling to rise.

'They often work in a gang, these hoodlums,' Mister Calder-

braith continued. 'Oh, yes. I've watched enough detective pro-
grammes to know how they operate.' He glanced from side to
side furtively.

'They've probably left their lookout nearby. Acting casual.'
He glowered menacingly at the passers-by.

They were closing in behind Mister Calderbraith. They peered
over his shoulder. Inhuman they cheeped and shrieked. I could
not understand a thing. Mister Calderbraith nodded at me, his
head pecking up and down. I reached out and pointed and a
dreadful magnetic force pulled me towards them. I was on my
feet in seconds.

Mister Calderbraith turned round and saw the three. He
shrank away from them.

'You don't mean these, surely?' he said. 'That is stretching it.
Have you been drinking? Tell me, were you on relief at the
spirit counter?'

'She's had a bit of a fall,' a passer-by said.

'I think she fell on her head,' Mister Calderbraith nodded.

Then turning to the spectators who had crossed from the bus
shelter, he reassured them that everything was all right.

'She is one of my staff members, it's all under control, I know
this young lady. Let me deal with it.'

The smallest nun, a tiny frail sparrow, hopped lightly towards
me, concern marked by the way she held her head on one side.
Her scrawny hand scratched at the ground and she caught up a
carrier bag that lay askew on the grass verge. The others
clucked solicitously. Then there was a stillness. All fluttering
seemed to stop. She handed the bag to me and I took it as my
voice returned to tumble out in hopeless apologies while my
face burned. Hugging the carrier bag to me, I stumbled towards
a taxi which had pulled up. I fell inside and slammed the door. I
breathed deeply, thinking that I was going to cry from embarrassment. Out of the back window I could see the nuns standing
with Mister Calderbraith who was looking about as if he had
lost something.

'Where to, love?' the driver asked.

My voice was thin and wavery as I told him. I put my head back and sighed. Only when we were halfway along the Dock Road did I realize that I was still hugging the bag. I peered inside. It was stuffed with pieces of meat, slivers of pork and ends of joints, all wrapped up in Mr Calderbraith's sandwich papers. There was a great knuckle of honey roast ham. It would be a sin to waste it.

Then I started to laugh. I couldn't stop. Tears ran down my face. Sister Mercy had told us that we had to be spotless, our souls bleached in God's grace. We had to repent our past and ask Him to take up residence in our hearts. I put my hand into the bag and drew out a piece of meat. I crammed it into my mouth. I swallowed my guilt, ate it whole and let it fill my body. As I chewed I wondered at how I still felt the same. I was no different, only now I had become the receiver of stolen goods. I wondered if Mister Calderbraith would be nicer to me? I would not be surprised if he let me have a go on the bacon slicer, next weekend.

'Are you all right love?' the driver asked.

I was choking on a piece of meat.

'I'm fine,' I coughed, scarcely waiting long enough before I stuffed another bit into my mouth. I ate with frenzied gulping sounds. When I looked up I saw the driver watching me in his mirror.

'God, but you must be starving,' he said.

I nodded.

'Well you're a growing girl. You don't know how lucky you are to have all your life in front of you.'

'I do, I really do,' I told him as I pulled another bit of meat off a bone with my teeth. Between mouthfuls I laughed. My one regret was that it wasn't a Friday — I could have doubled my sin then without any effort. Then I realized that I had subverted three nuns into being accomplices. What more did I need?

I slapped my knees and howled. God would have to be desperate to want me now.

As the taxi pulled up outside the house, I saw the curtains twitch. I did not know how I was going to explain losing my shoe, but nothing could lower my spirits, not even hiccups.

EILÍS NÍ DHUIBHNE
A Visit to Newgrange

Eilís Ní Dhuibhne (1954–) works as a keeper in the National Library of Ireland and as a lecturer in folklore. She has published a novel, The Bray House *and two collections of short stories,* Eating Women is Not Recommended *and* Blood and Water.

Mutti wrote to Erich. She would like to visit him in May. It had been two years since his last holiday in Bad Schwarzstadt and she was missing him. Besides, she was longing to see Ireland. A poster in the village travel agency depicted a scene in Connemara: a lake and hills and a donkey. The hills were so very green, she could hardly wait to climb them. And the sky was so very blue. And the donkey, so very friendly. It confirmed for her what she had always known, in her heart, about Ireland. She would arrive at 1.23 p.m. on the fourteenth, Flight E4327. Perhaps Erich could spare a few hours from his studies to come and meet her? She realized that he was very busy and if he couldn't manage it, why, she wouldn't mind. She was used to travelling alone now, ever since Vatti died (fifteen years previously). It was true that she was sixty-eight and suffered from severe arthritis of the hip. But she could get along very well on her own. Her English, at least, was rather good. That much she had to admit. She'd been taking lessons all winter, at the Bad Schwarzstadt Adult Education Centre. Of course, she'd never been to an English-speaking country before. Not since before the War, anyway, when she had stayed with a family in Devon, improving her command of the language. The father had been a doctor. He had died on D-Day, tending the wounded on a French beach.

She had written a long letter, apparently. I didn't see it myself. Erich relayed its contents to me, in a light, satirical tone he sometimes uses for comic effect. Probably he embroidered the details as he went along: he has a wonderful imagination.

Underneath his soft chuckles, however, lay a core of hysteria so blatant that I knew I was meant to take heed of it. Fear, I supposed it must be. Of Mutti. She was a little domineering, he had mentioned, once or twice? Oh, yes, indeed. With knobs on (Erich, like many speakers of English as a foreign language, possesses a rich store of colloquial expressions, and cannot resist employing them whenever possible). She was a real old battle-axe. Hard as nails. More demanding than a two-year-old Ayatollah. More conservative than Maggie Thatcher. A dyed-in-the-wool Lutheran. More puritanical than John Knox.

I would have to move out.

It was only temporary.

She didn't realize he was living with me and the shock would be too much for her. Her only son. It was only for two weeks. Why make an issue of it? For a mere fortnight.

What about my mother? I politely enquired. She was a dyed-in-the-wool Catholic, more conservative than John Paul the Second, more puritanical than Archbishop McNamara. She'd had to turn a blind eye on the fact that her daughter, her favourite daughter, her fifth daughter, was living in a state of mortal sin. She'd had to accept that life was different in Germany, different in Ranelagh, and soon would be different in Tuam, County Galway. And what about me, for heaven's sake? I was a dyed-in-the-wool Catholic, too, when you came to think about it, very deeply. Not just dyed, blued. Blued in the delicate, gauzy wool of the Virgin Mary's cloak: her blue-white, whiter-than-ordinary-white, artistically-draped, archetypal emblem of purity. A Child of Mary, that's what I actually was, called to her service in the chapel of Loreto on the Green when already a nubile impressionable fifteen-year-old. What about that? And what about integrity, courage and honesty, qualities which Erich claimed to prize above all others?

Mutti was sixty-eight. She had severe arthritis of the hip. It was only for two weeks. For heaven's sake.

On the thirteenth of May, I moved in with Jacinta who lives

around the corner. On the fifteenth, Erich invited me up for a cup of tea, and I was introduced to Mutti.

She moved swiftly towards me, hobbling a little on the hip, and encircled me in a warm embrace. I don't hug people's mothers, or touch them at all if I can avoid it, and I was put off guard. Oblivious of my confusion, she smiled radiantly, and effused:

'It is so nice to see you! Erich tells me all about you this morning. Such a nice surprise for me! I did not know Erich has a girlfriend, you see. In Ireland, that is!'

I shook her hand gently: slight, bony and hot, two rocky protrusions on its third finger bit into my palm. I held on for a second, and examined Mutti. She was about five feet tall and fragile, with bountiful curly grey hair, large gentian eyes, innumerable glittering teeth. A bygone beauty. 'Bygone' in my estimation, that is, although probably not in her own, if my experience of her type is anything to go on.

'Now, we have a nice cup of tea!'

She had motioned me towards the sofa, a handsome tweed one which I had bought the winter before in Kilkenny Design. We sat down, and Erich put on the kettle. Just a cup of tea. They'd had dinner in town, he explained. Yes, yes, acquiesced Mutti, such an excellent meal. I had not had dinner in town. I'd had nothing since lunch, and then I'd had two crispbreads and a slice of cheese.

I glared at Erich behind her back and he lilted: 'Perhaps you'd like a sandwich? Are you hungry?' 'Oh not at all,' I replied icily. 'Don't go to any trouble on my account.' My bitterness was wasted on him: he has weather-proof sensibilities, and can, at the flick of some interior zip, protect himself from all atmospheric variation. (This ability is one of the qualities which encouraged me to love him.) Blithely, he placed three mugs of tea, weak and tasteless, on the coffee table. We sipped it slowly, he and I marshalled up on the sofa opposite Mutti, who began her manoeuvres in oral English by requesting that I call her

Friederika (I'd die first). Then she gave a full report of her trip
from Germany and of the sightseeing tour she had taken that
day. Questions of greater significance followed: were my parents
still alive? What did my father do for a living? What was my
own occupation? Rank? Salary? Quick but efficient. The cross-
examination over, we ceded to her command that we watch
television, since this would aid her in her battle with the
language. Before I left, it was arranged that I should collect both
Mutti and Erich the following morning and drive them to
Newgrange, which Erich considered an essential ingredient of
any Irish tour worth its salt, as he put it himself. Mutti had
clapped her hands at the suggestion.

'Oh, yes. That would be so nice! Newgrange. I think Herr
Müller mentions it. Is it near Spiddal?'

A month prior to her visit, Mutti had borrowed a guide-book
from the public library in Bad Schwarzstadt. The work of one
Heinrich Müller, it was entitled *Ein kleines irisches Reisebuch*, and
she had studied it with single-minded diligence until she knew
its contents by heart. It was to be her inseparable vade-mecum
during her holiday, and her main criterion for enjoyment in
sightseeing was that the sight had been referred to by Herr
Müller.

Therefore she had merrily and gratefully limped through the
litter of O'Connell Street ('oh! the widest street in Ireland!'), but
the Powerscourt Centre had failed to arouse the mildest commen-
dation. The Book of Kells had won her freshest laurels, but to
the 'Treasures of Ireland' Exhibition, her reaction was one of
chilled disappointment. 'Please, what is the meaning of the word
"treasure?"' she had asked Erich, coming out of the museum
onto Kildare Street. 'We did not have it in class, I believe.'

Herr Müller had spent the greater part of his *Reise* in Spiddal,
and had devoted more than half his book, ten whole pages, to a
graphic account of that settlement and its environs. Few corners
of the western village were unfamiliar to Mutti, and she antici-
pated her sojourn there loudly and often and with the greatest of

pleasure. Unfortunately, it would occur at the end of her stay in Dublin and last for no more than two days.

I arrived at the flat on the following morning, having taken a day's leave from my job in the Department of Finance.

'We'll go through the Phoenix Park,' I recommended brightly, determined to get value for my time. 'It's much more interesting that way, and only a bit longer. The President lives there. It's the biggest park in Europe.'

'Ah, yes,' responded Mutti noncommittally, as she settled into the passenger seat and opened a map. 'Can you show me where it is?'

I tried to lean across the brake and locate it for her, but Erich beat me to it, and, from the rear, indicated the relevant green patch. Mutti took a pencil from her handbag, held it poised in mid-air, and smiled: 'Are we going now?' On, James.

I drove to Charlemont Bridge.

'That's the canal,' I exclaimed brilliantly, waving at it as we turned off Ranelagh Road.

'Canal?'

'You know, Mutti. Canal. Not a river. Made by man. *Ein Kanal*.' Erich proffered the translation with caution: Mutti had decreed that no German be spoken in her presence, since this might sabotage her chances of commanding the language.

'It's called the Grand Canal,' I continued, pedantically. 'There are two canals in Dublin, the Royal and the Grand. This is the Grand. It's quite a famous canal, actually. Poems have been written about it. Good poems. Quite well-known poems.'

Alas, it was not the leafy-with-love part of the canal, it was the grotesque-with-graffiti bit, and Mutti stared, bemused, at peeling mildewed walls and disintegrating furry corpses. Even if it had been picturesque, I don't think its high-falutin associations would have pulled any weight: Kavanagh had the misfortune to be post-Müller.

We drove towards Kilmainham in silence. The looming jail flooded my spirits with enthusiasm. The Struggle for Freedom was a favourite theme of Heinrich's, and Mutti, I had gathered from a few comments she had made, had also fallen victim to the romantic nostalgia for things Irish, historical, and bloody.

'Look!' I cried, 'there's Kilmain . . .'

But she had glimpsed the portico of the boys' school, which is impressive. And fake.

'Oh, Erich! How nice! Is it medieval, do you think?'

'Oh, yes, I think so, Mutti,' replied Erich, in his most learned voice. He knows nothing about Dublin, or architecture, or the Middle Ages.

'It looks like some of our German castles.'

'Look,' I pressed, 'that's Kilmainham Jail. The 1916 leaders were imprisoned there.' The light turned green. 'And shot,' I added, optimistically.

'In Bad Schwarzstadt we have two castles dating from the thirteenth century, Eileen, Marienschloss and Karlsschloss. They are so nice. People come to look from everywhere.'

'Really? I'd love to see them some day!'

The hint was ignored. I turned into the Park by the Island-bridge gate.

'This is the Phoenix Park,' the guided tour continued.

'Oh! A park. And we may drive in it. How nice.' Her tone was deeply disapproving. 'In Germany, we have many car-free zones. You know. Green zones, they are called. It is good without cars sometimes. For the health.'

At that moment, a Volkswagen sped around one of the vicious bends which are so common on the charming backroads of the Park. It took me unawares, and I was forced to swerve in order to avoid it. Swerve very slightly, and the Volkswagen was at fault.

'Oh, oh, oh, oh!' screamed Mutti, clapping her hands across her face. Through bony fingers her gentian eyes glared vindictively at me. I gritted my teeth and counted to fifty. Then I repeated fifty times 'a man's mouth often broke his nose', a proverb I had come across in *The Connaught Leader* a few weeks previously. Meanwhile, Mutti ignored the Pope's Cross, the clever woods, the flocks of deer gambolling in the clever woods, the American Embassy, the troops of travellers' ponies bouncing off the bonnet, the polo grounds and Áras an Uachtaráin.

'What town will we come to next?'

'Castleknock,' between one 'a man's mouth' and the next.

Scratch, scratch, went the pen on the map. Scratch scratch, through Blanchardstown, Mulhuddart, Dunshaughlin, Trim, past a countryside resplendent with frilly hedgerows, full-cream buttercups, fairy queen hawthorn, and, flouncing about everywhere, iridescent, giggling, fresh-from-Paris foliage. The sort of surrounding which sent many a medieval Irish monk into reams of ecstatic alliteration, as I liked to point out to my friends at this time of year, delicately reminding them that, even though I was a faceless civil servant, I had, in my day, sipped at the fountain of the best and most Celtic bards (taking a BA in Old Irish). Today I could practically smell the watercress and hazel. I could have taped the black-bird's song on my cassette. But I did not bother to emphasize the true Gaelic nature of the scenery for Mutti; tactfully leaving her to her own pedantic pursuits. Scritch scratch.

In County Meath we stopped for lunch. 'Ah,' gasped Mutti appreciatively, outside the 'olde worlde' hotel, 'this looks nice!' She guessed that an establishment with such a picturesque facade would have a high standard of cuisine. Alas, when we passed the promising threshold our eyes were greeted by a sign stating: 'lunch served in the bar', and our nostrils assailed by the ripe seedy odours of grease and alcohol. In Mutti's refined Lutheran opinion, drink was unspeakably Non-U, and her perfect nose wrinkled in disgust.

'Would you like something to drink, Mutti,' Erich asked, ordering two pints of Harp with great alacrity.

'Harp? What is that? Lemonade? Juice?'

'Well, no, it's a kind of light beer.'

'Juice. I will have some Harp juice, please. I am very thirsty.'

When the three drinks arrived, gleaming yellow and foaming over the edges, Mutti first clamped her lips together, then began to sip energetically. Service of the meal was slow, and she tapped her foot impatiently on the carpet.

'It is lucky I am not hungry. They are killing that pig for me, I think.'

In twenty minutes, the waitress arrived, bearing a dinner plate for Mutti, covered with slivers of pork and side dishes of carrots and cauliflower and cabbage and potatoes and gravy. She accepted generous helpings of everything ... 'I am not hungry but I pay' ... and, having dispensed with most of it, slid the leavings into a plastic bag which appeared, as if by magic, from her coat pocket: 'After all, we pay,' she said, not bothering to whisper. 'I eat this for lunch tomorrow. A little meat, that is all I need, now that I am older. I have a small appetite.'

Erich and I finished our salads hastily, and we proceeded to Newgrange.

It does not disappoint. Me. There are many among my acquaintance who hate it. They prefer Knowth and Dowth. Goethe. Shabby Victoriana. Woodworm. I relish the lambent, urbane face of immortality: Newgrange, pretentious crystal palace, lording it over the fat cowlands, the meandering fishbeds, reflecting the glory of the sun without a shadow of suburban modesty.

Erich, although he pays lip-service to its archaeological significance, belongs to the group of those who feel uneasy with this example of prehistoric PR; he senses that it is in dubious taste. I would not have been surprised to find Mutti of like mind. But no:

'It is very nice,' she gasped, to Erich, as we climbed the hill to the tumulus.

'I knew you'd like it, Mutti,' he simpered, his eyes rivetted to the figure of the guide, a slender and provocative one, neatly glazed in luminous yellow pants and white T-shirt. She posed on a standing stone outside the mound and outlined its history in a few well-chosen words, then led the creeping party of tourists along the narrow passage to the burial chamber. Mutti had been pleased by the outside of the grave, but she was in raptures within. The ice-cold room at the centre of the hill enchanted her soul, and she oohed and ahed so convincingly that the lemon-clad one directed her remarks expressly at her, catching her large eyes and ignoring the other, less charming, members of the little group. When her spiel was over and she made the mandatory request for questions, only one was asked, and that by Mutti:

'Are there any runic stones here?' How silly, I thought. But, of course, there were. It was possible that one stone at the side of the vault contained writing. Had the guide invented this titbit to satisfy Mutti? Hardly. She had an honest, if tarty, face.

After the tour, Mutti and I lingered in the burial chamber. The others left, gradually, but she seemed to want to stay, and I felt it my duty to remain, too. What with her arthritis. Gradually, however, I realized that I was happy to be in the cool greyness of the place. It has, I noticed for the first time, a curious intimacy, the character of a kitchen, a space at the centre of the home where people gather to sustain themselves. To survive. And, although it is as chill as a tomb . . . it is a tomb, after all . . . this room has a hearth, a focus: the guide had explained that once a year the sun would pour through the opening in the outer wall, stream along the entrance passage, and flood the chamber with light. Illumination for the immortal dead.

Mutti, tracing with her delicate fingers the spiralling patterns on the tombstones, turned to me:

'Imagine how nice it is here on December twenty-one. So very nice!'

Her eyes glowed with a candour they had not held before,

and for the first time since our meeting we looked at each other full in the face. We laughed. Mutti moved towards me slowly, because of the hip, and I had an impulse to run and embrace her, to kiss her. She would not have been embarrassed, that was the sort of thing she did. But I do not kiss people's mothers, or touch anyone at all, if I can avoid it. So I hesitated.

Erich crept into the chamber. Mutti hobbled over to him and clasped his hand.

'It's time to go,' he said. 'Haven't you had enough of this creepy old mausoleum?'

So brief are our moments of salvation. So sudden. So easily lost.

FERDIA MAC ANNA
From *The Last of the High Kings*

*Ferdia Mac Anna (1955–) lives in Dublin. He is the author of two
novels,* The Last of the High Kings *and* The Ship Inspector, *a
memoir,* Bald Head *and a play,* Big Mom.

After Da had left, Ma sent Dawn up to the Summit for two
Guinness and twenty Carolls. Then she withdrew to the kitchen.
She didn't even come out when Noelie threw a stone through
Mr Figgis's greenhouse window. Then she refused to open the
door when Frankie told her that Mr Figgis had threatened to
call the police if Noelie didn't get down from his garden wall.

'Take Noelie for a long walk,' she shouted from behind the
door.

So Frankie took Noelie by the hand and walked him up to the
Summit shops. They bought ice-pops. The bored shopgirl had
to move fast to stop Noelie taking a handful of chocolate bars
from the display counter.

'Ah-ah,' she said.

'Ah-ah,' Noelie mimicked, and immediately tried for one of
the sweet jars.

Outside, it was a bright, blowy day. There was a crowd
sitting around on the wooden benches outside the pub, drinking
beers and shorts and coloured minerals in tall glasses as they
looked out at the view. Noelie said 'hello' to everyone he
passed. Seconds later, in the same cheery voice, he told them to
'fuck off'. People just looked at him. Some girls tittered. An old
man said 'hello' back.

Noelie didn't mind; he had a big orange ice-pop to suck and
make slurping noises with, and a can of Heinz beans in his hand
to show people. He had his big brother by the hand and he was
going for a long walk.

They walked past the pub and turned the corner leading to

the Summit view, the car parks and the cliff walks. While Noelie sucked his ice-pop, Frankie gripped his brother's elbow and gently steered him out of the path of others.

At the top of the hill, a long line of cars was drawn up in a neat row in the public viewing area. Noelie walked along the low wall and waved and said 'hello' to the sightseers in every car he passed. It was wild and green and windy. People sitting on the grass were buffeted like palm trees in a hurricane. But the wind didn't bother Noelie; he walked and waved and shouted greetings, laughed and scratched himself, tripped and righted himself without breaking stride.

At the end of the wall, Noelie presented his licked-clean ice-pop stick to a plump old lady in a grey overcoat who was looking out at the sea.

'Why, thank you,' the old lady said and smiled graciously.

Then she walked away slowly with the ice-pop stick in her hand.

'He's a fine big fellow,' she called back against the breeze, 'what age is he?'

'Six,' Frankie answered without thinking — Noelie had been 'six' for over four years. 'No, he's ten,' Frankie yelled but the wind was howling and the lady had gone out of earshot. 'Ten,' Frankie roared anyway.

From the wall, Frankie could see the rolls of greenery winding down to the cliffs and the white-capped blueness. The only break in the wilderness was the creamy cone of the cliff light-house, rising up like a sentry from its slice of grey rock. The wind from the sea rocked him as he stood looking. It forced him to squint. But he could make out the lighthouse-keeper's house in the row of cottages at the far side of the bridge which joined the rock to the mainland.

Once, during a winter storm, a postman had been plucked off the bridge and blown out to sea, bicycle and all. Next day, they had found the postman's cap and a letter addressed to the lighthouse keeper, nothing else. It was a story everyone on the hill had known for years. Like the one about the party of schoolboys who had disappeared while searching for birds' nests along the cliffs. Or the tale about the drunken hardman who had gone down to the pier one night to drink beer and had fallen between a fishing boat and the harbour wall; when they had dragged him out next day, his blue hands had been clutching a six-pack.

Frankie's friend Nelson loved to tell the story about the two Hare Krishnas who had gone swimming off the east pier one gentle June morning, never to be seen again. Nelson said it was a sure sign that God wasn't too gone on Hare Krishnas.

In the midst of Frankie's recollections, something silver streaked through the air and narrowly missed the heads of a group of camera-toting Americans.

'Saaaay,' a big, purple-faced man in a billowing anorak shouted as he ducked.

The can of beans landed in the grass with a thud.

'Hello,' Noelie said warmly as he got down from the wall and retrieved his can. The American tourists stood and watched him, expecting him to throw it again at any second. 'Fuck off,' Noelie said with a smile and the tourists gasped.

Frankie jumped across the wall and grabbed Noelie by the hand. He escorted his brother off along one of the cliff paths before the tourists could recover from their shock.

'Hey, that's just great, buddy,' a large yellow-haired woman called after him, 'real nice country ya got here.'

When they got back, Ma was at the garden wall yelling at Mr Figgis. Dawn stood at her side holding her hand and looking up at the arguing adults with big innocent eyes. Ray was watching from the porch, practising his John Wayne stance. He gave Frankie a big wink.

'How dare you order my child down from her own family wall,' Ma said. 'This is our wall and my children have every right to walk along it whenever they wish.'

Mr Figgis was a tall confident man with thick black hair that

flopped down over his left eye. He began setting out his
grievances in a nasal English accent. He smiled to show that he
was a reasonable man.

That was a big mistake.

'Don't smile at me, mister – I'm not your Mammy.' Ma
glared and took a pull on her cigarette. She blew the smoke in
Mr Figgis's direction. 'You have no right to order Dawn down
from her own garden wall.'

'I'm not ordering anyone,' Mr Figgis said. 'All I'm saying is
that my wife and family deserve a little privacy. One of your
children has already broken a window in my greenhouse and
now the little girl is walking the wall making faces and rude
gestures at my children. Surely you can see my point of view.'

Ma shrugged. 'Imagine that,' she said. 'Well, these are Griffin
children. They're thoroughbreds. Pure Irish blood, descended
from the High Kings of Tara. You'll never understand that.
They can walk their 'Celtic' wall any time they want, day or
night. This is our land. We're a free people now – no thanks to
the likes of you.'

She gathered Dawn and Noelie and Ray to her and stood with
her head high and her long red hair blowing in the wind like a
warrior queen.

Mr Figgis attempted to make a few reasonable points. He
explained that it had all been a misunderstanding. He hadn't
ordered Dawn down from her wall at all, merely requested politely
that she refrain from spying on his family while they were at lunch.

'Spying, my god, spying is it?'

'Well, I only meant . . .'

'Oh yes, that's a good one all right – the English accusing the
Irish of spying. Well, this is one family ye'll never conquer – ye
West Brit *Bloodsucker*.'

Shocked, Mr Figgis took a step back. For a moment, he
seemed to think that Ma was about to leap the wall and come at
him. Then he shrugged off the thought and smiled to show that
he forgave Ma's outrageous statements.

'Madam, I believe you're under a misconception . . .' he began.

'Mister, you *are* a misconception,' Ma said.

Then she threw her cigarette at him.

It was like slow-motion in a movie, Frankie thought: the cigarette bobbed gracelessly through the air like a runaway rocket, trailing a thin wisp of smoke; then ash fell away as its tip flared pink; halfway there, it appeared to swerve in order to pick its spot; finally, it struck Mr Figgis on the cheek with a splash of sparks, then dropped like a nail.

Mr Figgis looked at Ma in horror. Then he looked at the cigarette on the ground at his feet. He touched the black smudge on his cheek where the missile had hit.

He opened his mouth to say something, then changed his mind and walked away.

Ma twirled with a triumphant smile. She slapped her hands together like a child who'd just been awarded a prize. Frankie stared at her in shock. Even Noelie was struck dumb.

'You should be honoured to have Griffins walking this wall,' Ma shouted after Mr Figgis. 'Who cares about your old greenhouse anyway?'

As soon as Mr Figgis had slammed his front door, Ma ordered her children to get up on the wall.

'Aw God, Ma . . .' Frankie said.

Ma shushed him with an imperious flick of the wrist. 'This is our wall and we're going to walk it.'

She made Frankie cup his hands to give her a hoosh up onto the wall. Once up, she wobbled defiantly in her high heels until the others had joined her.

'Now children,' she said and started off along the wall towards the back garden. Frankie and Roy and Dawn and Noelie skittered after her like Penguins across a wet plank. Parnell ran along the ground, barking.

They passed their neighbours' kitchen window. Inside Mr Figgis and his wife and their bespectacled daughter May and horn-rimmed son Harold looked up in astonishment as the Griffin family paraded past along the wall.

'Hello,' Noelie said cheerfully and gave them a big wave. 'Fuck off.'

PATRICK McCABE
From *The Butcher Boy*

Patrick McCabe (1955–) was born in Clones, County Monaghan. In 1979 he received the Hennessy Award for a short story and has had short stories published in the Irish Times *and the* Cork Examiner. *He has published a children's story* The Adventures of Shay Mouse, *and three novels,* Music On Clinton Street, Carn *and* The Butcher Boy. *In 1992,* The Butcher Boy *was nominated for the Booker Prize.*

There was some good laughs in them days, me and Joe at the river with our noses in the water, hanging over the edge. You could see the dartboard eyes and the *what do you want me to do* faces of the fish. Hey fish, Joe would say, fish? Fuck off! What do you think of that, fish? we'd say.

Then we'd go off on our travels.

It was all going well until the telly went. Phut!

That was that then, a blank grey screen looking back at you. I fiddled with it but all I got was a blizzard of snow so I sat there looking at that in the hope that something would come on but it didn't and there was still nothing when da came home. How did it happen he says and I told him. I was just sitting there the next thing – out like a light. He pulled off his greatcoat and it fell on the floor. Right, he says, all business, let's have a look at this now. He was humming away to himself happy as Larry about it all. Then he says you know there's not as much into these televisions as the likes of Mickey Traynor makes out. He had bought it off Mickey Traynor the holy telly man that was because he sold holy pictures on the side. He fiddled about with it for a while but nothing happened then he shifted it over by the window and said it could be the aerial but it only got worse there. He hit it a thump

and then what happened even the snow went. After that he
started to rant and rave about Mickey. He said he might have
known better than to trust the likes of Traynor, him and his holy
pictures don't fool me. He'll not sell me a dud television and get
away with it. He'll not pull any of his foxy stunts on Benny
Brady. I'm up to the likes of Mickey Traynor make no mistake.
He smacked it with his hand. *Work!* he shouted. Look at it – I
should have known it'd be no good. Work! How long have we
got? Six months that's how long we have it, bought and paid for
with my hard-earned money. But I'll tell you this – Traynor will
give me back every cent I paid him every cent by Christ he will!

He drew out and out his boot through it, the glass went
everywhere. I'll fix it, he said, I'll fix it good and fucking
proper.

Then he fell asleep on the sofa with one shoe hanging off.

There wasn't much I could do then I got fed up watching the
birds hop along the garden wall so I went off up the street. I
said to myself well that's the end of John Wayne I knew it'd lie
there glass and all and nobody would ever bother coming to fix
it. Ah well, I said sure Joe can always tell me what happens and
it was when I was thinking that I saw Philip and Mrs Nugent
coming. I knew she thought I was going to turn back when I
saw them. She leaned over and said something to Philip. I knew
what she was saying but I don't think she knew I knew. She
crinkled up her nose and said in a dead whisper: *Just stands there on
the landing and lets the father do what he likes to her. You'd never do the
like of that would you Philip? You'd always stand by me wouldn't you?*

Philip nodded and smiled. She smiled happily and then it
twisted a bit and the hand went up again as she said: *Of course
you know what she was doing with the fuse wire don't you Philip?*

She thought I was going to turn back all red when she said
that but I didn't. I just kept on walking. Ah there you are Mrs
Nugent I says with a big grin, and Philip. She looked right

through me and it was one of those looks that is supposed to
make you shrivel up and die but it only made me grin even
more. I was standing in the middle of the footpath. Mrs Nugent
held on her hat with one hand and took Philip with the other
would you let me by please she says.

Oh no I can't do that I said, you have to pay to get past. She
had all these broken nerve ends on her nose and her eyebrows
went away up nearly meeting her hair what do you mean what
on earth do you mean she said and I could see Philip frowning
with his Mr Professor face wondering was it serious maybe,
maybe something he could investigate or do a project on. Well
he could if he wanted I didn't care as long as he paid. It was
called the Pig Toll Tax. Yes, Mrs Nugent I said, the pig toll tax
it is and every time you want to get past it costs a shilling. Her
lips got so thin you really would think they were drawn with a
pencil and the skin on her forehead was so tight I thought
maybe the bones were going to burst out. But they didn't and I
says to Philip I'll tell you what Philip you can have half. So
what's that then one shilling for Mrs Nooge, I said and twopence
halfpenny for Philip. I don't know why I called her Mrs Nooge,
it just came into my head. I thought it was a good thing to call
her but she didn't. She got as red as a beetroot then. Yup, I said
again, ya gotta pay the old tax Mrs Nooge, and I stood there
with my thumbs hooked in my braces like a Western old timer.
She got all heated up then oh yes hot and bothered. Philip didn't
know what to do he had given up the idea of investigating the
pig toll tax I think he just wanted to get away altogether but I
couldn't allow that until the pig toll tax was paid, that was the
rules of pig land I told them. I'm sorry I said like they always do
when they're asking you for money, if you ask me its far too
much but that's the way it is I'm afraid. It has to be collected
someone has to do it ha ha. She tried to push her way past then but
I got a grip of her by the sleeve of her coat and it made it all
awkward for her she couldn't see what was holding her back.

Her hat had tilted sideways and there was a lemon hanging
down over the brim. She tried to pull away but I had a good
tight hold of the sleeve and she couldn't manage it.

   Durn taxes, I said, ain't fair on folks. When I looked again
there was a tear in her eye but she wouldn't please me to let it
out. When I saw that I let go of her sleeve and smiled. Right, I
says I'll tell you what, I'll let you by this time folks but
remember now in future − make sure and have the pig toll tax
ready. I stood there staring after them, she was walking faster
than Philip trying to fix the lemon at the same time telling him
to come on. When they were passing the cinema I shouted I
ain't foolin' Mrs Nooge but I don't know if she heard me or
not. The last thing I saw was Philip turning to look back but
she pulled him on ahead.

A fellow went by and I says to him do you know what its a bad
state of affairs when people won't pay a tax to get by. Who are
you he says. Brady I said.

   He was wheeling a black bike with a coat thrown over the
handlebars. He stopped and rested it against a pole then dug
deep in the pocket of his trousers and produced a pipe and a tin
of tobacco. Brady? he says, would that be Brady of the Terrace?
That's right I says. O, he says, I see. You see what, I said. Your
father was a great man one time, he says. He was one of the best
musicians ever was in this town. He went to see Eddie Calvert,
he says then. I said I wanted to hear no more about Eddie
Calvert. You don't like music, he says, do you think the town
will win again Saturday? I told him I wanted to hear nothing
about football either. You don't think its a great thing the town
won the cup? he says. No, I says. I said it was a pity they didn't
lose. I see, he says, well what's this tax you're talking about, you
seem to care about that. He was all on for a discussion about the
government and the way things had gone. There was a smell of
turf fires and buttermilk off him. He tapped the bowl of his pipe
against his thigh and he says which tax would this be now.

He thought it was some outrageous tax the government had brought in and he was about to say its time this quit or they have the country destroyed when I said ah no its not the government at all. It was invented by me, and its only the people I say.

And who are you, he says.

Francie Pig the Toll Tax Man, I says and he shook his head and tapped the pipe again, that's a good laugh he says.

Laugh, I said, I don't know where you get the idea its a good laugh. Then he said tsk tsk and you're an awful man altogether. He puffed on the pipe. Pig Toll Tax, he says, that's the first time I ever heard that now. He kept opening and closing his mouth over the brown stem like a fish smoking. Oh you needn't worry your head about it I said, it has nothing to do with you. What it really should have been called was The Mrs Nugent and Nobody Else At All Tax but I didn't tell him that. I see he says well in that case I'll be on my way.

His index finger jumped off his forehead *gluck now* he said and away off up the town with the bike sideways and the wheels ticking.

I went into the shop. The whine of the bacon slicer and the shopgirl licking a pencil stub racing up and down a wobbly tower of numbers on the back of a paper bag. The women were standing over by the cornflakes saying things have got very dear. Its very hard to manage now oh it is indeed do you know how much I paid for Peter's shoes above in the shop. When they seen me coming they all stopped talking. One of them moved back and bumped against the display case. There you are ladies I said and they all went right back on their heels at the same time. What's this? I says, the woman with three heads? When I said that they weren't so bad. Flick – back come the smiles. Ah Francie, they said, there you are. Here I am I said. They leaned right over to me and in a soft top secret voice said how's your mother Francie? Oh I says she's flying she's above in the garage

and it won't be long now before she's home. They're going to
give her a service I says, hand me down the spanner Mike! Ha,
ha, they laughed, that was a good one. Yup, says I, she has to
come home shortly now to get the baking done for Uncle Alo's
party. So your Uncle Alo's coming home! they said. Christmas
Eve I said, all the way from London. Would you credit that
now says Mrs Connolly with a warm little shiver, and will he be
staying long? Two weeks says I. Two weeks she says and smiled
I was going to say do you not believe me or something Mrs
Connolly but I didn't I had enough on my plate with Mrs
Nugent without Connolly starting. He did well in London,
Francie, your Uncle Alo, says the other woman. Then they all
started it. Oh he did well surely he did indeed, a great big job
and more luck to him its not easy in these big places like
London. It is not! Mrs Connolly'd say and then someone else
would say the same thing over again. It was like The History of
Alo programme. But I didn't mind. I said now you're talking
and all this. Mrs Connolly said: I saw him the last time he was
home with a lovely red hankie in his breast pocket and a
beautiful blue suit.

I seen him too, he was like someone in the government or
something.

He was indeed. It takes the Bradys, they said.

Every time, I said.

Good man Francie, said the women.

I'll tell Alo to call down and see you when he comes home, I
said, you can have a chat with him about London and all.

Do that Francie, they said. I will indeed, I said. Then I said
well ladies I'm afraid I can't stay here I have to be off on my
travels.

Dear dear aren't you a ticket Francie? they said.

I'm away off up the town on business to do with the toll tax.

Toll tax? I never heard tell of that now Francie. What would
that be?

Oh it's invented by me, I told them. But of course Nugent

won't pay it. You might as well be trying to get blood out of a stone.

Nugent? says Mrs Connolly, *Mrs* Nugent?

Yes I said. Well, be it on her own head. She won't be getting by so handy the next time.

They were all ears when they heard it was to do with her.

Getting by? But getting by *where*, Francie, they kept saying.

On the footpath I said where do you think, where else would you want to get past?

The footpath? they said.

Yes, I said again, *the footpath*. You'd think the three of them had gone handicapped all of a sudden the way they were staring at me.

I could see Mrs Connolly fiddling with her brooch and saying something out of the side of her mouth.

Then she said: There's no denying it Francie, you're a rare character!

The other two were hiding behind her now I think they must have thought I was going to stick them for a few bob tax as well.

Oh now I said and off I went out the door as I went by the window I could see Mrs Connolly saying something and the other women nodding then raising their eyes to heaven.

AIDAN MATHEWS
Nephritis

Aidan Mathews (1955–) began his fiction career with Adventures in a Bathyscope, *a collection of short stories which was shortlisted for the GPA book award and which John Banville – the eventual winner – described as 'the product of a unique talent . . . a very exciting debut'. His published work includes a novel,* Muesli at Midnight, *and a second collection of stories,* Lipstick on the Host. *He has won several awards for his poetry and for his plays,* The Diamond Body *and* Exit/Entrance.

'It begins with nephritis,' the consultant said, 'and it goes on from there.'

Jonathan could not decide the word he was looking for. Was it *terminal* or *terminus*?

'Is it fatal?' he asked.

'Yes,' the consultant said. 'We call it . . .' but just then the nurse who had shown Jonathan in and given him the *National Geographic* to examine for a half-hour, put her head round the door.

'Doctor,' she said, 'your wife says fine, but where and when, and is it all right if she leaves your off-white shirt out?'

'8.00 at Robbie's,' the consultant said, 'and no, it isn't. The cream one won't go with the club tie. Tell her this is senior faculty. Tell her the whiter-than-white one.'

Jonathan was afraid of asking the consultant a second time what he was dying of.

'So it begins with nephritis and it goes on from there,' he said.

'You got it,' the consultant said.

On the way out, the nurse called Jonathan over.

'Mr Wursmelt,' she said. 'On your Bluecross it says Wursmert; on your Mastercharge it says Wursmelt. What is it?'

'Wursmelt,' Jonathan said.

'Wursmelt is much nicer,' the nurse said.

Who could he tell this great thing to? Beth would not want to know. It had been five years since the divorce, and two since they had last slept together. Anyhow, he didn't know where she was now, or who she was with. There was his brother in Boulder, but Chuck would not know what to say, and it was unfair to put a person in a spot. One could not simply lift the phone and say 'Hi, Chuck, I am dying of something that begins with nephritis and goes on from there.' It would be an imposition.

Jonathan stopped at Just Browsing, the bookstore two blocks away from the Angel of Intercession Hospital. There was a coffee-bar at the back near the Science Fiction alcove where everybody brought the sex books to leaf through; and behind that, there was a men's room where he went and sat down in a cubicle with his trousers round his knees for a half-hour, and stared into space and read the graffiti and noticed a telephone number that was almost the same as his own.

People came and went. Jonathan was afraid to come out of the cubicle while someone was in the men's room: they would be sure to notice that he had done nothing. He tried to do something, but nothing happened. So he waited until the last hand-dryer had stopped working. Still, when he did come out into the coffee-bar, he knew that everyone was looking at him very obviously. The bookstore manager kept an eye on him too. Jonathan took a book on astrology from a shelf, and began to read Chapter Five.

'I want a piece of coffee-cake and a coffee too,' he said, avoiding the stare of the bookstore manager.

'The man wants a piece of coffee-cake and a coffee too,' the waitress said, serving him.

Jonathan's eyes watered.

'I am dying of something called nephritis,' he said.

'So?' the waitress said. 'I'm dying of boredom. The manager

is dying to get home. You're dying of whatever. We're all dying. Meantime, you owe me.'

But she came back a moment later.

'You look on the level,' she said. 'You mean it?'

'Would I lie?' Jonathan said.

'Not here,' the waitress said. 'Not in here you're not. I get off at 5.30, I have a date for 6.30, my hair's a mess, and my horoscope says at all costs avoid stress.'

Next morning, Jonathan called his psychiatrist.

'Long time no weepie-weepie, Jon,' Dr Smudgeon trilled. 'You fancy a weepie-weepie?'

'I'm dying,' Jonathan said, 'of something that begins with nephritis and goes on from there.'

'No kidding?' Dr Smudgeon said. 'You get your nephritis round here at 4.15, and we'll straighten it out.'

When Jon arrived at 4.15 Dr Smudgeon was squeezing in a saxophone player with a halitosis problem. He sat in the anteroom, and examined the *National Geographic* he had examined the day before. There was an article on a Zulu enthronement, a piece on a mining industry in Nebraska, and a shorter piece on the courtship ritual of the ant-eater. He whiled away the time, looking at the boobs of the Zulu women, and wondering.

Dr Smudgeon took some convincing. Jon had to tell him the consultant's fee before he believed him. Then he folded his hands; his face fell.

'This pains me, Jon. I am pained by what you tell me.'

Jon's eyes watered.

'There are four stages,' Dr Smudgeon said, 'each clinically observable. First, you're confused. Then you get mad. Then scared. Then mean. Then fat-al-is-tic.'

'That's five,' Jonathan said.

'What are we talking?' Dr Smudgeon said. 'Numbers? There are four stages, Jon. You are at Stage One. You feel this can't be happening.'

'No,' Jon said. 'I know this is happening. And I feel shy.'

'Jon, Jon,' Dr Smudgeon said. 'Who's the expert?'

When Jon got up to leave, Dr Smudgeon slid a book across the desk.

'For you, Jon,' he said. 'Tolstoy's *The Death of Ivan Ilyich*. It tells the story of a failure, a little man who has done nothing, experienced nothing, loved nothing, cared for nothing. He is told he is going to die. Bedoinng! It might help. It might help you, Jon.'

Jon gave a farewell party for his relatives and friends. Also, he wrote to Beth. 'Dear Beth,' he wrote, 'I am dying of something that begins with nephritis and goes on from there. I am giving a farewell party for my friends and relatives. I know it is five years since the divorce, and two since we last got together, but you are more than welcome. You know that. Your affectionate ex-husband, Jon.'

Beth did not come. Chuck could not make it either. But Jon's boss made it, and his wife and her boyfriend and his boyfriend. Most everyone made it. Jon went out onto the balcony and thanked God that there were so many people he could call on, and to think that he had called them on the Wednesday for the Friday coming. He mentioned this in his speech.

'I feel very humble that you should all make it,' he said. 'There is plenty of food and plenty of booze too. I want to see it all gone. And I should like to say a special word of thanks, of real appreciation, to the caterers. Thank you, one and all, those whom I have known a long time, and those whom I have come to know and to value by meeting them here for the first time tonight.'

Everyone was very nice, going. And the boss's wife, who had always only nodded at Jon so that the celery stalk in her mouth bobbed up and down, pressed his hands as she left, and said 'I think you're just *wonderful*.' Not alone that, but when she came back a minute later to retrieve her doeskin glove that she had mislaid in the bedroom, she had said it again.

Jon lay back on his pillow, smelling a faint trace of eau-de-cologne on the border of the duvet, and decided to remember the whole evening again, from the very first to the very last moment.

The next day, he called Dr Smudgeon.

'I am going to Italy,' he said. 'I am going to die in the Eternal City, or some nice resort where I can hear church-bells.'

'That's nice,' Dr Smudgeon said. 'That's constructive, Jon.'

A half-hour later, the doctor called back.

'Jon,' he said. 'I'm interested in your case. I'm writing up my PhD on Bereavement Structures, and I want to lighten it, leaven it, get a little of the Small Man, the Middlebrow, into it. Jon, send me postcards: how you feel, what you're going through, what angers you.'

'You think that could be useful?' Jon said.

'Jon, I'm talking National Book Awards.'

'I would be honoured,' Jon said, taking more care than usual not to use contractions. 'I would be honoured, Dr Smudgeon.'

When the phone rang the third time, Jon was startled. He had not noticed it was getting dark already.

'Jon,' Dr Smudgeon said. 'My kid collects stamps. Why not? Kids go through a stamp phase, they go through a coin phase. My kid's at the stamp phase. So, on the postcards, Jon, as many *different* stamps as you can manage. For Timmy. Maybe some Vatican stamps if you're in Venice. I joke, Jon, I joke. The psychiatrist is not without a sense of humour. As many stamps as poss., OK?'

'Shall do,' Jon said.

The resort he chose was on the Adriatic. It was called Poggio, but that was all right. Jon would have preferred a more sonorous name, but, in every other respect, Poggio looked just like what a Mediterranean port should look like. There were men with moustaches, women in black with enormous boobs, cafés where sailors stubbed their cigarettes on white metal table-tops, children that peed against the running boards of old motor-cars, fat nuns, thin nuns, tall priests, short priests, fishing nets on the wharf that people stood beside to have their picture taken, and American students with Canadian flags on their backpacks to whom Jon would always reply in the one bit of Italian – or was it Spanish? – that he knew.

'Che sera, sera,' he would say, whenever they approached him.

Mostly he walked the waterfront; sometimes, he sat in bars. Once or twice, while he was sitting down, he had the feeling that he was in an elevator that was descending too quickly. Then he would order a beer, and not finish it. How strange it was to think that, out of all the people in the place, he alone had been singled out to be afflicted (or was it inflicted?) with something that began with nephritis and went on from there.

He met a young French woman, who had known two people at the Sorbonne. Her name was Suzanne. She had wet lips, fingernail polish on her toe-nails, and was a little tubby from a high-dosage oestrogen pill. She was in Poggio to make lire in order to journey on to Athens to make drachmai by minding babies for women who could afford that kind of thing. Then she would travel by train, boat, and foot, to Istanbul. When she got there, everything would work out.

'Perhaps not,' he said. 'You may be seized, and locked into a harem. You may be violated abundantly.'

'Slower, please,' she would say. Finally, she asked him. 'And you, what do you do in Poggio?'

'I die,' he said, 'of a sickness.'

'You what?' she said.

'I go aaaahhh!' he said, clutching his side.

At last, she seemed to understand. After that, they slept together. She would lie her head on his shoulder; all night her mouth wet him. He would play with her as she slept, and walk his fingers up and down her back when the sheet fell off her down the side of the bed.

Jon needed to be certain. He had the desk-clerk translate for him. 'I am dying of something that begins with nephritis and goes on from there,' he said to her. She answered hurriedly. Her distress was very obvious to Jon. His eyes watered.

'She say,' the desk-clerk began, 'that she suffer for you. She say that she will not believe this to be so. She say you are too strong, too handsome, to be sick. She ask: is it contagious?'

A Franciscan monastery had not quite closed at the top of a hill overlooking Poggio. Jon went there, in the funicular. He found a young monk – or was he a priest? – sitting, twirling the rotative postcard stand.

'I am dying of something that begins with nephritis, and goes on from there,' he explained. 'I want to lay my head down in this place, if that is permissible. I would, of course, make a contribution towards whatever.'

'My son,' said the monk, 'level with me. Are you for real?'

'Would I lie?' Jonathan said.

'I believe you,' the monk said. 'I believe you. The important thing is not to be morbid. The Christian stands for affirmation. Christianity is about struggle, about immersion in a world in which the proletariat of the industrial West and the living dead of the Third World are ground down beneath the feet of the consumer capitalist. Do you realize how many people in this world would *eat* Purina Cat Food? And you talk to me about nephritis.'

'It's not nephritis,' Jon said. 'It begins with nephritis.'

'It has to begin somewhere,' said the monk. 'You have to let it grow. You have to make it an experience of growth. Only then can it be a growth in experience. You want to stay, you got a bed. Any questions?'

'Yes,' Jon said, 'St Francis . . .'

'Probably gay,' said the monk. 'Rome has the files.'

'What I mean,' Jon said, 'is this: did St Francis say Brother Death or did he say Sister Death?'

'He was very flexible,' the monk said. 'He was a very understanding man.'

When Jon returned to the hotel, the assistant manager was waiting in the foyer with the desk-clerk.

'Mr Wursmelt,' the assistant manager said. 'I'm so sorry, so very sorry. Nephritis, they tell me. Still, you must understand: this is a family hotel. If anything – God grant otherwise – were to happen; if, in short, you were to become acutely nephritic, other guests might think it was the food. My competitors would make hay of your most lamentable illness.'

'It's not nephritis,' Jon said. 'It only begins with nephritis.'

'But where does it end, Mr Wursmelt? Is that not the question? Where does it end?'

Later that evening, after the beef stroganoff, after the apple-strudel, after the cappuccino with peppermint schnapps, after the blue pill and the green pill and the vermilion pill, Jon sat in his chair in the dining-room of the hotel, and felt the elevator feeling. When it passed, he went to reception and settled his account.

'You will come again to Poggio,' said the girl at reception.

'I am going aaaahhh!' he said, clutching his side.

'I understand,' the girl at reception said. 'You are right. It is very beautiful.'

When he went to his room, Jon called the hotel operator.

'I want to make a collect call, long-distance,' he said. 'To a Dr Smudgeon in Manhattan.'

'Give me the number, sir,' she said. 'I ring you back.'

Minutes passed. In the background, the radio clock blinked.

'Dr Smudgeon says he can't take collect calls, Mr Wursmelt.

He says that it's very important that you should understand his reasons. They are strictly financial.'

'Of course,' Jon said. 'I'll pay.'

'Shall I put it on your bill, sir?' she said. 'Your account says Worsmelt, but I notice that your Masterchage says Wursmelt. What is it?'

'It begins with nephritis,' Jon said, 'and then it gets so much worse.'

BRENDAN O'CARROLL
From *The Mammy*

Brendan O'Carrol (1955–) was born in Dublin and grew up in Finglas. He is now one of Ireland's most famous and controversial comedians. The Mammy is his first novel.

29 MARCH 1967 – DUBLIN

Like all government buildings, the interior of the public waiting room in the Department of Social Welfare was drab and uninviting. The walls were painted in three colours: 'Government green,' as it was known to all in Dublin, on the bottom half, and either cream or very old white on the top half, with a one-inch strip of red dividing the two. The only seating consisted of two pew-like wooden benches – these were covered in gouged-out initials and dates. Lighting was provided by one large opaque bowl-like fixture hanging from a six-foot cable in the centre of the high ceiling. The outside of the bowl was dusty, the inside yellowed and speckled with fly shit. In the bottom of the bowl lay a collection of dead flies.

'Serves them right,' said the woman staring at the globe.

'What? Serves who right, Agnes?' her companion asked tenderly.

'Them, Marion.' She pointed to the globe. 'Them flies ... serves them right.'

Marion looked up at the globe. For a couple of minutes they both stared at the light.

'Jaysus, Agnes, I'm not with yeh ... serves them right for what?' Marion was puzzled and not a little concerned about Agnes's state of mind. Grief is a peculiar thing. Agnes pointed at the globe again.

'They flew into that bowl, right? Then they couldn't get out, so they shit themselves and died. Serves them right, doesn't it?'

Marion stared at the globe again, her mouth slightly open, her mind trying to work out what Agnes was on about. Agnes was now back scanning her surroundings; the wall-clock tick-tocked. Again, she looked at the only other person in the room. He was a one-legged man, half-standing, half-propped up at the hatch. She heard him making his claim for unemployment benefit. He was a 'gotchee', a night watchman on a building site. He had just been sacked because some kids had got on to the site and broken the windows. The girl was 'phoning his former employer to ensure he had been sacked and had not left of his own accord. Agnes was trying to imagine what it must be like to be sacked. Being self-employed, she had never been sacked.

'Fuck them.' Marion broke the silence.

'Who?' asked Agnes.

'Them flies,' Marion pointed. 'Fuck them, you're right, shittin' on everything else all their lives. Serves them right! Oh Agnes, is this fella goin' t'be much longer? I'm bustin' for a slash.' Marion had a pained expression on her face. Agnes looked over the man's shoulder. The girl was just putting the phone down.

'She's nearly finished. Look, there's a jacks outside in the hall, you go on, I'll be all right. Go on!'

Marion bolted from the waiting room. At the same time the girl returned to the hatch.

'Right then, Mr O'Reilly. Here's your signing-on card. You will sign on at hatch 44, upstairs in Gardiner Street at 9.30 a.m. on Friday, okay?'

The man looked at the card and then back at the girl. 'Friday? But this is Monday. Yer man wouldn't pay me and I've no money.'

The girl became very business-like. 'That's between you and him, Mr O'Reilly. You'll have to sort that out yourself. Friday, 9.30, hatch 44.'

The man still did not leave. 'What will I do between now and Friday?'

The girl had had enough. 'I don't care what you do. You can't stand there until Friday, that's for sure. Now go on, off with you.'

'He's a bollix,' the man told the girl.

She reddened. 'That's enough of that, Mr O'Reilly.'

But he hadn't finished. 'If I had me other leg I'd fuckin' give it to him, I would!'

The girl bowed her head in a resigned fashion. 'If you had your other leg, Mr O'Reilly,' she snapped, 'you would have caught the children and you wouldn't be here now, would you?' She closed the doors of the hatch in the hope that Mr O'Reilly would vanish. He gathered himself together, slid the card into his inside pocket, put his glasses into a clip-lid box and propped his crutch under his arm. As he made for the exit he said aloud, 'And you're a bollix too!' He opened the door of the waiting room just as Marion got to it.

'That one's only a bollix,' he said to her and, surprisingly quickly, headed off down the hallway.

Marion looked after him for a moment and then turned to Agnes. 'What was that about?' she said as she took her seat beside her friend.

Agnes shrugged. 'Don't know. Did yeh go?'

'Yeh.'

'All right then?'

'I'm grand. Jaysus, the paper they use here cuts the arse' off a yeh.'

'That auld greaseproof stuff?'

'Yeh, it's like wipin' your arse with a crisp bag.'

'Well, what are you waitin' for?'

'I was waitin' on you to come back. Come on.'

The two women went to the hatch. Agnes pressed the bell. They heard no sound.

'Press it again,' said Marion.

Agnes did. Still no sound. Marion knocked on the hatch doors. Behind, they could hear the sound of movement.

'Someone's comin',' whispered Agnes. Then, as if she was preparing to sing she cleared her throat with a cough. The hatch opened. It was the same girl. She didn't look up. Instead she opened a notebook and, still with the head down, asked, 'Name and social welfare number?

'I don't have one,' Agnes replied.

'You don't have a name?' The girl now looked up.

'Of course she has a name,' Marion now joined in. 'It's Agnes, after the Blessed Agnes, Agnes Browne.'

'I haven't got a social welfare number.'

'Everybody has a social welfare number, Missus!'

'Well, I haven't!'

'Your husband – is he working?'

'No, not any more.'

'So, he's signed on, then?'

'No.'

'Why not?'

'He's dead.'

The girl was now silent. She stared at Agnes, then at Marion.

'Dead?' Both women nodded. The girl was still not giving up on the numbers game. 'Do you have your widow's pension book with you?'

'I haven't got one, that's why I'm here.'

'Ah, so this is a new claim?' The girl felt better now that she had a grasp of what was happening. She lifted a form from below the counter. Both women shot glances at each other, a look of fear crossing their faces. They regarded the answering of questions on forms as an exam of some kind. Agnes wasn't prepared for this. The girl began the interrogation.

'Now, your full name?'

'Agnes Loretta Browne.'

'Is that Browne with an "E"?'

'Yeh, and Agnes with an "E" and Loretta with an "E".'

The girl stared at Agnes, not sure that this woman wasn't taking the piss out of her.

'Your maiden name?'

'Eh, Reddin.'

'Lovely. Now, your husband's name?'

'Nicholas Browne, and before you ask, I don't know his maiden name.'

'Nicholas Browne will be fine. Occupation?'

Agnes looked at Marion and back at the girl, then said softly, 'Dead.'

'No, when he was alive, what did he do when he was alive?'

'He was a kitchen porter.'

'And where did he work?'

Again, Agnes looked into Marion's blank face. 'In the kitchen?' she offered, hoping it was the right answer.

'Of course in the kitchen, but which kitchen? Was it a hotel?'

'It's still a hotel, isn't it, Marion?' Marion nodded.

'Which hotel?!!' The girl was exasperated now and the question came out through her teeth.

'The Gresham Hotel in O'Connell Street, love,' Agnes answered confidently. That was an easy one. The girl scribbled in the answer and moved down the form.

'Now, what was the cause of death?'

'A hunter,' Agnes said.

'Was he *shot*?' the girl asked incredulously. 'Was your husband shot?'

'By who?' Agnes asked this question as if the girl had found out something about her husband's death that she didn't know herself.

'The hunter, was your husband shot by a hunter?'

Agnes was puzzled now. She thought it out for a moment and then a look of realization spread over her face.

'No, love! A Hillman Hunter, he was knocked down by a Hillman Hunter – a car!'

The girl stared at the two women again, then dismissed the

thought that this was Candid Camera. These are just two gobshites, she told herself. 'A motor accident . . . I see.' She scribbled
again. The two women could see that she was now writing
on the bottom line. They were pleased. But then she turned the
form over to a new list of questions. The disappointment of
the women was audible. The young girl felt it and in an effort
to ease the tension of the two said, 'That must have been a
shock.'

Agnes thought for a moment. 'Yeh, it must have been, sure
he couldn't have been expecting it!'

The girl glanced around the room, wondering could it be
possible that there *was* a hidden camera after all. Again she
dismissed it.

'Right, then, let's move on. Now, how many children do you
have?'

'Seven.'

'Seven? A good Catholic family!'

'Ah, they're all right. But yeh have to bate the older wans to
Mass.'

'I'm sure. Eh, I'll need their names and ages.'

'Right! Let me see, Mark is the eldest, he's fourteen; then
Francis, he's thirteen; then the twins, there's two of them,
Simon and Dermot, twelve, both of them; then Rory and
he's eleven; after him there's Cathy, she was a forceps, very
difficult!'

'It was, I remember it well. You're a martyr, Agnes,' Marion
commented.

'Ah sure, what can you do, Marion. She's ten; and last of all
there's Trevor, the baby, he's three.'

The form had been designed to accommodate ten children so
there was plenty of space left. The girl ran a line through the last
three spaces and moved on to the next section. In the back of
her mind she wondered what it was between 1957 and 1964 that
gave Mrs Browne the 'break'!

'Now, when did your husband die?'

'At half-four.'

'Yes, but what day?'

'This mornin'.'

'This morning! But sure, he couldn't even have a death certificate yet!'

'Ah no, not at all – sure he didn't even go past primary!'

'No, a *death* certificate. I need a death certificate. A certificate from the doctor stating that your husband is in fact dead. He could be alive, for all I know.'

'No, love, he's definitely dead. Definitely. Isn't he, Marion?'

Marion agreed. 'Absolutely. I know him years, and I've never seen him look so bad. Dead, definitely dead!'

'Look Mrs . . . eh, Browne, I cannot process this until you get a death certificate from the hospital or doctor that pronounced your husband dead.'

Mrs Browne's eyes half-closed as she thought about this. 'So, if I can't get this until tomorrow, I'll lose a day's money?'

'You won't lose anything, Mrs Browne. It will be back-dated. You will get every penny that's due to you. I promise.'

Marion was relieved for her friend. She poked her in the side. 'Back-dated, that's grand, Agnes, so you needn't have rushed down at all.'

Agnes wasn't convinced. 'Are you sure?'

The girl smiled. 'I'm absolutely sure. Now look, take this form with you – it's all filled in already – and when you get the death certificate, hand them both in together. Oh, and bring your marriage certificate as well, you'll get that from the church that you married in. In the meantime, Mrs Browne, if you need some money to get by on just call down to the Dublin Health Authority Office in Jervis Street and see the relieving officer there.'

Agnes took all this in. 'The relieving officer, Jervis Street?'

The girl nodded. 'Jervis Street.'

Agnes folded the form. She was about to leave but she turned back to the girl. 'Don't mind that one-legged "gotchee". You're very good, love, and you're *not* a bollix!'

With that, the two women stepped back out into the March sunshine to prepare for a funeral.

NOEL McFARLANE
Lucky Singing

Noel McFarlane (1956–) is a journalist with the Irish Times. *He has written screenplays, essays, humorous columns and short stories. 'Lucky Singing' appeared in* True to Type, *a collection of short fiction by* Irish Times *journalists.*

Dear Jacob,

It appears that I've just returned from my Christmas sortie to Dublin, Ireland, but really, that's only a guess. I remain seriously disoriented. I seem to be in my apartment as I write, by the window where we've talked so often. A slow, immensely silent fall of snow has just begun to fill the night here now, smothering the lights of the Jersey Shore, falling lazily through the street-light amber, falling endlessly into the black Hudson.

My mind is spent utterly, everything has an ethereal aura. I look like a bum.

I do not have memories of those three days, I re-experience a series of bizarre tableaux. I perceive them chiefly through a haze of unprofessional, exasperated puzzlement, and a new, autumnal, 'artistic' melancholy. I still smell alcohol. They clubbed me to my knees with drink.

Jacob, I could not really figure one of the bastards out, they would not stop spinning, they would not stop singing. Geraldine says: Why do you have to poke, fiddle and feck (trans: to touch interferingly) at everything and everyone? Weren't they only enjoying themselves, sure wasn't it Christmas? But Jacob, it wasn't Christmas, it was them. Three hundred dollars an hour I command, from the most celebrated and committed neurotics in Manhattan, and I could not get a functional, meaningful handle on one of 'her people'. One moment of deduced certainty would have fulfilled me. Instead, they crippled me with beauty.

As I wrote you previously, I went to Dublin with Geraldine

to 'display' for her family, my prospective in-laws. I think you met her once in the early stages (hair like polished sequoia, good teeth, great soul, tenacious mind, paradisal torso), you would remember if you had. Relax, she told me, they only want a lookatcha. And remember, these aren't your crowd from the Village, the painters that won't paint, the dancers that won't dance, the birds that can sing and won't sing, just give yourself a bit of a break out of that and relax.

I was indeed intent on relaxing, for calm is a requisite of intuitive seeing, as you know. I was keenly interested in the family as crucible. Well, you would, wouldn't you? But wait, Jacob, what a selfish schlemiel I am, even though I am beset. How was Hanukkah in Saudi? Your mother calls me for reassurance after every news show on 'the situation': whenever Henry Kissinger is on, I have to spot her fifteen milligrams of Valium. I do my best with her. I tell her you are quite safe out there, that the army doesn't put its expensively educated, newly graduated shrinks into battle zones. You know that she responds to pragmatism best – the brand of the camps, again. So I lie a little. It is for love.

Your last letter says you're working out of a tent. I can hardly imagine. My patients won't divulge their names unless they have their tushes in one of those thousand-dollar New Age pseudo-thrones from Ethan Allen, while surrounded by twenty-five thousand dollars worth of 'permission-indicating' South American folk art.

Geraldine despises them, I'm afraid. It's a difficulty. And, of course, immediately upon meeting her, they pant and drool after her effortless certitude: I know, she says, they're gas (trans: humorous). She had a wonderful time in Dublin, of course. She's sleeping now. When I saw her sleeping earlier, I could not rid my mind of what her father (aka Guard Tumelty, the Super Tumelty, Mister Tumelty) bayed at me over the endless, raucous communal singing and the blaring TV. He is a detective. His eyes rove constantly, like searchlights; I saw at once that they are utterly unconnected to his thoughts. He is a brute of a man, rigorously mercurial. He said: So, I hear tell you want my young one's hand, wha? Well, you've had everything else, doctor, be all accounts.

And then, an unselfconscious display of dentures, a jailer's cackle.

I slept through most of the flight (I had tap-danced for half-a-dozen of my very surliest suicidals all day). The passengers were clearly Irish, all right. I hazily recall great gales of mindless communal singing from various parts of the aircraft: 'Jingle Bells' and 'White Christmas' were popular, of course, as was a positively Bavarian concoction about 'The One Road'. But, from those who sounded drunkest, I'll stake my reputation on the fact that I heard Catholic hymns, bellowed, sourly, in Latin! A thought: how we love our jailers, for where would we be without them? Answer: terrified by freedom!

Serious turbulence brought me to semi-wakefulness at some point. I recall seeing an entire aisle of them, probably a family, all in desiccated Christmas party hats: they were staring wide-eyed at nothing, like snared animals, as they carefully rode the jolts. Empty bottles clinked at their feet, having overspilled their tables. I noted that while their left hands clutched glasses containing morbidly large doses of alcohol, their right hands fidgeted in the gloom under the seats – they were fingering their prayer beads!

However, my experience upon touching tarmac in Dublin was particularly unique. From the rumpled, suddenly grinning ranks came an explosion of intense applause! I was close to astonishment. Do they do that every time they touch down, I asked Geraldine. She supposed so. But what did it mean, I asked. Could it be that they were expressing gratitude to the pilot for, essentially, not killing them? She whitened her lips. If so, didn't this betray a very unusual group demeanour or picture of the group self, I mused. Give it a rest, Theo, Geraldine said. But surely they knew the pilot couldn't hear them, anyway, I said, it was like children applauding in the movie theatre. Now that's enough, Mr Cleverality, she hissed, and it the mouth (trans: threshold) of Christmas.

There appeared to be a thousand members of her extended family waiting in a wary silence in the airport: I felt like Michael Caine in 'Zulu'. I knew many from photographs. Geraldine is the third youngest, Jacob, in a family of nine, *nine!* the married members of which carry on the torch of unremitting reproduction. They had all been drinking.

As I neared the group and began the ceremonial handshakes, something unusual led me to peruse the faces twice. I suspected initially that they were congenitally wall-eyed, or maybe even drunker than they appeared, but then I began to accommodate the reality of the matter – they were staring, in helpless fascination, at my nose.

Even her father, standing there in Prussian, patriarchal hubris, relented momentarily in his compulsive professional scanning of the other passengers to fix speculatively on it. And how is the man? he asked enigmatically. Man, I thought, what man? So I hung clever and wished him happy holidays. What appeared to be a frisson of comprehension, or relief, immediately suffused the troupe.

Well, happy em holidays, they said, with pure Elizabethan vowels, as they shook my hand and stared at my hooter, many adding strangely: and fair play to you, fair play to you now.

Geraldine was obliviously aglow. As she approached her father, the giant looked warily left and right, allowed a momentary emotional liquefaction, muttered something about a chicken (strange!) and engulfed her. I immediately sought signals of sib jealousy among the others, but noted none, just an unusual stoic acceptance of the primary place I had always suspected her of occupying with 'Me Da'.

Outside, the peculiarly wet, piercing chill was a shock, but the atmosphere amid the airport throng, of Christmas bustle and warm expectation, almost dissipated it. The family poured itself into a series of illegally parked cars, and, to my surprise, a large blue official police truck driven by a furtive man in a rumpled uniform, who confused me deeply by exuding an aura of unrestrained criminality and stealth. How is the for-um, he demanded heartily, adding, and happy whatever you're havin' yourself.

Downtown Dublin on Christmas Eve called to mind the Day of the Dead in Mexico City, but without any apparent religious inhibitions. The young were everywhere. Inebriated battalions of them marched about aggressively, bawling songs. Reeling figures palmed off walls, like injured running backs trying to slip tackles. There was candid drinking on the sidewalks, urination, passionate embracing, vomiting, and this inevitable, unending, frenzied singing. Aw, she's hoppin' all right, said the uniformed man very rapidly (opaque, Scandinavian-style accent, I thought, and he seemed to flaunt it). I hear tell tis dog wild in the Shtates, he said. I agree, I said cleverly.

My description of the dwellings in their home neighbourhood (Wightwall or Whyhall or somesuch) as townhouses, sparked volcanic hilarity among the driver, Geraldine's punkish cousins and others whom I did not know in the wired-off back of what they called 'the wagon'. We drove through chilly, pungent smog in what seemed like a labyrinth in a labyrinth. We stopped outside a house, where Geraldine's father stood in wait like a murderous sentry. I noticed as I hurried indoors from what was clearly serious air pollution that the house did not have a Christmas tree in its front window, as did every other house on the block.

The scene inside was to become a commonplace over the next two days. It engulfed and drowned me.

A compact strata of children and infants writhed on the floor of 'the kitchen' like snakes in a pit. A vast, perplexing kaleidoscope of people drinking morbidly spoke *at* each other without listening (this, especially, Jacob, struck mortally at my personal

and professional heart) alternating swiftly between what was
termed 'the slaggin' and remarkable familial tenderness and
insight: and there was individual and choral singing, some of it
sublime and transporting (I recall, through the sparkling gaiety
of early drunkenness, the shady uniformed policeman suddenly
throwing wide his arms and exploding into Puccini a foot from
my face) and some of it was infantile, drunken drech.

And of The One Song that Redeemed All But Me, more
anon.

As soon as I entered the house I noted the curious absence of
any sort of Christmas decoration. Also, there were ghostly
rectangles on the papered walls, where, I was sure, pictures had
recently hung. The Super Tumelty, holding an unmarked bottle
of clear liquid and glasses (they looked like doll's house props in
his paws) quickly cornered me, a drop now in hearty welcome,
he said, and poured a huge measure. Geraldine had warned me
precisely, twice: Now don't refuse a drink or two – they'll think
you're either an oul' oddity or an alcoholic.

I drank as he did, quickly: it approximated to drinking fire.
The second shot tasted, I felt, of trees, then bluish, pristine air.
So, how is tricks anywah, he said cagily. Tricks? I said. The line
of work, he said. Oh, I said, fine, and you? He shook his great
head. Aw, sure our hands is tied, he said, our hands is tied at
every turn. He lumbered off, the bottle raised before him like a
prow.

I said to Geraldine: do you guys not put up Christmas stuff
in this house? It's gas, she said, they don't want to, like,
upset you. Upset me? I said. Well, she said, me Ma told me
she found out 'your people' don't believe in Christmas, she
even took down her Sacred Heart! I was staggered. She
sniggered.

I began to note a certain scintillation in the air, as though
mood, the sadness of the evanescence of the moment, could
sparkle in the very oxygen. Distance, then intellection, began to
fluctuate curiously. I recall then the Super Tumelty slicing

professionally through the throng towards me with the bottle raised; I recall laughing recklessly; I recall kicking accidentally against a carton pushed under the tub in the bathroom and finding the pictures there (Christ and his heart, Christ and his mother, Christ with his bleeding palms). I then recall the sudden silence as I handed them with formal care to Mrs Tumelty in the kitchen: Go ahead and hang these up, I had said (according to Geraldine), let each believe in anything, for I believe in everyone. Anyway, it's his birthday, isn't it? A storm of laughter, backslaps, I was a terrible man, an awful man, a great man for 'a nerve doctor', they wouldn't be up to me, givis a song, have another and then a flood of childhood regression, the encompassing smell of my father, the smell of safety, as I was carried bodily by the Super Tumelty to a dark room filled with other sleepers — no, they were coats.

I woke with no hangover, but with a feeling of lightness, of intellectual potency. Then, as I 'remembered', I uncovered a large scab of guilt. I went forthwith to the kitchen to confront this guilt. Picking through the carpet of children, I was shocked to find (1) that it was midday and (2) that many 'visitors' seemed to be still there (or perhaps they had left and returned) along with what Mrs Tumelty termed 'the second shift'. I expressed sorrow for my behaviour generally and was immediately awash in forgiveness (how else would anyone survive there?): Twas jit lag, twas jit lag, gushed the singing policeman, who now wore an utterly disreputable suit.

The family, I was confounded to learn, had already toured several graveyards that morning for a cheerful seasonal visit with their multitudinous dead. So, the Shinto angle! I resolved there and then to attempt to desist from any further professional evaluation. Compared to these people, Jacob, the Jews are an open book.

There was a Christmas tree in the 'parlour', smelling like Maine and as bright as Broadway. There were ridiculous Santas on the walls, Christ with his heart, Christ with palms displayed (Oi, I should be so lucky!) and drunken paper streamers on the ceilings. The Super Tumelty cornered me once more, holding a teacup. I made this tay with holy water, he said foxily. He cleared his throat (I felt the vibration). Don't mind me asking you, he said, but are you allowed turkey? Isn't it the pig ye're not allowed?

Acceptance defeats perplexity, I was learning, Jacob, and merely said yes.

A notable trio entered as I finished my second cup of 'tay'. Two were clearly detectives. They wore enormous, shapeless jackets and a sense of stoicism that I liked intuitively, or perhaps it was the tay about its work: the third man, a tired, shabby young man in denims, wore handcuffs.

The Super Tumelty, who had been reading a newspaper in a show of furious suspicion, greeted them heartily. He then offered the young man his chair! Well well! He left the room as the handcuffs were removed. Through the crowd, which was, I noted painfully, beginning to talk *at* each other again, I saw a child offer the trio cake from a plate. The disreputable policeman made his way surreptitiously across the room, shook hands with the young man, spoke to him briefly and then slyly folded money into the young man's breast pocket.

I had thought initially that the young man was unwashed, or badly birthmarked (they live with anything that doesn't kill them immediately) but as I headed for the bathroom I recognized the unmistakable stain of Kaposi's sarcoma on his jaded face, his neck, the back of his hand. His breathing seemed sadly laboured.

There and then, Jacob, there was an agreeable rediscovery of self and mission: I am proud to say that he looked just like my kinda guy; his eyes were my workshop, he could make his pain mine if he so wished.

The Super Tumelty re-entered, and with a self-conscious, botched attempt at a flourish, presented him with a crystal

goblet and quickly filled it. I introduced myself as I passed, I
was Theo Schrine, shrink and medical doctor, if there was
anything I could do, he could ask. Well now fair play to you, he
said. And then, to one of his 'escorts': Is this the Harry that
doesn't agree with Christmas? The policeman, quickly: Now
Lucky, whist like a good man.

I stood in acute puzzlement at the bottom of the stairs by
the front door, examining a plastic object which was screwed to
the wall and which seemed for all the world to be a small
fingerbowl. A fingerbowl on the wall? Well, even they wouldn't
put a bird feeder indoors, I decided. A voice spoke suddenly at
my ear. The stealthy policeman in the disreputable suit had
materialized soundlessly there. Ya bless yourself wihha, he said,
tis for holy water, I'd dimonstrate only I've a whole lohha drink
took and I wouldn't have an hour's luck. He undid the bottom
buttons of his steamboat gambler's 'waistcoat'. He said: No
doubt you know the young lad inside has the AIDS? I did, I
said. Ah, he's game ball, he said, and I'll tell you why. He has a
young lad of five years. Says he to me once, I'm happy enough,
Bat – I've someone to folly me other than the Drug Shquad! We
feel for him.

The one Song That Redeemed All but Me was called for in
defence of peace, as darkness gathered. The Super Tumelty
had broken up a scuffle using only a magic mantra: Ah lads,
lads, the holy season! While he had the gathering's attention,
he placed a paw on his massive chest elegantly, as though
about to sing. Instead, he boomed: And now, a parting song
before the bit of dinner. I call on Mr Lucky Burke to fill the
bill. Good order please. There was an immediate tumult of
urging, Man Lucky! More power Lucky! Sing out Lucky! Yes,
Lucky!
    Lucky, I thought, indeed.
    The young man seemed very drunk now, or weary. He placed

his crystal goblet on the floor and his hands on his knees. He
reclined his head slightly and began to stare directly ahead, with
extreme avidness. I suspected he was seeing things. He was,
Jacob – I know that now. He was communing with whatever
transcending thing, with whatever wordless, vital cognizance
that had banished his anger and filled him with a sweet
acceptance.

For Jacob, I heard this sweetness overflow into the waiting
silence. He began to fill the room with a brown river of sound.
It awed me. The intensity, the compass, was so new to me. The
song flowed with the slowness innate to deep things.

> *On Raglan Road, of an autumn day,*
> *I saw her first and knew*
> *That her dark hair would weave a snare*
> *that I might one day rue.*
> *I saw the danger and I passed*
> *along the enchanted way,*
> *And I said let grief be a fallen leaf,*
> *at the dawning of the day.*

I was mesmerized, smitten, then devastated – and this, Jacob,
is what abides. I could not but watch the Irish as he sang: some
closed their eyes, smiling with the pleasure of the pain of it,
weeping, drinking deeply, smelling their children's hair.

I did not know and do not know now, Jacob, if this is in
some way 'of' them particularly, this faculty to bear witness to
elemental sadness, this capacity to shape enigmatic acceptance
into what shines and is exquisite.

Geraldine was watching me. I knew she would be. She knew
that I knew that she knew my precise anguish and yearning as I
listened to dying Lucky singing: what he poured out so sweetly
into adoring silence, I was condemned to poke, fiddle and feck
for, amid self-doubt, resistance and insult. She came and kissed
me. It was almost enough.

Thus, old friend, the snow falls for me tonight like the

shattered atoms of something I had placed high above and worshipped.

I may have to go and live with them, you know, and learn to sing.

Love,

Theo

RODDY DOYLE
Vincent

Roddy Doyle (1957–) won the Booker Prize in 1993 for Paddy Clarke
Ha Ha Ha. *His other works include the novels,* The Commitments,
The Snapper *and* The Van – *known as The Barrytown Trilogy –* two
plays, War *and* Brownbread *and a screenplay,* The Family. The
Commitments *and* The Snapper *have been made into successful films.
This short story, 'Vincent', was published in the* Sunday Independent
in 1988.

It had never been this bad before, never this full. It was a bit like
coming up to closing time on a Sunday but – Vincent looked up
at the clock behind the bar and subtracted ten minutes – it was
only half-four; six hours to go still.

– Vincent!

– Hang on; I'm comin'.

He could hardly get to the tables because of the shopping on
the floor and the babies crawling all over the place and the oul'
ones throwing out their arms when they were singing.

– FIFTY-FIFTY CASH BACK.

– FIFTY-FIFTY CASH BACK.

– LA LA LA LAAA.

– LA LA LA LAAA.

Every time some of them got up to go to the jacks, that gang
of oul' ones over there, they sang that; shaking their arses and
screaming laughing.

– FIFTY-FIFTY CASH BACK.

– FIFTY-FIFTY CASH BACK.

They'd been there for hours, surrounded by their shopping
bags and buggies. Some of their older kids were in Vincent's
class in school. It was mad.

– Vincy!

– Comin'! said Vincent.

He didn't want to put too much on his tray. He had to climb
over bags and children and it was getting slippy. He'd never
walked on a slippy carpet before.

– Vincy!!!

Vincent didn't answer. He was on his way. He took his
change off Leo the barman – he liked Leo – and stuffed it deep
down into his pocket.

– Crips.

There was a little young fella pulling Vincent's trousers,
holding a fifty-pence piece up at him.

– Wha'? said Vincent.

– Crips, said the little young fella.

– Here.

Vincent picked him up – he was heavier than he looked – and
got him to hang on to the counter so he could see over it.

– Tell Leo, he said.

Then he was off, heading for the far corner where Bertie
Gillespie and his mates were waiting for him. They'd give him
a tip; they'd given him two already. He skidded on someone's
My Little Pony but the pints stayed on the tray. He was getting
better at it.

– Vincennnt!

It was one of the Fifty-Fifty Cash Back oul' ones. She could
wait.

Bertie saw Vincent.

– Here's John Wayne, compadres, he said.

– Good man, Vincent, said Mr Rabbitte – Did yeh bring one
for this man here?

He had a turkey sitting on the stool beside him, dead; but the
way he had its head held up with his putter and 8-iron made it
look nearly alive; and the cigarette stuck in its beak.

– D'yeh want a chicken samage with your pint, son? Mr
Rabbitte asked the turkey, and they all laughed, Vincent as well.

He unloaded the tray.

– Lovely, said Mr Reeves, and he rubbed his hands.

— Vincennnt!

— Comin'!

Bertie had a load of selection boxes on the floor beside him. He was selling two of them to an oul' one Vincent didn't know.

— What's the Best Before date on them? she was asking Bertie.

— Never mind the Best Before date, said Bertie. They're grand. I tried them ou' on my own kids at home; they're grand. The chocolate's the righ' colour.

— Vincent; for Jaysis sake!

— I'm comin'!

He was holding out the change for Mr Rabbitte to take it.

— No, you're alrigh', said Mr Rabbitte.

— Thanks, said Vincent, and he tried to get back to the bar without looking at any of the people that were shouting at him and waving. That was what he'd got last year for Christmas; a selection box. And a pair of trousers for school because he'd been suspended just before the holidays for not having the right ones. (— Vincennt! Over here, love!) This year was better, he was getting HiTec runner boots; but clothes weren't really a present.

— Grab hold o' the other one there, Mary, an' we'll make a wish.

One of the oul' ones, Mrs Foster, had grabbed Vincent's leg.

— Let go o' me!

Vincent could feel his face getting scarlet. They were nearly getting sick laughing. There were five of them. It would take ages to find out what they wanted to drink; they'd have to make their minds up all over again.

— A gin an' a tonic, please, Vincent, said Mrs Foster. Wha' d'you want, Kay?

Vincent looked down at Kay. She looked up, closed her eyes, opened her mouth and —

— MEM-ORIES —

Ah shite, Vincent said to himself.

I'll be here all bleedin' night now.

− CAN BE BEUUU-TIFUL AN' THEN −

No way.

He turned and nearly ran to the bar, like your man Indiana Jones trying to get away from the big Malteser. (− Come back here, you, Vincent O'Leary!) He was on again this year, Indiana Jones.

He remembered his da coming in once when he lived at home, around Christmas, and he looked in the corner of the room and stared and staggered a bit, and said, Where's the telly? but he was looking in the wrong corner. He got twenty quid from his da last year, sent to him. In February.

− SCATTERED PIC-TURES −

He made it to the bar. The sweat was running off him; the way your woman'd grabbed him; she wasn't that old.

Leo was waiting for him at the counter.

− Now, he said.

He leaned over closer to Vincent.

− Trot out there for me now like a good man and find out what won the last race in Haydock; now.

− Okay, said Vincent, already on his way.

− Vincent; come here!

− I've to go on a message!

He stepped over a buggy and stood on a little young one sitting behind it. He looked down at her: she was deciding if she'd start crying or not. He kept going. It was getting louder in here; nearly more singing now than talking or laughing.

− COULD IT HAVE BEEN ALL-LLL − SO SIMPLE THEN −

− Vincennnt!

He pushed against the door and out, and it was lovely, the cold, in under his shirt and on his face. He didn't like the shirt. It was a white one, for work only, and it scratched. He'd had to give his ma back the money for it after he got his first pay.

It wasn't as mad out here. The Folk Mass choir were over outside Crazy Prices singing Feed The World, the saps. Across the carpark in the Community Centre there was a special little kids' disco on and Donkey Geraghty was trying to get into it on his horse. He was always doing that. The window of Mark 'n' Mindys, the hairdressers, was all steamed up. Vincent rubbed it but the steam was on the inside. He tried to look through it. There was a young one worked in there he liked; Anita Healy. She was nice. She knew his name. She was a bit older than him, a year and a bit, but he didn't think she was going with anyone. She wasn't really gorgeous looking; just nice – a few spots and that but not big mad red ones – and she said Howyeh to him when he said Howyeh to her, when there were none of the lads around to slag him.

He couldn't see her, just Mark trying to make some oul' one's hair stay up. There was a picture of Kylie Minogue stuck up in the window with an arrow pointing at her head and £10 at the other end of the arrow. That was what he'd got for his sisters for Christmas, Kylie Minogue's tape; three; one for each of them.

He went on.

He hadn't got his ma anything. He didn't know what to. He'd got her two of those salt and pepper yokes last year and she'd just looked at them and said Thanks, just looking at them. They were in the back of one of the presses, behind everything. He checked to see sometimes.

The Chinese chipper was black, packed; people coming out the door nearly. They were mad in there, the Chinese. One of them was lovely looking though.

Christmas was on a Monday this year, two days away only.

He went into Corals. The door was open.

He had to wash the dishes on Mondays, but maybe she'd let him off doing them this time because it was Christmas.

He wasn't sure where to look for Leo's result.

No way; she'd made him do them the last time Christmas had been on one of his days, Friday.

He'd been here in the bookies before but never to do anything. It wasn't that full. The telly was on but some of the men were looking up at a speaker, listening to the voice coming out of it. It was a woman's voice but Vincent hadn't a clue what she was saying; it was all crackly.

A man near Vincent, Gerrah Murray's da, said Shite on it! and threw a piece of paper on the floor and walked out. Vincent's da had brought him in here once and let him bet a pound on a horse, ages ago.

There was a fella with a huge belly up on a platform writing numbers beside the horses' names but Vincent didn't understand it. Then he saw Haydock in big print and lists under it. He pointed at the 3.30 list.

– Is tha' the last race? he asked a man beside him.

– That's it, said the man, unless they've installed flood-lights.

– Thanks.

There was a 2 and a 3 written with black marker beside two horse's names and a sort of bracket beside another one. That must have been the winner. He didn't want to ask.

He looked at the name for a bit to remember it, then went to the door. It was good in here. He was going to come in after Christmas and learn how to bet.

He ran, past Xtravision and the Chinese chipper, because he was cold now. He jumped up going past Mark 'n' Mindys to see if he could see in over the steam, but he couldn't.

– Vincennt!

– Vincent, over here, please!

Vincent pushed and slid through people and got to the bar.

– I SAY BLUE MOON –

OF KENTUCKY –

A-KEEP A SHININ' –

That was Larry O'Rourke. Barrystown's Elvis he called himself but he looked more like Barrytown's Freddy Boswell, the state of him; he was buckled.

Leo was waiting for Vincent.

– SHINE ON THE ONE –

THAT'S GONE AN' LEFT ME –

BELL-UE –

– Now? said Leo.

FIFTY-FIFTY CASH BACK

– Porky's Appendix, said Vincent.

Leo didn't smile or frown or anything. He pointed at the trayload of Guinness on the counter.

– Mister Gillespie, was all he said.

Vincent picked up the tray, to see if he'd be able to carry it. There were six pints on it.

– WEH-ELL –

IT WAS ON ONE MOONLIT –

NIGHHH' –

– Good man, Larry!

Vincent pushed his back into the crowd behind him ('Xcuse me, he said) and they opened a way for him when they saw the tray.

– Thanks.

Jesus, it was heavy. 'Leo had put beermats on it to keep the pints from sliding. Some of the oul' ones were going home to make the tea. He wondered would his ma come up here later. He hoped not. She didn't get drunk and sing or anything but – he hated seeing her with men that weren't his da.

– Watch it!

– Sorry, son – Clear the way there for Vincent!

– SHINE ON THE ONE –

THAT'S GONE AN' LEFT ME –

BLUE-UE-UE

They clapped and cheered and whistled.

– Yeow, Elvis!

He made it. He felt like they were cheering and clapping for him. The men helped him get the pints off the tray.

– Ah, good man, Vinnie!

Hey, Bertie, said a man a few tables away. D'yeh've anny o' them bits o' Berlin Wall left?

– Sorry, Compadre, said Bertie. Sold ou'. Selection boxes's all I have today.

– Wha' abou' perfume?

– Sold ou' as well, said Bertie. My twist, is it?

Vincent waited while Bertie rooted in his trousers for his money. (– When you're ready, Vincent!) He saw one of the oul' ones crying, one of the ones that was leaving. (– Vincennt!) The others were trying to stop her, none of them laughing and singing now: people at the other tables looking.

– Is that enough pesos, Vinny? said Bertie.

– Wha'? – Oh, yeah; yeah.

– Thank Christ, said Bertie.

Vincent remembered – he was only ten – he came down-stairs to get a few more of those satsuma yokes but really to see if there were any new parcels, big ones, under the tree and he could hear his ma crying and he kept going although he was scared now and he got to the kitchen door (– Vincennt!!) and his da had his ma's hair in his fist like he was going to pull her head down to his knee (– Vincent; come here, will yeh!) and his da saw him and stared at him as if he didn't see him and then he said, What're YOU lookin' at?

– Jaysis, Vincent, are yeh deaf or wha'!?

– Bertie, said Vincent – How much are the selection boxes?

– Wha'? said Bertie. – Here; take one. Go on; take it. I insist, compadre.

– Thanks, said Vincent. Are yeh serious? Thanks very much.

– No problem, said Bertie.

Brilliant; he'd something for her now. He'd get wrapping paper for it tomorrow.

— WEH-ELL —

SINCE MA BABY LEFT ME —

His ma loved Crunchies.

MARY MORRISSY
Bookworm

Mary Morrissy (1957–) is a short story writer and a journalist with the
Irish Times. *Her first book of stories,* A Lazy Eye, *was published to
critical acclaim in 1993. She has just finished work on her first novel.*

When I was at school you could buy a black baby. The images
of those hollow-eyed, skeletal children, flies on their eyelids,
the mortifying protuberances of their wrist and ankle bones
were part of our growing up. In our darkened classroom,
captives of the mote-flecked beam, they stole over the familiar
contours of blackboard and crucifix to the drowsy whir of the
projector. When the blinds were lifted with a disconcerting
snap, the nun would pass around a white, wooden collection
box, a smiling black cherub squatting on the top. The thud of
our coppers – ah, coins of nostalgia – made them seem distant
already, as if they had started their journey to parched lands.
And, sure enough, some months later, we would see more
pictures. Different children this time, flashing broad white grins,
happy in ill-fitting cast-offs, gathered outside crude school-
houses or beside village wells. Their faces pressed up eagerly
close to the lens as if to convince us that our pennies had
bought their smiles.

Sometimes a nun newly returned from 'the missions' would
talk over the slides. Always dressed in white creaseless cotton,
these nuns stood out in every way against the dour serge we
were used to. They were young, animated. They talked to us,
almost blamefully, of these children, of their hunger for learning,
of how they sat barefoot at pitted wooden forms, inherited from
the more privileged, engraved with hearts, names and messages,
all foreign to them. Or of how they lustily sang *our* hymns
which we merely mouthed. I imagined their voices to be harsh
and clear like the light which suffused each picture of their

homeland – as if the sun itself had lodged in their throats. There
seemed to be a purity, a simplicity in their lives which we were
to be forever denied.

I was reminded of them again when I saw this child in the
bookshop. She was about four or five years old. She was not
black, more the smooth honeyed colour of a half-caste. Her
tightly fuzzed hair seemed grizzled in the artificial light. I half-
expected her to be barefoot, but it was winter after all, and she
was muffled up in a grey duffel coat. She wore a stout pair of
brown, lace-up boots, oddly old-fashioned, the sort you see
children wearing in ageing sepia photographs. Her socks, a
bright canary yellow, were rumpled around her tawny ankles,
falling over the edges of the boots like some tropical throw-
back. Two golden studs pouted in her tiny ear lobes. She was
singing in that seemingly absent-minded, but strangely concentrated way that children do, repeating the same phrase monotonously until you long to supply the cadence. She was wandering
up and down between the shelves, one hand extended, so that
sometimes her finger would catch at the corner of a paperback,
sending it clattering to the floor or else curling the cover
slightly leaving a vague crease. This might annoy you if you
were fond of books. I know some people who won't lend books
in case you spill tea or drop cigarette ash on them, or bend
down the right-hand corner of the pages to mark how far
you've read. Or, worst of all crimes, turn them face down,
fracturing the spines. Since I have no respect for books, these
things do not worry me. You might think that strange since I
have spent so much time stealing books. But it is just that
sepulchral atmosphere in bookshops that makes them an easy
target. It is presumed that if you go into a bookshop that you
must love all that shiny merchandise, the glossy sheen of newly-
published paperbacks, their pages sticking together with new-
ness. You see them, these book lovers, caressing the stippled
covers of hardbacks or running their pale fingers over colour

plates. Sickening. That's why I liked this child. She showed the same disdain for them as I did.

I started off in the clothing trade, favouring large department stores with communal dressing rooms. I would choose two or three items, shirts or skirts, and neglect to take one of them off, putting my own clothes on over it. But then they started issuing little plastic counters for each item or using those white lug-like attachments, drooping from the clothes as blameless as the ears of a cocker spaniel, but which set off a frenzied bleeping at the door when you tried to take them out.

Anyway, I had grown tired of all those mirrors, and the sadness of seeing women disrobe revealing tired underwear, flesh-coloured bras, unseemly rolls of flesh and puckered elbows, and always, a light film of sweat on their brows. Their own clothes, sloughed from them, lay crumpled on the floor while they preened themselves before the mirrors – going up close, then retreating, flattening bulging bellies, pivoting around to profile and sweeping their hair high up on their heads in a strangely voluptuous manner, as if to lend grace to the outfit. But that was impossible. How could those rows and rows of corduroy and gaberdine be anything but graceless in the end? I recall with a shudder the flimsy polyesters, which gave off a tinselled static, as if something small and defenceless had been skinned in its making, leaving only a faint, silvered echo of its screams. Even the bright, floral cottons, with their great splashes of scarlet and magenta, seemed to languish in the fevered jungle heat.

No, bookshops are so restful in comparison, and much more hopeful. You can feel the bristling energy of hope rising off the books. All those authors earnestly offering themselves, in slim little packages, crying out for recognition from people like me. I wonder what it is like for *them* to walk into a bookshop and see slivers of themselves as if a surgeon had peeled off a section of their skin, bottled it, labelled it and set it on a shelf with a price. You're imagining already that I'm one of them, a disgruntled

writer never rewarded, wreaking her revenge. Not so, I have
never written in my life except for this dictated effort which will
be counter-signed at the bottom by a guardian-of-the-law. You
are asking for reasons, motives, as he is, as the psychiatrist will
when he is called at the court hearing to explain my aberration.
No one, you see, can accept blamefulness these days. A disturbed
childhood, he will say, the crushing pressure to perform academi-
cally, the failed university career. Ah yes, he will nod understand-
ingly, your father, the authoritarian figure with the scant education – 'sure I only went to the hedge school' – who both
revered and despised books. I remember him, a big, ruddy-faced
man with strangely trusting brown eyes, thumbing through my
schoolbooks, plucking phrases from them like a magpie, and
repeating them until he had beaten them senseless. And there
was my mother who devoured romantic novels, borrowed from
the library, encased in grubby plastic covers and printed in
insultingly large print for the short-sighted. She became like the
other bent old ladies we used to see at the library, who shuffled
between the shelves, white-haired and slack-jawed, holding the
books to their dry bosoms as if they were scented bouquets.

   The library incident will of course be dragged up. How at
seventeen, I invaded the local library, a municipal, red-bricked
edifice, courtesy of Andrew Carnegie, which squatted on the
high street under the shadow of the town hall clock. I walked up
the polished wooden staircase and into the reading room. The
door swung closed behind me and I went up to the desk. It was
as hushed as a church. All those bowed heads and the faint
rustle of paper, the odd agitated cough smuggled through the
imposed silence. I felt I had stumbled into a meeting of a secret
sect there in that high room, squares of pale winter sky conspir-
ing at the windows. I would not have been surprised to find
incense hanging in the air. There they sat, these pale monsters,
supplicant, awaiting some kind of proclamation. 'She asked for
information about beetles,' the short fat girl behind the counter
would explain to my mother who was called to haul me away. 'I

turned to look up the index and she just went berserk, sweeping her way through the shelves, flailing at the books, knocking them onto the ground . . . she was shouting, it was very disturbing. They are students here, not used to this sort of thing.'

I remember her outraged little face to this day, the wounded tone of her voice, her fingers clutching the worn edge of the desk. Sacrilege was the word on her lips.

She was wrong about the beetles. It was lice I was after, the humble booklice, or *psocoptera*, to give them their proper name. Wingless, they live indoors among old books and papers feeding on traces of mould. There is a whole army of them, well over a thousand species, gnawing the binding – they are partial to the paste – and piercing the pages of books with small holes. Having worked undisturbed for centuries, they were finally 'discovered' in 1701 when their ticking was traced to source in an English library. I am fond of such small industrious creatures – like the spiders who live in my bathroom. There are at least three of them, one permanently camped on the methyl green stain left by a tirelessly dripping tap. The other two, more social beings, snooze on the nether slopes of the enamel. I often sit on the bowl and watch them. They fight sometimes or perhaps it is some elaborate form of foreplay. Their tiny legs toy with one another, then lock in a vicious embrace. And then they part, retreating to resume their watchful torpor, lying motionless for hours. They disappear inexplicably for days, leaving the bath unembroidered. I often wonder what sprees they go on while they are away.

The spiders drove the last tenant out. She was terrified of them, and as if sensing her terror, they played malevolent tricks on her, lodging themselves under the light switch so her fingers would brush against their spongy bodies in the dark. She would run out into the hallway, hysterical, the neighbours tell me.

I like the squalor of the place. It is an old Georgian house, subdivided now, with sloping floors as if the mason who built it had been drunk or one-eyed. I prefer to think the structure has sagged in sympathy with those who tenant it. Even the rooms are lopsided, large windows squinting at both sides of thin partition walls, light bulbs dangling way off-centre, stucco work breached in midstream. The house overlooks the canal which is completely frozen over now. Winter dredges up the underworld debris. The rusty carcasses of cookers, cars, beds pierce the surface, always upended, Alp-like and ghostly. When it thaws they are submerged again, their season over.

My flat, of course, will throw more light on my activities. Like the tabloid image of suburban murder (the red-bricked house harbouring a grisly secret – a dismembered body, a bloodied hatchet?) the tools of my trade are innocuous enough – scissors and a blender. With the clothes there was no ritual of destruction. I tried hacking them with scissors or renting them with my bare hands, but they resisted. And, anyway, they looked more pathetic in their ragged pieces, they had more power over me. But there was mastery in destroying the books. I would first tear off the covers, then rip the pages out in clumps. I would cut each page into long thin strips and feed them to the blender. When they emerged they were like Michaelmas-daisies. I would stow them away in large plastic bags and weekly, I would leave the shredded offerings down on the street below, to be collected by dustmen. They would lie there beside the other bulging bags of tins, cartons, uneaten dinners and soggy tea-leaves. My bags were pristine, clean, as pure as a child in a christening robe. I would imagine their journey, mangled and crushed in the grinding, toothed lorry, smeared with the wretched saliva of household refuse, to be tipped out at the large dump by an angry, white-capped sea. Perhaps one or two pieces would remain unsullied, only to be haggled over by peevish seagulls, themselves the only white, clear beings on a landscape of greying, disintegrating humanity.

If that doesn't provide them with explanations, they may turn

to my politics, looking under my mattress for subversive literature. A socialist, perhaps, they will think, indulging in a warped
attack on materialism. Maybe. I once visited Moscow (more
evidence) but all I remember are the vegetable stores, miles of
shelves filled with cabbages, every one the same, and yet the
housewives mulled and hesitated, feeling this one and that,
weighing one against the other, as if *their* choice would make a
difference.

It is all vanity. My vanity was to look too long at a prissed-
up, coloured child in stout boots with a coarse accent and a
jabbing, accusing finger. 'Mammy, mammy, look at her, look,
she's taking them books.' And there I was, admiring the exotic
and imagining it untouched. I hesitated – the downfall of the
kleptomaniac – allowing the image of her sturdy, lithe limbs and
the dark pools of her eyes to capture me.

MICHAEL CURTIN
From *The Plastic Tomato-Cutter*

Michael Curtin lives in Limerick with his family. He has written four comic novels, The Replay, The Self-Made Men, The League Against Christmas *and* The Plastic Tomato-Cutter.

THE SOCIETY OF BELLRINGERS

There had always been a chaplain attached to the Society of Bellringers – a lame duck, a codger, an alcoholic, someone with a weakness best kept within the community. According to Donat, when he and Sam Brown and Charlie Halvey were newcomers, the incumbent was an ex-child molester. Occasionally – once in a blue fucking moon according to Charlie – we had a boss who was unremarkable. In the tower only Sam Brown failed to see the office as a sinecure. Clutching the hem of a cassock a new chaplain climbed the steps to the ringing chamber, cleaved a presence through the trap door and said: God bless the men. He was shown the photographs on the walls of all the ringers down through the years and sometimes went on up the ladder from the ringing chamber to see the actual bells. And then the chaplain withdrew, puzzled by the complexity of change ringing and was not seen again until the token appearance at the Christmas community dinner. No more was expected of him. Except by Sam.

On this hot and humid August Saturday evening we were coming out of a three month interregnum and expecting a new chaplain, Father Brock, a retired missioner. Hence my suit. The jacket hung from my finger over my shoulder as I strolled up the town. The peal was for the novena to Our Lady of Perpetual Succour, a crowded sodality of supplicants seeking a cure for cancer or the luck to pass exams – the simple largesse for which at some time or another we all thrust out the palm. I passed four houses of worship on the way and had left two more behind me, all within the city. Throw in half a dozen schools, two libraries, a few cinemas, a theatre, the enmeshed shopping and commercial sector, the pubs; one was all the way swaddled in the municipal cloak. The beauty of so much grey stonework held its own with the Georgian medical district when Donat reigned. The town then blended quickly into the necessary evil of the suburbs, but only for an acceptable distance before you were mercifully released into the countryside.

When I raised my eyes the tower and steeple of the Redemptorist church dominated and I was part of its elevation and on my way to play that part. Me, an agnostic Londoner. Going up the steps to the tower I slipped my arms through the sleeves and adjusted the knot of the tie. I was early but Sam Brown was there before me. He was wearing his best suit. Sitting down, smoking, apparently relaxed, Sam didn't fool me. He was excited. He lived for the bells. I walked around with my hands in my pockets. I didn't smoke, not since the day Jimmy Johnston took twenty quid off me in the Fulham Cosmo and told me the weed murders your game. Jimmy Johnston once took a ton off Tony Meo. So I gave them up when I was fifteen.

'New chaplain tonight, Sam.'

Sam waved his cigarette: 'For all we'll see of him, Tim.'

But I caught the hope in his voice. He shook his wrist free of the white cuff to see the time. 'We'll be lucky to have six with this heat.' That was settling for the worst muster. By Sam's standards all eleven members should have been present to meet the new chaplain, all wearing their best. We heard quick steps on the stairs. I opened the trapdoor. I said; 'Charlie.' But Sam knew Charlie Halvey's steps as those outside the bells might know another man's knock. Charlie owned the Statue of Liberty bar. He was a small man, stocky, and though he had thick grey hair he always wore a hat, a check, peaked affair with a tassel on top, the type beloved of otherwise sane golfers. Tonight he wore purple sneakers with yellow laces, the bottom of a green tracksuit and a red T-shirt. As he came through the trapdoor, he winked. 'God bless the men.'

Sam exploded: 'I suppose you think you're a comic, do you, Charlie? I suppose you think wearing rags worse than your usual rags is a blow for the tower, do you?'

Charlie dismantled his grin. 'Fuck me pink! Are you listening to him, Harding? You black English Protestant, do you hear him? I leave my fine pub in the hands of criminals, Jesus Christ Johnny Skaw is robbing me blindfold while I'm standing here and what do I get for thanks? I get shit for thanks. Sam Bollix Brown, I'm here, aren't I?'

'You could have put on something. Just for tonight. It wouldn't have killed you.'

'Like you? A suit? In this fucking heatwave? A tie strangling my neck and for what? Go on, where's the law says you're better dressed than I am, Sam Brown, get out the book, show me where it's written down.'

Sam would never be on Charlie's wavelength. And Charlie wouldn't bend. Sam looked at his watch again. 'Dr Donat's always here by now . . . five minutes . . .'

'. . . Dr Bollix . . . Dr Cunt . . .'

Outside of Sam, Donat and myself, all the other ringers were capable of arriving with seconds to spare. Charlie walked around, whistling, scratching his balls. Charlie sings in bank queues; he shouts at people across the street; roars up at painters on ladders. '. . . there's old Sloan . . . Jasus, will you look at the cut of Phil Thompson . . . look at bollix Yendall coming up the street . . . Simpson, smile and give the face an excursion . . .' Sam lit another cigarette. More footsteps. I turned to Sam: 'Paddy, George.' Sam took off his jacket. When they came through he asked immediately: 'Any sign of Dr Donat?' They both wore suits. No. No sign of Dr Donat. We all stripped – except Charlie – then Midge came. He didn't rush the stairs. He was the oldest since Jack Molyneaux retired. By the time Midge had his sleeves rolled up – a summer shirt inside a sleeveless jumper, Sam couldn't win them all – we were ready to ring. Only six. No Dr Donat. No chaplain. Mine was the number four bell over the trapdoor. I looked at Sam. He was sweating from more than the heatwave, the tower was cool. He nodded at me, said: 'Right.' I closed the trapdoor and we stood to our ropes.

Just as Sam was about to ease the treble out of its socket we heard a very slow step. I opened the trapdoor again. I said: 'Must be the chaplain, Sam.' Sam came to stand beside me watching the new chaplain negotiate his inaugural wheeze up the stairs. Sam greeted him. 'Father Brock, welcome to the Society.' Sam only had time to introduce himself and add his own title, Secretary. Brock sat down, out of breath. Sam launched us on the treble.

Standing on the trapdoor, ringing the number four in a six bell peal, I had the best seat in the house: I could watch Paddy, George and Sam in an arc to my right and when I was obliged by the changes to face left I had Charlie and Midge in my sights. And the new chaplain sitting. Brock had a bullet head with the vestiges of an old gym-hand's crew cut, accentuated by a round, fleshy face that he grabbed and pulled meditatively throughout the peal. But I could not tell if he was interested or just feigning attention. Sam's face was needlessly red since we were all good ringers and there was no danger of a clanger – for all his iconoclasm Charlie Halvey took his rope seriously. We finished the peal and Sam introduced Brock to 'the men'. Then Sam showed Brock the photographs. Sam was in most of them, from the early short back and sides to his present trendy if sparse fullness. Then Brock showed his jowled good humour: in response to Sam's invitation he looked mischievously up at the ladder leading to the belfry. He pleaded his age and said: 'Mr Brown, if you say the bells are up there I'll take your word for it.' Paddy, George and Midge laughed, the obedient appreciation of any old *mot* issued by those in authority. Charlie hated the black army. Sam was hurt. I didn't laugh. Then Sam started: 'It's a pity you missed our Dr Cagney, Father . . .' Charlie slid out of his mouth: 'Dr Prick.' Brock nodded away at Sam until he was able to shoot in: 'Well, I must thank you all so much, most enjoyable, I'll say goodnight to you now . . .' Even before Brock reached the foot of the stairs Sam was sitting with his fags out. 'He's not going to get in our way,' Sam said, loosening his tie.

I walked down town with Charlie. 'Harding, you black English Protestant, tell me how you stick it here. If I had your looks, your hair – Jesus to swap London for this kip – and that accent, I'd ride all round me. I'd shove it up from one end of the day to the other . . .'

'Charlie –'

'. . . when do I get my hole? I have to go to London for it. Know what a city is, Harding? All I want from a city? Fuck art galleries, and cathedrals and all that bollix I'll tell you what's a city. Give me an apple stand, a chipper and a brothel, that's a city and fuck the rest. To have the horn in this heat . . .'

'Charlie, I felt sorry for Sam tonight.'

'Fuck Sam. Did you see that big fat cunt back from the missions with the chubby cheeks and the belly. And they telling us all our lives don't have your usual full slice of bread and dripping during Lent, cut down on this, give up that, say your prayers to the statues in case you'd think of a pair of tits and your mickey'd stand up. Brock the bollix. And Sam's tongue hanging out to lick his fat arse. Oh, such a pity you didn't meet our Dr Cagney, Dr Donat. Dr Bollix . . . There's the Wank Mitchell, hey, Wank, how're they hangin' . . .'

'Thirty for a tenner, Charlie?'

'Fuck off. Forty. You black English Protestant robber.'

Outside the Drapers' Club Charlie grabbed my arm. 'It's sinful, isn't it, Harding, going in to a stuffy room to play snooker with the sun splitting the rocks. Fuck 'em. All the years they walked on us, you should be out jumpin' ditches in this fine weather, you should be on your knees, you should be in bed, you should be holy, you should be this, that and the other fucking thing. C'mon, we'll commit sin.'

The five tables were taken up. We watched old Simpson, Phil Thompson, Butsey Rushe and Wally Kirwan shuffle around in a four-hand. They seemed to take a month. When we were setting up the balls Charlie tried to psyche me. 'Get your tenner ready, Harding.'

I ate him. Charlie had to go to his Statue of Liberty. I went on to meet Donat in the Professional Club.

The Professional Club dated back to the turn of the century. Dr Donat Cagney was now its president, as his father, Dr John, had been before him. A founder member had given over the top floor of his Georgian town house for the Club's purpose. It was a place where the professional class met for a drink. Nothing more. But today the rest of the building was let in offices and the Club was a shabby couple of rooms catering for billiards and cards. It was a stipulation of the beneficent member's will that the top floor be retained by the Club through its trustees in perpetuity at a shilling a year. The professional class was an elastic term – doctors, solicitors, judges, Protestant clergymen, undertakers, dentists and later – by a nose – accountants, until Donat was finally goaded to sneer: 'Today, Tim, judging by our membership, auctioneering has become a profession. And building contractors. *Building contractors*, by Jove.'

It was early for the Club. I had a half of Guinness. De Courcy, a solicitor, and a guest were at the billiard table but of course they were playing snooker. I heard Donat once refuse De Courcy: 'Snooker? I'll have you know I'm a doctor, not a bookie.' In the far room I could see the television shadows flicker on the wall – a condition of its admittance had been that the set would not be visible or audible from the bar. I sat back in the cushioned armchair and waited for Dr Donat Cagney of Sexton Square.

He was carrying his bag which accounted for his absence from the tower. He wore a white flannel suit against the heat. Sockless sandals – attended at his Sexton Square residence every fortnight by a chiropodist. He was as handsome as he often said he was, the blond hair streaked with silver yet full of growth, curling over his shirt collar and around his ears. His affectation – a blond moustache – was nicotine stained. He bought his gin, sat in the chair opposite me, languid leg hanging over the arm.

'We lost Granny Eades, Tim.'

'I guessed we lost someone when you didn't make the bells. The new chaplain was there.'

'Lung cancer. She didn't smoke, remember that.' This as he took out his Players Medium. 'Her delirium aside, she would have resented a locum.'

'Good family?' I had heard him talk often enough with Jack Molyneaux about this Granny Eades.

'I interpret your inflection, Tim. I don't believe it becomes you. Yes, good family. We have a new chaplain?'

'Father Brock. Ex-missionary. He didn't go up to see the bells. Sam's disappointed again.'

'I wish you wouldn't warm to that fellow –'

'I wish you would.'

'A bony head.'

'I'm a bony head myself then.'

'Not with your blood.'

Jack Molyneaux came in. I hadn't known him in the bells. The stairs to the tower had caught up with him at seventy-five, yet at eighty he could make the top floor of the Professional Club. He was an undertaker. His sons and grandsons ran the business now – sorry, profession. It was one of only two undertaking firms in the city, over a hundred years in operation. It was not a business one broke into. People did change doctors nowadays – in their *Reader's Digest* wisdom according to Donat – but they were not so adventuresome over the last lap. Donat got him a drink.

'Granny Eades,' Molyneaux pronounced as he eased into his chair. He was reduced to a glass of stout.

'You've been there?'

'Just after you. The house is private. Sad, but I can understand, Donat. Not many of the old stock left. I prepared the insertion myself, one of the few I do now. Those "bony heads" as you call them, they swarm all over reception these days to compose their own. Imagine it, factory workers and the like, every one of them an instant obituarist with heads clipped out of dress dance snaps. I leave those to the grandsons. And how is young Tim, tonight? Not content to hunt the treble indifferently, I trust?'

'Of course not, Mr Molyneaux.'

'That's the lad. And how was Kilkee, Donat? Twice – no, three times – I was only down three times this year. Not able for the grandchildren, I'm afraid. Too lively. In my day you'd cower if your grandfather looked out over his glasses at you.'

'Kilkee is finished, Jack.'

'You don't say?'

'Caravans. What they are pleased to call mobile homes. How one wishes they were mobile and they might move – out of one's sight.'

Molyneaux shook the head. 'I said it years ago, Donat. Giving every Tom, Dick and Harry the vote. Every idler, nincompoop and chit of a lass. Without distinction. Such nonsense! But you're fortunate, Donat, your lodge is well away.'

'They pass by on their way to the Pollock Holes. I hear talk of a site behind me. I shall damn well sell out.'

'Donat!'

'What can one do? As you know I breakfast in the garden after my swim. Last weekend Molly had no sooner put the orange juice before me when there is a pair of heads looking in over the wall. Two bingo women, I've no doubt. I shouted at them: "Mind your business."'

'Quite right, Donat.'

'They guffawed. By the power invested in them by their medical cards, they guffawed.'

A few more came in. Soon we would have a circle around us, Donat the centre, cocktail conversation. I would be out of it.

'I'll leave you gentlemen,' I said, standing up. Donat raised the old eyebrows. I bent down and whispered: 'The pub fuck.' That hurt him. But then I hated being his son.

Two snobbish old farts like Donat and old Jack Molyneaux would have driven me to the Statue of Liberty if I was never in search of the pub fuck. Charlie's was crowded. It always is. On the shelf behind Charlie's head as he serves you is scrawled on cardboard: THE MANAGEMENT RESERVES THE RIGHT TO SERVE EVERYBODY. That included all three sexes; the arty crowd; criminals; the slummers; the pseuds; the characters; the respectable; the poor, and above all anyone barred from another pub or from every other pub. Charlie told me that he was torn between calling the pub the Statue of Liberty or The Three Cripples. He wasn't so far out tonight in that only Bill Sykes and Bullseye were missing. Phil Thompson – the Steve Davis of his day according to Charlie – was nailed to the counter surrounded by the newsboy Butsey Rushe and Wally Kirwan. You could sit on a high stool at the long bar where Charlie was helped by his sister, Hannah, or you could stand by the fireplace or sit back against the wall or squeeze into a corner or just stand up in the middle of the crowded floor. My spot was in the corner by the fireplace where I could reach up to my drink safe on the ledge. The minute I went in Charlie caught my eye and served me a quick pint and muttered: 'Don't do it to me tonight, Harding, please. Don't let me see you.' He meant the pub fuck. Said it grigged him. I sat down to suss out the prospects.

It's hardly a challenge in the Statue of Liberty. You could throw one over your shoulder and take her home in the fireman's grip. But I prefer to cope with some sort of obstacle course, however token. I like a leg and there I was handicapped by the arty crowd who wore dungarees, or clown's trousers held up by braces, or minis that give it all away brutally. Monica was at the bar and she had it all, legs, tits, lipstick and a gobbler's mouth. I knew from Charlie that she was game ball: 'Harding, what is this world coming to? Monica Miller was here the other night. After hours. Nicely pissed. I said, Charlie, now's your chance. So I sidled up to her. "Any chance of the ride, Monica?" Nice and pleasant. What does she do? Ups off her stool. Shouts at me: "You male chauvinist pig." Can you imagine it, Harding? Male chauvinist pig. I said what's wrong with you. I only asked for the fucking ride. She makes a swipe at me with her handbag. Half the town rides her, Harding, but I'm a male chauvinist pig. Why? Because I'm not good-looking enough for her.'

Monica would do. But if it was going to be a hot Monica night, then I wanted to time my race for the pub fuck. It isn't done on one and a half pints. You need six or seven and the other party four or five gins, or whatever takes your fancy. Anything goes wrong, blame the drink. When both are married there are mutual interests to protect, no recriminations and no coming back for more. One married, one single, run a mile from it. Both unattached, use a johnny. Otherwise it's a free world and how can you go wrong? I went down on my pint and held up the finger to Charlie. He knows what I'm up to when I drink quickly. On my third pint the pub darkened and Monica glowed and I had to slip my hand in my pants pocket to flatten the stiff prick against the abdomen. Monica was with a crowd – no contest there – and it was time to start giving her the look.

And then *she* came in. Excused herself through the crowd to the counter beside Phil Thompson and his mates. She was taller than I am, a velvety jade cloche hat with a brooch perked on fair hair that reached straight down to her shoulders, shoulders carrying the pads of the clinging, heat-wave, thirties style patterned dress. Long and slim and unbusty, she flaunted her height in jade stiletto heels. She stretched her neck to get Hannah's attention. In the crowded pub one of the queers did have to be leaning on the fireplace giving the smile down to me. They give me the creeps and I don't care who knows it. As

Charlie puts it: Gay my arse, those fuckers are bent. I was propelled to move towards my vision precipitatively. I carried my glass and managed to squeeze through just as Hannah was putting the small whiskey on the counter. 'Please let me,' I cut in with a smile and a beseech of the eyebrows. She smiled at me in turn, ever so sweetly, bent close, and hiss-whispered in my ear: 'Get lost, Buster.'

Her smile was gone and I was looking at steel. And then at her back. Instead of showing what a great PF man I was, my glass was up to my mouth as a crutch and I found myself edging back through the crowd to my mercifully still vacant corner seat. I put the pint back up on the ledge and was grateful for the friendly presence of the hovering queer who had the hots for me. She did not turn round once in another twenty minutes, but I caught her voice above the racket a couple of times talking to Hannah. 'Oh it was so divine' and 'It was absolutely wonderful.' And her voice was divine and wonderful to me.

My next full pint was unsipped on the ledge and Monica forgotten when I noticed the queer bloke miming the offer of a fag. I was so rattled by her nibs that I took the cigarette, my first in thirteen years. I accepted a light, coughed, just like the very first time ever: And then the OOPS happened. My friend the fagman's arm slipped along the top of the fireplace and upset my pint, which came cascading down over my head on to my suit and shirt. And as he made a grab at the glass to try and save the day, he tipped over the pictureless frame that was all so typical of Charlie's appointments. So there I was with my head sticking out of the frame, dripping, the cigarette sogged, the suit and shirt destroyed and himself trying to wipe me down. The bar roared, everyone's head thrown back. Except hers. She alone looked at the comicality without laughing. The other asshole was calling a replacement pint. I assured him I was fine, no I would not let him pay to have the suit cleaned, porter didn't stain and so on. It blew over. She turned back to her whiskey. Reading the entrails I was not dealing with pub fuck

material. But she was, after all, a woman, a fine one, and if I had
to work for my oats then so be it. Charlie came out collecting
glasses and feeling half the customers and he had the big grin on
his face. 'Your lovely suit, Harding, that you put on in this heat
for Sam and that fat prick missioner.' I pulled Charlie's arm
until his head came down and I could whisper: Who is she?

'Forget it, Harding. That's Sloan's daughter.'

NINA FITZPATRICK
In the Company of Frauds

Nina Fitzpatrick is of Polish–Irish ancestry and studies at University College, Galway. Her first collection of short stories, Fables of the Irish Intelligentsia *won the* Irish Times *prize for fiction in 1991 but the prize was later withdrawn when her Irish origins came into dispute. She has since published a novel,* The Loves of Faustyna.

(1)

Sesame O'Hara was a poor hoor. She had spent the most wretched twenty years of her life at the University in Galway explaining and obfuscating the work of Irish writers, A.T. Harrington among them.

For all these years she suffered the birth pangs of a theory that poetry was not, as the best French critics had it, phallic/priapic but rather vaginal/Venusian. The fruit of her labour was a foetus in formalin, a study of Irish poetry from Alice Milligan to A.T. Harrington entitled *The Well and the Pump*. The book never got beyond the proof stage. Sesame chopped and changed it constantly. She kept expanding the vulvar aspects and contracting the phallic and then by turns expanding the phallic and contracting the vulvar.

Few of her students were impressed by her search for perfection. The majority were sure that she no longer knew her arse from her elbow. One Christmas they sent her a green-veined dildo made of Connemara marble in a black velvet box. O'Hara prayed to St Sesaimh of Kinvara (anglicized Sesame) for release.

She always felt guilty. The vulvar theory was much against the grain of her Catholic upbringing. She would blush when asked to explain the gist of her research. More and more she was troubled by the indecency of her subject. Less and less was she able to endure the parasitism of her profession. The poet A.T. Harrington, for example, was a tree. She was the ivy. That's what occurred to her as she retyped for the umpteenth time her chapter 'The Modality of Desire in Harrington's Recent Verse'.

It was Harrington's *oeuvre* that caused all the problems. His poetry bulged with male Irish thuggery and threatened to wreck her theory at every turn. She tried to subdue him with words like 'discourse', 'desire', 'semiosis' and '*jouissance*'. All in vain. In spite of his extraordinary talent for inwardness, Harrington remained feral and stank.

One night after a meeting of the International Association for the Study of Anglo-Irish Literature (Austrian Section) O'Hara got drunk. She emptied a bottle of contaminated Klosterneuburger at a reception hosted by the governor of Styria in the last Rosicrucian palace in Europe. She sat in a baroque bay window all on her own. She felt full of wind, piss and quotations.

'Shame, Sesame, shame,' she quoted her father, 'you rump-fed ronion you.'

She found it increasingly difficult to think and speak without quoting somebody. She felt another quote coming on, this time from Harrington.

Suddenly it occurred to her that the quotation didn't sound right. As a matter of fact it wasn't Harrington at all. It was her very own. That's how she discovered that she could write poetry.

That night she smoked forty Gitanes and wrote five better-than-Harrington poems.

She felt sick in the morning. But her mind was in a ferment. She declaimed aloud a page of Harrington and a sheet of O'Hara. She was delighted. Harrington's verses unstitched themselves down the page like old woollen socks. There were holes and runs in them. They betrayed a shameless indecision. Hers, by contrast, were diaphanous stockings. They had definite seams, an amber transparency, a feminine pungency.

(2)

DEAR SIR,

Please find enclosed a sequence of poems inspired by recent events in Lebanon. They are a continuation of the work which you published last year in the spring issue of *Cosmos*.

Yours

ALAN T. HARRINGTON

This letter provoked one of the more vicious imbroglios in the recent history of Irish literature in English. It was concocted by Sesame O'Hara and it led to a curious vulvar period in the work of Harrington. The one-time eulogist of bed, booze, brothels and fornication in graveyards became the celebrant of Mother Gaia. She tightened her teeth on him and opened her swamps, her dark oozings seeping and softening his cough.

SIR,

What the hell do you think you're doing? I'll sue you for printing these abortions under my name in your last issue. Lebanon *my arse*.

A. THURLEY HARRINGTON

Harrington was to regret that letter for the rest of his natural life. Word of the appearance of a pseudo-Harrington reached *Horizon, The New York Review of Books, Encounter, The Clare Champion* and *Poetry Ireland*. All five rejected his just completed work on the grounds of uncertainty of authorship.

He tugged the hair that grew between his teeth. He cursed in Munster Irish. The famous bronchitis thickened in his chest. His coughing, spitting and sweating drove his lover away. But he

was no fool. He had difficulty enough getting published as it
was. Any further complications would shaft his chances of
winning the American National Poetry Award. In the end he
kicked for touch by pleading insanity.

DEAR SIR,
Please, disregard my ill-tempered epistle of 21 May. In confidence
I must tell you that I have had something of a breakdown and
my left hand, so to speak, didn't know what my right hand was
doing. The poems you published are, of course, mine, and here-
with I enclose an epilogue to my Lebanon sequence. Such a sad
country!

Yours,
A.T.H.

Harrington boomed. The Peace Movement invited him to
Acapulco to address a symposium on Suppressed Nationalities
of the World; Swedish feminists elected him an honorary life
member of the *Bara for Kvinnor Association* and he turned down
the offer of a Doctorate of Literature (*honoris causa*) from University College Galway.

(3)

During this vulvar period of his work Harrington never once
slept alone.

(4)

Sesame O'Hara wrote and wrote. Harrington, who hadn't read
anything in twenty years, was faced with the distasteful task of
rummaging through literary periodicals to find out what he had
published. He couldn't make head or tail of his new work. He
tried reading the critics for clarification. The critics said, for
example: 'It follows that a central concern of his [Harrington] is

the restoration of female energy to its appropriate position in the scheme of things, and, by the same token, the need for a transformation of male energy as we know it today. Here is the savage economy of hieroglyphics.'

This frightened him. He was fit to be tied.

The inevitable happened. That year the male coquettes of the International Association for the Study of Anglo-Irish Literature assembled in Munich for their quintennial conference. They needed one another. They needed Harrington.

He came in defiant Bermuda shorts and Palestinian shawl. He chaired the opening session and thereby managed to say nothing.

Professor Sesame O'Hara was there as well. When she saw Harrington she trembled and ran to the Fräuleins to check if her hair, her eyes, her cheeks and her lips were in their right places. She wanted to talk to him but it was impossible because of the innovative set-up of the conference. In the dining hall there were twelve tables. One of them was covered with a black table cloth. The others were in white. Anybody who sat at the black table was excused from talking or socializing in any way (the director of the conference got the idea from a café in Istanbul). Harrington sat at the black table.

Sesame invoked St Sesaimh of Kinvara who answered her prayer.

When nobody was looking she switched the tablecloth. Harrington, whose attention was focused on exploring inner space, didn't notice the difference. He sat in his usual place looking like Ho Chi Min before the fall of Saigon.

Sesame joined him and introduced herself.

'Hi, there, wanker,' he greeted her and slobbered his soup.

She stared at him, bottomified.

'Bollocks,' she breathed, frightened of herself.

Harrington was delighted. He offered her a glass of Madeira and a slice of lemon.

The IASAIL delegates who observed the encounter were

pleasantly dismayed to see Harrington's bony hand crawl over
Sesame's back and shoulders. A little later they watched the two
of them shamble out of the dining hall swathed in muslined
conversation.

Harrington's room stank of beer and incense. O'Hara
struggled to turn their conversation to post-modernism. But
Harrington was randy. He bolted the door and shouted 'Open
Sesame!' He started to poke at her which she found embarrassing. She could take *plaisir du texte* but not *plaisir de
l'homme*.

In an effort to divert his attention and finally come to
the point she started to praise his recent work. She would give
an arm and a leg, her professorship even, to produce such
stuff.

'Your professorshit!' exclaimed Harrington and released
her. He had been drinking for days and felt like a full
cistern in need of a good flush. It came in a torrent of green
venom.

'Your professorshit,' he repeated. 'I've hardly written a thing
for eight years.'

Sesame startled.

'How do you mean?' she enquired.

She had only been writing under his name for the previous
fifteen months.

'I'm a fraud,' said Harrington, relishing his words. 'You see
there's this creature writing my stuff better than I could ever do
it myself.'

Sesame's heart stopped.

'Who's he?' she asked in a small voice.

'It's a she,' Harrington chuckled. 'Maisie MacMahon. A
small farmer's wife in the County Leitrim with too much
time on her hands. She isn't bad. But a year or so ago
she developed this feminist kink. At first I wanted to stop her
but then I thought, what's the use, a change is as good as
a rest.'

Sesame gazed at him blankly, her mind dry and toxic as a puff-ball.

'I'm a fraud,' repeated Harrington with glee. 'But she's got what it takes. What odds: every man should have a smart woman like that in his life.'

Is fearr beagán don ghaol ná morán don aitheantas.

MOYA RODDY
The Day I Gave Neil Jordan a Lift

*Moya Roddy (1959–) was born in Dublin and grew up in Walkinstown.
She is the author of several screenplays, numerous short stories and a
novel,* The Long Road Home. *She lives in Galway.*

I was driving to work thinking the usual thoughts, how boring
life was, how we'd all cop it if it wasn't for a bit of fantasy. I
mean take my life. I get up every morning, get the kids ready
for school, Mike – the husband – is in bed, he works nights and
gets home about six in the morning so I never see much of him
until I get back in the evening. I walk the kids to the school
bus, say hello to the other parents, complain about the weather,
it's always too hot or too cold or too wet and then back home
to get ready for work. To be honest, first I have a cup of coffee.
I sit while I'm drinking and stare out the window, allowing
thoughts or nothing at all to float round me mind. If a worry
comes along like how are we going to afford the kids' schoolbooks or whatever, I give it its marching orders. 'Piss off,' I tell
it, 'this is my time.' When the coffee's finished I put on me face.
These days I stand a little further back from the bathroom
mirror – that way I still look as young as I did ten years ago.
Moisturizer. Foundation. Blusher, just a little. Eyeliner. Mascara.
Lipstick. Then earrings. I have a tray-full and I pick a different
pair every morning depending on me mood. I couldn't exactly
say what kinds of moods I have but I always know which
earrings to put on. Then I'm ready. Since I have to wear a shop
coat in the bakery it doesn't really matter what I put on but I
take a bit of care all the same. After all this is for me. That's
what Teresa doesn't understand. Teresa works with me at the
bakery. She's a bit older but looks ancient. If she combs her hair
that's about the size of it. Of course she's in sandwiches and
I think that makes a difference. There's not much glamour

attached to sandwiches is there? I'm in cakes and pastries. I'm selling dreams, that's what I told Teresa. Women and girls come in to me all day hoping to buy a dream. They gaze longingly at the chocolate eclairs and strawberry creams, or if they're a bad case the meringues and the cream trifles. Then they hand over their money and carry their treasure out lovingly. You don't see anyone fling a cream cake into a shopping bag like the office girls or the factory workers do with their sandwiches. No. The cream cake is carried home carefully. I imagine them – the baby finally gone to sleep or the unemployed husband gone out at last to the pub – putting on the kettle and ceremoniously opening the white cardboard box. Like the genie in the lamp, escape stares them in the face. Quickly they lay out the cup and plate, the spoon and the knife and then the cake is levered gently out. One bite and they're dreaming. Just for a few minutes, just enough to recharge the batteries. And it's worth it even if they put on a few pounds. I mean, if you could indulge and not put on a few pounds where's the danger?

But who'd buy a dream from Teresa, that's what I think, although I'd never say it to her. She's very sensitive. Whenever I waltz into the shop she always looks at me as if I'm getting at her. As if I've dressed up to annoy her. To highlight her drabness. She doesn't believe it's for meself. That I have me own fantasies.

Anyway, like I was saying, I was driving to work thinking me usual thoughts when I saw him. A sort of a smallish fellow in a dark green mac, there was a bag of some kind by his feet and he had his thumb out hitching. As a rule I never give a lift to men, even on their own, you just can't tell these days. But there was something about him, his face looked so familiar that I'd stopped before me brain caught up with itself. The smile he gave me! He was lit up. As he got into the car it came back to me. I couldn't believe it. But it was him alright. The guy who'd won the Oscar on the telly. What was his name? No use, I couldn't remember. For the film. I couldn't remember the name of that either. I hadn't seen it. And here he was in my car!

'Thanks very much. I didn't think anyone was going to stop.' He had a Dublin accent, I'm from Dublin meself, we only moved down the country when me husband was made redundant so I knew I was right. Your man on the telly was from Dublin.

I smiled. I was trying to decide whether to tell him or not. Or what I should say. I know these people hate being recognized. I remember reading about whatever her name was from that soap who had to wear dark glasses all the time even to go shopping. He'd probably be really pleased if I said nothing. All the same it would be nice to let him know he was known, appreciated here in his own country. I remember he'd said something about having to work in Hollywood when he won. At the time I thought nice work if you can get it. But that's the thing about reality – everyone else's always seems better than yours. That's why we need a bit of escape.

'Listen,' I said, 'I know you don't want to talk about it but I know your films and the Oscar and all.'

He smiled and I could see he was delighted I'd mentioned it.

'I only saw one.' I racked me brains for the name – Mike got it out on video. It came to me. 'Mona Lisa, great. I loved it.' To be honest I could hardly remember it but what was the point of saying that?

'You liked it?'

'Brill.'

I was still trying to think of his name. And how great it was going to be telling Teresa about him, and Mike – although I'd have to pretend there was a woman with him, he doesn't like me picking up men either.

'Are you making another one?'

He nodded.

'It's kind of a secret what I'm doing. I shouldn't even be here. You understand.' He looked uneasily out the window.

'Where are you heading?'

'Naas. I work in the bakery.'

By that time we were on the dual carriageway and I was

having to concentrate on me driving. There's a lot of fools about trying to get to Hell or Heaven and not caring if they take you with them. But I could see him studying me out of the corner of his eye. It pays to take care of yourself I thought. Then it struck me: why would someone as rich as him be hitchhiking? He must have a fleet of cars to his name. I was about to ask him when I realized he was probably doing research for his next film. That's what they do now, there was an article in the hairdressers', they like to go and see how ordinary people live. Film directors and that. He was probably making a film about someone hitchhiking and wanted to see what happens.

'You're doing some work for your new film?'

'Sort of . . .'

'I won't say a word to anyone promise. You couldn't give us a clue, just a hint what's it about?'

I could see him trying to make up his mind.

'Not a word, you promised remember? It's about hitchhiking. This guy is hitchhiking and he gets a lift with this woman, she's beautiful and they fall madly in love and run away together.'

What did I tell you, I said to meself. Not that I couldn't have made up a better idea if I had to. It makes you wonder sometimes.

'She doesn't happen to work in a bakery?'

He roared laughing.

'Why not?'

We were almost in Naas now.

'Where can I drop you? I usually leave the car in a car park down the end near the shop. You can get out there if you like or . . .'

'I'll come to the car park.'

We got there and as I turned off the ignition he touched me arm.

'Listen, can I ask you a big favour?'

'Sure.'

'You know what I was telling you about everything being secret. Well, I have to get to Dublin, I should've been there yesterday it's that urgent but I don't want anyone to know. I was wondering if I could borrow your car?'

'The car?'

'Look you know who I am. There's no problem. I'll leave it back later. It's not every day you pick up Neil Jordan.'

'That's your name!' It was out before I could stop meself. I felt really embarrassed. 'Sorry, I just couldn't remember it. It was on the tip of me tongue. I saw you on the telly when you won the Oscar.'

'Anyone can forget. What about the car?'

'I have to have it back by five o'clock. Me husband needs it for work tonight.'

'Like I said, no problem. I'll get one of the secretaries to return it. You'd really be helping me out.'

I stared at him, smiling all over. 'I can't believe it. Neil Jordan! Wait 'til I tell Teresa. She won't believe me.'

'And I thought you promised not to tell anyone. At least not until tomorrow. Nobody knows I'm here. I'm supposed to be in Hollywood.'

'You're tying up a deal, is that it?'

He nodded. I thought for a minute then handed him the car keys.

'It's a pleasure Mr Jordan.'

'I don't know your name.'

'Let's leave it like that. Just a sec.' I leaned across him.

Opening the glove compartment I pulled out me stilettos.

'For the shop.'

I shook me flatties off and shoved them into the compartment before squeezing me feet into the high heels.

'Don't your legs get tired standing all day on them?'

'Yeah but it's worth it, the customers like to see a bit of glamour. Like in the pictures, ye know.'

I got out and when I reached the stairs I turned and gave me biggest smile to Neil Jordan.

All day I was bursting to tell Teresa, but I didn't, although she knew something was up. She kept questioning me but I wouldn't budge. After all I'd promised. But she could see the smile on me lips and all the customers kept asking if I'd won the lotto or something. Tomorrow, I thought, I'll tell them.

As the day wore on though I began to have me doubts. Why didn't he hire a car or go by train? I mean, even if he drove his own car how would anyone know where he was? On the other hand, why would he pretend to be someone he wasn't? I made a secret pact I'd never tell anyone about the day I gave Neil Jordan a lift if the car was there. When I got to the car park it wasn't.

I caught the bus home and Mike wasn't a bit pleased when I came in.

'I'm late for work,' he growled. 'Where's the car? Did you have a breakdown? Why didn't you ring?'

All this before I'd time to take off me high heels.

The kids were screaming too, wanting to know what had happened.

'I gave the car to Neil Jordan,' I said as calmly as possible.

'Neil who?'

'You know, the guy from Dublin who won the Oscar a few months ago. He makes films in Hollywood.'

Mike stared at me.

'You gave our car to someone who makes films in Hollywood. Did he not have enough of his own?'

The kids all hooted at this.

'He asked me to lend it to him. He said he'd bring it back before five. He'll probably bring it back later.'

For a moment I thought he was going to hit the ceiling. Then he burst out laughing.

'Let's get this straight – you lent our car to Neil who . . .? where did you meet him?'

'I gave him a lift.'

'You gave a lift to some bloke who said he was . . .? I don't believe it. Your mammy's finally cracked kids. Are you out of your head or what? Film directors don't go round hitching lifts and asking for cars. You've given away our car to some bloody perfect stranger. I'm ringing the guards.'

'But he said he didn't want anyone to know it was him.'

'Bloody sure he did. It's probably been used in some bank robbery by now or on its way to England or sold. I don't believe this, we haven't even paid for it yet.'

'Who's Neil Jordan?' Cathy our twelve year old asked as Mike talked to the guards.

I shook me head. I could hear Mike's voice getting more and more hysterical on the phone. It was obvious the police didn't believe him.

At last he came back into the kitchen.

'Jesus but we'll be the laughing stock of the place when this gets out. I'm going to work. They'll ring back if they hear anything.'

I watched him go then went into the bathroom, locked the door and had a good cry. Me mascara ran all down me cheeks, Why shouldn't it be Neil Jordan, I asked the mirror.

Late that night the phone rang. An official sounding voice asked if I owned a silver Toyota Corolla.

I told them I did.

It had been found in Dun Laoighaire. Abandoned. We could come to the barracks anytime and collect it. I tried not to imagine Mike's face when I told him we had to go to Dublin to pick it up.

On our way up the following Saturday Mike warned me not to say a word about picking up a film director or any such nonsense. He'd already told the local guards I was playing a joke on him. Everyone knows I'm a bit of a dreamer anyway. I agreed and was really grateful when I saw the car hadn't been damaged. The first thing I did when we drove out of the station was open the glove compartment to get me flatties. Me feet were really killing me after three days of stilettoes. As I took them out a piece of paper with something scribbled on it fell to the ground. I picked it up and read it.

SORRY IT HAD TO END LIKE THIS. TOP SECRET. NJ.

Smiling, I shoved the note in me bag. I knew it was Neil Jordan all along.

EOIN McNAMEE
The Lion Alone

Eoin McNamee (1961–) was born in Kilkeel, Co. Down. His poetry and prose have been widely published in Ireland and he is the author of two acclaimed novels, The Last of Deeds *and* Resurrection Man *and a novella,* Love in History.

The sky over Tigers Bay was as dull as milk. It was overcast and warm. It had been warm for a week and the smell of rotting horseflesh and lion shit greased the rust-coloured bricks of the houses, draped the telephone wires, and threaded fingers of odour in the crudely-welded wire mesh that covered the windows of the shop on the corner.

Gus Ferguson emerged from the shop clutching two comics and a sherbet dip. Ignoring the smell he opened a comic on the windowsill of the shop and dipped the liquorice stick into the sherbet. The jungle doctor, he read, gunned his zebra-striped jeep through the bush. It was a race against time, but the jungle doctor braked hard and gaped in awe as the apeman swung himself, hand over hand, to the top of the tallest tree in the continent. Shading his eyes Gus Ferguson looked up at the towering gantry of the shipyard crane behind the houses. The apeman roared and pounded his chest.

Because of the smell Mrs Dorcas Wilson from No 72 had opened the telephone directory and noted the numbers of the police and the city zoo.

But the smell did not concern the lion for in the endless eye of his mind all was lion. The smell, the man who brought his meat, the ten feet by ten feet square of yard where he was lion and lion alone, the street, the city, the sky were endless lion without horizon, the pap of its bones.

Buck Spence worked on the docks. He was a timid man who had kept a lion in his back yard for so many years its origin had been forgotten. Perhaps it had come on one of the big African freighters, their holds dreaming with the green weight of African bananas.

Every Saturday morning an abbatoir van would halt at the kerb in front of No 70. The driver wore white oilskins. Buck Spence helped him to unload slabs of horsemeat which they would shoulder and carry down the narrow corridor which led from the front of No 70 to the rear, piling them in a corner of the back kitchen. As they worked Buck Spence complained about the weight, or the price, or the blood which ran from the larded sides of meat, congealing the fibres of the carpet into bristles.

Every Saturday afternoon Buck Spence walked the lion to the corner of the street and back, his head almost level with the undulant joint of the lion's shoulder, the reflection of the street held in the great mongoose circle of the lion's eye. Every Saturday afternoon Mrs Dorcas Wilson watched them with increasing bitterness. She did not hold with lions. Her yard was separated from Buck Spence's yard by a wall of breezeblocks topped with a wire mesh fence. She had tolerated lion hairs which penetrated the fence and were carried into the house to irritate her husband's allergy, but this time things had gone too far.

Despite the heat she put on the tweed coat with the leather buttons before stepping into the street to knock on the door of No 70.

Buck Spence opened the door. At his back the smell from the corridor loomed, a roar of blood and gristle.

– You have my heart scalded with the smell of that bloody cat, she told him.

– The smell's terrible, Buck Spence agreed, and he has me eaten out of house and home.

– My Wilfred is distracted with it, she went on, disconcerted, the whole street thinks your head is cut.

– My head must be cut, he concurred gloomily, lions is

unpredictable. One blow of a paw would gut you. I'm living in constant danger.

Mrs Dorcas Wilson's mouth, slotted with age, tightened under the stress until she was gilled like a fish. She shook her finger in Buck Spence's face until the knuckle rattled inside the hollow flesh like dice in a cup.

– I'll not be responsible, she warned.

Gus Ferguson turned the pages of the comic, his fingers sticky in the afternoon heat. In the yard of No 70 the lion yawned a watering-hole yawn and stood to unleash a dusty stream of lion's piss. Tigers Bay stank like the ribcage of a half-eaten beast on a plain without shade or mercy.

Mrs Dorcas Wilson sat by the window.

– I'm foundered, she told her husband, that damn Ferguson boy is hanging about the shop again. He should be in school.

– It's Saturday, Wilfred said, without taking his eyes from the television.

Mrs Dorcas Wilson watched Fiona Taggart from No 80 walk down the street, her brown breasts bobbing adams-apple tight against her chest.

– The cut of her, Mrs Dorcas Wilson snapped, it's enough to drive a body wild.

It was warm. Buck Spence dragged a sweating carcass from the pile in the back kitchen and pushed it through the back door. He listened for a moment to moist scuffles and devout grunts, sighed, then went into the front kitchen where he took the tea caddy from the shelf. Under a framed print of Isambard Kingdom Brunel Buck Spence began to make tea.

It was ominously quiet outside the compound, Gus Ferguson read. There had never been so many blossoms on the Frangipani. The dustbowl that surrounded the tiny compound was empty but soon it would be swarming with endless spears and he had only a handful of men. He composed himself to write a letter to his wife.

At exactly half past four Buck Spence and the lion left No 70, walked to the end of the street, turned and came back. Mrs Dorcas Wilson reached for the telephone.

At six o'clock a police landrover entered Tigers Bay and parked at the kerb opposite No 70. Shortly afterwards a small, white van pulled up behind the landrover. A policeman walked from the landrover to the van and talked to the driver, then the driver and the policeman walked to the door of No 70. Fiona Taggart came to the doorway of No 80. When she saw the policeman her mouth made an O as round and brown as the brown egg breasts basketed against her chest.

– Gawking at a peeler, the scut, Mrs Dorcas Wilson said, smacking her lips.

When Buck Spence answered the door the vandriver stepped forward.

– Are you the boy that has the lion? he asked.

– That's who I am, Buck Spence said in a small voice, the boy who has the lion.

– Have you the licence? the vandriver asked.

– Damn the licence he has, Mrs Dorcas Wilson said from the doorway of No 72.

– Wilful possession of a wild beast without a licence is an offence under section 30 (c) of the act, the vandriver said, making a note on a clipboard.

– Nobody told me, Buck Spence said.

– And a public nuisance, the policeman said.

– Nuisance is not the word, Mrs Dorcas Wilson said.

– It's a bloody menagerie, the policeman said.

– I was called out once to a case where a man kept a vulture in his living-room, the vandriver said as he walked back towards the van, a bird of carrion.

He returned with a rifle. He patted the barrel.

– .22 loaded with a hypodermic shot. Hit them anywhere in the body and over they go, out for the count. Accurate up to a hundred yards.

– Sterling sub-machine gun, standard issue, the policeman

said, holding up his gun, a hundred rounds a minute. Not accurate though. It sprays bullets.

– Right, the vandriver said, slipping off the safety catch, let's go.

He led the way down the narrow corridor followed by the policeman, then Mrs Dorcas Wilson, then Gus Ferguson, then Buck Spence.

Ten minutes later they emerged in reverse order. No-one spoke. The policeman looked thoughtful.

The vandriver broke the silence.

– You didn't have to shoot it.

– It was about to spring at your throat, the policeman said.

– It was yawning, Gus Ferguson said.

The vandriver snapped open the rifle and removed the hypodermic cartridge.

– I could sue, Buck Spence said. The policeman looked at Buck Spence, then looked at Gus Ferguson.

– Children, he said, were at risk. And he went to the landrover to fetch chalk so that he could draw an outline of the dead lion on the concrete surface of the yard. When that was done he helped the vandriver to drag the body of the lion down the narrow corridor. The corpse was put in the back of the small white van and they drove off. Gus Ferguson ran after them as far as the corner.

– Good bloody riddance, Mrs Dorcas Wilson said, and closed the door of No 72.

– Eaten out of house and home, Buck Spence said, but the street was empty.

Mrs Dorcas Wilson cooked tea for Wilfred. Rashers lean and dark, sausages plump, fried bread and eggs. Wilfred ate slowly, with little relish. When he left the table Mrs Dorcas Wilson gathered the scraps carefully. Salty rinds and one fat sausage, stowed and wrapped in a handkerchief.

Slowly she went up the stairs. At a certain point where the wall was thin she stooped to listen but there was no sound from

No 70. She went into the bathroom at the top of the stairs, closed and locked the door carefully behind her.

The book from the library had said that alligators preferred to eat meat that they had killed themselves but gradually she had persuaded him to accept household scraps. He almost filled the bath now, measuring five feet from the pointed tip of his snout to the end of his scaly tail. His stillness was immeasurable until he opened his mouth to receive the scraps.

The street had cooled a little at nightfall. Fiona Taggart, dressed to kill, left her house and saw a pampas moon. Two salamanders waited without noise in the shadow of a chimney. A fruit-eating bat gobbled a squashed tomato in the gutter outside the shop. Fiona Taggart began to walk towards the city and as she walked the hard, brown meat of her breasts whispered. On the distant shoulder of Cavehill mountain the wolves answered with their craving silence.

BRIDGET O'CONNOR
Here Comes John

*Bridget O'Connor (1961–) was born in London of Irish parents. She has
had stories published in several magazines and newspapers. Her story,
'Harp' won the* Time Out *prize for new writers.* Here Comes John,
her first collection of stories was published in 1993.

I remember my first one. Nineteen sixty-nine. He was called
John. A fine body of a man with his Go on, punch me *right
there*, the reddish ripple of muscle, that covering hair. It was all
over his stomach and all over his back. It used to crawl over his
collar and out of his cuffs. The man was a mat, but I suppose
some women must like it. *I* must have liked it. Before my brain
grew. And isn't it the way with them, the ones that slap at first,
then punch, then give you a right good kicking (keep you
straight), it's all mouth. Took him two seconds with drink in
him, three without. If I timed it right I could set my tea down
steaming and after, after I'd cleared up the mess a bit, it would
be just right. Very nice with a fag. And of course he'd be
exhausted, fairly whacked, bushed. And it would be, Can't you
give me a moment love? (oh, I thought that was one) or Jeezus!
You a nymphomaniac or what?

And if you don't learn nothing from that you don't learn
nothing.

Cos nothing changes that much does it? The Seventies, the
Eighties, the Nineties. It all boils down to tit men (look at the
conkers on that) or cunt men, or leg men. They still like to
divide you up. And it don't make no difference if it's squash
now stead of rugger, Bacardi not lager, they've all got mental
hair on their shoulders, red in the middle, wee white legs.
They're still all John. Old John and New John. And even in the
Nineties, where it's all talk dirty, they still can't manage it,
beckoning you over in a pub with their pinkie and off you trot,

ever hopeful, and it's, If I could make you come with my finger
think what I could do with my *whole* body. Or they'd spend all
evening, and a couple of quid, breathing in your ear even
though your hearing's perfect cos they've read some comic says
you can do this and it's like foreplay and we won't expect
nothing much later. Which brings me nicely round to John.

John was a fine body of a man, all dressed up. My ear would
be that wet sitting next to him I'd have to keep swapping places
for fear I'd get water on the brain. Now you're probably
thinking I'm talking about some motor mechanic or builder as
they're usually the ones with the tartan middles and luminous
legs, cept you'd be wrong. I'm talking about The Johns. The
millions of them. They're all stockbrokers, they're all Tories,
they're all married (you put a scratch on me I'll lay you out)
they're all BORING and so you're probably thinking, so why
do you bother and my answer to that is, well, why do you
think? Listen. This is how I met John.

Nineteen ninety-three. I was sitting in Rumours under a palm
tree nursing a gin and thinking I could jack it all in soon and
feeling this cold sore bubbling up on my lower lip, sort of
humming, 'Wish I was pretty, Wish I was rich,' when in walks
this bloke. Oh-oh, I thought, Here comes John. Oh-oh, I
thought, a bit later, fourth gin (no t), John reads the *Independent*.
Cos it's not all what's a gorgeous bird/chick/bit/bint doing in an
etcetera. It's all uni-this and multilateral-that and IMF and
ERM and ECU so you've got to read up a bit for these yuppy
Johns and you've got to know your way round shares and
things cos they might be tit, cunt and leg men but now they
want *brain*. And *brain*, girls, is what I've got. See this necklace?
John got me that. These earrings? John got me that. These
shares in British Telecom, British Gas, British Steel, British
Airways, British fucking everything, you name it, they sell it,
I've got it, cos I bloody well earn it.

So anyways, to cut the eye contact and the, If I could make
you come with my etcetera, there's John, finally sitting next to

me, soaking my lug hole, boring me to sweet Jesus, and I'm doing my Wiggle On The Seat bit (they like you to wiggle, it reminds them of studs and fillies) and to look at me you wouldn't think my brain had just atrophied cos I'm well into automatic and I look interesting. You've got to look interesting! It's all Nineties clean, it's Anneka Rice. So what you need girls is glasses to take off and on, a lot of hair half pinned up and something collarless and well cut and that's me down to a t – with a gin in it. And don't get drunk. Know your limit. He can get legless but you've got to hold your own cos You Need Your Wits About You.

Listen. Here we go.

This is what Johns do. They come straight out with it two seconds before last orders, giving it the old Nigel Havers eyebrow and it's, I feel this strong attraction to you . . . and I think you're an interesting woman but I . . . I better tell you I *am* married. Pause. And then its the old spaniel 'isn't life cruel' eye dodge and the quicky glance at you cos here's where everything hangs in the balance. This is *the* crucial moment, so watch out girls, watch me girls and *learn* – get it off by heart:

I flinch ever so slightly to show I've got scruples and morals and I'm not *that* kind of a girl cos you see they don't like *that* kind of a girl these yups, they don't really like any kind of a girl but they do like disguises. Everything nicely wrapped up. So here's where I go all foxy and silent and fight an inner battle that is highly visible (they're thick – you've got to ham it up) and, My Aunty's Knickers, this one turns out to be one of those Who-Hurt-You? merchants and I almost blow the whole job. Gin goes down one lung and out my nose (I'm getting careless, I've had three too many) but still I *am* an artist so I splutter just in time and turn it into a sort of highly-charged sob like he'd hit the nail right on the head. It works. Of course it works. Off he swaggers to the bar with his tight little arse grinning through his Chinos and I take a breather.

What's it all about? you wonder. That's what I wonder too sometimes, cos what's a brain like me doing with pricks like him? But then I look at my bank balance and think, come on girl, you're getting there.

What's it all about? you wonder. What d'you think? It's about sex, like it's always been, cept now it's better cos it's about Safe Sex. *I love Safe Sex.*

Now these Johns are so afraid of Aids they won't put it in you and God, what a blessing for the thinking girl. You don't have to take your clothes off. You don't even have to let him into the house (I want you so much John, we might get carried away). All you've got to do is put up with an earful of spit, a load of highly dodgy right-wing conversation and act like you're dying for it – and the last bit's how you get your pressies cos Johns feel guilty about denying it to you. Makes you laugh.

And this is an important bit: Johns *love* romance. They want you to romance them. They get off on all that dark corner bit and putting on a silly business voice when you ring them at home (ring them at home, they love it, ring them in the middle of the night, they thrive on guilt) and they can't get enough of slumming it off the stockbroker belt, Del-boys and cafés, holding hands under tables. And you don't even have to kiss them – tell them you've got mouth ulcers. And what keeps the whole ball rolling is they can't resist telling their mates: 'I'm having an *Affair*' – cos what's the use in being naughty if you've got no one to confess to? And John can pretend he does IT. John is not afraid of AIDS.

Which brings me, horribly, back to John.

Here comes John now, my last John, my grand finale and it's swaying, it thinks it's got it made, it's sort of brimming and relaxed and it doesn't spill a drop, and here comes John now, thank Christ it's my last one, and it's lowering down and watch this smile play on my lower lip, I've got it down to an art it's sort of trembly and yes, it says, I'm all heart, and here comes

John now and it's totally pleased, it thinks it's totally safe and listen girls, I am going to take this John for *every* little thing it's got.

ANNE ENRIGHT
Revenge

Anne Enright (1962–) has worked as a television producer/director with RTE. Her collection of short stories, The Portable Virgin *was nominated for the* Irish Times/Aer Lingus Literary Award *in 1991. She has also written a novel,* The Wig My Father Wore.

I work for a firm which manufactures rubber gloves. There are many kinds of protective gloves, from the surgical and veterinary (arm-length) to industrial, gardening and domestic. They have in common a niceness. They all imply revulsion. You might not handle a dead mouse without a pair of rubber gloves, someone else might not handle a baby. I need not tell you that shops in Soho sell nuns' outfits made of rubber, that some grown men long for the rubber under-blanket of their infancies, that rubber might save the human race. Rubber is a morally, as well as a sexually, exciting material. It provides us all with an elastic amnesty, to piss the bed, to pick up dead things, to engage in sexual practices, to not touch whomsoever we please.

I work with and sell an everyday material, I answer everyday questions about expansion ratios, tearing, petrifaction. I moved from market research to quality control. I have snapped more elastic in my day etcetera etcetera.

My husband and I are the kind of people who put small ads in the personal columns looking for other couples who may be interested in some discreet fun. This provokes a few everyday questions: How do people *do* that? What do they *say* to each other? What do they *say* to the couples who answer? To which the answers are: Easily. Very little. 'We must see each other again sometime.'

When I was a child it was carpet I loved. I should have made a

career in floor-coverings. There was a brown carpet in the
dining room with specks of black, that was my parents' pride
and joy. 'Watch the carpet!' they would say, and I did. I spent all
my time sitting on it, joining up the warm, black dots. Things
mean a lot to me.

The stench of molten rubber gives me palpitations. It also gives
me eczema and a bad cough. My husband finds the smell
anaphrodisiac in the extreme. Not even the products excite him,
because after seven years you don't know who you are touching,
or not touching, anymore.

My husband is called Malachy and I used to like him a lot. He
was unfaithful to me in that casual, 'look, it didn't mean
anything' kind of way. I was of course bewildered, because that
is how I was brought up. I am supposed to be bewildered. I am
supposed to say 'What *is* love anyway? What *is* sex?'

Once the fiction between two people snaps then anything goes,
or so they say. But it wasn't my marriage I wanted to save, it
was myself. My head, you see, is a balloon on a string, my
insides are elastic. I have to keep the tension between what is
outside and what is in, if I am not to deflate, or explode.

So it was more than a suburban solution that made me want
to be unfaithful *with* my husband, rather than *against* him. It
was more than a question of the mortgage. I had my needs
too: a need to be held in, to be filled, a need for sensation. I
wanted revenge and balance. I wanted an awfulness of my own.-
Of course it was also suburban. Do you really want to know our
sexual grief? How we lose our grip, how we feel obliged to *wear*
things, how we are supposed to look as if we mean it.

Malachy and I laugh in bed, that is how we get over the
problem of conviction. We laugh at breakfast too, on a good

day, and sometimes we laugh again at dinner. Honest enough
laughter, I would say, if the two words were in the same
language, which I doubt. Here is one of the conversations that
led to the ad in the personals:

'I think we're still good in bed.' (LAUGH)
'I think we're great in bed.' (LAUGH)
'I think we should advertise.' (LAUGH)

Here is another:

'You know John Jo at work? Well his wife was thirty-one
yesterday. I said. "What did you give her for her birthday
then?" He said, "I gave her one for every year. Beats blowing
out candles." Do you believe that?' (LAUGH)

You may ask when did the joking stop and the moment of truth
arrive? As if you didn't know how lonely living with someone
can be.

The actual piece of paper with the print on is of very little
importance. John Jo composed the ad for a joke during a
coffee-break at work. My husband tried to snatch it away from
him. There was a chase.

There was a similar chase a week later when Malachy brought
the magazine home to me. I shrieked. I rolled it up and belted
him over the head. I ran after him with a cup full of water and
drenched his shirt. There was a great feeling of relief, followed
by some very honest sex. I said, 'I wonder what the letters will
say?' I said, 'What kind of couples *do* that kind of thing? What
kind of people *answer* ads like that?' I also said 'God how vile!'

Some of the letters had photos attached. 'This is my wife.'
Nothing is incomprehensible, when you know that life is sad. I

answered one for a joke. I said to Malachy 'Guess who's coming to dinner?'

I started off with mackerel pâté, mackerel being a scavenger fish, and good for the heart. I followed with veal osso buco, for reasons I need not elaborate, and finished with a spiced fig pudding with rum butter. Both the eggs I cracked had double yolks, which I found poignant.

I hoovered everything in sight of course. Our bedroom is stranger-proof. It is the kind of bedroom you could die in and not worry about the undertakers. The carpet is a little more interesting than beige, the spread is an ochre brown, the pattern on the curtains is expensive and unashamed. One wall is mirrored in a sanitary kind of way; with little handles for the wardrobe doors.

'Ding Dong,' said the doorbell. Malachy let them in. I heard the sound of coats being taken and drinks offered. I took off my apron, paused at the mirror and opened the kitchen door.

Her hair was over-worked, I thought – too much perm and too much gel. Her make-up was shiny, her eyes were small. All her intelligence was in her mouth, which gave an ironic twist as she said Hello. It was a large mouth, sexy and selfish. Malachy was holding out a gin and tonic for her in a useless kind of way.

Her husband was concentrating on the ice in his glass. His suit was a green so dark it looked black – very discreet, I thought, and out of our league, with Malachy in his cheap polo and jeans. I didn't want to look at his face, nor he at mine. In the slight crash of our glances I saw that he was worn before his time.

I think he was an alcoholic. He drank his way through the meal and was polite. There was a feeling that he was pulling back from viciousness. Malachy, on the other hand, was over-familiar. He and the wife laughed at bad jokes and their feet were confused under the table. The husband asked me about my job and I told him about the machine I have for testing rubber squares; how it pulls the rubber four different ways at high speed. I made it sound like a joke, or something. He laughed.

I realized in myself a slow, physical excitement, a kind of pornographic panic. It felt like the house was full of balloons pressing gently against the ceiling. I looked at the husband.

'Is this your first time?'

'No,' he said.

'What kind of people *do* this kind of thing?' I asked, because I honestly didn't know.

'Well they usually don't feed us so well, or even at all.' I felt guilty. 'This is much more civilized,' he said. 'A lot of them would be well on before we arrive, I'd say. As a general kind of rule.'

'I'm sorry,' I said, 'I don't really drink.'

'Listen,' he leaned forward. 'I was sitting having a G and T in someone's front room and the wife took Maria upstairs to look at the bloody grouting in the bathroom or something, when this guy comes over to me and I realize about six minutes too late that he plays for bloody Arsenal! If you see what I mean. A very ordinary looking guy.'

'You have to be careful,' he said. 'And his wife was a cracker.'

When I was a child I used to stare at things as though they knew something I did not. I used to put them into my mouth and chew them to find out what it was. I kept three things under my bed at night: a piece of wood, a metal door-handle and a cloth. I sucked them instead of my thumb.

We climbed the stairs after Malachy and the wife, who were laughing. Malachy was away, I couldn't touch him. He had the same look in his eye as when he came home from a hurling match when the right team won.

The husband was talking in a low, constant voice that I couldn't refuse. I remember looking at the carpet, which had once meant so much to me. Everyone seemed to know what they were doing.

I thought that we were all supposed to end up together and perform and watch and all that kind of thing. I was interested in the power it would give me over breakfast, but I wasn't looking forward to the confusion. I find it difficult enough to arrange myself around one set of limbs, which are heavy things. I wouldn't know what to do with three. Maybe we would get over the awkwardness with a laugh or two, but in my heart of hearts I didn't find the idea of being with a naked woman funny. What would we joke about? Would we be expected to do things?

What I really wanted to see was Malachy's infidelity. I wanted his paunch made public, the look on his face, his bottom in the air. *That* would be funny.

I did not expect to be led down the hall and into the spare room. I did not expect to find myself sitting on my own with an alcoholic and handsome stranger who had a vicious look in his eye. I did not expect to feel anything.

I wanted him to kiss me. He leant over and tried to take off his shoes. He said, 'God I hate that woman. Did you see her? The way she was laughing and all that bloody lip-gloss. Did you see her? She looks like she's made out of plastic. I can't get a hold of her without slipping around in some body lotion that smells like petrol and dead animals.' He had taken his shoes off and was swinging his legs onto the bed. 'She never changes you know.' He was trying to take his trousers off. 'Oh I know she's sexy. I mean, you saw her. She is sexy. She is sexy. She is sexy. I just prefer if somebody else does it. If you don't mind.' I still wanted him to kiss me. There was the sound of laughter from the other room.

I rolled off the wet patch and lay down on the floor with my cheek on the carpet, which was warm and rough and friendly. I should go into floor-coverings.

I remember when I wet the bed as a child. First it is warm then it gets cold. I would go into my parents' bedroom, with its smell, and start to cry. My mother gets up. She is half-asleep but she's not cross. She is huge. She strips the bed of the wet sheet and takes off the rubber under-blanket which falls with a thick sound to the floor. She puts a layer of newspaper on the mattress and pulls down the other sheet. She tells me to take off my wet pyjamas. I sleep in the raw between the top sheet and the rough blanket and when I turn over, all the warm newspaper under me makes a noise.

JOSEPH O'CONNOR
The Wizard of Oz

Joseph O'Connor (1963–) is the author of two novels, Cowboys and
Indians *and* Desperadoes *as well as a collection of short stories,* True
Believers. *A collection of his journalism,* The Secret World of
the Irish Male, *was a bestseller in Ireland.*

So I phoned up Ed and introduced myself. It took ages to get
him on the line. This really awful woman kept telling me in her
sing-song Cockney voice that he was 'in a meeting' or 'tied-up'.
Old Ed seemed to get tied up more often than the Marquis de
Sade. But eventually, on the sixth call, he agreed to talk to me.
He didn't seem to know who I was at first. Then he said, 'Oh,
so it's you, Dave, so you're the wizard of Oz.' This particular
joke was one I'd heard about five billion times since I got back
– from the old man, my friends, Noreen, everybody, but I had
to laugh really. In the circumstances, there was no option. We
chatted away for a few minutes and eventually he said, 'OK,
listen, Dave, let's do lunch, wait till I get my paws on the old
filo.' He told me he had a spare window tomorrow. Scruples,
he said, a little wine bar, did I know it? I didn't.

   That's how I came to be there, in Scruples wine bar on
Charing Cross Road, with Ed. I recognized him as soon as he
walked in. Like all Irish yuppies, especially the ones that escape to
London, he looked slightly uncomfortable in an expensive suit.
He looked a bit like he was making his Confirmation or something, you know? He walked over and shook my hand, said, 'Hey,
Dave, I knew you'd be the one with the suntan.' He sat down
at the table, clicked his fingers at the waiter, said, 'Mein host,
por favor.' The second thing I noticed, after the suit, was that
he had this terrible grating laugh. I buried my face in the menu,
because just about everyone in Scruples was staring at us. It
really was a heavy case of beam-me-up, Scotty. Christ, that laugh.

So I said to him, 'Whatever you're having, Ed,' because whatever he wanted to order was fine by me. Then, just in case he got any ideas about who was footing the bill, I said, 'He who pays the piper calls the tune. Right, Ed?'

'Dave,' he said, 'I like your attitude. Absolutely.'

He told the waiter, a little guy with a persistent nervous blink, to bring a bottle of the seventy-five Chablis, real cold, real crisp, and 'a salvo of ham sandwiches all round'. He shovelled handfuls of peanuts into his mouth while we sat there eyeing each other up. I couldn't take my eyes off the poor waiter and his blink. It really was bad. I felt like slapping him right in the face. I just thought one short sharp shock might do the trick.

'Anyway, Dave,' Ed said, 'how is the old sod, and I'm not talking about Charlie Haughey.' I laughed, and told him the old sod was still the same as ever, although I'd only spent a week back there before getting straight on the plane over to London, inflation, cuts, unemployment, all of that. Ed shook his head ruefully while I was speaking. 'Same old story, Rory,' he said, 'same old story.' He told me he'd never regretted coming over here, he'd got out when the going was good, never looked back since he got his ass onto that boat.

I had to listen to fifteen minutes of this, all about Ed's great rise to power, how the Irish were doing very well in England these days, wasn't like the fifties anymore, how he could walk out of his job tomorrow morning just like that and get something else just as highly paid by high noon.

'Advertising, Dave,' he said, 'it's just wide open, man, wide open. It's anybody's ballgame.' The waiter came over and changed the ashtray. He winked. I grinned back at him, wishing I had stayed in bed that morning.

'Anyway,' he goes, 'that's enough about me. Tell me about yourself, guy, what you been doing?' He lit a very long cigarette. I noticed that like a lot of Dubliners over here, for some reason, Ed puts on this slight American accent when he talks.

Let's see. What had I been doing?

'Good question, Ed,' I told him. He did his annoying laugh again. I said I'd been to Sydney, course he knew that, worked in a bar, lots of responsibility, no customers.

'Oh, right,' he went, 'g'day sport.' I laughed. 'Fair dinkum, mate,' he said, 'Charlenes and Sheilas.' I laughed again. 'Koylie Meenowg,' he said. I saw a couple in the corner leaning across the table and whispering to each other. They got up and left.

Before he could get on to the inevitable Crocodile Dundee gags I told him they had a clock on the wall in this bar where I worked with all the cocktails written round the edge. I thought Ed might get a kick out of that. Then I told him about the night me and my cousin drank our way all the way around to quarter-past nine.

He did the laugh and said, 'Get outta here, you're pulling my wire, Dave.'

'No, Ed,' I said, 'I'm not pulling your wire.'

Then I told him about the houseboat and the crazy woman who stole our stuff when we went out. And how I wasn't going with the same girl any more, because she decided to stay over there. Well, I didn't feel like pouring out my heart all over the tablecloth, specially not to Ed.

Ed owns this big place in Docklands, one of those converted warehouses. I suppose he isn't exactly a yuppie.

'Yuppie's such a redundant concept,' he says. What he is is a nipple. New Irish Professional Person in London. Yes, Ed was one hell of a nipple. He was, in fact, the biggest nipple I've ever seen. Foxrock, Blackrock College, Trinity, Progressive Democrats, BMW, doesn't exactly agree with Maggie but my God she's sorted the fucking Unions out, you have to give her that. That's the type of guy he was. He's the kind of guy who says the word 'Yeah' after everything, followed by an ever so slightly inflected '?' So let's run this concept up the flagpole, see if anyone salutes, yeah?

Now you get the picture. And he's also the kind of guy who

holds his fingers in the air to make that infuriating inverted commas gesture.

He poured a glass of wine, knocked it back and went 'Cor blimey, kills all known germs dead, yeah?'

He's a friend of my sister, Noreen. They knew each other in Trinity, or 'Trinners' as he calls it. He says Noreen is 'a real sport' and that she's 'easy on the eye'. I think he's got the hots for her, but no point, she's engaged now. My sister Noreen is a bit of an operator, actually, came over to London three years ago, got on the property ladder with the money she got for the accident, bought a place for thirty-two K, just sold it for fifty-three fifty, now she's engaged, for God's sake, *engaged*, with a car, and shares in British Telecom, votes for the Greens because she fancies Jonathan Porrit, against apartheid of course but has to admit she thinks there's too many blacks in London, all of that, and I still haven't even got a damn *job*. Jesus.

When I got back from Oz my mother started nagging me to death. Dad was cool enough but she was just getting tyrannical so I came back over here pretty pronto and Noreen set up this meeting with Ed, to see if Ed could get me a job. Ed is the kind of guy who has a lot of contacts in the City. Or Ed is the kind of guy who *tells* people he has a lot of contacts in the City, quite a different thing.

So this guy with the blink brings the sandwiches over and Ed says, 'Preciate it.' Jesus. You should have seen the sandwiches. Lettuce, parsley, bits of celery, tomatoes cut up to look like rosebuds. The damn plate looked like the Amazon rain forest or something, or what's left of it. And right slap in the middle, kind of nestling, like almost *hiding* under the lettuce leaf, like they were scared, these two minuscule toasted ham sandwiches with the crusts cut off. Mine had a slice of pineapple on the top, and Ed's had a slice of orange, little cherry in the middle, plastic cocktail stick shaped like a sword. Three-Jesus-fifty, the most expensive damn piece of pineapple this side of Carmen Miranda.

He speared my cherry with his cocktail stick.

'Dave,' he said, 'you've just lost your cherry.'

'Right, Ed,' I said, 'good one.' He laughed away at that for a few minutes, wiping his eyes on the serviette. When he threw back his head I noticed that he had hair in his nostrils.

I'm not sure whether you were supposed to eat the pineapple, but I did. In fact I almost ate his orange as well I was so hungry.

'So you like this place, Ed?' I asked.

'Ish,' he nodded, mouth full of parsley. The conversation stopped while he held one hand in the air and tried to swallow. 'It's a bit ho-hum but it's convenient.'

'Yes,' I agreed, knowledgeably, 'it's a bit ho-hum alright.'

'But it's very U, Dave, if you know what I mean.' He held four fingers in the air and made inverted commas again. 'You get me,' he said, 'as opposed to non-U, yeah?'

'Oh, right,' I said. 'I'm with you now.'

Then, all of a sudden, I mean totally out of the blue, of all things, we started talking about this woman, Pamella Bordes, some high-class call girl who was in the news. Ed said, 'Ho ho, Dave, you've come to the right city for that carry-on.' He said for a few quid in Soho, you could have the time of your life.

'Is that right?' I asked. 'So how come you know, Ed?'

'Contacts, Dave,' he said, tapping his nose. '*Vorsprung Durch Technik*, eh?' I told him I thought it was all a bit sexist, actually, and he said, 'Oh yes, Noreen told me you were a bit of a bolshie.' Then he reached across and touched my arm and said, 'Hey, relax, Dave, only pulling your wire.' He went on, 'So hey, Davey, let's talk turkey, Noreen tells me you want to get into the City.'

I said, 'Yeah, Ed, that's the story.'

He went on for a few minutes then about how great Noreen was. That's Noreen for you. Everybody think she's so bloody great. They don't actually know the first thing about her but they all think she's Mother Teresa crossed with Marilyn Monroe or something. Then he said, 'Well, look, Dave, I took the liberty, right, I called this little chumette of mine who runs a rather interesting little unit trust outfit, who as it happens is looking for some willing hands to do a bit of cleaning at the moment, and I mentioned your name, said we were good mates, did the whole business.' He sat back while he was saying all this, with his hands behind his head and a smug look on his face, expecting me to fall down dead with appreciation or something. In fact, I almost gagged on my parsley sprig.

I said, 'Well, thanks, Ed, but cleaning isn't really what I had in mind.'

He said, 'Look Dave, everyone has to start somewhere.' He told me, as if I hadn't heard it a million times from Noreen, all about how Richard Branson started Virgin Records from a telephone box. I mean, he just went on and on, the whole bit, you have to start on the first rung, you name it. So I said, OK, I'd give it a try. Well, he looked so hurt, I had to say that. Noreen would have slaughtered me otherwise.

Then we had coffee. Four pounds for two cappuccinos. I ask you.

'Anyway,' he said, 'got to split, Dave, I'm feeling totally Melvinned.'

'Oh,' I said, 'what does that mean?'

'Melvinned,' he said, correcting himself, 'oh sorry, we have this rhyming slang in the office. Melvyn Bragged, you know. It means shagged. Gas, eh?' I agreed with Ed that it certainly was gas. He had one of those gold credit cards, and that's what he used to pay the bill. He told me to give him a call any time and let him know how things were going. He'd be expecting a few shares when I made my first million.

The next day I lay in bed in Noreen's place until twelve-thirty. Then I phoned Ed's chumette, and she said to come round at ten to clean the office. When I hung up I walked into Noreen and James's bedroom and had a bit of a search around the place, you know, the way you do. Some very interesting reading material in the bedside locker, *very* interesting indeed. I

made a mental note to remember all this the next time she tried
to nag me. I would blackmail her with the threat of telling my
mother. I could just see her face. It's called *The Joy of Sex*, Ma,
maybe you should give it a browse.

I hung around the flat all day watching television. I hadn't
enough money to go out. I had my Tube fare, and that was it.

I arrived at Jerusalem House at ten-thirty and there was
nobody around. I hammered on the glass and eventually this
black security guy let me in, locked the door, said his name was
Floyd and he'd be down in the basement smoking a joint if I
wanted him, which he sincerely hoped I wouldn't. He was
wearing tartan slippers. He said to start up on the twenty-second
floor.

I pressed the button for the lift, but nothing happened. So I
started to walk up the stairs. The building was quiet and cool
and everything seemed to be the same shades of matt black and
grey and silver. The first two floors seemed to be advertising
agencies or something. There were framed posters on the walls.
Advertising posters. That guy in the launderette showing off his
boxer shorts. Another one for the privatization of water. Another
one with a picture of a soldier with his arms in the air, and
words saying, 'This is Labour's Defence Policy; Vote Conservative'. Another one in the same series, long, long queue, 'Labour
isn't working'. That reminded me of good old Charlie. Health
Cuts hurt the Old, the Sick, the Handicapped. Yeah, Charlie,
great. I was looking at that one when suddenly there was a clank
and the lift started moving. I missed it on the second floor,
sprinted up to Equities National Suisse on the third and just
caught it in time.

When I walked into the office I saw this huge open-plan space
with maybe thirty desks, all flowing with computer print-outs and
pink pages from the *Financial Times*, plants and half-full polysty-
rene coffee cups everywhere. A light was on in the back office,
and a man's jacket was hanging on a chair. But I called out loud
and still nobody came. The lights hummed. I called out again.

My heart started to pound. I knew something was going to happen.

I don't know what got into me. I felt weird all of a sudden. I just kind of touched his jacket at first. That's all I wanted to do. Then I took it off the back of the chair and tried it on. I looked at my reflection in the side of a kettle. I turned around and looked at the back of it, over my shoulder. I could feel the sweat on my face. Then, although I tried to pretend I wasn't doing it, I reached slowly into the inside pocket. I really don't know what came over me. His wallet was fat. I took it out and smelt it. Then I opened it, real casually, so that if somebody came in I could say I was just looking for a name and address. Six fifties, five twenties, and more plastic than you'd find in Elizabeth Taylor's face. Jesus. Imagine leaving that much stuff lying around. That guy must have money to burn, he really must. I mean for these people, a couple of hundred is just nothing, small change.

I walked over to the window and stared out over London. Far in the distance I could see the top of Saint Paul's, all lit up with yellow light, a big silly hat on the head of the city. And a cruiser meandering along the river, like a little centipede or something, all made of coloured bulbs. Rain was falling gently against the windows, but they were so thick that you could hear no noise. I imagined I was down on the ground looking up at this black-glass building, with me in the bright window, and all the other lights in the building turned off. London looked like something out of *Star Trek*, all the weird lights flashing, lasers in the sky, reflecting on the river, and the cranes and the concrete walkways all over the place.

I started to tidy round but that damn noise from the lights started to get to me, and I'd no idea which bits of computer print to throw out and which to keep, and anyway I just got fed up. I wasn't feeling well. I walked home to Lewisham in the rain, all the way home, all six miles. I must have seen Pamella Bordes about sixty billion times. When I stopped for the burger

they wrapped up my chips in her. Then I saw her again, all over
the television shop window, sixteen of her. Then I saw her on a
billboard in Peckham. That damn woman just seemed to be
everywhere. She was like the Virgin Mary or something, in
Ireland. Ubiquitous.

I rang Ed up in his car the next morning.

'Yo, Dave,' he said, 'what's shaking?'

I said, 'Nothing's shaking, Ed, I left the job.' Then he
laughed and went 'boom boom', and I laughed too.

Then he said, 'You *are* kidding, aren't you?' and I said, 'No,
Ed, I'm not kidding.' There was silence for a few seconds. I
could hear the car engine over the crackle of the phone.

He said, 'Look, Dave, I'm having total sense of humour
failure on this one.'

I said, 'I'm sorry, Ed, but that building just gave me the
creeps.'

'But Dave, you utter Barclays Banker, I went out on a limb.'

'I appreciate that, Ed, I'm sorry.'

'You're *sorry*, whaddayamean, "sorry"? Jesus, Dave, like
beam-me-up, Scotty, or what?'

'Can I meet you, Ed?' I said. 'Today or something.'

'Sorry, Dave, no can do.'

'Come on, Ed,' I said, 'give me a break.'

'Time is money, Dave. I can't take time out to help you when
you drop me bollock deep in the brown stuff like this.'

I said, 'Come on, Ed, please.' More silence.

'OK, OK, but look, I can't see any blank space until *mañana*
at the earliest.'

'Tomorrow's fine, Ed,' I told him. 'And I won't be late.'

Ed said he couldn't give a Castlemaine Four X whether I was
late or not, it was my loss. Then he said Jesus Christ again and
put the phone down.

By the statue of Eros I sat down in the sunshine. I was tired
and still feeling funny. I opened my wallet. I took out six fifties,
five twenties, and more plastic than you'd find in a MacDonald's

hamburger. And I walked up the side streets of Soho, determined
to find myself the good time that Ed had told me about.

Some good time. I went into a peepshow and put a coin in
the slot. I saw this woman, maybe about forty, lying on a bed
with no clothes on, wearing nothing except a pair of sunglasses.
She was reading a paperback novel, *First Among Equals* by
Jeffrey Archer. With her other hand, she was smoking a cigarette. The ash on the end was long, and just as she moved to
flick it onto the floor it broke off and fell onto her bare
stomach. She didn't seem to mind, though. She brushed it out
of her navel with the book and turned another page. I noticed
she had this thin blue scar across her abdomen. The little cubicle
smelt of disinfectant and it made me feel like throwing up. No
matter how many pound coins I put in there, I still didn't feel
any better. Eventually some dude in a chequered suit came
banging on the cubicle door and I had to get out. I went outside
and sat on the pavement with my head in my hands.

I spent the rest of the afternoon trying to find a newspaper
that had some news about the Irish election. I was wondering
whether Charlie was going to get his majority or not, really
praying that he wouldn't. I found an *Irish Times* in the end, and
I sat in a coffee bar reading the results and lighting one cigarette
off the end of another, until it was time to go home.

On the way, I went to Leicester Square Tube station. There
was a bit of a commotion outside, this ambulance with a big
crowd of people around, four policemen struggling up the deep
steps from the Underground with a stretcher. They carried this
guy about my age, with a punk-rock haircut and tartan trousers,
up the stairs towards the street. A fat man in a uniform was
pumping up and down on his chest. He looked more unhealthy
than the guy on the stretcher. Every four or five steps they'd
stop and heave up and down on his chest again. The fat man
kept shouting 'stabilize' and 'release' and 'stabilize' again. They
had cut the young guy's shirt open. His chest was tattooed with
a crucifix. They carried him right up past me and I saw that his

lips were very light blue and his eyes, although they were open, were still and white like a fish's eyes when it's boiled. It reminded me of when we went fishing as kids, down on Dun Laoghaire pier in the summer. That's terrible I know, but sometimes you just think a thing, you can't help it. I mean, what can you do?

James and Noreen took me out to dinner that night, but they were having an argument about the wedding or something, so it was strictly a case of maintaining a tactful silence over the carbonara. I hadn't got a great appetite to tell you the truth.

Next morning I called into Ed's office. I had to wait for about half an hour to see him, in the same room as the woman who answered his phone. She kept offering me coffee, and I kept saying no thanks. She put me sitting on this big black leather armchair that farted every time I moved. She went back to doing the *Telegraph* crossword. Every so often she asked me for help with a clue but I'm useless at those things. Eventually the thing on her desk buzzed and she told me to go into Mr Murphy's office. On the door were these two little stickers. The first one said 'Ed's Den'. The second one said 'You don't have to be crazy to work here, but it helps'.

Ed was at his desk, holding the telephone between his chin and his shoulder, with one hand over the mouthpiece. He gave me his keys and told me to pop down to the old motor and collect his briefcase for him. He didn't even say hello or anything, just pushed the keys across the desk at me, spun around in his chair and put his feet up on the windowsill.

I walked down to the car park and found his car. The registration number was 'ED M 1'. Noreen had told me he paid £1,500 just to get that registration plate. I opened the door, and the inside smelt new and clean. I saw his briefcase on the passenger seat, but I just sat in there anyway. Just to see what it was like for a minute or two. I clicked on his compact disc player, and Phil Collins came on. That was when I saw his carphone.

I picked it up and dialled Australia. Just like that. I dialled the speaking clock in Australia and I waited for the clicks to give way to the voice. Me and Louise, in all the months we were living together over there, we never got round to buying a clock. So I knew the speaking clock number off by heart. She used to go on at me about how ridiculously expensive it was and tease me because she always had to pay the bill. I sat in the driver's seat just listening to the voice and thinking about her. It was seven o'clock in the evening over there. She was probably just getting ready to go out with that musclebound thug of a boyfriend of hers. I sat there in Ed's car, just listening, for maybe five whole minutes, as the time beeped down the line, until tears started rolling down my face, I still don't really know why.

After a few more minutes I got my head together and dried my eyes on my sleeve. I suppose I just realized there was no point, and that everything she had said about the two of us that night we had too much to drink in the Cantina, it had all been right, pity she had to say it in the way she did I suppose, but still. I was going to put the phone back on the hook, but then I had a thought. It was one of those moments.

I put the phone down carefully, slowly, on the floor, underneath the seat, and I could still hear the voice. I made sure it wasn't disconnected. Then I climbed out, closed all the windows tight, clamped his briefcase under my armpit, locked the door. And as I walked across the car park I stopped, just for a second, to drop Ed's car keys down the drain. I heard him screaming at me, thirteen storeys up. I heard him hammering on the window and screeching my name. I looked up and waved at him. And then, just before I opened his briefcase and slowly emptied its contents all over the car park, I blew him a big kiss.

I walked straight out onto the road and hailed a taxi. I felt light-headed from the tears, stupid I know. Then I said something that I had been wanting to say all my life. The taxi driver's eyes scrutinized me in the mirror. In my mind's eye I saw Ed tumbling down the stairs and shaking with rage. Once again I knew something was about to happen.

'Take me to the airport,' I ordered, 'there isn't a moment to lose.'

KATY HAYES
Forecourt

Katy Hayes (1965–) was born in Dublin and is founder member and resident director of The Glasshouse Theatre Company. Her first collection of short stories is due to be published next year. This story came second in RTE radio's Francis MacManus short story competition.

I arrive and the garage is sleeping quietly. I have it open and ready for business by six thirty. I love my job. I got Summer holidays on June the sixth, and started work here straight away. I'm only working on the petrol pumps. You have to be here six months before they allow you to start being a mechanic. The manager is a friend of my older sister. She used to go out with him. He is very ugly. My sister's taste in men is fairly dreadful.

I always wear figure hugging denims to work. They make my bum look nice. I can usually see out of the corner of my eye that all the mechanics are looking at me and my ass. When it's sunny like today, I wear a little vest top with bare arms and a bare neck, I look at my reflection in the mirror. It's a bit clean looking, so I rub a bit of engine oil just over my right breast and on my cheek. It looks really cute. I got a new bra and it makes my boobs look great. It kind of raises them up a bit and points them outwards. Not like the boring yokes my ma gets for me. Sports bras. They're made out of plain white stretchy cotton and they kind of flatten out your tits and tuck half of them under your armpits.

My mother is a feminist. She keeps talking about equality in the workplace, and she says there should be more women in male dominated jobs. I thought she would be pleased that I had got a job as a petrol pump attendant, but I think she was thinking more in terms of brain surgery. My older sister Pam tells her not to be so bloody bourgeois. When Mary Robinson was up for the presidency my mam made all my brothers vote for her. She said there wouldn't be another hot dinner in our house unless that woman got into the Park. My brothers all joked and said they'd vote according to their conscience. My mother is their conscience. I am too young to vote but I would have voted for Mary Robinson if I could. I think she has great legs. When I'm as old as her I hope I look as good as her. Why can't my mam dress like her instead of wearing denims all the time. She doesn't have the figure for denims. I wish she'd dress her age.

I know all the regular customers. I have great chats with them. There's one man in particular. Colm Cronin is his name. I know 'cos it's written on his credit card. Lovely name. He drives a black BMW. He stares into my eyes as I hand him back his car keys, and winks at me before he drives out of the forecourt. When he asks me how I am, he seems to really want to know.

His missus is also gorgeous. She is like a model. Tall, blonde, lots of suntan. They have one kid, a little girl who is an absolute stunner. Long blonde curls, cute pout. The Missus comes in to me about as often as he does, but during the morning, on her way to do the shopping. She drives a bright red Toyota Starlet. Usually she doesn't pay me, but asks me to put her bill onto his when he comes in later on, and he pays for the lot with his credit card. I'm not really supposed to do that, but so far they haven't let me down. He's always made it in before the end of my shift, so the Boss can't possibly know that I do it.

Sometimes I imagine myself driving the Starlet. I look great in red. I drive home with my kid, I'd call her Saffron, to a beautiful house surrounded by trees, and I'd cook his dinner for him. Something posh out of me mam's Cordon Bleu book. Then he'd come home and fly into a jealous rage and throw the dinner on the floor, on account of him thinking that I'm having an affair with his business partner, but then he'd say he's sorry and couldn't help himself because he's so tormented with adoration for me. Then we'd slip into something more comfortable and lie in each other's arms listening to U2 singing 'All I Want is You', then we'd dive into bed and make glorious amazing mega-fabuloid love. No, we wouldn't get as far as the bed. We'd do it on the carpet. We'd devour each other with kisses and bites and eventually we'd do you know what, and afterwards we'd lie there panting.

Sometimes I feel a little bit guilty when I see his wife. I wonder has she any idea about me and him.

Though I like my job, it can be a little bit dull. I've figured out a way to keep myself amused. If I position the pump nozzle in such a way while I'm filling the petrol tank, and hold my crotch against the tubing, the vibrations caused by the petrol flowing through makes me feel quite excited. It's a lovely tingly feeling. I could do it all day. Especially on a hot day.

As morning becomes midday I am getting hot and sweaty. I spend my time tidying and thinking about what the mechanics would look like with no clothes on. Colm's wife comes in. I fill her up and she smiles at me and tells me that he'll be up later to pay me. When she smiles she is a real smasher, but her eyes are slightly glazed and she doesn't really see me. Most of the customers are like that.

My big sister Pam and her current boyfriend Podge call in to me and try to scab some free petrol. I take off my sister's Ray Bans and hide them under the counter. She'd kill me if she knew I had them. They're real, not fake. She got them in New York. Podge is the ugliest boy in Dublin. He has chronic acne. He is twenty three and he still has acne! I got a spot once, when I was thirteen. It lasted for two weeks and then it went away. I haven't had one since. Puberty, I suppose. Podge's spots are really angry looking. I once asked Pam did she close her eyes when she kissed him and she didn't speak to me for two days. He drives a rusty heap of shit. Honestly, it is primitive. Pam, as always, is looking lovely in a gorgeous red and white polka dot mini dress. There is no point in Pamela dressing up when she has the Incredible Hulk on her arm. I've tried to tell Pam that it is embarrassing for me that she has gone out with every ugly guy in Dublin. She told me that pretty boys are crap in bed. In my opinion, it isn't a problem if they're ugly in bed, you could switch the lights out, it's just when they're out on the streets in public that they should be presentable. Besides, you spend much longer with them out of bed than in it. Podge pours his own petrol and makes funny faces in the window at Pam, who is laughing loudly. The two of them would have really ugly kids. Pamela coming here annoys me. This is my place. My sister never leaves me alone. No matter what I do she comes along and pokes her nose into it. I'm sick of her.

My kiosk is mostly made of glass so when it is as sunny as it is today it becomes incredibly hot. I try and stand in the shade a good bit, 'cos my shoulders are beginning to burn. The sun is baking down and the air is incredibly still, no breeze at all. I begin to sweat. Colm. Colm. I can't get his face out of my mind. He'll be up later. She said so. Time mooches past in the still heat. He doesn't come. At half past three I begin my end of shift routine. I start to count the cans of oil and add up the money. My till is going to be ten pounds short because he hasn't come in to pay for her petrol yet. Never mind, I'll explain to Bob, the three stone overweight boy who takes over from me at four. At a quarter to four, I hear the unmistakeable sound of Colm's engine. I am bent over my figures. As his car comes to a halt I look up and my insides leap. I go out to his car window and he hands me his keys, I see small beads of sweat on his temples and wet patches under his armpits. I can smell him. His eye is caught by the oil smear on my right breast. I colour unnoticeably under the screaming sun, and I feel blood rush to my groin. I open the petrol tank, put the pump nozzle in, and squeeze the trigger. The temptation is irresistible, so I slide my crotch over to it and a shiver goes down my back. I've never done it with his car before. I can feel my breath get faster. He switches on the car stereo and suddenly the air is filled with 'All I Want is You'. I look at the meter. It reads fifteen ninety five and it's churning fast. The car holds twenty six pounds usually. The petrol fumes rise to my nose as the sun beats down on the back of my neck and Bono's voice rings out across the forecourt. I pass a point and I cannot stop and suddenly I explode and a noise erupts from inside me, loudly, I hear myself groan, like an animal, as the petrol tank overflows and petrol runs down my jeans, the pump shuts off automatically. I stand there for a moment, the nozzle in my right hand, dripping petrol on the concrete forecourt.

Autopilot takes over. I hang up the nozzle and walk to the car window. I am terrified of his face. He turns to look at me and his cheeks are as red as his wife's car, his expression astonished. I feel more weird than embarrassed. I feel like my body belongs to someone else. My right breast is still tingling.

I walk into the kiosk with his card and do out his credit slip. He follows me in to sign it. I can smell him really strongly now. He is still staring at me with a bewildered look, though there is a small smile threatening at the corner of his mouth. I look at him, desperate. He puts away his card and goes to give me the usual one pound tip. In mid gesture he catches my crazy eye and goes scarlet, the colour of his wife's car. He drops the coin and I bend down and he bends down to pick it up. Our heads crash against each other and we both reel backwards, and my head spins. He asks me if I'm all right, the pound coin forgotten on the oily floor. I close my eyes and pretend to faint, and he steadies me. I fall against his chest and he has no choice but to put his arm around me.

There are two other cars on the forecourt, beeping furiously in the afternoon heat but I don't care. I am in his arms. I am in his terrified arms and I don't care.

MIKE McCORMACK
Thomas Crumlesh 1960–1992: A Retrospective

Mike McCormack (1965–) was born in London. He has had short stories published in the Sunday Tribune *and the* Connaught Tribune. *He is the author of a collection of short stories,* Getting It in the Head.

My first contact with Thomas Crumlesh was in 1984 when he exhibited with a small artists collective in the Temple Bar area of the city. His was one of the numerous small exhibitions that hoped to draw the attention of the many international buyers who were in Dublin for the official Rosc Exhibition at the Guinness Hops Store. It was July, just a few months after Thomas had been expelled from the National College of Art and Design for persevering with work that, in the opinion of his tutors, dealt obscenely and obsessively with themes of gratuitous violence.

His exhibition, 'Notes Towards An Autobiography', had been hanging less than three days and already word had got around and quite a bit of outraged comment excited. It consisted of four box frames with black silk backgrounds on which were mounted his left lung, the thumb of his left hand, his right ear and the middle toe of his left foot. Crumlesh was present also and easily recognizable, he was standing by the invigilator's desk, his head and right hand swathed in white but not too clean bandages. He was pale, carrying himself delicately, and like most young artists, badly in need of a shave. After I had got over my initial shock I ventured a few words of congratulations, more by way of curiosity than any heartfelt belief in his work's merit. He surprised me with a lavish smile and a resolute handshake that contradicted completely his frail appearance. This was my first experience of the central paradox in his personality – the palpably gruesome nature of his work set against his unfailing good spirits and optimism. He surprised me further by telling me in conspiratorial tones that he planned to flee the country that very evening. Some of the criticism of his work had found its way into the national press and already a few people with placards had picketed the exhibition. He had even heard word that the police were pressing for warrants to arrest him under the obscenity laws. He confided that what really worried him was that he might fall foul of Ireland's notoriously lax committal laws; he quoted an impressive array of statistics on secondary committals in the Republic.

I ended this encounter by buying his lung. His enthusiasm and verve convinced me of its worth and his whole appearance told me that he was in need of money. Before I left he told me of the programme of work he had laid out for himself – a programme that would take him up to 1992, the year he hoped to retire. I offered to check his wounds, his bandages looked like they had not been changed in a few days. He declined the offer saying that he had not the time, he needed to cash the cheque and he was afraid of missing the ferry to Holyhead. We shook hands one final time before parting and I did not expect to see him ever again.

Our paths crossed again two years later. I was in London, attending a symposium on trauma and phantom pains in amputees at the Royal College of Surgeons. By chance, in a Crouch End pub, I picked up a flier advertising the upcoming festival of Irish culture and music in Finsbury Park. Near the bottom of a list of rock bands and comedians was mention of a small exhibition of avant garde work to be shown in a tiny gallery in Birchington Road. Thomas's name was mentioned second from the bottom. When I eventually found the gallery it was nothing more than two rooms knocked together on the third floor over a Chinese restaurant. Among the second rate paintings and sculptures Thomas's work was not difficult to recognize. It stood in the middle of the floor mounted on a black metal stand, a single human arm stripped of skin and musculature leaning at

an obtuse angle to the floor. The bleached bones of the hand
were closed in a half fist and the whole thing looked like the jib
of some futuristic robot. As I approached it the arm jerked into
life, the fingers contracting completely and the thumb bone
standing vertical. It had the eerie posture of a ghost arm
hitching a lift from some passing phantom car. It was untitled
but had a price of two thousand pounds.

Thomas then entered the room and recognized me instantly. I
attempted to shake hands – an embarrassing blunder since I had
to withdraw my right hand when I saw the stump near his
shoulder. As before, he was in good spirits and entered quickly
into a detailed explanation of what he called his 'technique'. He
had bleached the bone in an acid formula of his own devising to
give it its luminous whiteness and then wired it to electrical
switches concealed beneath the carpet which would be unwittingly activated by the viewer whenever he got within a certain
radius – he admitted borrowing this subterfuge from some of
the work of Jean Tinguley. He then circled the arm and put it
through its motions, four in all. Firstly, a snake striking pose
that turned the palm downward from the elbow and extended
the fingers fearsomely, the hitching gesture, a foppish disowning
gesture that swivelled the forearm at the elbow and threw the
hand forward, palm upwards, and lastly and most hilariously an
'up yours' middle finger gesture that faced the viewer head on.
He grinned like a child when I expressed my genuine wonder. I
had no doubt but that I was looking at a masterpiece. I little
knew at the time how this piece would enter into the popular
imagery of the late twentieth century, featuring on a rock album
cover and on several posters. I only regretted at the time that I
had not enough money to buy it.

But Thomas was not without worries. He confided that he
had found it extremely difficult to find a surgeon who would
carry out the amputation, he had had to be careful to whom he
even voiced the idea – the terror of committal again. It had
taken him three months to track down an ex-army medic,

taken him three months to track down an ex-army medic, discharged from the parachute regiment after the Falklands war, to where he ran a covert abortion clinic in Holloway. In a fugue of anaesthesia and marijuana, Thomas had undergone his operation, a traumatic affair that had left him so unnerved he doubted he would be able to undergo a similar experience again. This fright had put his life's work in jeopardy, he pointed out. He was looking me straight in the face as he said this; I sensed that he was putting me on the spot. He came out straight with his request then. What I need is a skilled surgeon I can rely on, not some strung-out psycho. He will of course be paid, he added coyly. I told him that I needed time to think on it, it was a most unusual request. He nodded in agreement, he understood exactly the difficulties of his request and he would not blame me if I refused him outright. We shook hands before we parted and I promised to contact him the following day after I had given his request some thought.

In fact I had little to think about. I had very quickly resolved my fundamental dilemma, the healing ethic of my craft set against the demand of Thomas's talent. One parting glance at the arm had convinced me that I had encountered a fiercely committed genius who it seemed to me had already made a crucial contribution to the art of the late twentieth century. It was obvious to me that I had an obligation to put my skills at his disposal; the century could not be denied his singular genius on grounds of personal scruples. My problem was how exactly I was to make my skills available. That evening I gave the problem much thought and I returned to the exhibition the following day with my plans.

I found Thomas in high spirits. The lead singer with a famous heavy metal band had just bought his arm and Thomas was celebrating with champagne, drinking it from a mug, trying to get the feel of his new found wealth, as he laconically put it. He poured me a similar mug when I declared my intention to help him. I explained my plan quickly. Before every operation he giving me two weeks to put in place the necessary logistics and paperwork at the clinic where I worked. I believed I would be able to perform two operations a year without arousing suspicion. He thanked me profusely, telling me he could rest easy now that his future was secure. In a magniloquent moment that was not without truth he assured me that I had made a friend for life.

He contacted me for the first time in November of that year telling me that he planned to exhibit a piece during the summer Bienniale in Paris. He needed to have six ribs removed before February, when would be the most convenient time for me. I wrote in reply that I had planned the operation for Christmas Eve and that he could stay with me over the festive period into the new year while he recovered. The operation itself, an elaborate thoracotomy, carried out in the witching hour of Christmas Eve, was a complete success and when I presented him with the bundle of curved washed bones he was thrilled; it was good to be back at work, he said. It was during these days of convalescence that our professional relationship moved onto a more intimate footing. Mostly they were days of silence, days spent reading or listening to music in the conservatory that looked out over Howth to the sea beyond. Sometimes a whole day would go by without any word passing between us. Neither of us thought this odd. The looming, inexorable conclusion of his art ridiculed any attempts at a deeper enquiry into each other's past. He gave me his trust and I gave him his bones and internal organs. That was more than enough for both of us.

On the third of January he returned to London, he wanted to get to work as quickly as possible. Five months later he sent me a photograph from some gallery in Paris, a close-up of a piece called 'The Bonemobile', an abstract lantern shaped structure suspended by wire. His letter informed me that although the piece had excited the inevitable outrage among the more hidebound critics it had also generated some appreciative but furtive comment. Nevertheless, he doubted that any buyer would rise to the fifty thousand francs price tag he had placed on it. He understood the fear of a buyer ruining his reputation by buying into what someone was already calling high class voyeurism. Still, he was not without hope.

That was the first of twelve operations I performed on Thomas between 1986 and 1992. In all I removed twenty-three bones and four internal organs, eighteen inches of his digestive tract, seven teeth, four toes, his left eye and his right leg. He exhibited work on the fringe of most major European art festivals, narrowly escaping arrest in several countries and jumping bail in four. In his lifetime he sold eight pieces totalling fifty thousand pounds, by no means riches, but enough to fund his spartan existence.

Inevitably, by 1989 his work was taking a toll on his body. After the removal of a section of digestive tract in 1988, a slumped look came over his body; since the removal of his right leg in 1987 he was spending most of his time in a wheelchair. Despite this his spirits never sank, nor did his courage fail him; he was undoubtedly sustained by the tentative compliments that were being spoken of his work. For the first time also he was being sought out for interviews. He declined them all, pointing out simply that the spoken word was not his medium.

His deterioration could not go on indefinitely. In March 1992 he wrote telling me of his resolve to exhibit his final piece at the Kassel Documenta. He travelled to Dublin the following month and spent a week at my house where he outlined the procedure I was to follow after the operation. On the night of the tenth, after shaking hands with appropriate solemnity for the last time, I administered to him a massive morphine injection, a euthanasia injection. He died painlessly within four minutes. Then, following his instructions, I removed his remaining left arm and head, messy work. I then boiled the flesh from the arm and skull in a huge bath and using a solution of bleach and furniture polish

brought the bone to a luminous whiteness. I then fixed the skull
in the hand and set the whole thing on a wall mount: 'Alas,
Poor Thomas' he had told me to call it. I sent it to Kassel at the
end of the month, Thomas already having informed the gallery
as to the kind of work they could expect. In critical terms it was
his most successful piece; when Kiefer singled him out as the
genius specific to the jaded tenor of this brutal and fantastic
century his reputation was cemented. This last piece sold for
twenty-five thousand D'marks.

When, as executor of the Thomas Crumlesh Estate, I was
approached with the idea of this retrospective I welcomed it on
two accounts. Firstly, it is past time that a major exhibition of
his work be held in his native country, a country that does not
own a single piece of work from her only artist to have made
a contribution to the popular imagery of the late twentieth
century; a prophet in his own land indeed. Secondly, I welcomed the opportunity to assemble together for the first time
his entire *oeuvre*. My belief is that the cumulative effect of its
technical brilliance, its humour and undeniable beauty will
dispel the comfortable notion that Thomas was nothing more
than a mental deviant with a classy suicide plan. The rigour
and terminal logic of his art leaves no room for such
platitudes.

Several people have speculated that I was going to use this
introduction to the catalogue to justify my activities, or worse,
as an opportunity to bewail the consequences. Some have gone
so far as to hope that I would repent. I propose to do none of
these. Yet, a debt of gratitude is still outstanding. It falls to very
few of us to be able to put our skills at the disposal of a genius,
most of us are doomed to ply our trades within the horizons of
the blind, the realm of drones. But I was one of the lucky few,
one of the rescued. Sheer chance allowed me to have a hand in
the works of art that proceeded from the body of my friend,
works of art that in the last years of this century draw down the

curtain on a tradition. His work is before us now and we should see it as an end. All that remains for me to say is, Thomas, dear friend, it was my privilege.

Dr Frank Caulfield,
Arbour Hill Jail,
Dublin.

SARA BERKELEY
The Catch

Sara Berkeley (1967–) has published two books of poetry, Penn *and* Home Movie Nights, *as well as a collection of short stories,* The Swimmer in the Deep Blue Dream. *She now lives in America.*

Eamon, Rory and the other mermen were all in The Fish Bar in Clontarf by 8 o'clock Friday as arranged. The last to arrive was the Birthday Boy, and when he did there were grunts of surprise among the lads. Billy approached their table rather awkwardly:

'Er – lads, meet the maid.'

Helen smiled at the company and nine pairs of merman eyes rested on her long slender tail as she tucked it gracefully in under the seat beneath her.

'Gentlemen,' she said quietly.

Billy, rubbing his hands nervously, seemed to think a little more explanation was in order. After all, few of the men were ever seen in public with their maids, except at church, or similarly boring parent–teacher meetings they were forced to attend.

'Uh – she's learning to drive,' he nodded in the direction of Helen and winked with the other eye. 'Thought I'd give her a bit of practice.'

'Ah Billy now,' said Joe, 'I thought I heard you'd a bit of an old smash-up in the motor. Brought her up on some rocks didn't you?'

'Yeah, well,' Billy looked round defensively. 'She was an old wreck of a boat. I only used her for getting me home. Redrock's a bitch to negotiate in rough weather . . .'

'What's your Birthday poison?' cut in Michael and Billy got up gratefully to follow him to the bar.

An Anthology of Irish Comic Writing

'I'll help you Mick. Ten pints of winkles' he told the barman, 'Oh, and a crab claw for the lady. 'Cos she's always crabbing at me,' he added with a nudge and a wink to Michael, who chuckled appreciatively and turned to the corner where the lads were.

'Great tail on her though,' he said.

'Yeah,' said Billy, sulkily. He was thinking of Helen standing in the hall, dressed to go out, refusing to let him go alone. Thinks I can't drive with a few pints on me, he thought bitterly. I'll drive *her*. The shame of it! Still, she had a great tail. And her voice wasn't bad either, when she sat like that on the rocks at the Bailey, combing her hair – if only she'd do it more often instead of wasting her time with this degree business.

Conch-bloody-ology! What more did the maid need to know about shells, for crying out loud? The world was full of them. Shells shells shells, for breakfast, dinner and tea. He planted three pints of winkles on the table in front of his mates and pushed the crab claw across to Helen. She raised her eyebrows but said nothing. In fact she'd said nothing so far this evening. As soon as Billy had gone to the bar, an awkward silence had fallen punctuated by snorts of suppressed laughter and the occasional muttered comment. Now the merman next to her pointed to the crab claw and cleared his throat.

'Into crab, then?'

'Well, I'd normally have something a little stronger, but I'm driving.'

'Right. Who's looking after the kids tonight then?'

'Dermot. Our eldest. He's sixteen now and we trust him.'

'Haven't you a daughter not much younger?'

'She's out tonight. They take turns.'

Rory shook his head. 'Mark my words, you'll regret that,' he said knowingly. 'Give the girls ideas and they'll never lift a finger for you again. Sure give the lad his bit of freedom, wouldn't you?' 'Hey Rory!' someone called from across the table. 'Where's the maid tonight?'

'Oh she had a pressing engagement.' Rory grinned, 'with the ironing!'

There were roars of laughter. Helen was studying the tiny whorled shell he wore in one earlobe. Pearly nautilus, she thought, a cephalopod mollusc. From the Greek *nautilus*, sailor, and *naus*, ship.

Three pints later the mermen were swapping jokes.

'What's the difference between a Northsider and Batman?' said Greg, who liked to frequent the waters round Killiney. 'Batman can go into town without robbin!'

Several heads at the bar turned.

'What does a merman in Dalkey say to his boss at the end of the day?' countered Billy. 'Night da!'

The twins from Baldoyle Flats slapped their tails appreciatively.

'Hey! What does a hungry merman do when his wife won't cook dinner? He batters her!' There were cheers and roars of drunken laughter. Helen took her bag and slipped off quietly to the Maids' room. In the mirror, she ran a hand down her thick glossy hair, remembering the time she had suggested to Billy that she cut it. It slows me down, she explained. Billy had been livid. 'Cut your hair?' he'd screamed. 'What would you have to comb while you sang to me?'

In the end, she had come round to his way of thinking, but only because of the singing he didn't know about – her secret night-time journeys to the Kish lighthouse where she sat for hours on the rocks, combing and singing away the sorrow of the day. Billy only knew about the regular everyday singing that she did to please him – the soul-less stuff, the type of songs fewer and fewer mermaids were content these days to sing for their men.

She leaned forward to the mirror with her hands on the rim

of the basin and looked herself intently in the eyes. Helen, she said to herself softly, sing your *own* song.

The Fish Bar finally closed its doors at midnight and the mermen stood around outside, some with half a pint of winkles left, which they knocked back in one to the whoops and jeers of the rest. Billy stood with a hand on the window to steady himself and belched generously.

'Have you the keys,' said Helen quietly to him.

'Night Billy! Hope your birthday finishes in style!' shouted Joe.

'Whoah there boy!' Eamon gave Helen a pat where tail met waist. 'Night now!' he winked at her. She turned coolly back to Billy. 'Come on Billy, the keys.' 'Ah now – I'll be fine taking her out into the harbour!' he said loudly. 'You can bring her round the rocks if you like,' he finished in a savage whisper to her.

'Thanks, I'll swim,' she answered and began to make her way to the harbour wall where men were calling goodnight and getting into boats.

'Helen – wait!' Billy followed her angrily and put his arm roughly round her shoulders. 'Come on. You're getting in the boat with me.' He pressed the keys in her hand and waved cheerily to the lads who were making catcalls. 'Sure she's getting the hang of it fine,' he said to the man in the next boat as Helen sat into the driver's seat. 'I just like to give her some practice.' Helen, who had been driving for eighteen years, guided the boat expertly out from among the others and cruised gently in the direction of Howth. By the time they rounded Redrock, Billy was noisily returning winkles to Dublin Bay.

Nothing marked the spot. Some families liked to mark their homes with a buoy or a rock if they were close enough inland. Helen had always been proud of her skill in diving at exactly the right spot and Billy, for once, had respected her wishes. It meant he could occasionally lose his way coming home and stop over at Kathy's place, which was unmistakeably marked with a shining red buoy.

Helen cut the engine and let the boat glide to a halt. They sat in silence for a few moments, looking at the lights of Dublin in their lovely horseshoe. 'Jeez it's lovely,' said Billy, a little tearful after the journey. Helen said nothing. 'And you make it lovelier,' he said awkwardly, placing a hand on her tail, and hiccuping softly. 'Shall we go down then love?'

They slipped over the side of the boat and, their tails making perfect figures-of-eight, swam into the deep.

An hour later, Billy sleeping deeply, Helen finished up some study and looked in on the kids. She stood at her bedroom doorway for a while, looking at her husband. 'Happy Birthday love,' she whispered and then set off, swimming north, close to the surface until she could see the searchlight through the moonlit water. Just northwest of the Kish was her favourite rock. She found it effortlessly and sat for a while breathing the salty air. A slight wind lifted the sea and sucked it back down the rock. Her hair was freed from the water and, lifting the comb to it she began to sing. There were no words, but no mermaid hearing it could fail to understand and be moved to join in with her own wordless song. She sang from her heart and bones the heavy burden of the day, the same sorrows and secrets, the hidden pain she sang to ease every night. I have this, she was thinking, I have this and no-one can take it from me.

A mile away, a Howth trawler rocked gently in the swell and two fishermen sat smoking on the deck.

'I sometimes think, Paddy,' said one, 'that even out here in the middle of bloody nowhere, the wife won't let me alone.'

'How's that?' said Paddy.

'The wind. Listen. It sounds like her singing in the bath.' The two of them laughed heartily and went below deck for the night.

READ MORE IN PENGUIN

In every corner of the world, on every subject under the sun, Penguin represents quality and variety – the very best in publishing today.

For complete information about books available from Penguin – including Puffins, Penguin Classics and Arkana – and how to order them, write to us at the appropriate address below. Please note that for copyright reasons the selection of books varies from country to country.

In the United Kingdom: Please write to *Dept. EP, Penguin Books Ltd, Bath Road, Harmondsworth, West Drayton, Middlesex UB7 ODA*

In the United States: Please write to *Consumer Sales, Penguin USA, P.O. Box 999, Dept. 17109, Bergenfield, New Jersey 07621-0120*. VISA and MasterCard holders call 1-800-253-6476 to order Penguin titles

In Canada: Please write to *Penguin Books Canada Ltd, 10 Alcorn Avenue, Suite 300, Toronto, Ontario M4V 3B2*

In Australia: Please write to *Penguin Books Australia Ltd, P.O. Box 257, Ringwood, Victoria 3134*

In New Zealand: Please write to *Penguin Books (NZ) Ltd, Private Bag 102902, North Shore Mail Centre, Auckland 10*

In India: Please write to *Penguin Books India Pvt Ltd, 706 Eros Apartments, 56 Nehru Place, New Delhi 110 019*

In the Netherlands: Please write to *Penguin Books Netherlands bv, Postbus 3507, NL-1001 AH Amsterdam*

In Germany: Please write to *Penguin Books Deutschland GmbH, Metzlerstrasse 26, 60594 Frankfurt am Main*

In Spain: Please write to *Penguin Books S. A., Bravo Murillo 19, 1° B, 28015 Madrid*

In Italy: Please write to *Penguin Italia s.r.l., Via Felice Casati 20, I-20124 Milano*

In France: Please write to *Penguin France S. A., 17 rue Lejeune, F-31000 Toulouse*

In Japan: Please write to *Penguin Books Japan, Ishikiribashi Building, 2-5-4, Suido, Bunkyo-ku, Tokyo 112*

In South Africa: Please write to *Longman Penguin Southern Africa (Pty) Ltd, Private Bag X08, Bertsham 2013*

READ MORE IN PENGUIN

IRISH INTEREST

Come the Executioner M. S. Power

'Exceptional pacing carries us through an underworld of double-dealing, safe houses and bland killers' – *Glasgow Herald*. 'Power takes the dirty tricks practised by the security forces as the catalyst for this superior version-of-the-Troubles thriller' – *Time Out*

Emily's Shoes Dermot Bolger

'A sensuous melancholy pervades; a child's impacted grief at his mother's death and unacknowledged mourning for the father he never knew are rendered with painful accuracy' – *Independent on Sunday*

Time and Tide Edna O'Brien

'Nell was once one of those country girls with green eyes ... now she is trapped in London, in mortal enmity with her husband, sustained only by her two small sons ... In this surpassing novel ... written with sensual precision and relentless integrity, with tenderness and sometimes comedy, Edna O'Brien records the crises of Nell's motherhood, her vital reserves of love and her innocence within' – *Observer*

A World of Love Elizabeth Bowen

Memories shimmer like mirages in *A World of Love* and emotions are heightened to breaking-point. Seldom have the inarticulate sensations of women in love been so forcefully – and so poignantly – conveyed. 'Electric and urgent ... she startles us by sheer originality of mind and boldness of sensibility into seeking our world afresh' – V. S. Pritchett

Other People's Worlds William Trevor

'A constantly surprising work, grimly humorous, total in its empathy and pungent with the scent of evil and corruption' – *New Yorker*

READ MORE IN PENGUIN

IRISH INTEREST

A Border Station   Shane Connaughton

'With its sparse yet melodic prose it is a skilful tribute to a way of life that is as uncompromising as it is unchanging' – *Evening Standard*. 'Comparison with work by John McGahern and Patrick Kavanagh is inevitable ... it is a tribute to Connaughton that his child's view of life holds its own with those two giants' – *Irish Independent*

The Railway Station Man   Jennifer Johnston

Helen has retreated to the remote north-west of Ireland to be alone and to paint the sea and the shore ... 'A very nearly perfect novel of broad, regretful vision and magical intimacy' – *Sunday Telegraph*

Lamb   Bernard Mac Laverty

'To deal convincingly with innocence and the impossiblity of innocence without being falsely naïve ... is a special gift, and Bernard Mac Laverty displays it with great skill' – *Observer*

The Penguin Book of Irish Folktales   Edited by Henry Glassie

This exhaustive collection of stories from a wide selection of literary sources represents all facets of the Irish identity: from the wild, western coast to the urban bustle of Belfast and Dublin, from the ancient world of the Druids to the Celtic Renaissance and the present day.

Tarry Flynn   Patrick Kavanagh

For Tarry Flynn – poet, farmer and lover-from-afar of beautiful young virgins – the responsibility of family, farm, poetic justice and his own unyielding lust is a heavy one. The only solution is to rise above it all – or escape over the nearest horizon.

READ MORE IN PENGUIN

Also by Ferdia Mac Anna

The Ship Inspector

A few weeks before Daniel's ninth birthday his dad, who hated goodbyes, drove off in his Triumph Herald and disappeared without trace. Twenty years on, Daniel is surviving the neon night-shift as a ship inspector at Dublin Airport. His mother has become a successful politician, his punk brother a new 'wild man' of Irish rock. His girlfriend Carla – another absent hero – is abroad on tour in London with The Silent Screams . . . Unable to forget his father, Daniel has been running his work, his love affair, his whole life on automatic pilot. Hilarious and touching, *The Ship Inspector* dramatizes days of reckoning in a family riven by loss.

'Mac Anna shares with Doyle a fictional milieu: both write comic accounts of working-class family life in Dublin . . . Mac Anna has a lovely ear for the deadpan Irish one-liner . . . A Beckettian bleakness . . . lurks behind the novel's warm nostalgia' – *Guardian*

'Funny, sad, plaintive and poignant, peopled by characters you are unlikely to forget . . . Do yourself a favour. Read it' – *Irish Independent*

The Last of the High Kings

An irresistible portrait of an utterly mad, modern Irish family . . .

'At last a novel of contemporary Dublin that is buoyant with optimism . . . Mac Anna introduces us . . . in an easy, open manner, to the zany world of the Griffin family and, particularly, of Frankie, a gawkish youth traversing the no-man's land between acne and adult responsibility . . . delightfully entertaining' – *Irish Times*